NCO Guide

4th Edition

Revised by
Frank Cox

The *NCO Guide* was preceded by
The Noncom's Guide, written by
LTC Charles O. Kates, USA (Ret.)

STACKPOLE
BOOKS

Copyright © 1992 by Stackpole Books

Published by
STACKPOLE BOOKS
Cameron and Kelker Streets
P.O. Box 1831
Harrisburg, Pa. 17105

All rights reserved, including the right to reproduce this book or portions thereof in any form or by any means, electronic or mechanical, including photocopying, recording, or any information storage and retrieval system, without permission in writing from the publisher. Address all inquiries to Stackpole Books, Cameron and Kelker Streets, P.O. Box 1831, Harrisburg, Pennsylvania 17105.

This book is not an official publication of the Department of Defense or Department of the Army, nor does its publication in any way imply its endorsement by these agencies.

Cover design by Tracy Patterson.

Color photographs of medals by Ken Smith.

4th Edition

Printed in U.S.A.

10 9 8 7 6 5 4 3 2 1

Library of Congress Cataloging-in-Publication Data

Cox, Frank, 1954—
   NCO guide / revised by Frank Cox.—4th ed.
     p.   cm.
   "The NCO guide was preceded by The Noncom's guide, published by Stackpole in 21 editions totaling nearly 300,000 copies and written by LTC Charles O. Kates, USA (Ret.)."
     Rev. ed. of: The NCO guide / Dan Cragg and Dennis D. Perez. 3rd ed. © 1989.
     Includes index.
   ISBN 0-8117-2565-0
    1. United States. Army—Non-commissioned officers' handbooks.
I. Kates, Charles O. Noncom's guide. II. Cragg, Dan. NCO guide. III. Title.
U123.C7   1992
355.3'38'0973—dc20   92-21936
                                                                                                        CIP

In Memory of

The brave soldiers killed or wounded in action during Operation Desert Storm in Southwest Asia
And to all who fell while serving the nation in previous conflicts.

THE NCO CREED

No one is more professional than I.
I am a Noncommissioned Officer, a leader of soldiers.
As a Noncommissioned Officer, I realize that
I am a member of a time-honored corps, which is
known as "The Backbone of the Army."

I am proud of the Corps of Noncommissioned Officers and will at all times conduct myself so as to bring credit upon the Corps, the Military Service, and my country regardless of the situation in which I find myself. I will not use my grade or position to attain pleasure, profit, or personal safety.

Competence is my watch-word. My two basic responsibilities will always be uppermost in my mind—accomplishment of my mission and the welfare of my soldiers. I will strive to remain tactically and technically proficient. I am aware of my role as a Noncommissioned Officer. I will fulfill my responsibilities inherent in that role. All soldiers are entitled to outstanding leadership; I will provide that leadership. I know my soldiers and I will always place their needs above my own.
I will communicate consistently with my soldiers and never leave them uninformed. I will be fair and impartial when recommending both rewards and punishment.

Officers of my unit will have maximum time to accomplish their duties; they will not have to accomplish mine. I will earn their respect and confidence as well as that of my soldiers. I will be loyal to those with whom I serve; seniors, peers and subordinates alike. I will exercise initiative by taking appropriate action in the absence of orders. I will not compromise my integrity, nor my moral courage. I will not forget, nor will I allow my comrades to forget, that we are professionals, Noncommissioned Officers, leaders!

Contents

PREFACE	ix
1 THE ROLE OF THE NCO	1

   Leadership
   Discipline
   Training
   Duties
   Responsibilities
   The Chain of Command and the NCO
   The NCO and the Officer
   Precedence and Relative Rank
   Comparable Rank among the Services
   The New Manning System (NMS)
   Staff Assignments
   Casualty Notification, Survivor Assistance, and Body Escort Detail

2 THE PAPER WAR	33

   Information Sources
   Duty Rosters
   Classified Information
   The World of Supply

3 PROFESSIONAL DEVELOPMENT 44
The Noncommissioned Officer Development Program (NCODP)
Programs for Training
The Noncommissioned Officer Education System (NCOES)
Functional Courses
Education and Training
Membership in Professional Organizations
Applying for a Commission or a Warrant

4 EVALUATION AND MANAGEMENT SYSTEMS 68
NCO Evaluation Reporting System
The Qualitative Management Program
Physical Fitness

5 PROMOTION 90
Authority to Promote
Advancement to Private E-2 and Private First Class
Criteria for Promotion to Specialist or Corporal
Promotion to Sergeant and Staff Sergeant
The Paper Work
Assignments and How They Affect Promotions
Selection and Promotion to Senior NCO Ranks
Frocking
Reductions in Grade

6 PERSONAL AFFAIRS 113
Legal Assistance
Your Will
Power of Attorney
Personal Affairs Record
Military Records
Bank Accounts
Insurance Programs
Your Personal Property
Income Taxes
Personal Conduct
Deciding Where to Live
Army Community Services (ACS) and Army Emergency Relief (AER)
The Army Family Action Plan

7 CONTEMPORARY PROBLEMS 127
Counseling
Sexual Discrimination
Racial Prejudice
Substance Abuse
AIDS

8 THE UNIFORM CODE OF MILITARY JUSTICE 145
Nonjudicial Punishment
Courts-Martial

Contents   vii

9 COURTESY, ETIQUETTE, AND CUSTOMS   162
Courtesy
Etiquette
Customs

10 UNIFORMS AND INSIGNIA   182
Wearing the Uniform
Uniforms
Personal Appearance
Distinctive Uniform Items
Distinctive Unit Insignia and Heraldic Items
Enlisted Insignia of Rank

11 AWARDS AND DECORATIONS   219
Criteria
Time Limitation
Precedence
Wearing of Medals and Ribbons
U.S. Army and Department of Defense Unit Awards
Service Medals Described
Non-U.S. Service Medals
U.S. Army Badges and Tabs
Appurtenances
Foreign Individual Awards
Certificates and Letters

12 PAY AND ENTITLEMENTS   250
Pay
Benefits
Public Holidays

13 ASSIGNMENTS   277
Personnel Action Request
The Enlisted Personnel Assignment System
Career Development Programs
Overseas Service
Relocation Assistance

14 TRANSITIONS   296
The Drawdown
Discharges
Transfer Points and Facilities
Retirement
Veterans' Rights

INDEX   319

Preface

Credibility. Achieving and maintaining it takes much more than appearing spit-polished in a pressed set of BDUs with sergeant's chevrons and rockers affixed to the uniform's collar. To serve as an effective, productive, contributing member of the Total Army, and to gain and hold the respect of soldiers who are more educated today than ever before, a noncommissioned officer must exude the confidence that comes only from knowledge and years of experience. You will not gain experience from reading what is between the covers binding this publication, but if you apply yourself, you can gain knowledge.

As you read the *NCO Guide, 4th Edition*, do so with the following in mind. Information, which comes from myriad sources and leads to knowledge, is constantly subject to change. What is current in the *Guide* (or any official publication) today may be superseded, rescinded, or obsoleted tomorrow. Readers must therefore use the *Guide* as a springboard. From it you will need to jump into Army regulations, field manuals, other official Army documents, and the ongoing changes made to them to ensure that you remain fully and correctly informed.

Having stated my disclaimer, let me now tell you just how valuable the *Guide* is as an account of timeless truths, tips, and otherwise salient points about sergeant's business. Through its initial printing and three revisions, this unofficial guide has been published to serve the professional NCO. It contains narrative and anecdotal material about leadership, training, administration, supervision, and other aspects of the NCO's universe that will not be found in official documents. Former sergeants major Dan Cragg and Dennis D. Perez, retired LTC Charles O. Kates, and others previously credited for the contributions they have made to the *Guide* have over time constructed a work worth keeping readily available.

You *should* keep this guide handy for many reasons. As a serving NCO, you never know when you will be called upon to provide survivor assistance. Or, one of your soldiers may want to know where to obtain this or that accountable item through the complex Army supply system. Another NCO, perhaps a close friend, may be considering career options and want to speak intelligently with you about the subject. You may serve in an over-strength MOS that has been targeted for further reductions during the Army drawdown, and you may need information about transition assistance. You could have a legal concern about your will, a special or general power of attorney, taxes, or other personal affairs. It is possible that you subconsciously have the wrong attitude about the opposite sex, or you believe that you have been a victim of sexual harassment. Or, what about that medal or special skill badge you think that you are authorized for taking part in operations as recent as the Persian Gulf War? The *NCO Guide* will inform you about all of these matters and more. It contains the answers to many common questions, and it will lead you to sources of more current and specific information on more complex issues.

AIDS, racial prejudice, counseling, alcohol and drug abuse, nonjudicial punishment and courts-martial, your rights, pay and allowances and entitlements, military customs, awards, decorations, promotions—it's all here, the negative and the positive, in condensed form. Learn all you can from the *Guide*, spring from it when necessary, and over time you will serve more and more credibly among your peers, in front of your superiors, and when leading, supervising, counseling, or guiding your subordinates.

I thank my wife, Kelly, for her encouragement (for late-night snacks, neck massages, and for keeping our children occupied) as I worked on the revision. I also thank Ann Wagoner, my editor at Stackpole Books, for giving me latitude and an achievable deadline. I am in debt to Department of Veterans Affairs employees Barbara Cantwell and Alice Bachman for their rapid assistance. I am grateful for timely information provided by representatives of the Defense Finance and Accounting Service, the Association of the United States Army, the Noncommissioned Officers Association, the Army Continuing Education System, and the Army Community Services. I am also indebted to fellow members of the NCO Corps who have freely offered advice about various technical aspects of the *Guide*.

Frank Cox

1

The Role of the NCO

> I can't think of anything in the United States Army today that sergeants should not be involved with or aware of.... I want sergeants to be aware of all aspects of their soldiers, and nothing is off limits. "Sergeant's business" as we use it today applies to the things that are primary concerns: training, maintaining, caring for soldiers, discipline standards, the Noncommissioned Officers Education System, and families."
>
> —SMA Richard A. Kidd

LEADERSHIP

Leadership is a term relative to its application by combat arms, combat support, and combat service support sergeants. The infantryman, in one situation, may rely on his tactical savvy to overcome his fear on a battlefield. When he exhibits his skill and with it fights his fear, the infantry sergeant is viewed as a capable leader, and soldiers will follow. The combat engineer NCO, in another situation, may deftly supervise the handling and employment of blasting caps, fuses, and high explosives during a bridge demolition exercise. His soldiers see a leader who is cool under pressure, and they react accordingly. And a personnel sergeant, in yet another situation and entirely different environment, may calmly and efficiently supervise an administration, management, records, and personnel action operation during the surge of activity associated with a division mobilization. Her soldiers know they can rely on the NCO to lead them through a turbulent period.

Regardless of where, when, under what circumstances, or by whom it is used, leadership throughout the Army boils down to getting soldiers to willfully carry out orders and accomplish the mission. The more expert and credible the leader, the more likely his or her soldiers are to follow and be successful.

In time of peace or war, the NCO must be able to motivate and inspire his or her soldiers to relinquish self-interest—possibly even to sacrifice their lives—to carry out missions for the greater good of the unit, the Army, and the country. In order to inspire soldiers, an NCO must know how to lead. Good leaders do not come by leadership attributes naturally. They acquire these attributes through a never-ending process of self-study, education, training, and experience.

Although the Army consists of well-trained soldiers, the most current weapons and equipment available, and the world's most efficiently structured military organizations, coupled with battle doctrine and policies aimed at winning the next conflict, all is for naught without good leadership. Only efficient and caring leaders can bring all of these elements together to make them work.

Military leadership is a process whereby you as a leader influence other soldiers to accomplish various mission-related tasks. Although many principles of leadership exist, the ability to lead by example has stood the test of time and rigors of battle.

Leadership Competencies

The nine leadership competencies every NCO should possess are communications, supervision, teaching and counseling, soldier-team development, technical and tactical proficiency, decision making, planning, management technology, and professional ethics.

A good leader knows himself and continues to seek self-improvement. Therefore, you should strengthen your attributes and know your soldiers and your unit.

Always be technically and tactically proficient. Techniques and tactical knowledge are important to leadership. As a leader, you must be proficient with your weapon and all other pieces of equipment in your unit. Develop your technical and tactical skills and knowledge through practice and study.

Seek responsibility and take responsibility for your actions. Take the initiative: pay attention to what is going on around you, figure out what needs to be accomplished, and take responsibility for doing it.

Make sound and timely decisions. Problem solving, decision making, and planning are all part of a good leader's responsibilities. Identify the problem, analyze and develop courses of action, make a plan, decide on a course of action, implement your plan, and assess it. Implementing your plan will task your abilities to communicate, coordinate, supervise, and evaluate your plan. This seven-step problem-solving process is described in FM 22-100, *Military Leadership*.

Know your soldiers and look out for their well-being. Show that you sincerely care for the well-being of your troops. You do not have to be a behavioral scientist to motivate. Make the needs of the people in your unit coincide with unit tasks and missions. Reward individual and team behavior that supports unit tasks and missions. Develop good morale and esprit de corps in your unit by alleviating causes of personal concern so that your soldiers can concentrate on their jobs. And most important, ensure that your soldiers are properly cared for and that they have the proper equipment and tools to do their work well.

Keep your soldiers informed. Your ability to communicate up and down the chain of command and with your peers can sometimes be the difference between success and failure. Be available to your troops. Discuss upcoming training and other mission-

The Role of the NCO

related events with your soldiers. Implement a way of receiving feedback from your soldiers. And make sure that short- and long-range training plans are available to your soldiers to help them plan for leave and other personal situations.

Develop a sense of responsibility in your subordinates. Challenge your soldiers by giving them more responsibilities—especially those soldiers who exhibit the potential to handle more than their assigned tasks and responsibilities. Delegate. Do not be afraid of losing some of your power or authority, for in fact, by delegating, you actually increase the power of your unit and yourself because you give your subordinates a chance to think and carry out their plans and thus increase their motivation and your means of accomplishing your mission.

Ensure that your subordinates understand the task, and that they have good supervision so that they can accomplish this task. Employ good communication techniques. Try to eliminate psychological and physical barriers that can sometimes inhibit good communication. Often, even differences in rank block clear communication. Remember that communication coordinates and controls all parts of a unit so that they act in harmony to accomplish a mission. Only a leader who has the ability to provide accurate and timely information, especially information that flows from soldier to soldier, can manage effective communication.

Train your soldiers as a team. All of the Army's successes depend on team cohesiveness. Cohesion demands strong bonds of mutual respect, trust, confidence, and understanding among soldiers in your unit. Cohesion and discipline go hand-in-hand. True cohesion often rests on union of thought and information among all soldiers when performing a unit's mission.

Employ your soldiers and your unit according to their capabilities. Develop these capabilities through individual and unit training under your leadership and guidance. Be aware of fatigue and the draining effects of other negative characteristics, such as fear. Train your soldiers to meet unit standards.

If you have the necessary desire, you can develop into an increasingly efficient and effective leader. Becoming an effective leader is a continuous process that will last your entire career and beyond. The study of leadership techniques, theories, anecdotes, military history, and human behavior along with sincere concern for your troops will improve your chances for success.

DISCIPLINE

AR 600-20 defines discipline as a function of command. It is the responsibility of all leaders, whether they are on duty or in a leave status, to see that all military personnel present a neat and soldierly appearance and to take action in cases of conduct prejudicial to good order and military discipline by any military personnel that may take place with their knowledge.

The senior officer, warrant officer, or noncommissioned officer present at a scene of disorder must act promptly to restore order. One of his initial actions should be to call for the military police if they are readily available.

When any offense that endangers the reputation of the Army is committed anywhere in public, you may request the civilian police to take the offender into custody when no military police are available. Make on-the-spot corrections of uniform or courtesy violations wherever possible, and never refer matters to an individual's commander that should be handled by a member of the NCO support chain. Exercise good judgment in all cases.

Noncommissioned officers are authorized to—and must, when they have knowledge of any quarrel, fray, or disorder among persons subject to military law—take action to quell these disorders and apprehend the participants. In order to fulfill your duty, you may have to risk physical injury, so you should proceed with judgment and tact, but *you must take action*.

You must exercise your military authority with promptness, firmness, courtesy, and justice. One of your most effective nonpunitive disciplinary measures is extra training or instruction.

The training or instruction given to an individual to correct deficiencies not only must be directly related to the deficiency observed, but also must be oriented to improving the individual's performance in his or her problem area. Requiring a road march for soldiers who have unclean equipment, for example, would be improper, but such a road march would be proper if the soldiers had allowed themselves to lapse into poor physical condition. A useless requirement, like digging and filling in holes, would be improper as well.

Corrective measures may be taken after normal duty hours.

These disciplinary measures are not an exclusive listing of what is and what is not permissible. These measures have the nature of training and instruction, not punishment, and authority to employ them is part of the inherent powers of command that you as an NCO have been delegated. If you abuse them, you will lose them.

Noncommissioned officers have the authority to apprehend under UCMJ, Article 7(c), page II-18, MCM; and paragraph 5-5, AR 600-20. NCOs may also be authorized by commanders, in accordance with the UCMJ, Article 9(b), to order enlisted persons into arrest or confinement. This authority is often limited to first sergeants, charge of quarters, or other duty positions. Noncommissioned officers do not, however, have the authority to impose nonjudicial punishment upon other enlisted persons. However, the recommendations of NCOs are considered by unit commanders before imposition of nonjudicial punishments.

TRAINING

> You don't get excellence, you don't get pride in service, and you don't get opportunities for career advancement through haphazard training programs administered by NCOs with size 32 waists and size 4 hats. As an infantryman, I know the importance of having soldiers who can shoot, but I say, give me soldiers who can *think* and I'll train them to shoot and I'll train them to be leaders. When a soldier stops thinking for himself and ceases to try to improve himself, then he is no longer qualified to lead.
>
> —Former SMA William G. Bainbridge

The noncommissioned officer plays a vital role in training soldiers. This role is active in that NCOs are responsible for accomplishing training objectives rather than for managing training, which is the responsibility of officers. The NCO's scope of responsibility may be narrower than that of the manager, but it is more concentrated and more exacting.

The NCO's duties as a trainer include the requirement to prepare, conduct, and evaluate individual or collective training. Training is hard work, and the NCO cannot afford any substitutes or shortcuts during preparation. In all training situations, always look for the answers to these three questions.

1. WHERE AM I GOING? What must my soldiers *do* as a result of their training?
2. WHERE AM I NOW? What can my soldiers do *now* compared to what I want them to be able to do as a result of training?

The Role of the NCO

3. HOW CAN I BEST GET FROM WHERE I AM TO WHERE I SHOULD BE? What techniques, training methods, and organization offer the most effective and efficient use of available resources?

Performance-Oriented Versus Conventional Training

This section deals primarily with performance-oriented training. Therefore, it is necessary that you understand the differences between performance-oriented training and what is called conventional training.

Performance-Oriented Training	Conventional Training
Uses short demonstrations and "learning by doing" as its main means of instruction.	Uses lectures as chief method of instruction.
Makes the soldier active and centers training on him, giving him the time and support needed to learn.	Places the instructor in the central active role.
Digests content into a set of high priority skills that are important for soldiers to learn in the time allotted for training.	Selects content in relation to what the instructor can present or cover in a certain amount of time.
Sets standards all soldiers must meet; when soldiers do not meet the standards, they practice until they can.	Uses grades to rate what the soldier has learned.

The Purpose of Performance-Oriented Training

The purpose of performance training is to prepare soldiers, teams, and units for job performance. It is that simple. But because it is so obvious, trainers sometimes forget and allow "eye wash" to prevail; some get so bogged down in the techniques of training that they forget their objective. Lecture techniques, lesson plans, training aids—as important as they are—are merely tools and secondary to what your soldiers are to do during and at the end of their training.

Remember that the purpose of training is *preparation for performance.* The question "Does this training really prepare my soldiers to do their jobs?" should become your guide as you prepare for performance training. The objective is the key to training. For any given skill, a properly structured and formulated training objective is both the training and the test. An objective can also contribute to your evaluation of the training needed and conducted. This approach can be described like this:

TRAINING OBJECTIVE = TRAINING + TEST + EVALUATION

A properly constructed training objective consists of three elements: task to be performed, conditions of performance, and a training standard of acceptable performance.

Stated differently, the training objective answers three questions: *What skill do I want my soldiers to acquire? Under what conditions do I wish my soldiers to demonstrate that skill? How well do I expect these soldiers to perform?*

An airborne soldier in ground exercise.

Learning motivation is very important if your training is to increase your soldiers' knowledge and skill. To learn best, your soldiers must:
- Realize the needs for training.
- Understand what is expected of them.
- Have an opportunity to practice what they have learned.

The Role of the NCO

- Get reinforcement that they are learning.
- Progress through training presented in a logical sequence.
- Be willing to learn.

Preparing and Conducting Individual Training

Specific training guidance should consist of the following elements:
- The commander's training objectives.
- Who will receive the training.
- The dates and times the training is to occur.
- Where the training will take place.
- The reasons why the commander decided that this training is necessary.

Remember that your expertise in the subject, bearing, appearance, manner, and desire to help your soldiers learn are vital motivation factors. You must involve yourself continually in the training, supervising and critiquing to ensure that your standards are met. Use the faster learners to help the slower ones. Make sure your soldiers can execute the fundamentals, the intermediate objectives of your training program. Conduct a post-training evaluation to determine your training effectiveness and efficiency.

Pay close attention to the contents of the Soldier's Manuals, which specify the critical performances essential for any given military occupational specialty, duty position, and skill level.

But the objective of performance training is not simply to enable your soldiers to pass the SDT in their particular MOSs, but to ensure their survival under real conditions.

The training of the individual soldier is the basis for the collective training of squads, sections, platoons, and companies. Field Manuals 25-100, *Training the Force*, and 25-101, *Battle Focused Training*, detail the essential components of the training process.

As the Soldier's Manual is to individual performance-oriented training, the Army Training and Evaluation Program (ARTEP) is to collective training. Each ARTEP consists of a series of training and evaluation outlines. Each outline specifies for a particular element of a battalion or separate company the following information.
- Unit (crew, squad, platoon, company, battalion) the outline applies to.
- Mission to perform.
- General conditions (situation) under which the unit will perform the mission.
- Primary training and evaluation standards for evaluating satisfactory or unsatisfactory unit performance.
- Collective training objectives, guidance for estimating support requirements necessary to conduct formal evaluations, and tips to trainers and evaluators.

DUTIES

Walking down the road one day at Fort Benning, I saw a group of airborne trainees in the front-leaning-rest position. Their arms were shaking and quivering, and I heard one call out in a weak and plaintive voice, "Sergeant . . ."

This massive airborne NCO leaned over him and yelled in his ear, "You don't need to call me 'sergeant,' soldier, 'cause I'm your friend. I'm your friend."

—Former SMA William G. Bainbridge to the
USMA Class of 1979, 17 April 1979

Of course, the airborne sergeant was really only joking. The special relationship between good sergeants and their soldiers goes far beyond that of friendship. Establishing this relationship is one of the most important responsibilities that any noncommissioned officer must face, but there are many others as well.

All soldiers, from the rank of private to that of general, have "duties and responsibilities," and no soldier should take them lightly. If you are a young soldier, you may well wonder whether you can handle all of them. Perhaps you will find, in time, that you cannot handle them, or perhaps you will discover that you can manage some better than others. There are two basic factors that will determine how well you handle your NCO duties and responsibilities: your initiative in accepting the challenge and responsibility of your grade; and your experience in exercising your duties and responsibilities.

There is a difference between duties and responsibilities. For instance, it is the supply sergeant's *duty* to issue equipment and keep records of the unit's supplies; it is the first sergeant's *duty* to hold formations, instruct platoon sergeants, and assist the commander in supervising unit operations; it is the *duty* of squad/section/team leaders to account for their soldiers and ensure that they receive necessary instructions and are properly trained to perform their jobs.

Responsibilities are those things for which you are held personally accountable. Any duty you have because of the position you hold in a unit includes a *responsibility to perform that duty*. But in addition, the mere fact that you wear the insignia of grade of an enlisted leader charges you with responsibility that goes far beyond ensuring that the soldiers under your supervision work as a team to further your unit's assigned mission.

Promotion Boards

Local promotion boards are generally convened by commanders to consider personnel for advancement to sergeant and staff sergeant (although some commanders may hold boards to consider specialist and corporal promotions). Promotion boards are convened monthly (except during those months when no personnel are being recommended) and may consist of commissioned, warrant, and noncommissioned officers, or all enlisted members. Board members are appointed in writing, and a board consists of at least three voting members and a recorder without vote. The senior member presides over the board's operation.

The senior member of a mixed board must be an officer, preferably field grade. The senior member of an all-enlisted board must be a command sergeant major or a frocked CSM. The board members must be senior in grade to those being considered for promotion. The recorder should be from your organization's personnel and administration center or military personnel office or be someone qualified in military personnel procedures. Inasmuch as the recorder has no vote, he or she does not need to be senior in grade to the personnel being considered for promotion.

The board must have at least one voting member of the same sex as those being considered. When this is not feasible for good reasons, the recorder must record the reason in the board proceedings. The appointing authority must also appoint members of minority ethnic groups within the command as voting members, even though the board may not be considering soldiers of minority ethnic groups. There is, however, no specific number or ratio of these soldiers to serve on any given board.

The board president (the senior member) calls the board to order and briefs it on the proceedings to be followed. Generally, the president will contact the board members somewhat in advance of convening to assign them specific areas on which to examine the candidates (or the recorder will be assigned this duty).

The president may decide to vote, or he may use his vote only to break a tie. The president may put specific questions to candidates, but generally the president's function is to direct general opinion-type or personal ("Where did you take your basic training?") questions at the candidates, put them at ease, and orient them toward the proceedings.

Each voting member completes a DA Form 3356, *Board Member Appraisal Worksheet*, on each soldier. The worksheet allows the member to rate each candidate in six areas of evaluation: personal appearance; bearing and self-confidence; oral expression and conversational skill; knowledge of world affairs; awareness of military programs; knowledge of basic soldiering; and attitude. The maximum number of points that can be awarded is 200, which is one-fifth of the soldier's overall promotion points.

Each voting member signs the worksheet recommending or not recommending the soldier for promotion. The recorder then collects the worksheets and checks them. If there is a tie, he so informs the president; otherwise, he completes DA Form 3357, Board Recommendation, which the president signs. Finally, the recorder completes the remaining portion of part III, DA Form 3355, Promotion Point Worksheet.

Know what the Promotion Point Worksheet contains. Basically, the maximum allowable points for promotion are 1,000: 800 administrative and 200 from the promotion board examination. The administrative points break down into six major categories: 200 for duty performance; 200 for SDT scores; 50 for awards and decorations; 150 for military education (NCOES, NCOA, correspondence courses); 100 for civilian education (business/trade school, college, GT and GED score improvements); and 100 for military training (marksmanship and physical readiness test scores).

Noncommissioned officers exercise significant influence in all of the areas cited above. NCOs are the primary evaluators of soldiers' duty performance; soldiers do well on their SDT if they are trained well by their NCOs; soldiers who are well trained and well led invariably attain special skill badges and are recommended for decorations by their NCO leaders; noncommissioned officers run the NCOES and constantly emphasize education and training.

All these "NCO influences" come together when that soldier appears before you at his promotion board. A good showing before the promotion board can assure a soldier of the promotion points he or she needs to make sergeant or staff sergeant, and attaining these grades is an important factor in a soldier's deciding whether he or she will make a career of the Army. Your duty is to keep the outstanding soldiers by identifying them when they come before you. Likewise, you must be fair to them by identifying those soldiers who do not measure up.

When asking questions, never ask ones that are not pertinent or realistic, such as "How many trucks are there at Fort Myer?"* If you are questioning clerks on a headquarters staff, do not expect them to know technical information about the care and operation of the M-60 machine gun, for instance.

Pay close attention to the soldier's personal appearance and bearing. Although you may not be asking the questions in a particular area (world affairs), pay attention to each candidate's responses, and if you are not sure of the answer yourself and the questioner gives no indication whether the soldier's responses are correct, find out the answer after the individual is dismissed.

---

*The correct answer is "two." A "truck" is a small wooden disk or block with holes for flag halyards.

BOARD MEMBER APPRAISAL WORKSHEET

For use of this form, see AR 600-8-19; the proponent agency is ODCSPER

1. NAME (Last, First, MI)	2. RECOMMENDED GRADE	3. PRESENT PMOS	4. RECOMMENDED CPMOS

5. Board Interview and Evaluation

AREAS OF EVALUATION	POINT SPREAD				TOTAL
	AVERAGE	ABOVE AVERAGE	EXCELLENT	OUTSTANDING	
A. Personal Appearance, Bearing, and Self-Confidence	1-15 POINTS	16-20 POINTS	21-25 POINTS	26-30 POINTS	
B. Oral Expression and Conversational Skill	1-15 POINTS	16-25 POINTS	26-30 POINTS	31-35 POINTS	
C. Knowledge of World Affairs	1-10 POINTS	11-15 POINTS	16-20 POINTS	21-25 POINTS	
D. Awareness of Military Programs	1-10 POINTS	11-15 POINTS	16-20 POINTS	21-25 POINTS	
E. Knowledge of Basic Soldiering (Soldier's Manual) (See note.)	1-15 POINTS	16-25 POINTS	26-35 POINTS	36-45 POINTS	
F. Soldier's Attitude (includes leadership and potential for advancement, trends in performance, etc).	1-15 POINTS	16-25 POINTS	26-35 POINTS	36-40 POINTS	
			G. TOTAL POINTS AWARDED (MAXIMUM 200 POINTS)		

NOTE: Questions concerning the knowledge of basic soldiering will be tailored to include land navigation, survival, night operations, inclement weather operations, adverse environment, and terrain.

6. REMARKS

7. I DO ☐ DO NOT ☐ recommend the soldier for promotion.

8. SIGNATURE OF BOARD MEMBER	9. RANK	10. DATE

DA FORM 3356, APR 91   DA FORM 3356, MAR 85 IS OBSOLETE

DA Form 3356 is designed to be used by field promotion boards for evaluation and recommendation of personnel being considered for promotion to sergeant and staff sergeant.

The Role of the NCO

Rating personnel in such areas as personal appearance, bearing, self-confidence, oral expression, and attitude is difficult and largely judgmental and subjective. Often, board members tend to mark higher in these areas than in those that require specific answers to direct questions. With younger soldiers, consider that a little tension or nervousness is natural and may tend to dampen their enthusiasm. Put them at ease by introducing yourself and perhaps commenting on the individual's background (generally, you will have an opportunity to screen each candidate's personnel record before examining him). Explain what area you will be examining the candidate in, and give him or her sufficient time to answer your questions fully.

Do not sit stiffly and stone-faced and put your questions in a rapid-fire, drill-field tone of voice. Relax. Let the candidate know how he or she has done in response to your questions, and when wrong answers are given, give the correct ones before the candidate leaves the room.

Look for honesty in response to opinion-type questions rather than "party-line" answers. The soldier who has the courage to state forthright views before a promotion board is either a leader of exceptional potential or crazy, depending on the question asked. (A soldier who admits to a love relationship with the Nazi party or the KKK should cause even the most case-hardened command sergeant major to arch an outraged eyebrow or two.) But never mark down soldiers who are critical of military policies or procedures, providing their views are intelligently expressed, logical, and objective. It is from people such as these that our best leaders come.

Remember this and apply it to your own situation as a leader: *Soldiers who make a poor showing before a promotion board were poorly prepared for it, and this poor showing reflects not upon the soldier, but upon the noncommissioned officer who is that soldier's leader or supervisor.*

When preparing your own soldiers to appear before a promotion board, impress upon them that those initial few seconds as they cross the room, come to attention before the president of the board, salute, and report are crucial. A sloppy performance here may very well leave a bad impression on the individual members that will affect their overall evaluation. There is just no "trick" to doing well before promotion boards. One must simply look and act sharp, be relaxed but confident, and *be prepared*.

Your personal assurance of confidence in your soldiers' ability to do well before a promotion board is the best thing you can give them. An NCO can provide material to study, explain how boards operate, even conduct dry runs, but if a candidate does not believe his NCO is 100 percent behind him, he probably will not do well.

Soldier Boards

These boards are convened by local commanders to select outstanding soldiers for special reward and recognition, and as such, they are exceptionally important factors in boosting morale within a unit or a command. They fall into three types, and the degree of reward and recognition is based on an ascending scale of achievement.
- Soldier-of-the-month boards
- Soldier-of-the-quarter boards
- Soldier-of-the-year boards

Competition before these boards is very tough, perhaps tougher than it is for many promotion boards. To be considered for soldier of the year or even soldier of the quarter is a distinct honor by itself.

These boards generally proceed along the same lines as promotion boards, although their deliberations are often less formal than those of promotion boards because the benefits are conferred locally and do not involve the expenditure of public funds (money for bonds, plaques, certificates, and such are obtained from non-appropriated funds).

Unit Fund Councils

Unit funds contribute significantly to the morale and welfare of soldiers because through them commanders are able to obtain the money needed to furnish day rooms and purchase recreational gear as well as finance unit parties and picnics. The money for unit funds is disbursed by a Central Welfare Fund, which in turn draws upon nonappropriated funds, which come from sources like PX profits.

Unit fund councils, which decide how the money is to be spent for the greatest benefit of the greatest number of personnel in each unit, consist of an officer (usually the unit commander) and several enlisted personnel who represent all the enlisted persons in a unit. Money is disbursed to units at a fixed rate according to the average strength of enlisted and warrant officer personnel assigned or attached each month.

No matter where a noncommissioned officer is living, no matter what his or her duties may require, he or she is assigned to a unit and is obligated to participate in the social life of that unit, whether by attending unit-sponsored recreational activities or by sitting on the unit fund council, deciding how the money should be spent, and then actively planning and carrying out the arrangements.

RESPONSIBILITIES

While officer and noncommissioned officer responsibilities may be shared, the tasks necessary to accomplish them should not be. Noncommissioned officer responsibilities are divided into twelve broad categories, the bible of the NCO Corps:

1. *Individual training of soldiers in MOSs and in basic soldiering skills.*
   - Train soldiers to fight, win, and live.
   - Teach soldiers the history and traditions of the Army, military courtesy, personal hygiene, appearance standards, and drill and ceremonies.

2. *Personal and professional development of soldiers.*
   - Recommend that the good soldiers attend service school specialist or career development courses as needed and as appropriate.
   - Fix responsibility. Assign to subordinates the responsibility for appropriate tasks: give soldiers tasks they can do based on their abilities, experience, and know-how. Train your soldiers to take on increasingly difficult or complex tasks.
   - Train your soldiers to replace you, just as you yourself train to replace your superiors. Begin today; once the shooting starts, it may be too late.
   - Develop a sense of responsibility in your soldiers by holding them responsible for their actions.
   - Ensure that required publications are available and convenient for the soldiers to use.
   - Help soldiers cope with personal problems. This means more than referring them to another person—the chaplain, a doctor, or counselor. Until the problem is resolved, you have a soldier with a problem in your unit, so it is your problem, too.
   - Counsel soldiers on their strengths and weaknesses; build on their strengths

The Role of the NCO

A drill sergeant instructs a recruit in the handling of a grenade. U.S. Army photo

and help them strive to overcome their weaknesses.
- Recommend soldier promotions and awards through the NCO channel of support.
- Do not promise promotions and awards you cannot guarantee.
- Develop your own ability to deal with personal and professional development of soldiers of both sexes.

3. *Accountability for the squad, the section, or the team.*
   - Know what each soldier in the unit that you lead is doing during duty hours (and off-duty hours as well when there is a problem that spreads from off-duty to on-duty).
   - Know where each soldier lives and how to contact him.
   - Know why a soldier is going on sick call or other appointments, how he or she is treated, and what is wrong.
   - Use the team, the squad, or the section as a unit to accomplish as many missions as possible, *but never volunteer your troops for missions to make yourself look good in the eyes of your superiors.* Know your team's limitations.
   - Know the readiness status or operating condition of the weapons, vehicles, and other equipment with which your soldiers and your unit do your unit's job.

4. *Military appearance, physical conditioning, and training of soldiers.*
   - Make corrections on the spot when you see something wrong *wherever* you may be and to *whomever* is concerned. Always be polite and diplomatic.
   - Supervise the physical fitness training and development of your soldiers, in accordance with FM 21-20, *Physical Fitness Training*, and AR 350-15, *The Army Physical Fitness Program*.
   - Ensure that you and your soldiers meet the army's weight and body fat standards in accordance with AR 600-9, *The Army Weight Control Program*.

5. *Physical and mental well-being of the soldier and his or her family.*
   - Know your soldiers' family situations and help them if they have problems.
   - Make sure your soldiers know what services and benefits they and their families are entitled to; if you do not know, find out. Your personnel officer or personnel service NCO can provide this information.

6. *Supervision, control, motivation, and discipline of subordinates.*
   - Counsel your soldiers and maintain your own counseling records.
   - Support actions of your subordinate NCOs when you have any. Similarly, when they are wrong, tell them so, but do it privately.
   - Teach your soldiers about the Uniform Code of Military Justice.
   - Recommend commendations and passes.
   - Recommend bars to reenlistment or elimination actions if appropriate. Weeding out the bad soldiers will encourage the good soldiers to stay.
   - Conduct corrective training when required.
   - Keep your soldiers informed—do not let them be surprised by extra duty details, field training exercises, special inspections, or other events.

7. *Communication between the individual soldier and the organization.*
   - Use, and insist that your soldiers use, the chain of command and support channels.
   - Listen and act on soldiers' suggestions and complaints when possible, but you must be able to distinguish between mere belly-aching and serious complaining. Do not let your zeal for demonstrating concern for your soldiers let you go off half-cocked.
   - Support and explain the reasons for current policies.
   - Try to develop a feeling of loyalty and pride in your team and your unit.
   - Do not complain to, or in the presence of, your soldiers.

8. *Plan and conduct day-to-day unit operations within prescribed policies.*
   - Provide input to the schedule for individual skill training.
   - Conduct team training.
   - Supervise daily events as required by training schedules.

9. *Maintain established standards of performance for soldiers and NCOs.*
   - Explain clearly what you expect from your soldiers.
   - Conduct special training to correct training weaknesses.
   - Train your soldiers to the standards set by the soldiers' manuals and other training literature.
   - Provide up-to-date information for appropriate levels of skill qualification tests.

The Role of the NCO

* Be an example of the professional NCO in action. If you are, many of your soldiers may also want to be sergeants some day.

10. *Maintenance, serviceability, accountability, and readiness of arms, clothing, vehicles, and equipment.*
    * Inspect your soldiers' and the unit's equipment often. Use the manual or approved checklist. Hold your soldiers responsible for repairs and losses.
    * Learn how to use and maintain the equipment your soldiers use. Be among the first to operate new equipment, whether tanks or word processors.
    * Enforce maintenance and supply system procedures for the chain of command.
    * Encourage economy and deal summarily with soldiers who abuse their equipment.
    * Keep up-to-date component lists and set aside time for inventories. Know what you have on hand and turn in excess or unserviceable equipment.

11. *Appearance and condition of unit billets, facilities, and work areas.*
    * Inspect these areas often and supervise their maintenance.
    * Conduct fire and safety inspections and drills.
    * Set and enforce cleanliness standards.
    * Eat in the mess hall and observe mess operations.

12. *Advise on, support, and implement policy established by the chain of command.*

THE CHAIN OF COMMAND AND THE NCO

The importance of the chain of command to the success of tactical operations and organizations is nothing new in military affairs. The extent to which any social institution works depends for the most part upon how effectively orders and information are passed from top to bottom and back. The old joke about the spaceman landing in a farmer's pasture and telling the mule, "Take me to your leader," while saying nothing about how intelligent beings on other planets may organize their affairs, certainly says something about the universal concept among us humans that somebody has to be in charge. When things do not work this way chaos is the result. The role of the noncommissioned officer in making the chain of command work is absolutely vital.

The chain of command is defined as the succession of commanding officers from a superior to a subordinate through which command is exercised. There is only one chain of command in the Army, but it is paralleled and reinforced by the NCO support channel. Both are channels of communication used to pass information up and down the unit. Neither is a one-way street, nor are the two entirely separate. In order for the chain of command to work, the NCO support channel must be operating.

In addition to the chain of command and the NCO support channel, most units have staff and technical channels. The most well-known example is that of the battalion staff, but variations on this theme occur throughout the Army. The battalion staff consists of these staff members: S1, personnel and administrative staff section; S2, intelligence; S3, training and operations; and S4, logistics. Each section includes commissioned and noncommissioned officers who work for the battalion commander and with subordinate units.

Essentially, the staff and technical channels provide the commander the information needed to implement decisions, but they provide no control over the activities of subordinate units.

The NCO Support Channel

The NCO support channel begins with the command sergeant major and ends with the squad/section chief/team leader. Between these points, it works through intermediate levels, such as company first sergeants and platoon sergeants. In addition to passing information, this channel is used for issuing orders and getting routine, but important jobs done. This NCO channel leaves the commander free to plan, make decisions, and program future training and operations.

The CSM is the senior enlisted advisor to the commander, and although he is not in the chain of command, he knows what instructions are being issued through it, and this knowledge helps him supervise the NCO support channel. He has the commander's ear and vice versa.

An important aspect of the NCO support channel is the periodic "NCO Call" or "First Sergeant's Call," which enables the NCOs of a unit to assemble and discuss items of mutual interest. This traditional method of keeping the members of the NCO support channel informed works whether that channel serves a battalion organization or a major command staff.

The NCO support channel is a formal entity, directive in nature. But regardless of where information or tasks begin, the officer counterpart in the chain of command at that level must be kept informed to prevent duplication and issuing conflicting orders.

Command is not normally delegated to enlisted soldiers, although any unit that is temporarily without officers may actually be commanded by an enlisted person, as sometimes happens in platoons or platoon-sized units. Nevertheless, commanders have the specific responsibility of ensuring the equitable delegation of authority and responsibility to noncommissioned officers by their subordinates, whether officers, warrant officers, or other noncommissioned officers.

The Sergeant Major of the Army

The Sergeant Major of the Army is the senior sergeant major grade of rank and designates the senior enlisted position of the Army. The individual who occupies this office serves as the senior enlisted advisor and consultant to the Chief of Staff of the Army in the following areas: problems affecting enlisted personnel and solutions to these problems; professional education, growth, and advancement of NCOs; and morale, training, pay, promotions, and other matters concerning enlisted personnel.

The Command Sergeant Major

The Command Sergeant Major (CSM) is the senior noncommissioned officer of the command at battalion or higher level. He or she executes established policies and standards pertaining to the performance, training, appearance, and conduct of enlisted personnel. The CSM provides advice and initiates recommendations to the commander and staff in matters pertaining to enlisted personnel. The activities of the local noncommissioned officer channel emanate from the CSM of a unit, an installation, or a state headquarters. This channel functions orally through the command sergeant's major or first sergeant's call and normally does not involve written instructions; however, either method may be used, and both are considered *directive in nature.*

The First Sergeant

The position of the first sergeant is similar to that of the command sergeant major in importance, responsibility, and prestige. The first sergeant is in direct and daily

The Role of the NCO

contact with sizeable numbers of other enlisted personnel, requiring of him or her outstanding leadership and professional competence. The first sergeant is the senior noncommissioned officer in companies, batteries, and troops. Normally, company commanders use the noncommissioned officer support channel for conducting many routine activities, particularly in garrison. The first sergeant conducts routine company administration and company operations as directed by the company commander.

The Platoon Sergeant

The platoon sergeant is a key person in the command structure of the Army. It is normal for platoon sergeants to become commanders during the absence or disability of commissioned officers of the platoon. When the platoon leader is present, the platoon sergeant is a key assistant and advisor.

Section, Squad, Team Leaders

Traditionally and habitually, noncommissioned officers fill the positions of section, squad, and team leaders. These soldiers are responsible for the personal appearance and cleanliness of their soldiers, for property accountability and maintenance, for the whereabouts of their soldiers at all times, and for the ability of the team to perform the primary mission at all times.

THE NCO AND THE OFFICER

> You are not only to entertain a hearty contempt for your officers, but you must also take care to communicate it to the soldiers. The more you appear to despise your superiors, the greater respect, you know, your inferiors will possess for you.
>
> —Captain Francis Grose, *Advice to the Officers of the British Army* (1782)

Too often the relationship between officers and noncommissioned officers is seen as an adversary one, with officers trying their best to muddle things up while hard-working and dedicated sergeants try their best to straighten them out. Captain Grose was not really advising the NCOs of the British Army to be contemptuous of their officers. He was satirizing a situation that he found all too common in the army of his day. If you look about you, you will find that there are still vestiges of this "advice" present in the NCO Corps of the U.S. Army even today.

It is also a fact that sometimes over-eager and inexperienced officers *do* make messes out of things, despite good advice from their NCOs. But ask yourself this question: Wherever there is an officer who is contemptuous of NCOs, might there not be, somewhere in that officer's past, a bad NCO? Unfortunately, it takes only one bad example to spoil things for everybody.

During the Vietnam War, something happened to the NCO Corps of the U.S. Army. Former Sergeant Major of the Army William A. Connelly, in an address before a TRADOC Command Sergeants Major Conference at Savannah, Georgia, in November 1977, put it this way.

> The years of Vietnam saw a decline in the role of the NCO. Officers took on many jobs formerly given to NCOs, perhaps because of a lack of faith in subordinates, or perhaps because many

from the "officer factories" of the '60s would have preferred to be NCOs in a more normal time and since they felt more comfortable doing the "running" of the outfit, they just did it. Vietnam was also the time of the "instant NCO," graduate of "combat leader courses" which turned out an E-6 with less than six months' service. Well, there is not now—nor was there then—any such thing as an "instant NCO," for the main ingredient—experience—is missing.

The root cause of that whole problem was not that officers "took" anything away from their NCOs, but that those NCOs relinquished their responsibilities. Former Sergeant Major of the Army William G. Bainbridge, in an unpublished essay titled "The Corps of Noncommissioned Officers," put this very succinctly in words that should serve as a guide for all noncommissioned officers in their relations with their officers.

> No officer ever took anything away from the noncommissioned officer—it was simply given away. The good noncommissioned officer has never been short in confidence—either to perform the mission or to inform the superior that he or she was interfering with traditional noncommissioned officer business. When a noncommissioned officer chose to relinquish some responsibility to a commissioned officer, he or she taught an officer that a sergeant couldn't or wouldn't perform a certain task.

The essence of the officer/noncommissioned officer relationship is best expressed in an old Army story.

An old major, a veteran of long service and some hard campaigns, was giving some officer candidates a practical exercise in how to lead troops. The problem involved putting up a flagpole. To do it, he had provided a sergeant and a detail of three privates with tools. But it was up to the officer candidates to figure out the best way to do the job.

They pondered the situation carefully. Several false starts were made; solutions were advanced and tried but failed because nobody seemed to be in charge; each candidate thought only he knew the right way and competed loudly with the others to be heard.

Finally, the old major stepped in and with a gesture silenced the babble. "Gentlemen," said he, "allow me to demonstrate how a good officer would do this job." He turned to the sergeant and said, "Sergeant, please have the men put up the flagpole." Nothing more was said and in a few minutes the pole was up.

The good officer knows that the good NCO gets the job done. The good NCO knows that the good officer will let him do it.

The Officer/Noncommissioned Officer Relationship

OFFICER	NONCOMMISSIONED OFFICER
The officer commands, establishes policy, plans and programs the work of the Army.	The NCO conducts the daily business of the Army within established orders, directives, and policies.
The officer concentrates on collective training that will enable the unit to accomplish its mission.	The NCO concentrates on individual training that develops the capability to accomplish the mission.

The Role of the NCO

The officer is primarily involved with unit operations, training, and related activities.	The NCO is primarily involved with training individual soldiers and teams.
The officer concentrates on unit effectiveness and unit readiness.	The NCO concentrates on each subordinate NCO and soldier and on the small teams of the unit—to ensure that each is well trained, highly motivated, ready, and functioning.
The officer pays particular attention to the standards of performance, training, and professional development of officers as well as NCOs.	The NCO concentrates on standards of performance, training, and professional development of NCOs and enlisted personnel.
The officer creates conditions—makes the time and other resources available—*so the NCO can do the job.*	*The NCO gets the job done.*

COMPARABLE RANK AMONG THE SERVICES

Commissioned Officers of the Army, the Navy, the Air Force, and the Marine Corps

Army, Air Force, and Marine Corps	Navy
General	Admiral
Lieutenant general	Vice admiral
Major general	Rear admiral (upper half)
Brigadier general	Commodore (lower half)
Colonel	Captain
Lieutenant colonel	Commander
Major	Lieutenant commander
Captain	Lieutenant
First lieutenant	Lieutenant (junior grade)
Second lieutenant	Ensign

Warrant Officers of All Services

Chief warrant officer, W-4
Chief warrant officer, W-3
Chief warrant officer, W-2
Warrant officer, W-1

Cadet

Cadet	Midshipman

PRECEDENCE AND RELATIVE RANK

The determination of rank and precedence among enlisted personnel is sometimes not as critical as it is among officers (especially when deciding who will com-

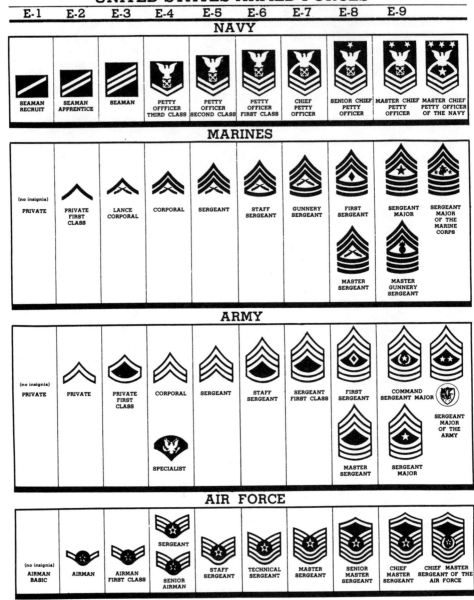

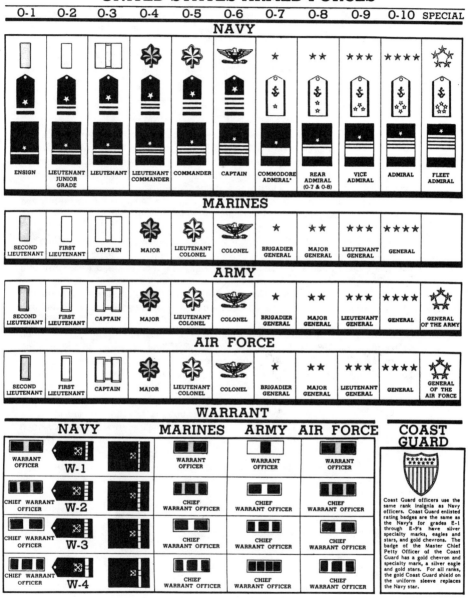

mand), but it is necessary to resort to some system on those occasions when determining among two or more individuals of equal rank which one will be responsible to a commander or a supervisor for functions within the enlisted support channel.

Among enlisted personnel of the same grade of rank in active military service, including retired personnel on active duty, precedence or relative rank is determined:
1. By date of rank.
2. When dates of rank are the same, by length of active service in the Army.
3. When 1 and 2 above are the same, by length of total active service.
4. When the foregoing tests are not sufficient, by age.

THE NEW MANNING SYSTEM (NMS)

One of the most traumatic experiences a soldier faces is that of reporting to a new outfit in a new location, making new friends, and getting to know new NCOs and officers. The New Manning System (NMS) is designed to minimize this turbulence in the Army's replacement system and to increase the stabilization in units of soldiers as well as add some predictability to their assignment pattern.

The objectives of the NMS are to reduce the personnel turbulence that often frustrated unit training and readiness goals and to allow soldiers to develop an enduring sense of *identity* with their units.

The NMS was developed in 1981. It is *not* a tactical system; it does not replace the combined arms team concept; it is a way of manning and training the Army. The NMS has two subsystems: the Cohesion, Operational Readiness, and Training system (COHORT) and the Regimental System.

The COHORT system has been applied to companies/batteries and battalions. Its objective is to provide for a more stable unit environment by reducing personnel and organizational turbulence. Under the company/battery COHORT system, soldiers destined for a COHORT unit train together during initial Entry Training (IET), after which they join their company cadre in a stateside COHORT unit. These cadre and the first-term soldiers stay together in the same unit for a three-year life cycle. The unit trains together in the states and then deploys as a unit overseas.

Soldiers in COHORT companies/batteries bound for a short-tour area spend 24 months together in CONUS before deploying; those going to a long-tour area remain in CONUS for 18 months before deploying. When the unit reaches the end of its life cycle, it is replaced by a new one. Its soldiers either separate from the Army or are reassigned on individual orders to CONUS or overseas locations, depending on how much time they have left on their active duty obligation or overseas tour.

Under the COHORT battalion movement concept, the first-term soldiers are stabilized for three years as are soldiers with companies, but the cadre are stabilized with the unit for 48 months from their date of arrival. Some COHORT battalions also are designated as nonrotating units, and soldiers assigned to them can expect to spend at least three years in the same unit at the same location.

The Regimental System is a grouping of like battalions in CONUS and overseas with the same regimental designation, according to AR 600-82, *The U.S. Army Regimental System*, June 1990. Regiments are formed to allow affiliation and recurring assignments to the same units and geographical locations. In June 1990, the Army had 184 regiments. Since that time, and because of ongoing force reductions, the number of regiments has been declining.

NEW MANNING SYSTEM

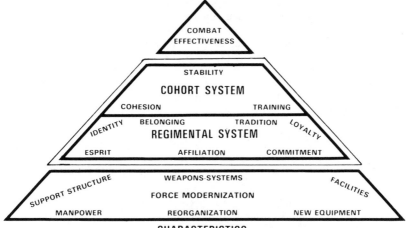

CHARACTERISTICS

COHORT

- MORE STABLE UNIT ENVIRONMENT
- REDUCED PERSONNEL TURBULENCE
- EXTENDED SOLDIER-LEADER INTERFACE
- REDUCED ORGANIZATIONAL TURBULENCE
- GREATER STRUCTURAL COMPATABILITY

REGIMENTAL SYSTEM

- RECURRING ASSIGNMENTS
  - SAME UNITS
  - SAME LOCATIONS
  - SAME PEERS
- INCREASED PROFESSIONAL SPECIALIZATION
- GREATER SENSE OF BELONGING IDENTITY
- INCREASED PREDICTABILITY
- INCREASED FAMILY SUPPORT

STAFF ASSIGNMENTS

The military staff is divided into the categories of combined, general, integrated, joint, parallel, and special. The two kinds of staff assignments you are most likely to draw are those on the general and joint staffs. The others are defined in JCS Pub 1, *Department of Defense Dictionary of Military and Associated Terms.*

General staff. General staff officers are in the headquarters of an Army division or larger size unit that assists the commander in planning, coordinating, and supervising operations. A general staff may consist of four or more principal functional sections: personnel (G-1); military intelligence (G-2); operations and training (G-3); logistics (G-4); and civil affairs/military government (G-5). A particular section may be added or eliminated by the commander, depending on need. In Army brigades and smaller units, staff sections are designated S-1, S-2, and so on. Similarly, a joint staff may be designated J-1, J-2, and so on.

Joint staff. A joint staff is really a general staff operating under very special conditions: It is the staff of a commander of a unified or specified command, or of a joint task force, which includes members from the several services composing the force. Positions on a joint staff are divided so that service representation and influence generally reflect the service composition of the force. A unified command is one with a broad continuing mission under a single commander and composed of significant assigned components of two or more services; a specified command normally consists of the forces of one service.

You will adjust quickly to duty on an Army general staff because it is duty with your own service. Joint staff duty, however, can be a whole new world, especially if the commander is from a service other than the Army. If, for example, you should be assigned to a job with Commander in Chief, Pacific (CINCPAC), you will be working for the Navy.

The ultimate in joint staff duty is with the Joint Chiefs of Staff at the Pentagon. The JCS takes on the coloration of none of the military services because the chairman is changed every four years. There is nothing else in the military like the JCS because it operates under a distinct set of rules evolved over the years. That is why you are said to wear a "purple suit" when you are assigned there: you lose the "coloration" of your service, and when you return to the Army, you undergo what is called a "regreening process" in order to catch up on what has been going on in your own service.

Like death and taxes, nobody avoids service on the staff, especially the senior noncommissioned officer. Your turn may come, though, even before you have reached those grades, so be prepared. How you do in a staff assignment will determine the rest of your career.

Wherever you may pull staff duty, the following lessons, gleaned over the years by NCOs who have served on Army general staffs at all levels and joint staffs in several theaters, will be of great help to you. The following bits of advice have come from those who have gone before. Read them and heed them, but above all, remain flexible.

You have been picked to serve on the commander's staff because somebody thinks you are pretty good. Now you'll have to prove it. If you've been leading troops up to now, you're in for a *big* change. It's only temporary, but if you cannot accept it, you are in for trouble.

Accept that you are now a small cog in a very big wheel and that you are going to make mistakes — especially if you have little or no administrative experience. Do not try to hide your ignorance or bluff your way through things you do not understand. Learn from those who have been there for a while, and don't be too proud to ask for advice. If, for instance, you have been a hard-charging platoon sergeant up to now but yesterday found yourself installed as battalion operations sergeant, look to your clerks first: If you are blessed with good ones, treat them with the respect they deserve; otherwise, get clerks you can rely on. One good clerk can keep you afloat in your new job until you learn the ropes; a bad one can torpedo you quickly.

You are going to be required to do a lot of things below your ability and not commensurate with your grade or specialty, such as typing, filing, and errand running. Enlisted people on the staff have traditionally done those jobs. That is changing, but if you prove incompetent at any of these chores, your boss will not trust you with more important jobs, and you will wind up doing the menial ones until he can get you replaced.

If you are assigned to a major headquarters staff and you are really good, you could perform some action officer duty. A staff action officer is the lowest creature in the world, to hear him tell it. Nobody likes what he writes, nobody listens to what he says, and nobody cares if he lives or dies. He is expected, however, to be at his desk

The Role of the NCO

eighteen hours a day, seven days a week, and if that's not enough to get the job done, he works overtime. And that's what the lieutenant colonels do.

The ability to read and write is necessary for anybody who serves on the staff. As a writer, you are probably no Shakespeare. Don't sweat it; nobody else is either, although you may run into some staff officers who think they are. Write in short, simple sentences. Keep a dictionary handy and use it. Remember that generals like to go straight to the core of the problem. Make sure you are never the problem. The key to good staff work is based on the "KISS principle": Keep It Simple, Stupid. Never make things more complicated than they are, and let sleeping dogs lie.

Learn the language of the staff. Get to know the buzzwords and acronyms. But be careful where you use such language. The rest of the world doesn't understand it, and if you write your sweetheart about prioritizing the logistical requirements of this weekend's date in order to define the fiscal parameters of the problem, you'll probably be going out by yourself.

If you are replacing somebody, get rid of him as soon after you arrive as you can. After two or three days, his continued presence will hold you back. If he stays around just long enough to show you where things are and to introduce you to the people you need to know, that's enough. Do not be annoyed if he forgets to tell you something vital. Chances are he's as anxious to be gone as you are to be in, and once you find out how hard he worked, you won't hold it against him that he didn't leave you a detailed SOP on how to get the job done.

Learn the priorities. Staff work consists of knowing what to do first. When every action has a suspense that was due yesterday, you need to develop a good sense of what comes first. Keep track of what's due, and if you can't make a suspense, let someone know. There really is no such thing as a "drop dead" date on an Army staff paper, although this fact is a jealously guarded secret at every headquarters. Coordinate your actions thoroughly with everyone concerned, be honest if you're having a problem, and don't be afraid to ask for an extension if you need one.

Do not be disappointed if your best work goes for nothing. Crises on the staff come like huge waves, rolling in and knocking everything out of kilter, then rolling on and leaving you getting ready for the next one. What is a comber today is only a puddle tomorrow, and by then, everybody's forgotten all about it.

Remain physically fit. Desk work will make you soft and fat if you let it: Don't. Work out a regular exercise schedule and keep to it. Commanders and staff officers realize the necessity of keeping physically fit. No matter how busy you are, short of real combat operations, you can always find time to exercise.

Do not get in the habit of eating at your desk. Get out of the office for a spell, if only to walk around the headquarters area. This will break up the monotony and give you a few minutes of badly needed relaxation. It will give you a chance to think and calm down, and there will be many days when you will need to do that.

Keep up your personal appearance. Duty away from troops is no excuse to let yourself grow sloppy. Wherever you go, set the standard for military bearing and appearance.

On the staff, you get to know officers as you've never known them before. What may shock you is that some may even want you to be on a first-name basis with them. Don't. Your special status as a noncommissioned officer will suffer if you become too familiar with your superiors. This familiarity begins when you start calling them by their rank instead of "sir" or "ma'am." Maintain that distance. This admonition does not mean you cannot be easy with them, but a good NCO always observes the courtesies and, by giving the proper respect, gets it back.

Every major staff system includes plenty of civilian personnel who serve commanders in support roles. Sometimes these people are relatively high-ranking individuals with many years of government service. Get to know them. Civilians are the "corporate memory" of the staff; military people come and go, but the civilians stay forever.

To be a good all-around NCO, you must know how the staff works. That knowledge will be priceless to you when you're back with the troops and on the receiving end of staff decisions. Staff and field have traditionally hated each other. The typical staff officer thinks troops in the field are dirty, ugly, and stupid; the typical infantryman thinks the staff officer is arrogant, lazy, and purposely isolated from reality. The soldier who can cross those lines is ready for anything the Army can throw at him.

CASUALTY NOTIFICATION, SURVIVOR ASSISTANCE, AND BODY ESCORT DETAIL

The chances are that at some point in your military career you will be detailed to act as a casualty notifier or a Survivor Assistance Officer (SAO) or a body escort. You will find the experience one of the most difficult and trying duties you will ever face. If you perform these duties well, you will receive a deep sense of personal satisfaction from knowing that you have helped someone in distress.

Notification of Next of Kin

As a casualty notifier, you represent the Secretary of the Army. You are expected to be courteous, helpful, and sympathetic, and your presence should soften the blow, if possible, and show the Army's concern for its soldiers, their dependents, and their next of kin.

Department of the Army policy is to make personal notification of the next of kin of all deceased and missing soldiers. As far as possible, the deceased soldier's desires for notification of next of kin listed on DD Form 93 *(Record of Emergency Data)* will be followed.

Paragraph 5-4, AR 600-8-1, prescribes that enlisted personnel in the senior grades may be used as notifiers providing an officer is not available and the grade of the enlisted person used is equal to or higher than that of the deceased.

If the person to be notified is not fluent in English, a qualified interpreter should accompany you. The linguist should interpret only what is spoken between you and the next of kin and should not engage in side conversation. Contact your installation personnel officer in cases that require a linguist.

Be prepared for an adverse reaction on the part of the person being notified. If you know beforehand that the next of kin has a medical problem, consult the family doctor. If one cannot be identified, consult any physician in the area where notification is to be made. If you feel it is best, get the doctor to go with you when you make notification. Army Medical Corps doctors cannot accompany you on these calls, although they may be consulted if they have been treating the person being notified. Just in case, be sure to have with you the telephone numbers for a local hospital, ambulance service, and fire department rescue squad.

If the person being notified does suffer an adverse medical reaction as a result of the news, you must follow certain procedures to keep your casualty commander notified. Additionally, all personal notifications must be confirmed promptly by commercial telegram. These details are set forth in Department of the Army Pamphlet 608-33,

The Role of the NCO   27

Casualty Assistance Handbook, a copy of which should be provided to you at the time you are selected for this duty.

Be careful to observe the following basic guidelines.
- Present the best possible military appearance that you can.
- Make your visit to the next of kin promptly after receiving casualty information, but your visit should take place only during the hours from 0600 to 2200, unless otherwise directed.
- Be as natural as possible in speech, manner, and method of delivery. What you say and the sincerity with which you say it are of the utmost importance.

The Army recommends you say these words:

> "The Secretary of the Army has asked me to express his deep regret that your (relationship) (died/was killed in action) in (country)/(state) on (date). (State the circumstances briefly and succinctly.) The Secretary extends his deepest sympathy to you and your family in your tragic loss."
>
> or:
>
> "The Secretary of the Army has asked me to inform you that your (relationship) has been reported (missing/missing in action) in (country) since (date). (State circumstances.) When we receive more information, you will be promptly notified. The Secretary extends his deepest sympathy to you and your family during this trying period."

- If the next of kin is alone at the time of your visit, offer to call someone or ask a neighbor to step in.
- You may inform the next of kin that survivor's assistance will be rendered, but do not specify date or time on which such a visit will be made.
- Advise the next of kin that a confirmation of your visit will be sent by telegram. Advise that there may be up to a 24-hour delay and verify the next of kin's name and mailing address.
- In cases of death, if the remains have been recovered, tell the next of kin that a message on the disposition of the remains will be coming. The normal time for the return of remains from overseas to their final destination is from seven to ten days; for shipment of remains within CONUS, three to four days. If the remains have not been recovered, tell the next of kin how memorial services are conducted (see AR 600-8-1).
- If the next of kin are not at home when you visit, make every reasonable effort to locate them, using neighbors or local authorities, as necessary. Be most discreet not to compromise the purpose of your visit, especially if you are forced to deal with friends or neighbors of the next of kin. You may find it necessary to go in search of the next of kin, even to traveling out of town, if the distance is not prohibitive. Should the next of kin be on vacation and too far away for you to carry out your visit, redirect action at once by telephone through the casualty reporting chain of command.
- Remember, once you begin notification action, you must continue to completion.
- You may inform the primary next of kin that personal notification will be made to the secondary next of kin if required. When notifying the secondary kin, you may inform that the primary kin have already been informed.
- Inform the next of kin that a letter from the soldier's commander will give more complete details (see Chapter 6, AR 600-8-1).

Be careful to observe the following prohibitions:
- DO NOT notify by telephone.
- DO NOT call for an appointment before making the visit.

- DO NOT hold notes or a prepared speech in your hand when approaching the residence of the next of kin.
- DO NOT disclose the purpose of your visit or the contents of your message except to the next of kin.
- DO NOT leave word with neighbors or others to have the next of kin contact you, should you find them away from home.
- DO NOT speak hurriedly or continually refer to notes when talking to the next of kin.
- DO NOT pass on any gory or embarrassing details surrounding the circumstances of the soldier's death.
- DO NOT use code words or acronyms or military jargon when speaking with the next of kin. (See Table 3-2, AR 600-8-1, for definitions of the code words used in the casualty reporting system.)
- DO NOT touch the next of kin unless there is extreme shock or fainting.
- DO NOT discuss entitlements at this time. Advise that the SAO will be in touch later, but make no specific statements or commitments.
- DO NOT discuss disposition of remains or personal effects.
- DO NOT inform the secondary kin that they will receive an SAO visit.
- DO NOT commit either your organization or the Department of the Army to carrying out any action or obtaining any information by a given time.
- DO NOT, under ANY circumstances, "fortify" yourself with alcohol or any other substance before making the visit.

Survivor Assistance

As a Survivor Assistance Officer, you are charged by the Secretary of the Army to render all reasonable assistance necessary to settle the personal affairs of a deceased soldier. Keep the thoughts and feelings of the next of kin uppermost in your mind at all times. Above all, be *prepared*. Nothing can reflect more adversely upon you than to demonstrate ignorance or indecision when dealing with the next of kin. Should you be asked questions for which you do not know the answers, remain cool and assure the next of kin that you will get the answers. But a thorough study of the references given to you by your local casualty office should ensure that you are not caught unprepared for any contingency.

Your main point of contact as an SAO will be the local casualty section. You may also receive assistance from the staff judge advocate, surgeon, provost marshal, public affairs officer, and finance, housing, and transportation officers. You are expected to make contacts with these officers, as required, without referral by the casualty section.

The Casualty Branch of your local Adjutant General Office should furnish you a complete packet relating to your duties as notifier/SAO at the time you receive a case for action. This packet should contain a detailed SOP pertaining to the services available to you locally to assist you in the efficient completion of your duties. The SOP, as a minimum, should include a telephone directory of the services available to you locally as well as most of the information sources listed below. Remember that the Casualty Branch is there to *advise* and *assist* you, but not to do your work for you.

Reference Materials for SAO

DOD Military Pay and Allowances Entitlements Manual.

AR 37-104-3, *Military Pay and Allowances Procedures: Joint Uniform Military Pay System (JUMPS—Army).*

The Role of the NCO

AR 40-121, *Uniformed Services Health Benefits Program.*
AR 600-8-1, *Army Casualty and Memorial Affairs and Line of Duty Investigations.*
AR 600-25, *Salutes, Honors, and Visits of Courtesy.*
AR 608-2, *Servicemen's Group Life Insurance (SGLI); Veteran's Group Life Insurance (VGLI).*
AR 608-50, *Legal Assistance.*
AR 640-3, *Personnel Records and Identification of Individuals, Identification Cards, Tags, and Badges.*
AR 672-5-1, *Military Awards.*
DA Pam 55-2, *Personal Property Shipping Information; It's Your Move.*

Body Escort Detail

Body escort detail is an extremely important and responsible duty. Soldiers selected to act as escort for a deceased member of the Army represent the U.S. Army and the United States itself. Being selected for this duty is an honor. The escort's mission is to see that the remains of the deceased reach the final destination chosen by the next of kin and that they are treated with honor, respect, and dignity during the time they are being transported.

Maintaining a highly correct state of personal appearance while acting as an escort is of primary importance. The uniform for this duty is the Army green uniform, with necktie (or necktab) and low-quarter shoes. The uniform should be cleaned and pressed and shoes well shined. If you are selected for escort duty, be sure that you take along enough clothing so that you will look well groomed at all times. Neatness and cleanliness of your person are a part of the respect shown for the dead.

Before you depart on this detail, you will receive a briefing concerning your duties. At that time, you will also receive a packet containing papers necessary to your assignment, including VA Form 40-1330 *(Application for Headstone or Marker)* and DD Form 1375 *(Request for Payment of Funeral and/or Interment Expenses).* You will also receive a Statement of Condition of Remains (a locally reproduced form) and the deceased's death certificate, which you should give to the funeral director when you arrive at your destination. You will receive an advance on your travel pay. If this amount is not enough, use your own money and file a claim for reimbursement when you return to your home station. You will need only one round-trip ticket. The casket is shipped on a transportation request (TR).

You are responsible for the remains from the time you sign for them to the time you obtain a receipt for them from the funeral director at your destination. The statement of the condition of the remains serves as your receipt.

When remains are to be transported in a casket, they may be sent by air or by rail, although the latter is used less often than air transportation. But regardless of how the remains are being shipped, you should be at the terminal well before the time of departure.

If the remains are going by air, check into the airline ticket counter to confirm your reservation. Determine at that time where you should go to make sure that the casket has arrived (this will be the operations room at the airport or the baggage room at a railway station). Examine the casket and check the label that shows the deceased's name and social security number. The label is located at the head of the casket. Sign your name on the label to show that you have checked it. Be sure that no cargo is placed on the casket.

When the casket is placed in the cargo compartment of an airplane, it is moved in a feet-first position. On the aircraft, the body should be placed in a head-first position, with the head toward the nose of the aircraft. The airline employees should be reminded of this. In a railcar, the remains are placed feet-first.

Salute the casket while it is being loaded on the carrier.

When traveling by airplane, tell the flight attendant that you are escorting a deceased person and wish to be the first to leave after landing. Do not discuss your escort duty with anyone during the journey. If there are transfers during the journey, use the ones arranged by the carrier's agent. Do not ask for any special arrangements to be made.

When the casket is being moved, you should accompany it to ensure proper handling and to make sure that the remains do not become separated from you.

If any emergency or unavoidable delay occurs, notify the receiving funeral home by telephone. Pay for this call and claim reimbursement when you file your travel voucher. Also call the mortuary officer at the shipping installation. You may call this officer collect. Give him the information about the cause of the delay and where it occurred. Be sure to include the new arrival time and flight number of the airplane on which you will arrive.

When you reach your destination, go immediately to watch the casket being unloaded. As soon as the remains arrive in the terminal, drape the flag over the casket with the blue-starred field above the left shoulder of the deceased. The remainder of the flag should be draped evenly over the casket. Secure the flag on the shipping case with the elastic flag band. If the casket was shipped by rail, remove the baggage tag and turn it in at the baggage room.

The funeral director will meet you at the terminal. The remains will be loaded into a hearse for transfer to the funeral home. The casket should be moved feet-first. *Salute the remains before the door of the hearse is closed.*

Ordinarily, the family of the deceased will not be present at the terminal when you arrive, and your first contact with them will not occur until you have reached the funeral home. But should they be present at the terminal, be sure to introduce yourself to them at that time. Should there be an SAO present, be sure to make yourself known. He or she may be of great help to you if you should need assistance.

You should accompany the funeral director in the hearse. Use this opportunity to find out all you can about the next of kin and the other relatives of the deceased whom you shall meet at the funeral home. Try to find out their attitude and any other facts that will help to make your assignment easier.

When you arrive at the funeral home, salute the casket as it is being unloaded.

Once at the funeral home, you and the funeral director will fold the flag that has been draped over the casket. You are responsible for returning this flag to the mortuary division of the installation that shipped the remains. Next, the two of you should inspect the outer casket cover or shipping case for damage. The flag to be used during the funeral service is in a plastic case under the shipping cover. This flag is draped on the casket at the funeral home.

The funeral director will inspect the casket to see that it has not been damaged during shipment. If the remains are to be viewed, he also opens the casket for inspection. You are responsible for inspecting the uniform and decorations of the deceased to see that everything is in place. If the casket is to be closed, arrange the flag as you did at the terminal. If it is to be half or fully open, use the methods shown in the accompanying illustration.

When you and the funeral director have completed these steps, he will prepare the statement of the condition of the remains and sign it. You are responsible for returning the statement to the supervisor of mortuary operations at the installation that prepared

The Role of the NCO

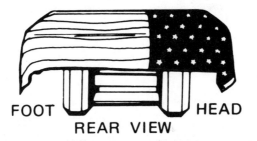

FOOT   HEAD
REAR VIEW

CENTER THE FLAG ON THE CASKET SO THAT THE BLUE FIELD IS AT THE HEAD AND OVER THE LEFT SHOULDER OF THE DECEASED.

HEAD   FOOT

CLOSED CASKET OR SHIPPING CASE.

the remains. You will also give the funeral director the certificate of death, which will have been included in your packet.

Do not push yourself on the family of the deceased. If there is an SAO present, he or she will handle all matters pertaining to insurance, back pay, casualty information, awards, military funeral arrangements, and such. If an SAO is not present, offer the family your assistance and sympathy, but remain quiet, tactful, and dignified. Offer to remain for the funeral services. If the family wants you to stay, you are required to do so.

If burial is to be made in a private cemetery, show the family VA Form 40-1330 and DD Form 1375. If the remains are consigned to a funeral director before interment in a government or national cemetery, show the family DD Form 1375. Explain to the next of kin that the forms should be filled in as soon as possible and mailed to the military activity listed on the form.

When you have completed your assignment, you are to return to your duty station. After your return, you are required to submit a short report in letter form concerning your escort duty. Be sure to include any problems that may have arisen during your escort duty and how they were taken care of. You should also include any special requests made by the deceased's next of kin. Be sure to state whether they were satisfied with the arrangements and mention any unusual situations that may have occurred.

Cremated remains are shipped in an urn placed inside a shipping box that you hand-carry and keep in your possession at all times during the journey. You will also carry along the flag, folded and in a plastic case; you do not place or drape the flag on the shipping box.

When you arrive at your destination, you will remove the urn from the shipping box. During the interment service, the flag may be taken out of its case, folded to resemble a cocked hat, and placed in front of the urn. At the end of the service, it is put back into its case and presented to the next of kin.

When escorting cremated remains, you will obtain from the funeral director a receipt for the remains instead of a statement on the condition of the remains.

In all other respects, the details of escort duty for cremated remains are the same as for escorting a body in a casket.

2

The Paper War

No noncommissioned officer can function without some knowledge of Army administration. As you rise in rank, your ability to understand and perform administrative tasks becomes more and more important. *Every senior noncommissioned officer must also be an administrator.*

INFORMATION SOURCES

Almost every situation that will arise in the administration of an Army unit or office is covered somewhere in Army regulations or other publications. Knowing where to look for guidance is therefore almost as important as knowing the answers. Some soldiers pride themselves on their ability to memorize large portions of pertinent regulations, and they amaze everyone by accurately quoting the most up-to-date information on a wide variety of subjects, verbatim. Most soldiers, however, have neither the time nor the capacity for that sort of thing and must therefore be content to stumble through various indexes when searching for information sources. There is nothing wrong with this approach, so long as you know where to look and have the appropriate references at hand. The following resources are essential for the NCO administrator.

AR 310-1, *Publications, Blank Forms, and Printing Management.*
AR 310-2, *Identification and Distribution of DA Publications and Issue of Publications.*
DA Pam 25-50, *Consolidated Index of Forms and Publications.*
DA Pam 310-12, *Index and Descriptions of Army Training Devices.*

DA Pam 310-13, *Posting and Filing Publications.*
AR 310-25, *Dictionary of U.S. Army Terms.*
AR 310-50, *Authorized Abbreviations and Brevity Codes.*
Manual for Courts-Martial, 1984 (includes UCMJ).
JCS Pub 1, *DOD Dictionary of Military and Associated Terms.*

Each MOS has a corresponding set of publications that are the basic references for that MOS, and the effective NCO will know them and what is in them, even if he or she cannot quote all their contents from memory. But the series listed above are basic to every good publications library, and no orderly room or office should be without a set. In addition, the Learning Resource Center and the MOS Library are valuable sources for these and other publications.

DUTY ROSTERS

AR 220-45, *Duty Rosters*, very clearly and succinctly states the rules for preparing and maintaining DA Form 6, the duty roster. These rules are very logical and easy to understand, and anybody of average intelligence can memorize them in a matter of only a few minutes. Yet accurately putting them into practice requires the most meticulous attention to detail and sometimes the patience of Job.

Duty rosters are kept for recording the duty performed by each person in an organization in order to make an equitable determination of duty assignments. Commanders are authorized to establish methods and procedures that will best suit the needs of their organizations; however, they must comply with the spirit and intent of AR 220-45: the longest off duty, the first on, and absolute impartiality in the assignment of duties to individuals.

The "From" date on the roster is always the date immediately following the "To" date on the previous roster and is entered at the time the new roster is prepared. The "To" date is always the date of the last detail made from the roster and is entered when the roster is closed. Intermediate dates are entered as details are made, and no date will be entered for any day that the detail was not made. For instance, a charge of quarters is required for every day of the month, but an officer or NCO may be needed to perform body escort or SAO duties only several times a year—only those dates on which an individual is actually detailed to perform body escort duty or SAO duty would be entered on such a roster.

Duty rosters contain only the names of those personnel required to perform the duty involved. When a new roster is prepared, all names are entered *alphabetically by rank*, beginning with the highest ranking person and using the appropriate grade of rank as shown in Table 1-1, AR 600-20. Subsequent names are added to the bottom of the roster.

Generally, the person longest off the duty will be the next one selected for it. It does happen, however, that soldiers are not always available—for various reasons—and when this situation happens, the next person eligible on the applicable duty roster who *is* available will be detailed to perform or complete the duty. Frequently, rosters are published somewhat in advance of the time the duty is to be performed, and when absences of personnel already assigned duty occur, they always seem to occur at the last moment.

Many commanders will allow personnel to substitute for one another on various details, and in some units, individuals make extra money by selling their services as substitutes. Where this is permitted, the individual primarily designated for duty is completely responsible if the substitute does not appear for the duty or performs it badly. Trade-offs are also frequently permitted on a "gentleman's agreement" basis. In

DUTY ROSTER		NATURE OF DUTY		ORGANIZATION	FROM (Date)	TO (Date)
		Charge of Quarters		Co A, 3d Infantry	14 Feb	

		Month	February												March					
GRADE	NAME	Day	14	15	16	17	18	19	20	21	22	23	24	25	26	27	28	1	2	3	4	5
SFC	Bierce		8	9	10	11	1	2	12	13	3	3	14	4	15	2	3	4	5	6	7
SFC	Le Faneau (7)		10	11	12	13	3	4	14	1	4	5	1	5	1	2	6	7	3	4	5
SSG	Dunsany (3)		7	8	9	10	11	1	A	A	A	2	12	13	14	1	1	4	5		
SSG	Hawthorne (4)		9	10	11	2	2	3	3	14	4	5	5	1	2	3	4	5	7	8	
SSG	Lovecraft		3	4	5	6	7	7	8	9	10	9	10	11	2	13	4	11	2		
SSG	O'Neill (1)		1	1	A	8	1	9	10	3	11	2	14	13	1	2	3	1	2		
SSG	Yitzaina		11	12	13	14	12	13	1	14	1	2	3	1	4	5	6	7	8	2	3
SGT	Arnold		1	2	3	4	5	6	6	7	7	8	7	10	8	9	10	11	12	9	10
SGT	Bolce (8)		1	2	3	4	6	7	7	8	8	9	9	10	5	6	7	8	4	3	4
SGT	Couperin		12	13	14	13	1	2	3	4	1	2	5	6	7	8	4	3	4		
SGT	Falstaff (10)		2	3	4	5	7	8	6	7	9	9	10	11	12	13	14	12	13		
SGT	Percy		13	14	1	10	11	2	3	12	4	5	3	4	6	7	3	A	1		
SGT	Woolsey		4	5	6	7	9	10	8	9	11	10	11	12	2	13	1	2	14		
CPL	Boswell (11)		3	4	5	6	8	9	7	8	10	9	10	3	9	10	1	2			
CPL	Johnson (7)		14	1	2	14	3	4	5	6	2	3	7	8	9	10	11				
CPL	Pope		6	7	8	9	5	6	10	11	7	12	13	1	2	3	4	10	11		
CPL	Spenser (2)		A	5	A	A	6	8	9	7	8	9	10	11	12	13	14	15	13	14	
SSG	Fairleigh (5)																	1	2	3	1	6	1	2
CPL	Queen (6)																		1	2	3	1	2

This is a consolidated duty roster. Therefore, 18, 19, 22, 25 and 26 February and 4 and 5 March are holidays.

The following remarks go on the back of the roster:

(1) Sick in quarters
(2) 72 hour Pass (soldier of the month)
(3) Leave 21-24 Feb
(4) Assigned and joined
(5) Relieved as company clerk
(6) Excused-detailed as company clerk
(7) AWOL
(8) PCS
(9)
(10) Leave 2-9 Mar
(11) Dead

DA FORM 6, 1 JUL 74   PREVIOUS EDITIONS OF THIS FORM WILL BE USED UNTIL EXHAUSTED.   SEE REMARKS ON REVERSE.   For use of this form, see AR 220-45, the proponent agency is The US Army Adjutant General Center.

all such cases, the person who maintains the duty roster must be notified of any changes, and recovery of any promised compensation is strictly up to the individuals concerned.

The duty roster is posted only for those days on which a detail is made. When a detail is made, all other persons on the roster are charged on that day with the number of details missed since the last time they were selected, excluding any nonchargeable days. The following abbreviations are used to indicate those personnel not available for duty. *No others are authorized.*

• Those who are absent or otherwise not available because of leave, pass, special duty, temporary duty, illness in line of duty, or any other authorized reason (not misconduct) will be indicated by the letter "A."

• Those eligible for detail who cannot be selected because of previous detail or other duty will be indicated by the letter "D."

• Those not available because of being AWOL, in arrest, or in confinement or sick as a result of misconduct will be indicated by the letter "U."

Whenever the abbreviation "A" is used, the numbering sequence of days off will be interrupted. Whenever the abbreviations "D" or "U" are used, the numbering sequence will continue, and the appropriate number will be included with the abbreviation.

Consolidated weekday-weekend-holiday duty rosters are maintained whenever practical. When consolidated rosters are used, separate numbering sequences may also be used to distinguish weekends and holidays from regular weekdays; these entries may be entered in red or some other distinguishing color to eliminate confusion. It sometimes happens that a soldier will become eligible for weekday and weekend duty back-to-back. This may be inconvenient for the soldier, but it is not reason for an excusal.

Details of *units* are made the same as they are for individuals, in turn according to one roster. However, commanders are authorized to use other methods, providing that equity is maintained.

The diagonal lines in the right corner of any block indicate duty on that date.

The numbers in parentheses immediately following a person's name refer to a corresponding explanatory remark on the reverse of the roster. A remark *must* be made to explain the reason an individual's name is added to or deleted from a roster, but the authority responsible for the preparation and maintenance of the roster determines the necessity or desirability of using an explanatory remark each time an individual is not available.

A number is used with the abbreviation "A" in the column for 14 February to indicate the last number charged, as shown on the previous duty roster, before the person entered upon the nonchargeable status. Entering these numbers in the first column of a new roster eliminates the necessity for referring constantly to the old one when individuals return to a chargeable status.

The duty roster should be available at all times for the inspection of commanders, supervisors, and the personnel concerned. If you are charged with the responsibility for maintaining a duty roster, do not feel that your integrity is being impugned when a soldier subject to detail according to the roster asks to see it.

Publish your rosters as far in advance as possible to give all concerned fair warning as to when they are coming up for duty. Be consistent when you publish your rosters. If you post the detail announcements on Monday, always post them on Mondays. Smart soldiers will always contact the person responsible for the duty roster when making plans, so never discourage personnel from doing this. Thinking ahead benefits everyone.

Above all, remain flexible. Never abandon the spirit of the regulation when it comes to preparing the duty roster and never, never play favorites, but so long as you keep your roster fairly, try to be accommodating.

CLASSIFIED INFORMATION

At some point in your Army career you will require access to classified information. AR 380-5, *Department of the Army Information Security Program Regulation*, defines "classified information" as material that is owned by, produced for or by, or under the control of the U.S. government, and determined pursuant to Executive Order 12065 ("National Security Information," 28 June 1978) or prior orders and AR 380-5, to require protection against unauthorized disclosure, and so designated.

You are individually responsible for complying with the provisions of AR 380-5 in all respects.

Classification Designations

Information or material that requires protection against unauthorized disclosure in the interest of national security is classified in one of three designations: Confidential, Secret, or Top Secret. "For Official Use Only" and "Limited Official Use" markings are not used to identify classified information.

Confidential. This classification applies only to information or material the unauthorized disclosure of which could reasonably be expected to *cause identifiable damage* to the national security. Examples would include the compromise of information that indicated strength of ground, air, and naval forces in the U.S. and overseas areas; disclosure of technical information used for training, maintenance, and inspection of classified munitions of war; and revelation of performance characteristics, test data, design, and production data on munitions of war.

Secret. This classification applies only to information or material the unauthorized disclosure of which could reasonably be expected to *cause serious damage* to the national security. Examples would include disruption of foreign relations significantly affecting the national security; significant impairment of a program or policy directly related to the national security; revelation of significant military plans or intelligence operations; and compromise of significant scientific or technological developments relating to national security.

Top Secret. This classification applies only to information or material the unauthorized disclosure of which could reasonably be expected to *cause exceptionally grave damage* to the national security. Examples would include armed hostility against the United States or its allies; disruption of foreign relations vitally affecting the national security; the compromise of vital national defense plans or complex cryptologic and communications intelligence systems; the revelation of sensitive intelligence operations; and the disclosure of scientific or technological developments vital to national security.

You are most likely to be exposed to classified information of an operational, intelligence, or technical nature, generally at the Secret and Confidential levels, but do not let that fact lull you into thinking that you may not someday be entrusted with classified information of the utmost sensitivity. No one knows where his or her assignments may lead, and as you progress in rank and experience, you may well find yourself handling war plans with regularity.

Follow these rules when dealing with classified information and you will avoid problems.

- Never discuss classified information outside the work environment or with anyone who is not properly cleared or who has no reason to know about the information entrusted to you, *even if that person is cleared for access to classified information.*
- Never leave classified material unattended unless you work in a secure environment (walk-in vault).
- If you are charged with classified material, never give it to anyone else without obtaining a receipt for it. Some people may bluster about your insistence on obtaining a receipt, especially in environments where large volumes of classified material circulate, but if you have signed for it, make the other party sign for it as well.
- Read the appropriate Army and local regulations on security, and be sure that you comply with them at all times.
- Never allow magazines, newspapers, bags, or packages around classified material. It is too easy for a classified document to be inadvertently included among the pages of a newspaper that winds up in the unclassified trash basket, and it would be a great shock if you should ever open a shopping bag on the way home and find a Top Secret document crammed in with your new shirts.
- Always keep classified and unclassified trash separate. If you have an unclassified trash receptacle in your area, check it periodically (especially before securing work for the day) to make sure that classified material has not been put into it by mistake.
- Check your work area frequently to be sure that classified material or documents have not been put into drawers, regulation binders, or correspondence trays or among collections of unclassified papers or materials.
- Follow security checks meticulously. People have a tendency to take security checks rather lightly. *Take them very seriously.* A safe left open because you are rushing to get home at the end of the day can cost you your career. Counterintelligence agents make periodic unannounced after-hours inspections of all work areas where classified information is handled, and they know their business. A call late at night to come back to work because of a security violation will freeze your blood and your chances for ever getting another promotion.
- Above all, use common sense whenever dealing with classified materials. Your common sense should tell you that when you become lax, you are setting yourself up for trouble.

THE WORLD OF SUPPLY

Everyone in the Army, from private to general, is accountable and responsible for some amount of government property; the amount of property a soldier is responsible for generally increases in value as he or she advances in rank. As with classified documents, safeguarding government property requires basically lots of good old-fashioned common sense.

Classes of Supply

Supplies are all items necessary for the equipment, maintenance, and operation of a military command, including food, clothing, equipment, arms, ammunition, fuel, materials, and machinery of all kinds. Supplies are divided into 10 basic categories

The Paper War

called "classes" and into lettered subclasses known as "material designators" (A through T).* For example, Class I C supplies are combat rations.

Class I—Subsistence, including health and welfare items. Subclassifications include inflight rations, refrigerated subsistence, nonrefrigerated subsistence, and combat rations.

Class II—Clothing, individual equipment, tentage, organization tool sets and tool kits, hand tools, administrative and housekeeping supplies, and equipment. Subclassifications include weapons, power generators, textiles, and so on.

Class III—Petroleum, oils, and lubricants.

Class IV—Construction materials.

Class V—Ammunition, including chemical, biological, radiological, and special weapons.

Class VI—Personal demand items, including beer and liquor ("Class VI Store" items).

Class VII—Major end items (a final combination of end products ready for intended use). Subclassifications include bridging and fire-fighting equipment, administrative and tactical vehicles, missiles, weapons, and special weapons.

Class VIII—Medical materials.

Class IX—Repair parts and components.

Class X—Material to support nonmilitary programs, such as agricultural and economic development.

Basic Principles

All persons entrusted with government property are responsible for its custody, care, and safekeeping. No commander or supervisor can assign a soldier a duty that would prevent him or her from exercising the proper care and custody of the property for which he or she is responsible.

When you assume accountability for property that is remotely located, keep records to show the location of the items and the person(s) charged with their safekeeping.

Army property will *not* be used for private purposes. Likewise, government property cannot be sold, given as a gift, lent, exchanged, or otherwise disposed of unless specifically authorized by law.

Giving or accepting an issue document, hand receipt, or any other form of receipt to cover articles that are missing, or appear to be missing, is prohibited.

It is a well-known fact of military life that all units accumulate varying types and amounts of equipment and supplies that are not reflected on the property books. These materials are intended for swapping purposes: If A Company has an extra buffing machine but no lawn mower while B Company needs a buffer but its lawn mower is excess property, sergeants are supposed to get together and make the appropriate trade so that A Company's grass gets cut and B Company's barrack floors shine like glass for inspection.

Only experts should play this game and then discreetly and with restraint. *Never* divert such property to personal use, and if you are ever afflicted with severe conscience pangs, turn the equipment in and get it on your unit's property book.

---

*For a detailed discussion of supply, see Edwards, *Combat Service Support Guide* (Stackpole Books, 1989).

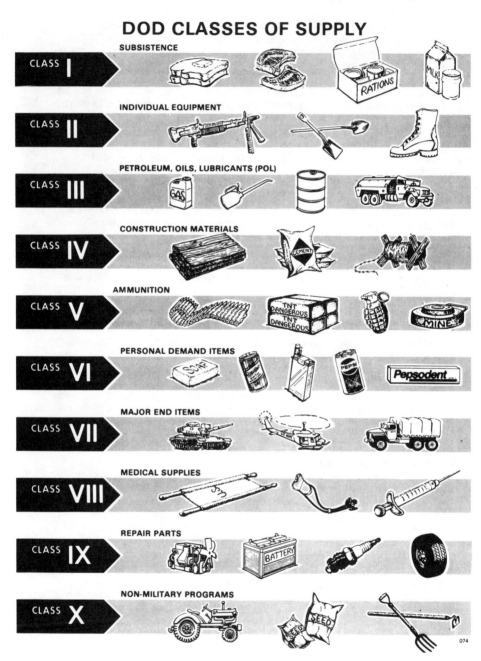

The Paper War

Accounting for Property

So far as most soldiers are concerned, property falls into three distinct categories:

• *Nonexpendable.* These items are property that is not consumed in use and that retains its original identity during the period of use. Included are all serial-numbered items, such as weapons, vehicles, office machines, and so on. Nonexpendable property requires formal accountability throughout its life and is accounted for at the use level by property book procedures. A continuous chain of receipts is required if these items pass between different persons.

•. *Expendable.* Generally, expendable supplies consist of office supplies, cleaning materials, and other supplies that are consumed upon issue. Expendable property does not require formal accountability except for some sensitive categories, such as drugs. Some items, because of their susceptibility to pilferage, are more tightly controlled in the issuing process than others.

• *Durable.* Durable property consists of certain kinds of hand tools worth five dollars and more. While durable property does not require property book control, these tools must be issued on a hand receipt.

Any found government property must be turned in to the supply system.

Responsibilities

Responsibility for property results from possession or the command or supervision of others who have possession of Army property. It involves a basic obligation for the proper custody, care, use, and safekeeping of government property. This responsibility may be assigned by appropriate authority in writing or orally.

Supervisors have the responsibility to ensure the safety and care of property issued to or used by their subordinates. This responsibility comes with the job and does not depend only on signed receipts. Supervisors are also responsible for maintaining the proper atmosphere that leads to supply discipline among subordinates.

Direct responsibility is a formal assignment of property responsibility to a person within the supply chain who has the property within his or her custody but not necessarily in his possession for his personal use. Accountable officers always have direct responsibility unless it has been specifically assigned to another person. An accountable officer maintains formal records that show, on a continuing basis, the balance, conditions, and location of all property assigned to a property account. Enlisted personnel who are sergeants or higher rank, when appointed by proper authority, may serve as accountable officers.

Responsibilities of Hand-Receipt Holders

Signing a hand-receipt, including signing for clothing and equipment, is probably the most familiar aspect of the supply system to most soldiers. It carries with it definite responsibilities; you can get into trouble if you do not use your head and follow these simple rules.

• Inventory on a periodic basis all equipment and supplies receipted to you.

• Have all property for which you have signed on hand or accounted for by a receipt, turn-in, or some other type of authorized credit document.

• Take active measures to prevent loss, damage, or destruction of any of the property under your control.

• When you turn an item in, be sure to get a receipt for it.

- Report any loss or theft to your immediate supervisor, commander, or first sergeant immediately.
- When you transfer, be sure all property is turned in or passed into the custody of your replacement or whoever succeeds you in custody for the property. This will require an inventory of all items for which you do not have receipts to show their whereabouts. This procedure can be very sticky if you have been careless about your record keeping. You will not be allowed to clear the installation until you have accounted for all the property for which you are responsible.
- Report to your supervisor, first sergeant, or commander any circumstances that make the proper security of property or equipment impossible. Failure to do so can result in your being charged for any loss or damage because you knew the facts and did not report them.

Statements of Charges and Reports of Survey

Statements of Charges (DD Form 362) and *Reports of Survey* (DA Form 4697) are the unpleasant methods the Army has of getting its money back from soldiers who have been careless or negligent in regard to their duty as property custodians.

A *Statement of Charges* is prepared in the following situations:
- Liability for loss, damage, or destruction of property is admitted.
- The charge does not exceed the monthly basic pay of the person being charged.
- Individuals do not offer cash payment to make good the lost, damaged, or destroyed property. (All military personnel and civilian employees of the Department of the Army who voluntarily admit liability may offer to replace the property through cash purchase.)

If the charges levied by a *Statement of Charges* exceed two-thirds of an individual's monthly basic pay, the unit commander will attach a letter requesting that the charges be prorated over a two-month or longer period.

A *Report of Survey* is required to account for lost, damaged, or destroyed property when it is known that negligence or misconduct is suspected and liability is not admitted. In addition, a *Report of Survey* is prepared in the following situations:
- A sensitive item is lost or destroyed (certain types of arms and ammunition as defined by AF 190-11).
- It is directed by higher authority or Army directives.
- Property loss is discovered as a result of change of accountability inventory (unless voluntary reimbursement is made for the full amount of the loss).
- The value of the damages or shortages in occupied government quarters (real property and furnishings combined) exceeds the responsible person's monthly basic pay.
- A person admits liability, and the loss, damage, or destruction exceeds the individual's monthly basic pay.
- A soldier refuses to admit liability and does not offer repayment.

Sergeants first class, master sergeants, and sergeants major may be appointed survey officers. Upon appointment, investigating the *Report of Survey* becomes that person's primary duty until the appointing authority has accepted the investigation as completed. Such investigations are painstakingly thorough. The survey officer is charged with finding out the facts surrounding the loss, damage, or destruction of government property, and he or she, based on the facts of the investigation, must recommend whether or not to fix responsibility upon specific individuals.

The Paper War

If you are ever the subject of a *Report of Survey* remember these guidelines:
• Keep calm, tell the truth, and cooperate fully with the survey officer.
• Remember that the survey officer is a soldier like yourself with a job to do; do not take anything he or she says personally.
• If the survey officer finds you liable to pay for the property in question, he or she must show you a copy of the report and explain your right to legal counsel and your right to appeal the recommendation if it is approved.
• If you appeal, take advantage of legal counsel; consult an Army lawyer even if you don't appeal.
• Remember that you may request remission of indebtedness or an extension of the collection period if the report is approved.
• Many *Reports of Survey* do not recommend affixing pecuniary liability upon an individual. If you have taken every reasonable precaution to protect the property in your possession, and you can prove it, you should have nothing to fear. If responsibility is fixed on you and the report is approved, then take your medicine because you probably deserve it.

Enforcement of Supply Discipline

Various disciplinary and administrative measures are available to a commander to enforce supply discipline and reduce the incidence of lost, damaged, or destroyed government property. When property for which a commander has responsibility is lost, damaged, or destroyed by a subordinate, the usual reaction is to reach for AR 735-5 and initiate a report of survey. This action may be appropriate or, in some cases, required.

Military discipline goes hand-in-hand with supply discipline. Commanders have the following administrative tools available for use in connection with the report of survey.

• An oral reprimand, a basic "chewing out." In more serious cases, a formal letter of admonition or reprimand may be used and, when appropriate, filed in the soldier's Official Military Personnel File.
• Noting a soldier's inefficiency or negligence in his or her NCOER.
• Article 15 or court-martial in cases of misconduct or neglect resulting in damaged or lost military property. For example, action may be taken against a soldier under Article 92, UCMJ, for dereliction of duty or for failure to obey orders or punitive regulations. Disciplinary action may also be taken under Article 108.

A report of survey is not a form of punishment nor a deterrent. Nonjudicial punishment, however, is both, and its use in conjunction with a report of survey may be indicated, depending upon the circumstances. Even when no pecuniary liability is found, the facts may warrant some form of command action. There is little doubt that strong measures should be taken against a supply sergeant whose stocks are found $10,000 short because of his or her misconduct or neglect. But similar action also would be appropriate against supervisors if investigation revealed inadequate supervision, such as if required inventories had never been made or verified.

3

Professional Development

Professional development is that improvement in your degree of qualification in the profession of arms that prepares you for higher and higher responsibility in that profession.

Professionalism, like virtue, is its own reward. The personal benefit that a soldier derives from the fruition of his or her professional development is an ever-increasing sense of satisfaction and self-fulfillment that comes from knowing that he or she is making significant contributions to the national defense. The promotions, the awards, the good assignments that come to the professional are merely pleasant tokens of faith and trust. The NCO who plans his military career merely to "get ahead" is a commercial schemer, nothing more. He may attain all the honors that good planning and hard work can bring him, but unless he has the heart of a soldier, he has nothing. The young specialist who returns to civilian life after only one enlistment, if he has caught the spirit, is more a professional soldier than any "career planner" who retires with 30 years of service.

Your professional development begins from the moment your drill sergeant instructs you in the facing movements of close-order drill, and it is never completed. The process of personal growth, which is the most important result of your development as a professional soldier, never stops.

Experience is another important factor in determining how far you will develop as a soldier. You can go to all the schools and academies, read all the books you want, and succeed in a wide variety of assignments, and, in even 20 lifetimes, never experience everything there is to know about the Army. But as you overcome a succession of challenges and prepare to go on to even more exacting trials, your experience will have

Professional Development

forearmed you and given you confidence.

Education is also important to the soldier. You must always retain an insatiable curiosity not only about your profession, but also about the world in general. The soldier does not exist in a vacuum.

To a very large extent, larger perhaps than you realize when you are young and new to the Army, you are in control of your military future. What you do and how you do it have a profound influence on your career. The better you understand how things work, the better are your chances to grow within the system.

Professional development is the synthesis of training, education, and experience provided by the Army to improve your overall ability to carry out your responsibilities as a team member of a fighting force. These elements must complement one another. It is your responsibility to anticipate what the Army expects of you as a dedicated NCO; therefore, your knowledge of the professional development system and its opportunities for the career soldier will assist you in your career development. You may not agree with all aspects of the system; however, knowledge of the system will assist you in making the system work for you. Conversely, you must function within the system.

For you as an NCO, job proficiency and MOS competence in both a combat and a peacetime environment are essential. You must also have the skills to train soldiers, make sound decisions, and enforce standards. To effectively perform as an NCO, you must have the ability to read, write, and speak effectively.* These skills, in conjunction with some basic mathematical skills, will enable you to train, counsel, and advise personnel, account for personnel and property, and write reports and recommendations for various personnel actions. This educational foundation gives you the confidence and ability to perform your primary job—training your soldiers to be a cohesive team, competent in their MOSs and physically fit to fight.

THE NONCOMMISSIONED OFFICER DEVELOPMENT PROGRAM (NCODP)

The NCODP is a leadership tool designed to be used at the battalion or equivalent level, equally applicable to TDA (Table of Distribution and Allowances, which are non-fighting) and TOE (Table of Organization and Equipment, which are fighting or supporting) units. NCO professional development training is scheduled and reflected on unit or organization master training programs and schedules and structured to the needs of the unit NCOs as assessed by the unit commander. Soldiers who demonstrate the potential for or are performing duty in leadership positions or are designated as acting NCOs participate in the NCODP, although separate classes may be conducted for senior NCOs.

The NCODP has the following objectives.
- Strengthen and enhance leadership development of the first-line NCO supervisor.
- Assist and provide guidance in the continuing development of NCOs.
- Increase the confidence of the NCO as a leader.
- Realize the full potential of the NCO support channel for the chain of command.
- Improve unit effectiveness.

Although the Enlisted Personnel Management System (EPMS) and the Noncommissioned Officer Education System (NCOES) provide a valuable foundation for the development of noncommissioned officers, the NCODP builds upon their contributions because only through the *practical application of skills* in the unit can soldiers achieve their goal of becoming truly professional noncommissioned officers.

---

*For help with writing, see McIntosh, *Guide to Effective Military Writing* (Stackpole Books, 1986).

Unit commanders are responsible for developing NCODPs that are responsive to the needs of their unit and the aspirations and development of their junior leaders. They provide the time and resources for the conduct of professional training, including formal periods of instruction and timely counseling of NCOs as an integral part of professional development. In addition, the unit commander ensures that there is, throughout his unit, a clear identification of those tasks that are noncommissioned officer business and that there is a clear and distinct NCO support channel that complements the supervisory chain of command.

NCODP training is programmed as an integral portion of formal and informal periods of instruction. It is implemented at the lowest level feasible, which may be company, troop, battery, or separate detachment. Unit programs complement formal training presented at military and civilian institutions, such as that offered by the NCOES and civilian schooling. Professional training includes instructions applicable to soldiers of all career management fields, as well as those specific NCO responsibilities outlined in FM 22-600-20 (see Chapter 1).

Portions of the NCODP may be formalized into periods of NCO development training that are institutionalized in all commands. The topics selected are attuned to the geography, mission, and needs of the unit, and they supplement professional training gained from daily, routine operations.

Appendix B, "Suggested Topics for NCO Training Program," of AR 350-17, *Noncommissioned Officer Development Program (NCODP)*, contains a partial list of references that may be used to conduct NCODP.

PROGRAMS FOR TRAINING

Individual Training and Evaluation Program (ITEP)

This program improves combat readiness by formalizing the training and retraining of the individual soldier in his MOS and item of equipment along with collective tasks critical to the unit's mission. Evaluation of such training improves unit cohesiveness and provides trainers, MOS proponents, and commanders information on the effectiveness of individual training. It measures performance against the Soldier's Manual and ARTEP standards.

The Commander's Evaluation, a hands-on test, provides the commander and others in the chain of command a method to assess unit proficiency on individual tasks critical to the unit's mission. During the application of this component, unit NCOs and other leaders test their soldiers' ability to perform certain tasks against standards delineated in the respective Soldier's Manuals. At the conclusion, results of the evaluation are discussed with the soldiers. The strengths and weaknesses are then recorded in the job book.

The *Common Task Test* includes 17 tests that primarily assess unit training. Also a hands-on test, this major training event evaluates the soldier's fundamental combat and survival skills. The results of this mandatory training for all soldiers from privates E-1 through sergeants first class regardless of MOS are often used by commanders and NCOs when preparing NCO evaluation reports, making recommendations for promotions, and taking other personnel actions.

NCO Self-Development Test, the SDT, was fielded throughout the active Army in FY 91, and in the Reserve and National Guard in FY 92. The SDT, which replaces the Skill Qualification Test, or SQT, must be taken by all sergeants through sergeants first class—annually by active NCOs, every two years by Reserve and Guard NCOs. The

Professional Development

SDT is designed to motivate NCOs to remain current on MOS requirements, to assist in preparing NCOs for future assignments, and to help make NCOs more versatile.

Skill level 1 soldiers do not take the SDT; instead, they are assessed for technical competence through a commander's evaluation.

The SDT, like the SQT, includes MOS-related questions. Unlike its predecessor, however, the SDT also contains questions about military leadership and training management. Sixty percent of the test questions relate to the soldier's MOS and come from the Soldier's Manual and supporting references. The remaining 40 percent is split evenly between questions about leadership and training. Leadership questions are taken from FM 22-100, *Military Leadership* (July 1990); FM 22-101, *Leadership Counseling* (June 1985); and FM 22-102, *Soldier Team Development* (March 1987). The leadership section of the test was developed by the Center for Army Leadership. Training management questions come from FM 25-101, *Battle Focused Training* (September 1990). To better comprehend FM 25-101, soldiers are encouraged to read its companion, FM 25-100, *Training the Force* (November 1988). The training section of the SDT was developed with the assistance of the U.S. Army Sergeants Major Academy.

Preparing for the two-hour, multiple-choice SDT is an individual responsibility. No unit training time is devoted to test preparation. Because test results will be used by promotion, assignment, and school attendance boards beginning in FY 93, and by the Enlisted Personnel Management System beginning in FY 94, commanders and senior NCOs have been instructed to make sure their subordinates understand the importance of the test.

Army Training and Evaluation Program

This program, as published in mission training plans of individual MOSs, provides unit leaders at each organizational level objectives critical to a unit's combat mission. It combines training and evaluation with its focus on what the unit trainers and leaders need to know in order to correct training weaknesses—what should be done tomorrow. These objectives include tasks, related conditions, and standards that the unit must meet to perform successfully on the battlefield. Unit NCOs participate in the planning, conducting, and evaluating phases of this program.

THE NONCOMMISSIONED OFFICER EDUCATION SYSTEM (NCOES)

The NCOES, in both its active and Reserve Components versions, is an integrated system of resident training (service school and NCO academy, supervised on-the-job training), self-study, and on-the-job experience that provides job-related training for NCOs and specialists throughout their careers. The NCOES is designed to provide, as required in each MOS, progressive, continuous training from the primary through the senior level.

NCOES training upgrades readiness, supports mobilization, and sustains the Army with trained leaders and technicians during wartime. It is an integral part of the Enlisted Personnel Management System (EPMS). The NCOES applies to all enlisted personnel of all components of the Army. NCOES and the ACES are complementary programs guiding the development of NCOs through their careers.

The EPMS, which the NCOES supports, is characterized by five skill levels, representing progressively higher levels of performance capability, experience, and grade. Five levels of training have been established in support of these skill levels. Completion of initial entry training provides the soldier the foundation of professional and

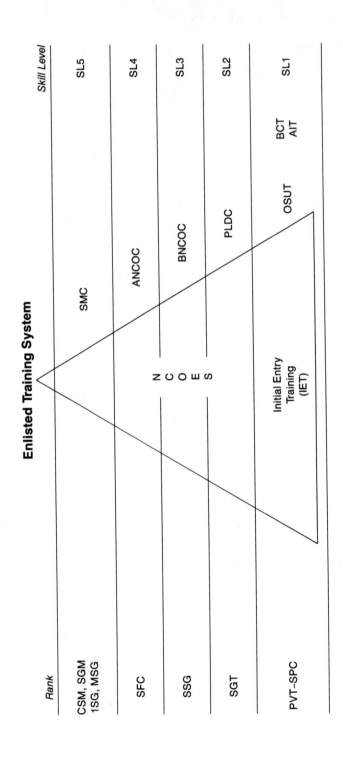

Professional Development

technical knowledge he or she needs to perform at his or her first duty station; combined with subsequent individual training in the unit, this soldier qualifies at skill level 1. The next four levels of training (primary, basic, advanced, and senior) are taught through the NCOES.

NCOES is designed to prepare soldiers to assume or perform duty at the next higher skill levels.

Battalion command sergeants major are key individuals in ensuring that soldiers who need training receive it: The right soldier receives the right training at the right time in his career. Soldiers who are not otherwise qualified will not be sent for training merely to fill a quota. In the past, the Army's NCO academies (NCOA) were plagued by soldiers who did not want to be there and often did not deserve to be there either.

While the U.S. Total Army Personnel Command (PersCom) schedules soldiers for resident training (other than for the 1SG Course), local selection authority governs attendance at PLDC and BNCOC. Soldiers are selected for these courses based on a battalion-level (or equivalent) Order of Merit List. To be eligible, a soldier must be trained on 70 percent of all MOS tasks in his individual soldier's job book within the past six months, must have passed the Army Physical Readiness Test within the past six months, must have passed the SDT within the past twelve months, must meet the physical fitness and weight standards, must be eligible for reenlistment, and must be recommended by his unit commander.

Primary Leadership Development Course (PLDC). This non-MOS-specific leadership course emphasizes how to lead and train and the duties, responsibilities, and authority of the NCO. This is a four-week course conducted at NCOAs in CONUS and overseas open to all enlisted MOSs who have not previously attended a primary-level leadership course. Currently, successful completion of PLDC is required for promotion to sergeant.

Basic NCO Course (BNCOC). The BNCOC provides a hard-hitting squad leader, section leader, tank commander, and weapons and equipment expert who can lead and train soldiers in combat. The length of the course varies according to MOS. BNCOC is conducted at NCOAs in CONUS and overseas. First priority goes to soldiers selected for promotion to staff sergeant and to those staff sergeants who have not previously attended. Promotable specialists and sergeants serving in staff sergeant positions are given second priority. BNCOC is mandatory for promotion to sergeant first class.

Advanced NCO Courses (ANCOC). These courses stress common core and MOS-related tasks, with emphasis on technical and advanced leadership skills and knowledge of military subjects required to train and lead other soldiers at the platoon or comparable level. Course lengths vary with the requirements of the particular MOS. ANCOCs are presented in CONUS service schools. Selection is by DA selection board, and the program is centrally managed by PersCom. The sergeant first class ANCOC selection board evaluates personnel for attendance. Attendance from an overseas command in a TDY status is authorized providing the soldier's oversea-tour length exceeds 13 months and he or she will have a minimum of six months remaining in the command after completing the course. Successful completion of this course is required for promotion to master sergeant.

Overweight soldiers who report at any of the four NCOES courses are tape-tested by instructors (small group leaders) to determine body fat content. If they are over the limit for their age, gender, and height, they are denied enrollment and sent home.

Soldiers who show up exceeding their body fat standard cost small group leaders time away from their classes and cost the Army round-trip tickets and other expenses.

When an overly fat soldier returns to his or her unit, that individual will soon receive bad news. The soldier's first general officer in the chain of command will already have been informed, via a memorandum from the NCO Academy commandant, that the soldier failed to maintain the standard. Subsequently, the soldier will be barred from reenlistment or be separated if he or she fails to make satisfactory progress in the weight control program after six months.

U.S. Army Sergeants Major Academy (USASMA). This course is the capstone of the NCOES. USASMA prepares master sergeants and first sergeants for troop and staff assignments throughout the defense establishment. Being selected to attend the USASMA is a great honor and a big step forward in an NCO's career because it paves the way for eventual selection for command sergeant major.

The course's objectives are to prepare students to assist in the solution of command problems; to improve senior NCO capability to develop and maintain discipline; to instruct students in tactical, administrative, and training operations; to update them on contemporary Army problems; to improve their communication skills; to develop intellectual depth and analytical ability; to increase their understanding of military management practices; to sustain high physical conditioning and appearance standards; and to prepare students to develop and conduct physical readiness training themselves.

The USASMA is held at Fort Bliss, Texas, is 22 weeks long, and is attended in a permanent-change-of-station status. Prerequisites are as follows.

• Be a master sergeant or 1SG (E-8) with at least one year time in grade as of 1 August, but not more than five years time in grade as of 13 July of the calendar year in which the USASMA Selection Board convenes.

• Have 23 years or less time in service as of 31 August of the calendar year following the calendar year in which the board convenes.

• Have not submitted an application for retirement or separation.

• Have not been selected for the nonresident course.

• Reenlisted or extended current enlistment to meet the 19-month service-remaining requirement.

Because senior NCOs selected for attendance at the USASMA must move to Fort Bliss, Texas, then move elsewhere to assume duties as a sergeant major, preparation is a key element, especially for married soldiers.

Selection is based on records, potential value to the Army, and ability to absorb and profit from the course. All personnel eligible for selection are considered available to attend. Soldiers selected who are later determined to be unavailable will be deferred for attendance to the next class following the end of their unavailable status. Students are notified by PersCom annually and, once elected, must submit acceptance statements within 30 days of release of the selection list for primary selectees or activation of the alternate list.

Once a soldier has been selected, he may not decline. Soldiers eligible for selection who do not want to attend must submit a statement of declination through command channels to PersCom. Approved declinations, for either the resident or nonresident courses, become a permanent part of the soldier's official military personnel file. Soldiers declining either course will not be reconsidered for future USASMA attendance.

The USASMA Corresponding Studies Program closely parallels the content of the resident course and is designed to be completed in two years or less, depending on the

Professional Development

student's ability to accelerate the pace. The course consists of four nonresident phases and a two-week resident phase. The individual must volunteer for this course and not have completed more than 23 years of service. (The latter requirement, though, is waiverable up to 27 years as of the starting date of the class.)

FUNCTIONAL COURSES

First Sergeant Course. This course stresses training in the most critical tasks in the duty position of first sergeant. The course curriculum includes instruction in physical training and appearance, unit administration, logistics, security, field operations, discipline and esprit de corps, personnel actions, communications, and problem solving. No priority is given to MOS or unit status in the selection of students. All first sergeant designees and incumbents, sergeants first class, and master sergeants who have less than 18 months in a first sergeant position are eligible to attend. The major commands select about 90 percent of each class, and PersCom selects the other 10 percent. PersCom's selectees attend the course in a TDY en route status, generally to an overseas duty position. Candidates for this eight-week course must meet the physical fitness and weight standards. In addition, soldiers more than 40 years old must complete appropriate medical screening at the local installation before attendance.

Operations and Intelligence Course. This course trains senior NCOs (sergeants first class through sergeants major) for either operations or intelligence sergeant duties at the battalion or higher level. Student quotas are managed similarly to the first sergeant course quotas. The major commands receive allocations. Selectees attend this eight-week course in either a TDY or TDY en route to another assignment status.

Primary Technical Course (PTC). The PTC focuses on training for critical tasks listed in the skill level 2 Soldier's Manual for a given MOS. It is given in the resident service school or in an extension course. Length varies by MOS and mode of training. The resident PTC is open to soldiers who have been selected for promotion to sergeant, or sergeants who are performing in or being assigned in sergeant positions in their MOS. Second priority goes to those corporals or specialists performing in sergeant positions for which the training is necessary. The extension version is available to corporals, specialists, and sergeants who desire to establish a course of self-study as approved by their commanders.

Basic Technical Course (BTC). This course focuses on training critical tasks at the skill level 3 for a given MOS. Course length varies by MOS. The BTC is given at a resident service school or as an extension course. Soldiers are nominated by their commanders within 30 days of the time they attain staff sergeant promotable status. For the resident BTC, first priority goes to staff sergeant promotable and to those staff sergeants who are performing in or being assigned to skill-level 3 positions for which the training is designed (see DA Pamphlet 351-9). Second priority goes to promotable corporals, specialists, and sergeants who are performing in staff sergeant positions. The extension course is available to soldiers in the ranks of corporal or specialist through staff sergeant who have the approval of their commander.

Army Correspondence Course Program

A variety of exportable training courses specific to the CMF and MOS are available through this program. The courses are designed for your professional development.

They include individual subcourses on specific topics developed by their respective proponent schools. You may enroll in this program as an individual student or via the group enrollment program. Group enrollment allows an NCO to use these courses to supplement individual training. It provides a professionally designed training course for the NCO supervisor and awards promotion points for those who successfully complete each subcourse.

Army Training Extension Course (TEC)

This self-paced training medium is for individuals and groups. The training is oriented toward common skills and critical MOS tasks. Proponent schools develop TEC, and soldiers in the MOS validate them. Generally, soldiers use TEC in groups as part of unit training or individually for self-study. These courses are usually distributed to unit learning centers based on assigned MOS, but you can requisition individual TEC lessons. TEC lessons are designed in various formats: printed, audiovisual, audio, and job performance aids. Printed lessons are, however, the most predominant medium.

Noncommissioned Officer Academies (NCOA)

The mission of NCO academies is to provide NCOES training to qualified soldiers to train them in the fundamentals and techniques of leadership, prepare them to train subordinates, offer them increased career educational opportunities, prepare them for leadership in all kinds of environments, instill increased self-confidence and a sense of responsibility, and provide selected personnel with specific critical MOS training.

To ensure that all soldiers are provided an equal opportunity to attend available NCOES courses, the NCOA network has been divided into geographic training regions. Currently, there are 20 such regions established worldwide. Alaska, Korea, U.S. Army, Europe, Hawaii, and Panama are considered as separate regions with the remaining 20 regions designed to accommodate soldiers assigned within the continental United States. If certain NCOES training is not available within a region, that region's student population may receive its training at the nearest NCOA that offers the training. Appendix D, AR 351-1, lists the NCOA regions.

NCOA courses do not award an MOS, an additional skill identifier, or a higher skill level. Leadership courses offered in academies emphasize training students to train subordinates while developing training management and leadership skills that focus on senior and subordinate relationships, needs of the soldier, discipline, counseling, and techniques of soldier motivation.

NCOAs ensure that students maintain high standards of military courtesy, military conduct, and physical fitness. The level of discipline maintained by NCOAs should not, however, interfere with the learning environment, and treatment of students is designed to reflect favorably on the image of the Army and the objective of the NCOAs.

Dismissal from Courses. Students may be removed from NCOES courses by the service school NCOA commandant before course completion for disciplinary reasons, lack of motivation, academic deficiencies, or other valid reasons, such as illness or injury. Failure of a student to maintain established academic, physical fitness, conduct, and weight control standards at any time during a course is cause for elimination. Failure to maintain standards may constitute an infraction of the UCMJ or may indicate a lack of motivation or aptitude.

Students whose actions during training constitute a probable violation of the

Professional Development

UCMJ may be suspended, dismissed, or reported to the commander exercising court-martial jurisdiction. Students who show a probable lack of motivation will be counseled by either the training supervisor or the senior NCO (CSM or 1SG) of their parent units, wherever possible.

If disenrollment is determined to be appropriate and is adequately documented to sustain it, the student is notified in writing of the proposed action, the basis for the action, and the consequences of disenrollment. The student has the right to appeal but must submit any appeal within two days after receipt of written notification. Appeals are reviewed by a disinterested command sergeant major.

Soldiers eliminated from the 1SG Course and the USASMA are not eligible for reentry. Those eliminated academically from other NCOES courses will not be eligible for further NCOES training for a period of six months.

According to the Office of the Deputy Chief of Staff for Personnel, NCOs eliminated for cause from an NCOES course face a mandatory bar to reenlistment or separation proceedings. "For cause" can mean for lack of discipline or motivation, or for other problems like insubordination or alcohol abuse.

In the summer 1991 issue of *The NCO Journal*, SGM Dan Murphy, U.S. Army Sergeants Major Academy, wrote, "Soldiers dismissed from [NCOES courses] receive negative academic reports that go into their personnel records, scarce travel funds are needlessly depleted, and more qualified soldiers are denied the chance to attend courses." Murphy, in context, was referring to NCOs who report to an NCOES course and fail the APFT, but his comment applies equally to elimination for cause.

EDUCATION AND TRAINING

In today's increasingly complex and technological military environment, soldier education is vitally important. Although there is no MOS in the Army that requires an enlisted person to have a college education, and while no soldier should neglect his or her primary military duties in pursuit of advanced degrees, you would be remiss in your duty as a noncommissioned officer not to encourage soldiers to take advantage of all the wonderful educational opportunities the Army offers those who have the initiative to apply themselves.

Because graduation from an NCO education course is already a requirement for promotion to staff sergeant and master sergeant and appointment to command sergeant major, it is highly likely that other NCO course requirements will be implemented by 1990, according to Army planners. This major policy change—a highly prescriptive school-promotion link—will soon produce promotion potential soldiers with nearly identical qualifications. Where does this development leave the NCO who wants to be a cut above his peers with the goal of secondary zone promotions? The NCO evaluation report? Not likely because of the inflation factor. Therefore, postsecondary education—in some cases, a college education—will soon be the mark of an NCO who is on the move.

In fact, AR 621-5, *Army Continuing Education System (ACES)*, Chapter 1-9, states that soldier educational goals include mastering basic educational skills necessary to perform duties in their PMOS, earning a high school diploma or equivalent before completing the first enlistment (88 percent of new recruits are high school graduates), and earning an associate degree or completing 60 semester hours in a field related to one of their specialties before the 15th year of active duty. Because completing an associate degree takes two to three years, the time to get involved in postsecondary education is now, not two to three years later when most of your peers will then begin to consider additional education through ACES.

NCO Development Time Line

This time line represents promotion, training, and assignment opportunities as a "generic" soldier progresses from initial entry through CSM. It can aid individuals in seeing where they stand and where they are going, and may assist leaders in counseling and advising their subordinates on professional development.

YOS	Promotion Potential	EXPERIENCE Assignments MOS and CMF	Other	TRAINING AND EDUCATION NCOES	Civil
0		PVT			Complete HS or GED or begin college HS graduate desirable
1	4–6 months	PFC			
2	6–12 months	SP4-CPL		PLDC	
3	12–26 months				
4	18 months–5 years	SGT			
5				BNCOC	Continue or complete work on college education as a personal goal
6	5–8 years	SSG	Recruiter		
7			Drill SGT	ANCOC	
8					
9					
10	9–13 years	SFC and PSG	SR Drill SGT		Continue or complete work on college education as a personal goal
11			RC Advisor		
12			ROTC Cadre		
13			Recruiter		
14	14–18 years estimated	1SG and MSG			
15				SMC	Continue or complete work on college education as a personal goal
16			RC Advisor		
17			ROTC Cadre		
18					
19					
20					
21					
22	18–22 years estimated	SGM and CSM	ROTC Cadre		Continue or complete work on college education as a personal goal
23			RC Advisor		
24					
25					
26					
27					
28					
29					

Professional Development

Army Continuing Education System (ACES)

The ACES is an integrated management system of voluntary educational opportunities. It helps soldiers grow professionally within the Army and to transfer knowledge and skill gained to productive post-service employment. It is an Army-wide system of relatively uniform educational opportunities, decentralized to post level, and operated within HQDA policies.

Participation in the ACES is voluntary and depends on individual goals, but all soldiers should be urged to achieve the following:

• Earn a high school diploma or state-issued high school equivalency by the end of the first enlistment.

• Have occupational skills certified that are learned through Army training and experience by taking part in an Army skill recognition program.

• Acquire an occupational skill through the skill development program.

The ACES consists of the Basic Skills and Advanced Skills Education Programs (BSEP, ASEP), the High School Completion Program (HSCP), the Associate Degree Program, the Baccalaureate and Graduate Degree Programs, and the Skill Recognition Program.

Basic Skills Education Program (BSEP)

This program is designed to develop educational competencies required for a soldier's job performance, skill qualifications, and career growth. BSEP develops job-related educational skills from a soldier's entry into active service through completion of the Advanced Course, Noncommissioned Officers Education System. It is implemented in three phases:

• *BSEP I* for soldiers in initial entry training.

• *BSEP II* for soldiers serving at permanent duty stations in MOS positions in skill levels 1 and 2.

• *Advanced Skills Education Program* (ASEP) for soldiers serving at permanent duty stations in MOS skill levels 3, 4, and 5.

BSEP is part of each unit's master training schedule and is conducted during normal duty hours at no cost to participants. Formal entry into the program is a commander's decision, made after coordination with the education services officer and discussion with the soldier concerned. Selection is based on whether the soldier is willing to learn and use this knowledge productively in the Army.

BSEP I provides basic literacy instruction in reading, writing, arithmetic, and language skills to support MOS training. It provides selected trainees a maximum of 180 hours of instruction in basic skills education for a maximum of six weeks.

BSEP II provides educational services to soldiers whose commanders evaluate as possessing high reenlistment, leadership, and promotion potential, and/or who need BSEP to meet current MOS and job requirements. It is also available to those desiring to raise their Armed Services Vocational Aptitude Battery (ASVAB) scores in order to qualify for a different MOS or for various Army service schools. The maximum length of BSEP II instruction is 360 hours of classroom instruction. Optimal classroom participation is four hours a day in classes ranging in size from 10 to 20 students to permit individualized instruction.

ASEP is a command, on-duty educational program designed to help NCOs meet their training responsibilities as supervisors, managers, and communicators. This program does not replace any element of the NCOES but complements and provides expanded opportunities in the NCO development process. Some of the specific subjects included in the curriculum are instruction on general and personnel supervision, human relations, basic management, personnel management and military management, management problems, business communication and communication skills, public speaking, technical and report writing, pubic relations, and vocational and general counseling.

First priority for ASEP enrollment goes to soldiers with PMOS requirements, then to those with duty MOS requirements, then to those with SMOS needs, and then to soldiers below skill level 3, who may be selectively placed in ASEP classes as requested by their commander.

High School Completion Program (HSCP). The HSCP gives soldiers a chance to earn a high school diploma or a state-issued high school equivalency certificate or diploma during off-duty hours. Soldiers may enroll, with Army tuition assistance, in locally available high school completion programs.

All soldiers who are not high school graduates are authorized tuition assistance (100 percent), to take part in off-duty high school completion courses. Soldiers may be enrolled in the BSEP and the HSCP at the same time.

Service Members Opportunity Colleges Associate Degree Program (SOCAD). Under the Service Members Opportunity Colleges (SOC), this is an associate degree program wherein a soldier is normally awarded an associate degree by a two-year community or junior college for an academic or technical course of study. Many four-year colleges also award associate degrees. The program was developed to provide common curricula in special disciplines related to Army MOS and career specialty programs. SOCAD programs are available to all military personnel where troop concentration and soldier interest support one or more of the curricula.

The SOC is a network of schools across the country and overseas that have recognized and responded to soldiers' expectations for postsecondary education. They must have liberal entrance requirements, give soldiers a chance to complete courses through optional nontraditional modes, provide academic advisement services, offer maximum credit for educational experiences obtained in the military service, have residence requirements that are adaptable to the mobility and special needs of soldiers, have a transfer policy that is generous in recognition of traditional and nontraditional learning obtained at other schools, promote the SOC in their catalogs and other media, and provide educational support to servicemembers and to local military posts.

Under SOCAD, the college must limit the residency requirement to a maximum of 25 percent of the total credits needed to complete a degree and offer a flexible curriculum that will require a maximum of 65 semester hours (97 quarter hours) for completion, require no more than 50 percent of the total required hours in prescribed courses, include a minimum of 50 percent of the total required hours in free elective courses or in broad areas that permit wide selection of learning experience, and accept credit for military training and experience.

Baccalaureate and Graduate Degree Programs. A baccalaureate (bachelor's) degree is normally awarded in arts and science or in certain professional fields on completion of a four-year college curriculum. A graduate degree refers to a degree beyond the bachelor's degree, normally a master's or doctoral degree.

The chance to complete or work toward a bachelor's or graduate degree while serving in the Army is an important incentive for recruiting and keeping highly motivated soldiers. This opportunity is made available at all posts. Each post usually has at

NCO LEADER SELF-DEVELOPMENT CAREER MAP

TITLE OF CAREER MANAGEMENT FIELD: FINANCE/ACCOUNTING

CMF NUMBER: 71 (MOS 73C, D, Z)

THE FOLLOWING ARE ONLY RECOMMENDATIONS. It may not be feasible to complete all recommended courses since assignments may preclude off-duty education. Alternate methods of achieving CMF course recommendations are possible (examinations, correspondence courses, and ACE-recommended credits). See an education counselor for assistance in completing recommended courses/goal.

OPERATIONAL LEADER DEVELOPMENT

RANKS, SKILL LEVELS & DUTY ASSIGNMENTS	PVT PFC SPC/CPL SKILL LEVEL 10	SGT SKILL LEVEL 20	SSG SKILL LEVEL 30	SFC SKILL LEVEL 40	MSG	SGM/CSM
	TEAM LEADER	RECRUITER/RETENTION / DRILL SERGEANT	OPS/INTEL SERGEANT		SKILL LEVEL 50	
		SQUAD LEADER	PLATOON SERGEANT		FIRST SERGEANT	

INSTITUTIONAL LEADER DEVELOPMENT

| INSTITUTIONAL TRAINING | BCT / AIT | PLDC | BNCOC | ANCOC | RECOMMENDED: BATTLE STAFF NCO &/OR 1SG COURSE | SERGEANTS MAJOR COURSE | CSM (D) |

LEADER SELF-DEVELOPMENT

RECOMMENDED NCOES-RELATED COURSES	**PRIOR TO PLDC** 1. English Composition 2. Basic Mathematics 3. Computer Literacy 4. Reading Recommended Reading Standard: 10 Achieve Writing Standard*	**PRIOR TO BNCOC** 1. Communication Skills 2. Personnel Supervision 3. Behavioral Science Recommended Reading Standard: 10 Achieve Writing Standard*	**PRIOR TO ANCOC** 1. Principles of Management 2. Organizational Behavior 3. Information Mgt Systems 4. Technical Writing Recommended Reading Standard: 10 Achieve Writing Standard*		**PRIOR TO SMC** 1. Research Techniques (Statistics) 2. Human Resource Management 3. World Geography Recommended Reading Standard: 12 Achieve Writing Standard*
RECOMMENDED CMF-RELATED COURSES AND ACTIVITIES	**Skill Level 10** 1. Intro to Business 2. Accounting 3. Keyboarding 4. Communications 5. ACCP: Finance Spec Crs; Military Accounting Crs	**Skill Level 20** 1. Algebra 2. Principles of Management 3. Computer Operations 4. Computer Hardware 5. ACCP: Programming & Budgeting Spec Crs; Intro to Disbursing Operations; Basic Level Technical/Sustainment Course	**Skill Level 30** 1. Speech 2. Supervisory Management 3. Algebra 4. Problem Solving 5. Human Relations 6. Decision Making 7. ACCP: Adv Level Tech/Sustainment Course	**Skill Level 40** 1. Applied Management 2. Planning 3. Organizing 4. Stress Tolerance 5. Interpersonal Skills	**Skill Level 50** 1. Public Relations 2. Business Communications 3. Organizational Effectiveness
RECOMMENDED CMF-RELATED CERTIFICATION OR DEGREE GOAL	**AA/AS IN:** Accounting, Finance, Management, Economics, Marketing, Mathematics, Banking, Communications, Public Administration, Statistics, Business, Data Processing, Payroll, Public Budgeting, Personnel Admin, Info Systems, Bookkeeping, Computer Science, Mgt Info Systems BY THE __10th__ YEAR OF SERVICE				**BA/BS IN:** Accounting, Finance, Management, Economics, Marketing, Mathematics, Banking, Communications, Public Administration, Statistics, Business, Data Processing, Payroll, Public Budgeting, Personnel Admin, Information Systems, Bookkeeping, Computer Science, Management Information Systems BY THE __16th__ YEAR OF SERVICE
NOTE	* See DA Pam 600-67. The Army Writing Standard is writing that can be understood in a single, rapid reading, and is generally free of errors in grammar, mechanics, and usage.			APPROVED BY: Commandant, U.S. Army Finance School	
LEGEND	ACCP - Army Correspondence Course Program CTBIS - Network Computer Instruction (Where Available) LC - Course found in Learning Center			DATE: 4 October 1991	

Career maps, like this one for finance and accounting soldiers, are new aids designed to illustrate MOS career tracks. Notice the CMF-related education goals.

least one bachelor's and one graduate degree program available to soldiers on post or within reasonable commuting distance. These programs are oriented toward the Army's requirements. Soldiers may, however, enroll in off-post programs of their choice. The New GI Bill, the New Army College Fund, the New GI Bill for Vietnam-era Soldiers, the Veterans Educational Assistance Program (VEAP), tuition assistance, and Department of Veterans Affairs educational benefits are all available to eligible soldiers for pursuit of under- and post-graduate degrees. For soldiers being considered for advancement up to staff sergeant, education is very important. A soldier with a bachelor's degree from a four-year college is eligible for the maximum award of promotion points based on civilian education—100 points. While a high school diploma or GED earns no points, a soldier who obtains one while on active duty, or improves his GED score, is eligible for 10 promotion points for education improvement.

For promotion to the senior enlisted grades, however, promotion boards consider many other factors besides education.

If you are thinking of pursuing or completing your college education while on active duty, do so. But remember that part-time college courses leading to a baccalaureate or graduate degree will have to be pursued on your own time, and that rule generally means attending class and doing your reading and writing and studying at night.

The people who sit on DA promotion boards are old soldiers who know when an individual is coasting in an assignment. "Ho-hum" efficiency reports and a variety of unchallenging assignments in the military backwaters of the world cannot be offset by a college degree when it comes to competing for promotion against soldiers who always think Army first. For more information, inquire about the Bachelors Degrees for Soldiers program at your local education office.

College Programs and Locations

Before a PCS move or before requesting a particular assignment or location, it is beneficial for a soldier pursuing a degree to know the availability of schooling at the new site. Many colleges offer courses on-post, at least on a limited basis. If an institution is close to an installation, it will sometimes elect to offer certain popular courses on site but will require students enrolling in smaller or more specialized courses to attend classes on campus.

Education centers at major posts sometimes serve smaller installations in the nearby region. High school and college preparatory course work is available at nearly all Army installations.

Schooling Overseas

Overseas assignments are serviced by contract institutions. In Europe, for instance, five colleges provide vocational, technical, associate, and baccalaureate programs for all Army installations. Five provide graduate programs as well, although there is overlap among the groups. Overseas assignments are listed by region.

Europe. The Army has education centers in Europe that service military communities. The educational program is a comprehensive package, with services provided to soldiers in even the most remote casernes and garrisons. Three colleges provide technical certificate and baccalaureate degree programs throughout the region: Big Bend Community College, Central Texas College, and City Colleges of Chicago. Embry-Riddle Aeronautical University and the University of Maryland also offer baccalaureate programs.

Professional Development

Graduate programs are plentiful. Embry-Riddle Aeronautical University, Ball State University, Boston University, the University of Oklahoma, and the University of Southern California offer degree programs at the master's level. Boston University expands its curriculum to post-master's work, as well.

As is true with stateside assignments, the soldier has a wealth of educational opportunities at the high school level, the Basic Skills Education Program (BSEP) level, and the Career Soldier's Education Program (CSEP) level.

Japan/Okinawa. Educational opportunities in Japan and Okinawa are more limited than those in Europe. A soldier can still complete his secondary education by GED, however, and can participate in college preparatory programs. Language programs include German and Japanese.

Only one undergraduate school, the University of Maryland, services this region. It offers associate and baccalaureate degrees. At the master's degree level, the University of Oklahoma and the University of Southern California offer limited graduate studies. Post-master's programs are not available.

Panama. Soldiers stationed in Panama can take advantage of a full range of course work at the secondary and college preparatory levels, including BSEP and ESL. Vocational/technical training is also available.

Four universities offer a wide range of associate, baccalaureate, and master's degree programs in this area.

Puerto Rico. The on-post educational opportunities in Puerto Rico are quite limited. A full curricular range is available, however, from the associate level to the post-master's level for students willing to travel to the off-post campuses located from three to fifty miles from Fort Buchanan.

Only two skill development programs offer certificates on post. These are Los Angeles Community College's emergency medical technician course, and the Manpower Business Training Institute's business skills program. Secondary and college preparatory programs on post include GED completion, BSEP, and ESL. Language training is available in Spanish and German.

South Korea. Soldiers stationed in South Korea can take advantage of a full range of educational opportunities without leaving the post, whether they are assigned in the northern region (Camp Red Cloud or Camp Greaves); in the southern region (Camp Pusan); or any of the 12 other camps in between.

The secondary level course work includes GED, high school diploma, college preparatory courses, languages (German, Japanese, and Korean), BSEP, and ESL.

Central Texas College offers certificates and associate degrees and the University of Maryland offers programs at the associate degree and the baccalaureate degree levels.

At the graduate level, two schools are available—the University of Oklahoma and the University of Southern California. Post-master's programs are not available.

The Skill Recognition Programs

The Skill Recognition Programs show ways to get recognition within the civilian sector for skills soldiers learn in the Army. This recognition can come in a variety of ways.

- **Accreditation of military experience.** The American Council on Education evaluates Army service school courses and recommends the number of semester hours of credit that civilian schools may wish to award based on a soldier's military training and experience. Examples include vocational, lower-level baccalaureate and associate degree, upper-level baccalaureate, and graduate level credits. These recommendations are published in the *Guide to the Evaluation of Educational Experiences in the Armed Services (ACE Guide)*.
- **Army apprenticeship.** This program provides participants documentation of apprentice skills acquired while in the Army that is understood by civilian industry, improves the performance and motivation of soldiers, provides a recruiting incentive for MOSs that are related to skills with apprenticeships, and improves the supervisor-soldier relationship.

Occupations with apprenticeships are those that are learned through experience and on-the-job training and are supplemented by related technical instruction. They involve manual, mechanical, or technological skills and knowledge requiring a minimum of 2,000 hours of work experience plus related instruction. They do not fall into the categories of selling, management, clerical, or professional skills requiring advanced knowledge and academic degrees. These occupations are identified in Department of Labor pamphlets and Appendix I, AR 621-5. The majority fall into engineer, quartermaster, transportation, and signal fields.

Enrollment is open to soldiers who perform satisfactorily on the job and possess an MOS (primary or secondary) that relates to the program and that has been registered with the Bureau of Apprenticeship Training. Also eligible are soldiers who possess a qualifying MOS in which they were initially registered but are no longer serving because of priorities and mission requirements.

- **Certification.** Some Army MOSs correspond to civilian occupations that require licensing or certification as a prerequisite for employment in certain states or businesses (truck mechanics, for instance, who may have to pass such tests as the National Institute for Automotive Service Excellence). Certification requirements and agencies are listed in Army apprenticeship or industry recognition pamphlets in the 621 series or in DANTES Examination Program Handbook.

Involvement in these programs is voluntary, but such involvement can foster professional development. It will not, however, result in duty assignments that are made solely to assist soldiers in fulfilling skill recognition program requirements.

Normally, certification or licensing through civilian agencies, if desired, will be done at the individual's expense. Exceptions occur when certification automatically follows successful completion of a course for which tuition assistance is authorized and is not a separate item of expense.

Army training programs will not be altered to meet civilian standards for skill recognition programs, but in some instances, civilian agencies, as a prerequisite to registration, certification, or formal recognition, might require additional nonmission-related training or experience before recognizing a soldier as fully qualified. When this training is necessary, the soldier must acquire the additional training and experience through local trade or vocational schools or other means.

Programs stress individual initiative on the part of the soldier to complete program requirements. An individual cannot be enrolled in more than one occupational skill area within an apprenticeship program at any one time. The soldier may, however, change to another occupational skill area or program as many times as desired, provided prerequisites are met.

Professional Development

Education Services Support

Education services support consists of counseling; participation in programs such as the New GI Bill, the New Army College Fund, the New GI Bill for Vietnam-era soldiers, the Veterans Educational Assistance Program (VEAP), VEAP-era Army College Fund, and the Servicemen's Opportunity Colleges Program; tuition assistance; VA educational benefits; DANTES; the Skill Recognition Program; and a full range of local educational opportunities available through the local Army education office (including language refresher training and MOS libraries). To determine what specific education program is available for you or your soldiers, consult with your local educational services officer.

One particularly valuable program is the Defense Activity for Nontraditional Education Support (DANTES), a Department of Defense activity that supports the services' voluntary education programs, with the Navy acting as the executive agent. It develops and sends out information on independent study programs and provides examination-for-credit programs available in the civilian education community.

DANTES services are available through education programs to all eligible active duty soldiers. One important aspect of the DANTES is the College Level Examination Program (CLEP), which also enables students to earn credit by examination. The examinations are not based on any particular textbook, syllabus, or set of readings. Instead, they measure knowledge of the basic concepts and applications involved in courses that have the same or similar titles. They are divided into two types: general examinations and subject examinations.

General examinations measure college-level achievement in five basic areas of the liberal arts: English composition, social sciences and history, natural sciences, humanities, and mathematics. The test material covers the first year of college, often referred to as the general or liberal education requirements. Through the CLEP general and subject tests, a student may earn many valuable college credits.

Subject examinations measure achievement in specific college courses and are used to grant credit for these courses. Examples of test titles include Introduction to Business Management, General Psychology, Western Civilization, American Literature, and so forth.

CLEP tests are kept on file for 20 years. Each institution has its own evaluating criteria for using CLEP test scores to determine credit. You should have official transcripts forwarded to the registrar of the college or university at which you desire to receive credit (some institutions require that a minimum number of semester hours of classwork be completed before CLEP credit will be accepted). Write to CLEP Transcript Service, College Entrance Examination Board, Princeton, NJ 08540.

Another type of subject test that, like CLEP, substitutes for college classroom work is the DANTES Subject Standardized Tests. Personnel who have not graduated from high school can earn either a high school diploma or an equivalency certificate by passing the General Educational Development (GED) test (if they also meet other state requirements).

Your post MOS library is a valuable job-related educational service available at the local education center. This library helps soldiers prepare for their SDT and for promotion board qualification. To supplement the Soldier's Manual, Training Extension Courses (TEC) are available. TECs are prepackaged video/audio taped lessons on a wide variety of military subjects. Additional library resources include Army regulations, pamphlets, field manuals, technical manuals, technical bulletins, training circulars, SDT Soldier's Manuals, and SDT test notification booklets. Library personnel also advise and assist with the selection of Army Service Correspondence Courses.

The U.S. Army operates perhaps the finest series of educational programs available anywhere in the world. The soldier who allows these educational opportunities to slip through his fingers is cheating himself and the Army. You must encourage your soldiers to take full advantage of these programs. The best way, as in most other things, is to set the example yourself.

Additional Qualification Training Courses

There are a number of additional qualification training courses for which a soldier may apply. (Soldiers are sometimes directed to take certain language training in connection with specific assignments.)

1. *Ranger Training.* This voluntary training conducted by the U.S. Army Infantry School, Fort Benning, Georgia, is designed to develop leadership skills and provide a knowledge of ranger operations involving direct combat with the enemy. Enlisted graduates receive a special qualification identifier ("V") for their MOS code. Ranger training is available on a voluntary basis for eligible male personnel. Applications should be submitted according to the instructions contained in AR 614-200.

2. *Airborne Training.* This voluntary functional training conducted by the U.S. Army Infantry School, Fort Benning, Georgia, is designed to qualify volunteers in the use of the parachute as a means of deployment and, through mental and physical training, to develop leadership, self-confidence, and aggressive spirit. Graduates receive an additional skill identifier ("P"). Airborne training is available on a voluntary basis for

Sound off! Soldiers march to class. *U.S. Army photo.*

Professional Development

enlisted personnel on assignment to airborne units. Eligible personnel volunteering for airborne training should submit applications according to the instructions contained in AR 614-200.

3. *Language Training.* The Defense Language Program is designed to provide personnel minimum essential professional linguistic skills to meet specific Army requirements. Basic language training is provided through the Defense Language Institute, Presidio of Monterey, California. Training requires full-time attendance. Courses are designed to provide the student a level three proficiency. Nonresident training is conducted in education centers, units, or established language training facilities using approved materials. Details of the management of the program are set forth in AR 350-20, AR 611-6, and AR 621-5. An additional skill identifier ("L") is usually awarded to graduates of the program.

4. *Equal Opportunity Training.* The Defense Equal Opportunity Management Institute at Patrick Air Force Base, Florida, conducts the 16-week training program. Selected officers and qualified enlisted volunteers are provided the skills and knowledge needed to assist the commander in increasing unit effectiveness and efficiency through improved racial harmony and equal opportunity. Enlisted personnel who successfully complete the training are awarded the appropriate additional skill and special skill identifiers. Details on eligibility and application for this training may be obtained from your local EEO NCO.

5. *Noncommissioned Officer Logistics Program (NCOLP) Training.* NCOLP training is conducted at the U.S. Army Quartermaster School, Fort Lee, Virginia. Its purpose is to provide program members a broad overview of logistics operations. Graduates are qualified for assignment to key logistic management positions that require technical knowledge of two or more logistics functions. NCOLP training is available for enlisted personnel in the ranks of staff sergeant through command sergeant major who possess the special qualification identifier "K," indicating NCOLP membership. Attendees must have at least nine months of service remaining upon completion of the course. Procedures for application are contained in AR 614-200.

MEMBERSHIP IN PROFESSIONAL ORGANIZATIONS

Membership in professional military organizations keeps you in touch with what other professionals are doing, provides a forum for the exchange of ideas through professional publications such as magazines and newsletters, offers you access to group life and medical insurance at rates competitive with those of the major insurance companies, assures you of a voice in national affairs through the appointed officers of your organization, and gives you a chance to meet periodically with like-minded persons at local chapter affairs.

Two such organizations you should consider joining are the Association of the United States Army (AUSA) and the Noncommissioned Officers Association (NCOA).

The Association of the U.S. Army (AUSA)

AUSA is a private, nonprofit, educational organization whose members join in supporting all aspects of the national security with emphasis on the Total Force Army and especially on the men and women who serve. The association has four objectives: public education about the Army; professionalism within the Army; industry liaison in support of the Army; people support for those in the Army.

As of April 1992, the AUSA membership consisted of 138,000 persons, military and civilian. Also, as of April 1992, 7,250 business firms held corporate (sustaining) memberships with the association. AUSA has 238 chapters: Most of them are in the United States, but some are located in Europe, the Pacific, South Korea, Alaska, and Japan.

The association's membership consists of officers, noncommissioned officers, and enlisted men and women serving in the active Army, National Guard, and Reserve, retirees of all ranks, and cadets. In addition, all grades of Department of the Army civilian employees and the civilian members of local communities who believe in what the Army is doing and in what the AUSA stands for are also eligible to become members.

The association also offers a variety of personal benefits to members, such as insurance and health care plans. For further information, write to AUSA, 2425 Wilson Boulevard, Arlington, VA 22201, or phone 703-841-4300.

The Noncommissioned Officers Association (NCOA)

The NCOA is basically a fraternal organization that offers a wide variety of benefits to its members and acts as a powerful voice in the U.S. Congress through its two registered lobbyists in Washington, D.C.

NCOA membership is open to all petty officers and noncommissioned officers in all branches of the Armed Forces, active, retired, Reserve, National Guard, and veterans. Associate memberships are available for the widows of NCOs and veterans (these are nonvoting memberships). As of April 1992, the NCOA had 155,000 members.

The NCOA is an effective lobbying organization in the nation's capital. It lends its support to a variety of programs designed to support national defense, pay and benefits for active duty personnel, and programs for the benefit of veterans and retired personnel. The association is a strong, unified voice for the noncommissioned and petty officers in all communities, as well as in Washington.

For more information on NCOA benefits and programs, write to NCOA International Headquarters, PO Box 33610, San Antonio, TX 78233, or phone 512-653-6161.

APPLYING FOR A COMMISSION OR A WARRANT

Applying for a commission or a warrant is not advancing the *noncommissioned* officer's career, which is the basic purpose of this guide. But no soldier worth his or her salt has not at some time—if only briefly—considered the prospect of becoming an officer. And subordinates will definitely ask you questions about applying for commissions, so to do your job effectively, you must know something about the process, even if you have no intention of taking advantage of it yourself.

You should encourage those subordinates you feel are qualified to apply for commissions or warrants. It is a good feeling to know that you have been instrumental in both helping a young soldier rise in the Army and providing the officer corps a talented and highly motivated young man or woman.

It is not easy to become an officer. The person who obtains a commission works very hard to attain the necessary qualifications. Young people—young officers, especially—are not necessarily endowed at the moment of their commissioning with more wisdom and judgment than their NCOs, but they can be counted on to have a high degree of self-confidence and determination.

Should you apply for a commission or a warrant yourself? The answer is an

Professional Development

unequivocal yes, if you qualify. But the older you are and the more rank you have as an NCO, the more careful you should be about accepting the status of a junior officer or warrant officer. Compare the current pay scales and allowances. You may find that there is really not that much difference in pay between what you are earning now and what you might expect to earn as a warrant or commissioned officer, and remember that to retire as an officer you must have at least 10 years' active service as a commissioned officer.

A soldier can pursue a commission or warrant in the following various ways.

Officer Candidate School

Officer Candidate School (OCS) is conducted at Fort Benning, Georgia. Each year, five 14-week classes produce second lieutenants in the Army Reserve. Approximately half the candidates are soldiers who were in the Army before applying. Approximately 60 percent of the applicants for these courses are selected. Once enrolled, a candidate is automatically promoted to the grade of sergeant, providing he or she held a lower grade before enrollment.

To be eligible for OCS you must meet the following criteria:
- Have at least two years of college.
- Be a U.S. citizen.
- Score 80 or higher on the English Comprehension Level Test.
- Achieve a GT score of 110 or higher.
- Score 90 or higher on the Officer Selection Battery.
- Be less than 30 years old on enrollment date.
- Have a favorable background security check.
- Meet the weight and physical standards contained in AR 600-9 and be otherwise medically fit according to the standards of AR 40-501.
- Not have been previously dismissed from OCS training.

United States Military Academy (USMA)

A soldier may attend the United States Military Academy at West Point in two ways: one is to seek nomination and selection as would any other U.S. citizen; the other, for those already in the Army, is to apply for the West Point Preparatory School at Fort Monmouth, New Jersey. Attendance at the Preparatory School does not, however, guarantee selection for attendance at the USMA, but it does improve your chances. The Regular Army has 85 appointments to the Military Academy each year, and attendance at the Preparatory School increases your chances to get one of those appointments.

For application to the West Point Prep School you must meet the following criteria:
- Be single.
- Have no legal dependents to support.
- Be younger than 22 before entering USMA (11 months following entry into the prep school).
- Be a U.S. citizen.

You apply by first filling out the basic application. See AR 351-12 for guidance. Do not be modest and do not leave any line blank. The following must accompany your application:
- Your commander's endorsement, which will include your Army Physical Readiness Test form, GT score, ETS, and MOS.
- Your high school transcript or GED scores and GED certificate.
- SAT or ACT test scores.

- Records of medical examination (SF 88) and medical history (SF 93).
- Your photograph (any type will do).
- Any college transcripts you may have.
- A personal essay discussing why you want to attend West Point and your personal goals for the future. Remember when writing these essays that the West Point motto is "Duty, Honor, Country."

For more information, write Commandant, USMAPS, ATTN: MAPS-AD-A, Fort Monmouth, NJ 07703.

Reserve Officer Training Corps (ROTC)

The ROTC program is a series of college elective courses and field training that, when successfully completed, leads to a commission as a second lieutenant in the Active Army, the Army National Guard, or the U.S. Army Reserve. Military science courses are taken in conjunction with an academic course load. You must be a full-time student to enroll in Army ROTC.

You enroll in ROTC the same time you enroll in college. Since you must be enrolled full-time as a student to enter ROTC, you may not concurrently serve on active duty. Most ROTC cadets first enroll in the two-year Basic Course and then in the two-year Advanced Course. As a veteran, you receive credit for the Basic Course and may earn your commission by enrolling in ROTC for two academic years and completing one six-week summer camp. You must complete your baccalaureate degree before returning to active duty as a commissioned officer.

High school graduates of any race or ethnic origin who will be enrolling in college for the first time may compete for a four-year scholarship at a historically black college or university (HBCU) such as Howard University in Washington, D.C. HBCU scholarship applicants must have SAT scores totaling 850 or an ACT of 19 to apply.

Students may compete for on-campus scholarships once they enroll in ROTC: Two- and three-year active duty scholarships and two-year reserve forces duty scholarships are offered. If you have completed two years of active duty before school starts and are accepted by a college or university as either a sophomore or a junior, you can compete for an active duty two- or three-year scholarship. You must have a GT score of 115 or higher to qualify. Applicants for a four-year Green-to-Gold scholarship must have SAT scores totaling 850 or an ACT composite score of 19 to apply and must attend a historically black college or university.

The Army ROTC scholarship annually pays up to $8,500 or 80 percent of college tuition, whichever is higher. Scholarship winners receive a tax-free subsistence allowance of $100 a month for up to 10 months for each year the scholarship is effective, and you still qualify for Veterans Assistance Education Program, GI Bill, or Army College Fund benefits you have earned. The scholarship application window each year is 1 December through 15 March. Scholarship cadets must be under 25 when commissioned. Veterans with scholarships get constructive credit for each year of active duty up to four years, thus allowing a scholarship winner to be up to 29 at commissioning.

If you accept an ROTC scholarship, you will give back to the Army eight years: four on active duty and four in the Reserve. While in school, you must rank in the top half of your ROTC class. If you receive such a scholarship, you will be discharged and enlisted in the Reserve. A scholarship offers full tuition plus a $1,000 living allowance each school year. Your Army ROTC contract provides for payment of tuition and lab fees and a flat rate for books, equipment, and supplies.

Professional Development

For more details visit your on-post education center. You may also find more information in AR 145-1 and AR 635-200 (Chapter 16). For information about ROTC programs in your area, call 800-USA-ROTC.

Direct Appointments

Direct appointments are offered to personnel who have the skills and managerial ability required of an Army officer. In order to qualify, soldiers must have served one year on active duty and have a college degree. The educational requirement is waived if a soldier has served six months as a warrant officer or in an enlisted grade above specialist.

Applications for direct appointments are submitted on DA Form 61; personal appearance before a local review board is required. The final decision to commission is made by PersCom, which also determines grade and branch assignment.

Check AR 135-100 for details about the program. If you are or think you may become a doctor, a lawyer, or some other type of civilian professional, a direct appointment may be just the thing for you.

Warrant Officer Appointments

A master list of all warrant officer specialties is included in AR 611-112; AR 611-85 explains how to apply for officer flight training. Warrant officers fill highly specialized areas that are incompatible with a commissioned officer's career progression (warrant officers are "specialists" while commissioned officers are "generalists").

Applications for warrant officer appointments (except applications for flight training) are submitted on DA Form 61.

4

Evaluation and Management Systems

NCO EVALUATION REPORTING SYSTEM

On 1 January 1988, the Army implemented an annual evaluation report that emphasizes Army values, NCO responsibilities, and counseling duties. The report does not include numerical ratings used by the retired 20-year-old Enlisted Evaluation Report (EER). Instead, this report focuses on the NCO's skills and Army-required attributes in conjunction with current and potential performance. This two-form system is used to evaluate all NCOs. DA Form 2166-7, *NCO Evaluation Report*, is used to evaluate CPLs through CSM. DA Form 2166-7-1, *NCO Counseling Checklist/Record*, however, is mandatory for only CPLs through SFCs/PSGs, although face-to-face counseling for all NCOs is required. DA Pam 623-205, *The Noncommissioned Officer Evaluation Reporting System "In Brief,"* provides detailed information on this system, which is the result of the NCO Professional Development Study Group's effort that began in 1985. This system is aimed at strengthening the ability of the NCO corps to meet the professional challenges of the future through Army values and NCO responsibilities. This system will improve selection of the best NCOs to serve in positions of increasing responsibilities because selection boards and other EPMS decision-making agencies will have more accurate information.

Evaluation and Management Systems

Performance Counseling/Checklist

The purpose of performance counseling is to inform soldiers via face-to-face counseling about their jobs and their expected performance standards. It also provides feedback on their actual performance. The ultimate goal of this part of the system is to assist all NCOs to be successful in their endeavors and to meet applicable standards. Although past performance must be acknowledged, the best counseling does not dwell on the past but rather looks ahead to the future and what can be improved.

Counseling at the end of the rating period is ineffective because no time remains to improve performance before evaluation; therefore, under this system, counseling takes place within 30 days of each rating period and at least quarterly thereafter. The first counseling session tells the rated NCO what is expected, and the quarterly sessions (active duty NCOs) tell the rated NCO what he or she has done well and what could be done better. After the initial counseling session, ARNG and USAR soldiers are counseled semiannually.

The NCO Counseling Checklist/Record is designed to be used with the NCOER as the only counseling support document. It includes all the necessary information needed to assist you in preparing and conducting a counseling session. It also provides a section to record results of the session. Upon completion of the counseling session, the rater keeps one checklist for each rated NCO until the end of the rating period. This counseling form is comprehensive. It includes reference material related to counseling, Army values, and NCO responsibilities. Read this form thoroughly before counseling.

Types of NCOERs

Only those types of reports authorized by AR 623-205 are submitted.

Initial Reports. Initial reports are prepared for soldiers three months after promotion to sergeant, providing minimum rater qualifications are met. Initial reports should not be signed by the rater prior to the first day of the month following the closing month.

Annual Reports. Annual reports are submitted 12 months after the ending month of the last report submitted. If 12 months elapse since the ending month of the last report, but the required three-month minimum rating period or rate qualification criteria have not been met, the annual report period is extended until the minimum requirements are met. Annual reports should not be signed before the first day of the month following the ending month.

Change-of-Rater Reports. Providing minimum rater qualifications are met and *no other reports have been submitted* in the preceding three months, change-of-rater reports occur when there has been a normal change of the designated rater, the individual has been on extended TDY, the rater has left the Army, or the rater is relieved or incapacitated. Change-of-rater reports may be signed at any time during the closing or following month of the report.

Complete-the-Record Reports. At the option of the rater, a complete-the-record report may be submitted on a soldier who is about to be considered by a DA centralized board for promotion, school, or CSM selection provided the soldier is in the zone of

NCO COUNSELING CHECKLIST/RECORD

For use of this form, see AR 623-205; the proponent agency MILPERCEN

NAME OF RATED NCO	RANK	DUTY POSITION	UNIT

PURPOSE: The primary purpose of counseling is to improve performance and to professionally develop the rated NCO. The best counseling is always looking forward. It does not dwell on the past and on what was done, rather on the future and what can be done better. Counseling at the end of the rating period is too late since there is no time to improve before evaluation.

RULES:
1. Face-to-face performance counseling is mandatory for all Noncommissioned Officers.
2. This form is for use along with a working copy of the NCO-ER for conducting NCO performance counseling and recording counseling content and dates. Its use is mandatory for counseling all NCOs, CPL thru SFC/PSG, and is optional for counseling other senior NCOs.
3. Active Component. Initial counseling must be conducted within the first 30 days of each rating period, and at least quarterly thereafter. Reserve Components. (ARNG, USAR). Counseling must be conducted at least semiannually. There is no mandatory counseling at the end of the rating period.

CHECKLIST – FIRST COUNSELING SESSION AT THE BEGINNING OF THE RATING PERIOD

PREPARATION
1. Schedule counseling session, notify rated NCO.
2. Get copy of last duty description used for rated NCO's duty position, a blank copy of the NCO-ER, and the names of the new rating chain.
3. Update duty description (see page 2).
4. Fill out rating chain and duty description on working copy of NCO-ER. Parts II and III.
5. Read each of the values/responsibilities in Part IV of NCO-ER and the expanded definitions and examples on page 3 and 4 of this form.
6. Think how each value and responsibility in Part IV of NCO-ER applies to the rated NCO and his/her duty position.
Note: Leadership and training may be more difficult to apply than the other values/responsibilities when the rated NCO has no subordinates. Leadership is simply influencing others in the accomplishment of the mission and that can include peers and superiors. It also can be applied directly to additional duties and other areas of Army community life. Individual training is the responsibility of all NCOs whether or not there are subordinates. Every NCO knows something that can be taught to others and should be involved in some way in a training program.
7. Decide what you consider necessary for success (a meets standards rating) for each value/responsibility. Use the examples listed on pages 3 and 4 of this form as a guide in developing your own standards for success. Some may apply exactly, but you may have to change them or develop new ones that apply to your situation. Be specific so the rated NCO will know what is expected.
8. Make notes in blank spaces in Part IV of NCO-ER to help when counseling.
9. Review counseling tips in FM 22-101.

COUNSELING
1. Make sure rated NCO knows rating chain.
2. Show rated NCO the draft duty description on your working copy of the NCO-ER. Explain all parts. If rated NCO performed in position before, ask for any ideas to make duty description better.
3. Discuss the meaning of each value/responsibility in Part IV of NCO-ER. Use the trigger words on the NCO-ER, and the expanded definitions on pages 3 and 4 of this form to help.
4. Explain how each value/responsibility applies to the specific duty position by showing or telling your standards for success (a meets standards rating). Use examples on pages 3 and 4 of this form as a start point. Be specific so the rated NCO really knows what's expected.
5. When possible, give specific examples of excellence that could apply. This gives the rated NCO something special to strive for. Remember that only a few achieve real excellence and that real excellence always includes specific results and often includes accomplishments of subordinates.
6. Give rated NCO opportunity to ask questions and make suggestions.

AFTER COUNSELING
1. Record rated NCO's name and counseling date on this form.
2. Write key points made in counseling session on this form.
3. Show key points to rated NCO and get his initials.
4. Save NCO-ER with this checklist for next counseling session.

CHECKLIST – LATER COUNSELING SESSIONS DURING THE RATING PERIOD

PREPARATION
1. Schedule counseling session, notify rated NCO, and tell him/her to come prepared to discuss what has been accomplished in each value/responsibility area.
2. Look at working copy of NCO-ER you used during last counseling session.
3. Read and update duty description. Especially note the area of special emphasis; the priorities may have changed.
4. Read again, each of the values/responsibilities in Part IV of NCO-ER and the expanded definitions and examples on pages 3 and 4 of this form; then think again, about your standards for success.
5. Look over the notes you wrote down on page 2 of this form about the last counseling session.
6. Think about what the rated NCO has done so far during this rating period (specifically, observed action, demonstrated behavior, and results).
7. For each value/responsibility area, answer three questions: First, what has happened in response to any discussion you had during the last counseling session? Second, what has been done well?; and Third, what could be done better?
8. Make notes in blank spaces in Part IV of NCO-ER to help focus when counseling. (Use new NCO-ER if old one is full from last counseling session).
9. Review counseling tips in FM 22-101.

DA FORM 2166-7-1, AUG 87

COUNSELING

1. Go over each part of the duty description with rated NCO. Discuss any changes, especially to the area of special emphasis.
2. Tell rated NCO how he/she is doing. Use your success standards as a guide for the discussion (the examples on pages 3 and 4 may help). First, for each value/responsibility, talk about what has happened in response to any discussion you had during the last counseling session (remember, observed action, demonstrated behavior and results). Second, talk about what was done well. Third, talk about how to do better. The goal is to get all NCOs to be successful and meet standards.
3. When possible, give examples of excellence that could apply. This gives the rated NCO something to strive for, REMEMBER, EXCELLENCE IS SPECIAL, ONLY A FEW ACHIEVE IT! Excellence includes results and often involves subordinates.
4. Ask rated NCO for ideas, examples and opinions on what has been done so far and what can be done better. (This step can be done first or last).

AFTER COUNSELING

1. Record counseling date on this form.
2. Write key points made in counseling session on this form.
3. Show key points to rated NCO and get his initials.
4. Save NCO-ER with this checklist for next counseling session. (Notes should make record NCO-ER preparation easy at end of rating period).

COUNSELING RECORD

DATE OF COUNSELING	RATED NCO's INITIALS	KEY POINTS MADE
INITIAL		
LATER		
LATER		
LATER		

DUTY DESCRIPTION (PART III of NCO-ER)

The duty description is essential to performance counseling and evaluation. It is used during the first counseling session to tell rated NCO what the duties are and what needs to be emphasized. It may change somewhat during the rating period. It is used at the end of the rating period to record what was important about the duties.

The five elements of the duty description:

1 & 2. Principal Duty Title and Duty MOS Code. Enter principal duty title and DMOS that most accurately reflects actual duties performed.

3. Daily Duties and Scope. This portion should address the most important routine duties and responsibilities. Ideally, this should include number of people supervised, equipment, facilities, and dollars involved and any other routine duties and responsibilities critical to mission accomplishment.

4. Area of Special Emphasis. This portion is most likely to change somewhat during the rating period. For the first counseling session, it includes those items that require top priority effort at least for the first part of the upcoming rating period. At the end of the rating period, it should include the most important items that applied at any time during the rating period (examples are preparation for REFORGER deployment, combined arms drills training for FTX, preparation for NTC rotation, revision of battalion maintenance SOP, training for tank table qualification, ITEP and company AMTP readiness, related tasks cross-training, reserve components annual training support (AT) and SIDPERS acceptance rate).

5. Appointed Duties. This portion should include those duties that are appointed and are not normally associated with the duty description.

DA FORM 2166-7-1, AUG 87

NCO Counseling Checklist/Record (continued).

VALUES/NCO RESPONSIBILITIES (PART IV of NCO-ER)

VALUES: Values are what soldiers, as a profession, judge to be right. They are the moral, ethical, and professional attributes of character. They are the heart and soul of a great Army. Part IVa of the NCO-ER includes some of the most important values. These are: Putting the welfare of the nation, the assigned mission and teamwork before individual interests; Exhibiting absolute honesty and courage to stand up for what is right; Developing a sense of obligation and support between those who are led, those who lead, and those who serve alongside; Maintaining high standards of personal conduct on and off duty; And finally, demonstrating obedience, total adherence to the spirit and letter of a lawful order, discipline, and ability to overcome fear despite difficulty or danger.

Examples of standards for "YES" ratings:

- Put the Army, the mission and subordinates first before own personal interest.
- Meet challenges without compromising integrity.
- Personal conduct, both on and off duty, reflects favorably on NCO corps.
- Obey lawful orders and do what is right without orders.
- Choose the hard right over the easy wrong.
- Exhibit pride in unit, be a team player.
- Demonstrate respect for all soldiers regardless of race, creed, color, sex, or national origin.

COMPETENCE: The knowledge, skills and abilities necessary to be expert in the current duty assignment and to perform adequately in other assignments within the MOS when required. Competence is both technical and tactical and includes reading, writing, speaking and basic mathematics. It also includes sound judgment, ability to weigh alternatives, form objective opinions and make good decisions. Closely allied with competence is the constant desire to be better, to listen and learn more and to do each task completely to the best of one's ability. Learn, grow, set standards, and achieve them, create and innovate, take prudent risks, never settle for less than best. Committed to excellence.

Examples of standards for "Success/Meets Standards" rating:

- Master the knowledge, skills and abilities required for performance in your duty position.
- Meet PMOS SQT standards for your grade.
- Accomplish completely and promptly those tasks assigned or required by duty position.
- Constantly seek ways to learn, grow and improve.

Examples of "Excellence":

- Picked as SSG to be a platoon sergeant over twelve other SSGs.
- Maintained SIDPERS rating of 98% for six months.
- Scored 94% on last SQT.
- Selected best truck master in annual battalion competition.
- Designated Installation Drill Sergeant of Quarter.
- Exceeded recruiting objectives two consecutive quarters.
- Awarded Expert Infantryman Badge (EIB).

PHYSICAL FITNESS AND MILITARY BEARING: Physical fitness is the physical and mental ability to accomplish the mission – combat readiness. Total fitness includes weight control, diet and nutrition, smoking cessation, control of substance abuse, stress management, and physical training. It covers strength, endurance, stamina, flexibility, speed, agility, coordination and balance. NCOs are responsible for their own physical fitness and that of their subordinates. Military Bearing consists of posture, dress, overall appearance, and manner of physical movement. Bearing also includes an outward display of inner-feelings, fears, and overall confidence and enthusiasm. An inherent NCO responsibility is concern with the military bearing of the individual soldier, to include on-the-spot corrections.

Examples of standards for "Success/Meets Standards" rating:

- Maintain weight within Army limits for age and sex.
- Obtain passing score in APFT and participate in a regular exercise program.
- Maintain personal appearance and exhibit enthusiasm to the point of setting an example for junior enlisted soldiers.
- Monitor and encourage improvement in the physical and military bearing of subordinates.

Examples of "Excellence":

- Received Physical Fitness Badge for 292 score on APFT.
- Selected soldier of the month/quarter/year.
- Three of the last four soldiers of the month were from his/her platoon.
- As Master Fitness Trainer, established battalion physical fitness program.
- His entire squad was commended for scoring above 270 on APFT.

DA FORM 2166-7-1, AUG 87

NCO Counseling Checklist/Record (continued).

LEADERSHIP: Influencing others to accomplish the mission. It consists of applying leadership attributes (Beliefs, Values, Ethics, Character, Knowledge, and Skills). It includes setting tough, but achievable standards and demanding that they be met; Caring deeply and sincerely for subordinates and their families and welcoming the opportunity to serve them; Conducting counseling; Setting the example by word and act/deed; Can be summarized by BE (Committed to the professional Army ethic and professional traits); KNOW (The factors of leadership, yourself, human nature, your job, and your unit); DO (Provide direction, implement, and motivate). Instill the spirit to achieve and win: Inspire and develop excellence. A soldier cared for today, leads tomorrow.

Examples of standards for "Success/Meets Standards" rating:

- Motivate subordinates to perform to the best of their ability as individuals and together as a disciplined cohesive team to accomplish the mission.
- Demonstrate that you care deeply and sincerely for soldiers and welcome the opportunity to serve them.
- Instill the spirit to achieve and win; Inspire and develop excellence through counseling.
- Set the example: BE, KNOW, DO.

Examples of "Excellence":

- Motivated entire squad to qualify expert with M-16.
- Won last three platoon quad inspections.
- Selected for membership in Sergeant Morales Club.
- Inspired mechanics to maintain operational readiness rating of 95% for two consecutive quarters.
- Led his squad through map orienteering course to win the battalion competition.
- Counseled two marginal soldiers ultimately selected for promotion.

TRAINING: Preparing individuals, units and combined arms teams for duty performance; The teaching of skills and knowledge. NCOs contribute to team training, are often responsible for unit training (Squads, Crews, Sections), but individual training is the most important, exclusive responsibility of the NCO Corps. Quality training bonds units: Leads directly to good discipline; Concentrates on wartime missions; Is tough and demanding without being reckless; Is performance oriented; Sticks to Army doctrine to standardize what is taught to fight, survive, and win, as small units when AirLand battle actions dictate. "Good training means learning from mistakes and allowing plenty of room for professional growth. Sharing knowledge and experience is the greatest legacy one can leave subordinates."

Examples of standards for "Success/Meets Standards" rating:

- Make sure soldiers-
  a. Can do identified common tasks.
  b. Are prepared for SQT and Commander's Evaluation.
  c. Develop and practice skills for duty position.
  d. Train as a squad/crew/section.
- Identify and recommend subordinates for professional development courses.
- Participate in unit training program.
- Share knowledge and experience with subordinates.

Examples of "Excellence":

- Taught five common tasks resulting in 100% GO on Annual CTT for all soldiers in directorate.
- Trained best howitzer section of the year in battalion.
- Coached subordinates to win consecutive soldier of month competitions.
- Established company Expert Field Medical Badge program resulting in 85% of all eligible soldiers receiving EFMB.
- Distinguished 1 tank and qualified 3 tanks in platoon on first run of tank table VIII.
- Trained platoon to fire honor battery during annual service practice.

RESPONSIBILITY AND ACCOUNTABILITY: The proper care, maintenance, use, handling, and conservation of personnel, equipment, supplies, property, and funds. Maintenance of weapons, vehicles, equipment, conservation of supplies, and funds is a special NCO responsibility because of its links to the success of all missions, especially those on the battlefield. It includes inspecting soldier's equipment often, using manual or checklist; Holding soldiers responsible for repairs and losses; Learning how to use and maintain all the equipment soldiers use; Being among the first to operate new equipment; Keeping up-to-date component lists; Setting aside time for inventories; and Knowing the readiness status of weapons, vehicles, and other equipment. It includes knowing where each soldier is during duty hours; Why he is going on sick call, where he lives, and his family situation; It involves reducing accidental manpower and monetary losses by providing a safe and healthful environment; It includes creating a climate which encourages young soldiers to learn and grow, and, to report serious problems without fear of repercussions. Also, NCOs must accept responsibility for their own actions and for those of their subordinates.

Examples of standards for "Success/Meets Standards" rating:

- Make sure your weapons, equipment, and vehicles are serviceable, maintained and ready for accomplishing the mission.
- Stop waste of supplies and limited funds.
- Be aware of those things that impact on soldier readiness e.g., family affairs, SQT, CTT, PQR, special duty, medical conditions, etc.
- Be responsible for your actions and those of your subordinates.

Examples of "Excellence":

- His emphasis on safety resulted in four tractor trailer drivers logging 10,000 miles accident free.
- Received commendation from CG for organizing post special olympics program.
- Won the installation award for Quarters of the Month.
- His constant instruction on maintenance resulted in six of eight mechanics earning master mechanic badges.
- Commended for no APCs on deadline report for six months.
- His learn and grow climate resulted in best platoon ARTEP results in the battalion.

DA FORM 2166-7-1, AUG 87

NCO Counseling Checklist/Record (continued).

consideration, has been in the current duty assignment under the same rater for at least three rated months, and has not had a previous report for the current duty assignment.

Special Reports. Special reports are submitted to recognize a deed, an act, or a series of deeds or acts that are so outstanding that they cannot await recognition through the normal reporting schedule or to reveal a performance deficiency so serious that it cannot await reporting through the normal reporting schedule. These are the *only* kinds of reports that may be submitted as special reports; they are not submitted in connection with an individual's consideration for schooling or promotion. Each special report must be approved or disapproved by a field grade officer who is in the direct line of supervision of the rated soldier and who will act as the reviewer for the report. Special reports may be signed at any time during the closing or following month of the report.

Relief-for-Cause Reports. Relief-for-cause is the early release of a soldier from a specific duty or assignment, directed by superior authority, and based on a decision that the soldier has failed in his or her duty performance through inefficiency or misconduct. The reasons for relief must be clearly explained by the rating official in his narrative portion of DA Form 2166-7 along with a statement that the soldier concerned has been informed of the reasons for the relief. When the relief is directed by someone not in the designated rating chain, that official describes the reasons for the relief in an enclosure to the report. The minimum rating period for these kinds of reports is normally 30 days, but a general officer in the chain of command (or the general court-martial convening authority) may waive this requirement and authorize the relief report to be written in clearcut cases of misconduct. Relief-for-cause reports are signed at any time during the closing or following month of the report.

Restrictions

A number of restrictions apply to the type of material that may be included in an efficiency report.

• The zeal with which a soldier performs duty as a member of a court-martial, counsel for an accused, or an Equal Opportunity NCO cannot be referred to in an efficiency report.

• No reference may be made to any unproven derogatory information in an efficiency report. Such information includes punitive or administrative action taken or planned against a rated soldier or *any* investigation concerning the soldier, unless such action or investigation has been processed to completion and adjudication and final action have been taken within the rating period. This prohibition prevents unverified derogatory information from being included in reports and guarantees the exclusion of information that would be unjustly prejudicial from being included permanently in a soldier's OMPF.

• Although incidents caused by alcohol or drug abuse (but not information derived from ADAPCP records) may be taken into account by rating officials, a soldier's participation in the ADAPCP is not normally mentioned in evaluation reports. Although paragraph 2-16, AR 623-205, authorizes raters to mention a soldier's voluntary entry into the ADAPCP and successful rehabilitation "as a factor to the rated soldier's credit," this kind of information should not be included in a report unless previous reports cited problems arising from substance abuse.

NCO EVALUATION REPORT

For use of this form, see AR 623-205; the proponent agency is DCSPER

SEE PRIVACY ACT STATEMENT IN AR 623-205, APPENDIX E.

PART I - ADMINISTRATIVE DATA

a. NAME (Last, First, Middle Initial) | b. SSN | c. RANK | d. DATE OF RANK | e. PMOSC

f. UNIT, ORG., STATION, ZIP CODE OR APO, MAJOR COMMAND | g. REASON FOR SUBMISSION

h. PERIOD COVERED				i. RATED MONTHS	j. NON-RATED CODES	k. NO. OF ENCL	l. RATED NCO COPY (Check one and Date)		m. PSC Initials	n. CMD CODE	o. PSC CODE
FROM		THRU					1. Given to NCO	Date			
YY	MM	YY	MM				2. Forwarded to NCO				

PART II - AUTHENTICATION

a. NAME OF RATER (Last, First, Middle Initial) | SSN | SIGNATURE

RANK, PMOSC/BRANCH, ORGANIZATION, DUTY ASSIGNMENT | DATE

b. NAME OF SENIOR RATER (Last, First, Middle Initial) | SSN | SIGNATURE

RANK, PMOSC/BRANCH, ORGANIZATION, DUTY ASSIGNMENT | DATE

c. RATED NCO: I understand my signature does not constitute agreement or disagreement with the evaluations of the rater and senior rater. Part I, height/weight and APFT entries are verified. I have seen this report completed through Part V. I am aware of the appeals process (AR 623-205). | SIGNATURE | DATE

d. NAME OF REVIEWER (Last, First, Middle Initial) | SSN | SIGNATURE

RANK, PMOSC/BRANCH, ORGANIZATION, DUTY ASSIGNMENT | DATE

e. ☐ CONCUR WITH RATER AND SENIOR RATER EVALUATIONS   ☐ NONCONCUR WITH RATER AND/OR SENIOR RATER EVAL (See attached comments)

PART III - DUTY DESCRIPTION (Rater)

a. PRINCIPAL DUTY TITLE | b. DUTY MOSC

c. DAILY DUTIES AND SCOPE (To include, as appropriate, people, equipment, facilities and dollars)

d. AREAS OF SPECIAL EMPHASIS

e. APPOINTED DUTIES

f. Counseling dates from checklist/record | INITIAL | LATER | LATER | LATER

PART IV - VALUES/NCO RESPONSIBILITIES (Rater)

a. Complete each question. (Comments are mandatory for "No" entries; optional for "Yes" entries.)

VALUES

PERSONAL
Commitment
Competence
Candor
Courage

ARMY ETHIC
Loyalty
Duty
Selfless Service
Integrity

	YES	NO
1. Places dedication and commitment to the goals and missions of the Army and nation above personal welfare.		
2. Is committed to and shows a sense of pride in the unit - works as a member of the team.		
3. Is disciplined and obedient to the spirit and letter of a lawful order.		
4. Is honest and truthful in word and deed.		
5. Maintains high standards of personal conduct on and off duty.		
6. Has the courage of convictions and the ability to overcome fear - stands up for and does what's right.		
7. Supports EO/EEO		

Bullet comments

DA FORM 2166-7, SEP 87   REPLACES DA FORM 2166-6, OCT 81, WHICH IS OBSOLETE

RATED NCO'S NAME (Last, First, Middle Initial)		SSN	THRU DATE

PART IV (Rater) - VALUES/NCO RESPONSIBILITIES — Specific Bullet examples of "EXCELLENCE" or "NEEDS IMPROVEMENT" are mandatory. Specific Bullet examples of "SUCCESS" are optional.

b. COMPETENCE
  o Duty proficiency; MOS competency
  o Technical & tactical; knowledge, skills, and abilities
  o Sound judgment
  o Seeking self-improvement; always learning
  o Accomplishing tasks to the fullest capacity; committed to excellence

EXCELLENCE (Exceeds std)   SUCCESS (Meets std)   NEEDS IMPROVEMENT (Some) (Much)

c. PHYSICAL FITNESS & MILITARY BEARING
  o Mental and physical toughness
  o Endurance and stamina to go the distance
  o Displaying confidence and enthusiasm; looks like a soldier

APFT   HEIGHT/WEIGHT

EXCELLENCE (Exceeds std)   SUCCESS (Meets std)   NEEDS IMPROVEMENT (Some) (Much)

d. LEADERSHIP
  o Mission first
  o Genuine concern for soldiers
  o Instilling the spirit to achieve and win
  o Setting the example; Be, Know, Do

EXCELLENCE (Exceeds std)   SUCCESS (Meets std)   NEEDS IMPROVEMENT (Some) (Much)

e. TRAINING
  o Individual and team
  o Mission focused; performance oriented
  o Teaching soldiers how; common tasks, duty-related skills
  o Sharing knowledge and experience to fight, survive and win

EXCELLENCE (Exceeds std)   SUCCESS (Meets std)   NEEDS IMPROVEMENT (Some) (Much)

f. RESPONSIBILITY & ACCOUNTABILITY
  o Care and maintenance of equip./facilities
  o Soldier and equipment safety
  o Conservation of supplies and funds
  o Encouraging soldiers to learn and grow
  o Responsible for good, bad, right & wrong

EXCELLENCE (Exceeds std)   SUCCESS (Meets std)   NEEDS IMPROVEMENT (Some) (Much)

PART V - OVERALL PERFORMANCE AND POTENTIAL

a. RATER. Overall potential for promotion and/or service in positions of greater responsibility.

AMONG THE BEST   FULLY CAPABLE   MARGINAL

e. SENIOR RATER BULLET COMMENTS

b. RATER. List 3 positions in which the rated NCO could best serve the Army at his/her current or next higher grade.

_____
_____
_____

c. SENIOR RATER. Overall performance
     1 2 3 4 5
     Successful Fair Poor

d. SENIOR RATER. Overall potential for promotion and/or service in positions of greater responsibility.
     1 2 3 4 5
     Superior Fair Poor

NCO Evaluation Report (continued).

Evaluation and Management Systems

Commander Intervention

When a commander learns that a report made by a subordinate or a member of a subordinate command may have been illegal or unjust or may have violated the provisions of AR 623-205, he or she must investigate the allegation. The commander may not, however, direct that a report be changed or use command influence to alter an honest evaluation.

When the commander's investigation finds that an error, a violation of the regulation, or some wrongdoing has occurred, the report is returned to the reviewer along with the results of the investigation. The commander then recommends to the rating officials that the report be corrected to account for matters revealed in the investigation. This recommendation is done with regard for the restrictions on command authority and influence mentioned above.

When a report has been corrected under the above circumstances, it is forwarded with no reference to the action taken by the commander.

Rater Qualifications and Responsibilities

The rater must be the first-line supervisor of the rated soldier for a minimum of three months (see paragraphs 2-10c and 2-11c, AR 623-205, for exceptions) and senior to the rated soldier either by grade or by date of rank. Members of other U.S. military services who meet these qualifications may also be raters.

Commanders may appoint U.S. civilian raters GS-6 and above when a first-line military supervisor is not available and when the civilian supervisor is in the best position to accurately evaluate the soldier's performance. The civilian rater must be officially designated on the published rating scheme established by the local commander. Members of allied forces are not authorized to be raters.

Raters must counsel rated soldiers on their duty performance and professional development throughout the rating period. They must assess the performance of the rated soldier, using all reasonable means to do so, and prepare a fair, correct report evaluating the soldier's duty performance and potential. The rater must also verify the personal data and duty description on the NCOER.

Without a doubt, you will find NCOER counseling of good soldiers a pleasant experience. Counseling bad soldiers is a bad experience, yet you must face up to it if you are to be a good leader.

Keep a record of your counseling sessions with problem soldiers, making notes of dates and matters discussed. If you have to give such persons bad NCOERs they may react vigorously and you must have your facts in good order. One or two sessions should be sufficient to straighten the problem performer out, but if not, you must do your duty and you must be ready to back up your ratings.

Senior Rater Qualifications and Responsibilities

The senior rater must be in the direct line of supervision of the rated soldier for a minimum period of three months and senior to the rater in grade or date of rank.

Members of other U.S. military services who meet the qualifications above may be senior raters, and civilians may be appointed senior raters providing they are the supervisors in the best position to evaluate the soldier's performance and their appointments are published in the rating scheme established by the local commander. Members of allied forces are not authorized to be raters. A senior rater is not required when the rater is a general officer or equivalent.

The senior rater must use all reasonable means to become familiar with the rated soldier's performance and prepare a fair and correct report. Like the rater, the senior rater evaluates the rated NCO, but he or she focuses on potential, oversees the performance evaluations, and serves as a mentor. Since the senior rater's evaluation directly impacts the NCO's performance and professional development, it must reflect the entire rating period and not an isolated incident.

To be fair, the senior rater must be familiar with the rated soldier's performance. He or she must also do the following: prepare a fair and correct report to evaluate the NCO's performance, professionalism, and potential; date and sign Part IIb of the NCOER; obtain the rated NCO's signature in Part IIc; ensure that bullet comments are fully justified in Part IVb–f; and ensure that "Do not meet minimum requirements" is entered in Part Ve if the senior rater does not meet the minimum time requirement.

According to former Sergeant Major of the Army Julius W. Gates, comments taken from members of eight DA selection boards held prior to January 1991 unanimously support that senior rater comments about potential are extremely valuable to the selection process. So, as DA Pamphlet 623-205 states, "The better you know the rated NCO, the better you will do your duty as senior rater. Check early to see that the rater is counseling and has a checklist for each rated NCO. This will be a matter of command and inspection interest. Don't get caught short.

"When it's time to rate, make sure the rater's bullets follow the rules, especially double spacing and no more than two lines per bullet. Also check to see that an excellence rating in Part IV is fully justified by examples."

Reviewer Qualifications and Responsibilities

The reviewer must be a commissioned or warrant officer, command sergeant major, or sergeant major in the direct line of supervision and senior in grade or date of rank to both the rater and the indorser. A field grade reviewer is required for special reports (see paragraph 2–10, AR 623-205). There is no minimum time period requirement for reviewer qualification.

Commanders may appoint officers of other U.S. military services as reviewers when the grade and line-of-supervision requirements listed above are met and when either the rater or senior rater is a uniformed Army official.

In cases in which both the rater and the senior rater are other than uniformed Army rating officials, and no uniformed Army reviewer is available, the report is reviewed by an officer in the rated soldier's military personnel office.

Commanders may appoint U.S. civilians GS-6 and above or other civilian pay scales when the grade and line-of-supervision requirements are met and either the rater or senior rater is a uniformed Army official.

Members of allied forces are not authorized to be reviewers, and a reviewer is not required when the rater or the senior rater is a general officer or equivalent.

The reviewer ensures that the proper rater and senior rater complete the report. The reviewer examines the evaluations and resolves discrepancies and inconsistencies. The reviewer also approves or disapproves special reports and ensures that the provisions for change-of-rater and relief-for-cause reports are complied with.

The reviewer also ensures that required comments have been made to explain low ratings on the NCOER and that allegations of injustice or illegality are resolved or brought to the attention of the commander. The reviewer is responsible for forwarding the report to the military personnel office.

Evaluation and Management Systems

Responsibilities of Commanders

Commanders are responsible for establishing controls to ensure that official rating schemes are published, by name or duty position, and are posted in the unit so that each soldier knows his or her rater, senior rater, and reviewer.

Commanders are also responsible for the following actions.

- Each rating official is fully qualified to meet his or her responsibilities and knows whom he or she is responsible to rate.
- Reports are prepared by the individuals designated in the published rating chain.
- Rating officials give timely counseling to subordinates on professionalism and job performance.
- Each rated soldier is provided a copy of his or her completed evaluation report.
- Soldiers receive assistance, if they request it, in preparing and submitting appeals.
- Reports are prepared fairly and carefully and submitted in time to reach the U.S. Army Enlisted Records and Evaluation Center (USAEREC) not later than 60 days after the ending month of the report.

Responsibilities of the Military Personnel Office

The Military Personnel Office (MILPO) initiates the report and forwards it to the rated soldier's commander for proper control. Returned reports are reviewed at the MILPO for completeness and administrative accuracy. The MILPO also makes copies of the reports and forwards them to the rated soldier, forwards them to the USAEREC, and assists soldiers in preparing and submitting appeals.

Appeals

The efficiency report appeals system exists to ensure fairness to the soldier, protect the Army's interests, and prevent unjustified attacks on the integrity or judgment of rating officials.

The burden of proof rests with the soldier making the appeal. Once NCOERs are filed in the soldier's OMPF, they are presumed to be administratively correct, to have been prepared by the proper officials, and to represent the considered opinions and impartial judgments of rating officials at the time they were prepared.

The mere allegation of error or injustice does not constitute proof. Clear and convincing evidence must be submitted to cause alteration, replacement, or withdrawal of a report from the OMPF. The decision to appeal an evaluation should not be made lightly. Frequently, clear and convincing evidence may be difficult to obtain, and in most cases, the appellant may be unable to analyze his or her own case objectively.

Normally, appeals are originated by the rated soldier, but in cases in which an appeal is originated by someone other than the rated soldier, it is not processed unless the rated soldier has been notified in person or in writing (by certified mail) and given the opportunity to submit statements pertaining to the case. Rating officials who claim "second thoughts" about ratings previously made have no grounds for submitting an appeal on behalf of the rated soldier.

Appeals alleging bias, prejudice, unjust ratings, or any matter other than administrative error will be adjudicated by the DCSPER Enlisted Special Review Board. The board's determination is final.

Board proceedings are administrative, nonadversary, and not bound by the rules of evidence for trials by courts-martial or other court proceedings, although the board is obligated to keep within the reasonable bounds of evidence that is competent, material, and relevant.

The appellant or his agent is not authorized to appear before the board, although the board has the right to obtain additional information from anyone with first-hand knowledge of the case.

Appeals based on administrative error only are adjudicated by the USAEREC Enlisted Evaluation Report Appeals Section.

To be considered, appeals must be received at USAEREC within five years of the date of the rated soldier's authentication or the MILPO's certification, if the soldier refused to sign the report. Appeals that do not meet this time restriction may be submitted to the Army Board for Correction of Military Records, in accordance with AR 15-185. Once the decision has been made to appeal an evaluation report, there are a number of steps that should be followed. You should know what they are because soldiers may ask you for help in preparing an appeal, or you may someday have to prepare one for yourself.

- Start by reading Chapter 4, AR 623-205, "Appeals."
- Write down clearly and specifically what will be appealed and why it should be.
- Identify specifically what evidence should be obtained to substantiate each part of the appeal.
- Determine what evidence can be obtained.
- Obtain the evidence. If statements from persons are necessary, make sure they clearly identify their roles at the time of the contested report and ensure that the statements make specific, not general, comments. Seek statements from senior personnel who have specific knowledge of the facts; avoid statements from subordinates or persons whose knowledge of the facts may be limited. Obtain sworn statements, if possible.
- Documentary evidence, if not original, should be in certified true copies.
- Prepare the appeal in military letter format.

THE QUALITATIVE MANAGEMENT PROGRAM

The Qualitative Management Program (QMP) is based on the premise that reenlistment is a privilege for those whose performance, conduct, attitude, and potential for advancement meet Army standards. The purpose of the QMP has four parts:

- To improve the quality of the career enlisted force.
- To selectively retain the best qualified soldiers.
- To deny reenlistment to nonprogressive and nonproductive soldiers.
- To encourage soldiers to maintain their eligibility for further service.

The QMP consists of two major subprograms that operate independently: qualitative retention and the qualitative screening.

The Qualitative Management Program is an effective way to rid the NCO Corps of personnel who do not measure up to Army standards. It is applied equally to all personnel, especially the Qualitative Screening Subprogram, which is conducted periodically for all personnel in ranks sergeant through command sergeant major. The only soldiers who have anything at all to fear from the Army's QMP are the poor performers and the bad actors of the NCO Corps.

Evaluation and Management Systems

Qualitative Retention Subprogram

The Qualitative Retention Subprogram consists of the use of reenlistment ineligibility points for each grade. Reenlistment ineligibility points are based on years of service. The reenlistment ineligibility point is the *maximum number of years of active federal service authorized for a soldier in a specific grade.*

Rank	Total Active Service
SPC, CPL	8 years
SGT	13 years
SGT (P)	15 years (effective 1 Oct. 93)
SSG	20 years
SSG (P)	22 years
SFC	24 years
SFC (P)	24 years
1SG, MSG	27 years
CSM, SGM	30 years

Specialists, corporals, and sergeants who are on the local order of merit promotion list will be considered for reenlistment under the criteria of the rank to which they will be promoted. Staff sergeants, sergeants first class, first sergeants, and master sergeants selected for promotion by Headquarters, Department of the Army, may voluntarily continue on active duty if they are not beyond the reenlistment ineligibility point for the grade to which they will be promoted. Those who are beyond the ineligibility point for the grade to which they will be promoted will not be considered for reenlistment extension.

Staff sergeants, sergeants first class, first sergeants, and master sergeants who are in DA-announced primary zones of consideration for promotion and who have reached or are beyond the reenlistment point may be voluntarily extended beyond their expiration term of service. Those with more than 20 years' service who have not received a waiver to their reenlistment ineligibility point and who were not selected will be retired by the third month after the promotion list is published. The first field grade commander in the chain of command will formally notify them and establish retirement dates.

Soldiers who apply for retirement before the announced zone of consideration will not be considered for promotion.

Extensions apply only to soldiers affected by qualitative retention. They do not apply to those who have a DA bar to reenlistment imposed by qualitative screening.

Qualitative Screening Subprogram

The Qualitative Screening Subprogram applies to enlisted members who are sergeants or higher rank. It does not apply to members who have completed 28 years of active federal service or to command sergeants major, regardless of time in service. Selection for elimination under this program results in a DA-imposed bar to reenlistment for those who do not meet Army standards.

Records are screened as follows:

For sergeant major   By DA Command Sergeants Major Selection Boards

For staff sergeant, sergeant first class, first sergeant, master sergeant | Regularly scheduled HQDA promotion selection boards

For sergeant | Regularly scheduled first sergeant and master sergeant selection boards—limited to those who have 11 or more years' active federal service

The appropriate DA selection boards review the performance portion of the OMPF maintained at USAEREC. From the OMPF, the board evaluates past performances and estimates the potential of each soldier to determine whether continued service is warranted.

Bars to reenlistment for those identified by the selection boards and approved by the Deputy Chief of Staff for Personnel (DCSPER) are imposed as directed by Commanding General, U.S. Total Army Personnel Command. The effective date is the date the bar to reenlistment letter is mailed from the USAEREC.

Soldiers selected for DA bar to reenlistment are informed by individual letters. Copies of documents in the individual's OMPF that most significantly contributed to the board's decision to impose the bar are attached in a sealed envelope as an enclosure to the letter. These documents are personal and are privileged information and must be treated with the utmost discretion during transmission to the affected soldier.

These letters are forwarded through the chain of command to the individual's commander (lieutenant colonel and above). *They are not delivered to soldiers who have retirement applications approved or pending.*

The individual's commander (lieutenant colonel and above) may, within seven days after receipt of the notification letter, request withdrawal of the bar if he or she believes it was improperly imposed or based on material error in the soldier's OMPF when reviewed by the board. A commander's request to withdraw the bar must provide specific information and documents to refute the board's action.

The individual's commander must personally interview the soldier and give him or her the letter, the enclosures, and his endorsement. He must also ensure that the soldier is counseled so that he or she understands the impact of the bar to reenlistment and the options available. The commander must also ensure that the soldier completes DA Form 4941-R, *Statement of Option*, within seven days of receipt and returns it through the chain of command to PersCom.

A soldier may appeal a bar to reenlistment. The soldier submitting an appeal must allow sufficient time for it to arrive at PersCom, not later than 12 months after the date of the bar letter. The soldier also must understand that this appeal is the only one he or she may submit, although this does not preclude the commander submitting an appeal on the soldier's behalf.

The appeal should address the items that served as a basis for the bar to reenlistment and the actions taken by the soldier to improve his or her performance to overcome other noted deficiencies. Documents that demonstrate improved performance or the resolution of a deficiency (MILPO-authenticated NCOER, award orders, revocation of a court-martial, removal of disciplinary data, and SQT results) should be attached to the appeal.

If the appeal is denied, the soldier's commander must reevaluate the soldier to determine whether there has been a demonstrated marked improvement in performance and potential. If the commander desires, he or she may submit an appeal to the

STATEMENT OF OPTION

For use of this form, see AR 601-280, the proponent agency is DCSPER.

DATA REQUIRED BY THE PRIVACY ACT OF 1974

AUTHORITY: Title 5 USC Section 301
PRINCIPAL PURPOSE: To determine and select option after bar to reenlistment.
ROUTINE USES: Information is needed to ensure that soldier's option statement is properly identified with his records.
DISCLOSURE: Disclosure is voluntary, however, failure to furnish information could adversely affect soldier.

THRU: (Include ZIP Code)	TO: Commander US Total Army Personnel Agency ATTN: DAPC-PDT-SA 2461 Eisenhower Avenue Alexandria, VA 22331-0400	DATE:

I WAS NOTIFIED OF MY DA BAR TO REENLISTMENT UNDER THE QUALITATIVE MANAGEMENT PROGRAM (AR 601-280) on _____. I HAVE CAREFULLY READ, HAVE BEEN COUNSELED, AND UNDERSTAND THE OPTIONS OPEN TO ME AS A RESULT OF THE DA BAR TO REENLISTMENT. I HAVE CHOSEN THE FOLLOWING OPTION AS INDICATED BY MY INITIALS AT THE BOX MARKED BELOW:

1. ☐ _____ I will submit an appeal. I understand this appeal must be submitted not later than 90 days after the date of notification. If my appeal is not received by DA 4 months after the date of the bar or the appeal is denied, HQDA will automatically change this option to option 2. Additionally, I understand that I can request an extension of service in order to process my appeal *(for a maximum of 9 months of service from the date of the bar letter)* as a separate action, provided the extension does not pass my Reenlistment Ineligibility Point.

2. ☐ _____ I intend to complete my remaining term of enlistment and will take no further action. I understand that I will be processed for separation *(IAW AR 635-200)* 60 days after the date of notification and that I may be separated prior to my current ETS. I understand I can change to option 4 or 5 at a later date.

3. ☐ _____ Under the provision of paragraph 16-5, AR 635-200, I request to be discharged on _____ *(Requested discharge date must be NLT 6 months from the date option is signed).* I understand that recoupment of unearned portions of Enlistment Bonus (EB)/Selective Reenlistment Bonus (SRB) is required. I also understand that once separated I will not be permitted to reenlist at a later day. If this request is approved, it may not be revoked. *(This option form will be forwarded to the discharge authority for approval/disapproval of this request.)*

4. ☐ _____ I intend to request immediate retirement, *(only those persons eligible to retire may choose this option, see AR 635-200.)* I understand my request for retirement must be submitted within 14 days of completion of the option statement for a retirement date not later than 12 months from date of submission.

5. ☐ _____ I had at least 18 years of active Federal service at the date of the DA bar to reenlistment letter and will retire upon attraining retirement eligibility *(20 years AFS)*. If necessary, I will request to extend for _____ months, as a separate action, to achieve 20 years AFS and will retire no later than the last day of the month in which I attain retirement eligibility.

PRINTED/TYPED NAME AND RANK	SSN	ETS

SIGNATURE	DATE

ON _____ I PRESENTED THE DA BAR TO REENLISTMENT, EXPLAINED THE AVAILABLE OPTIONS, AND COUNSELED THE SOLDIER ON HIS/HER RIGHTS UNDER AR 601-280 AND AR 635-200. AS THE COMMANDER, I HAVE CHOSEN THE FOLLOWING OPTION AS INDICATED BY MY INITIALS AT THE BOX MARKED BELOW:

1. ☐ _____ I will submit an appeal based on my determination that the soldier has overcome the deficiencies cited by the Selection Board or has so significantly improved his/her performance as to warrant reconsideration of the board's decision. I understand this appeal must be submitted within 90 days of the date I presented the DA Bar.

2. ☐ _____ This soldier has been assigned to my command for less than 120 days; he/she was assigned on _____. I will submit a supplemental DA Form 4941-R indicating my decision on my options NLT _____ *(NLT 120 days from date of assignment).*

3. ☐ _____ I will not submit an appeal. Action will be taken per AR 601-280 and AR 635-200 as necessary based on the soldier's selected option *(above).*

PRINTED/TYPED NAME, RANK AND BRANCH OF COMMANDER PRESENTING THE BAR	SIGNATURE	DATE

DA FORM 4941-R, MAY 88   EDITION OF NOV 87 IS OBSOLETE

bar to reenlistment on the soldier's behalf, but only after the individual's appeal has been disapproved.

For a soldier who had less than 18 months remaining until ETS at the date of the bar and who has not been granted an extension to provide for the 18 months, no reevaluation is required. If the commander desires to reevaluate the soldier, an extension for the amount of time originally required to allow the 18-month period may be granted.

For a soldier who has more than 18 months remaining until ETS on the date of the bar or for a soldier who was granted an extension to provide for the 18 months, the commander must reevaluate the soldier not less than 90 days before ETS.

Sergeants cannot be extended past 20 years' active federal service. Staff sergeants cannot be extended past 24 years. A soldier who has completed 18 or more years' service on the effective date of the DA bar letter may be extended to reach retirement eligibility.

The Command Sergeant Major Retention Program

The CSM Retention Program establishes procedures whereby outstanding CSM may be retained beyond 30 years of active service. The program provides the Army the benefit of their long years of experience, expertise, and continued outstanding service.

CSM who wish to be retained beyond 30 years of service must submit a request for retention to President, DA Retention Board, Fort Benjamin Harrison, IN 46216, during their 28th year of service. During the 29th year of service, a request may be reconsidered if the CSM submits a new one. All requests are sent through command channels for endorsement by the appropriate MACOM commander or designated representative. Declination statements will not be submitted. Only those who have requested retention will be considered. CSM who request retention will state on their application they will serve to 35 years of service before submitting for voluntary retirement.

CSM may be retained up to 35 years' active service or to age 55, whichever is first.

The selection board consists of five members, one of whom is the Sergeant Major of the Army. The board president is a major general. Volunteering does not automatically ensure selection. Selection is in part based on the individual's potential for outstanding service in positions of responsibility. Retention beyond 30 years is not a reward for past performance.

PHYSICAL FITNESS

In a speech before a group of TRADOC command sergeants major at Savannah, Georgia, in November 1977, former Sergeant Major of the Army Connelly stated the prime reason for soldiers to maintain their physical fitness. "Soldiers—and that means everyone in the Army—from private to senior officers—must maintain their physical condition. We are in a physically demanding business, and just because on his current tour, a soldier happens to sit behind a desk and push papers, does not guarantee that next week he may not be running for his life on a real battlefield." The soldier who is physically fit has a better chance of surviving in combat than the soldier who isn't.

The two essential elements of the Army's approach to physical fitness are weight control and physical conditioning.

Physical Conditioning

The Army needs soldiers who are capable of performing the physically demanding

Soldiers complete the running requirement of Army Physical Fitness Test. *U.S. Army photo*

tasks of combat. FM 21-20, *Physical Fitness Training*, lays out the approved methods of physical training that will allow individuals and units to reach their physical conditioning goals. This manual, along with AR 350-15, *The Army Physical Fitness Program*, provides guidance to ensure that all soldiers are physically fit.

As your career progresses, you undoubtedly will find yourself in an organization that allows you to do "PT" on your own. Do not take this time as a break from maintaining your standards. If you do, you will not be prepared when you return to a unit, and you will have a hard time getting back to your previous fitness level.

Successful completion of the APFT is required twice each year. In addition, passing the APFT is required for graduation from NCOES schools. The best advice is to get in shape and stay in shape.

Weight Control

Being out of shape does not necessarily mean being overweight, but usually the two go together. Losing weight can be difficult, and generally it is much harder for the obese person to get into shape than it is for a slim person. The Army Weight Control Program is designed to help soldiers maintain their fitness and health.

The program has two objectives: to ensure that soldiers are able to meet the physical demands of their duties under combat conditions and to present a trim military appearance at all times. Excessive body fat connotes a lack of personal discipline and detracts from military appearance. It also may indicate a poor state of health, physical fitness, or stamina.

Soldiers who exceed the following body fat standard for their current age group and the screening table weights indicated on the accompanying chart will not be allowed to reenlist or extend their enlistments.

Age Group	Male % of Body Fat	Female % of Body Fat
17–20	20	30
21–27	22	32
28–39	24	34
40+	26	36

Note that the Army *prefers* soldiers to meet the Department of Defense-wide goal, which is 20 percent body fat for males and 28 percent for females. Note also that soldiers who exceed their body fat standard (as defined in AR 600-9) will be considered nonpromotable (to the extent permitted by law), will not be authorized to attend professional military or civilian schooling, and will not be assigned to command positions.

Soldiers who fail to meet the program standards, providing there is no underlying medical reason for this failure, are given six months to get within the standard. During that time their progress is monitored very closely. If progress is made, the individual may be continued in the program; if not, the soldier's commander will initiate separation proceedings. If separation proceedings are not initiated or they do not result in separation, the soldier will be entered into or continued in a weight-control program. The time allowed to achieve these milestones has been reduced recently. Soldiers who fail to make satisfactory progress in the weight control program after six months—and those who fail to meet body fat standards within one year after removal from the program—will be denied reenlistment or separated.

Weight for Height Table (Screening Table Weight)

Height (in inches)	Male Age				Female Age			
	17–20	21–27	28–39	40+	17–20	21–27	28–39	40+
58	—	—	—	—	109	112	115	119
59	—	—	—	—	113	116	119	123
60	132	136	139	141	116	120	123	127
61	136	140	144	146	120	124	127	131
62	141	144	148	150	125	129	132	137
63	145	149	153	155	129	133	137	137
64	150	154	158	160	133	137	141	141
65	155	159	163	165	137	141	145	145
66	160	163	168	170	141	146	150	149
67	165	169	174	176	145	149	154	154
68	170	174	179	181	150	154	159	159
69	175	179	184	186	154	158	163	164
70	180	185	189	192	159	163	168	168
71	185	189	194	197	163	167	172	173
72	190	195	200	203	167	172	177	177
73	195	200	205	208	172	177	182	183
74	201	206	211	214	178	183	189	188
75	206	212	217	220	183	188	194	194
76	212	217	223	226	189	194	200	200
77	218	223	229	232	193	199	205	206
78	223	229	235	238	198	204	210	211
79	229	235	241	244	203	209	215	216
80	234	240	247	250	208	214	220	222
								227

Note: For screening purposes, body fat composition is to be determined in accordance with Appendix B, AR 600-9.

You cannot lose weight by exercise alone. People get fat principally because they eat too much of the wrong kinds of foods. Exercise will help you reduce up to a certain point, particularly when it comes to loss of body fluids. Frequently, people just starting an exercise program are pleasantly astonished by a rapid weight loss, but after a few weeks, their bodies reach a plateau. Losing weight after that is a combination of good diet and regular exercise, and *it is not easy.*

Overeating is a behavioral pattern and a very hard one to break. Obesity for the vast majority of people is not a disease. Out of every 100 overweight soldiers, perhaps one may have an endocrine problem that requires the special care of a physician. For all the others, those extra pounds are their own responsibility. Command responsibility lies in developing a sound program to educate and encourage overweight soldiers to overcome habits that may be ingrained from childhood.

As in all things, the good NCO should take the lead in keeping fit. Example is the best precept, so make yourself an example of a physically fit soldier. Do not wait for your commander or supervisor to tell you to get into shape.

Follow a sensible diet. Cut down on your consumption of alcohol, sugar, fat, and starch; eat high-protein foods; eat plenty of fresh fruit and vegetables; and get regular exercise. Don't kill yourself. If you have any doubt about your physical stamina, consult a doctor before commencing any kind of exercise program.

Pick an exercise program that suits you. Handball, squash, jogging, swimming, bicycling, even walking, are excellent ways to get the proper amount of physical exercise. The definition of what is the "proper amount" of exercise for any individual varies, but as a rule of thumb, to maintain physical fitness, exercise vigorously at least three times a week for a minimum of 20 minutes each time.

Your unit master fitness trainer will be of great help to you in planning a suitable physical fitness program. Remember to start slowly and gradually work your way up. If you push yourself, you may get hurt. If you jog, do not increase your speed or distance until you feel comfortable with your present level of exercise.

Soldiers over 40

A new set of guidelines for soldiers aged 40 and over was established in 1988. These guidelines are used during the periodic physical examination that screens soldiers for cardiovascular risk factors.

The guidelines focus on having all soldiers exercise regularly and adopt life-style changes to help decrease the risk of coronary heart disease. The program originally focused on detecting soldiers with heart disease who have no symptoms and at clearing those aged 40 and over for taking the Army's physical fitness test. That approach relied heavily on the use of treadmill testing. That test, however, could pick up only about 30 to 40 percent of those persons with heart difficulty who do not exhibit symptoms or problems. Now the new guidelines emphasize screening for coronary risk factors, provide advice and assistance for controlling risk factors, provide specific guidance for sedentary persons about regular exercise (of gradually increasing intensity) based on age, sex, pulse rate, and current level of fitness, and apply the treadmill test only to those in the highest risk category, which represents less than 15 percent of the total population screened.

Under the old program, soldiers were screened or cleared for taking the physical fitness test. Today, they are screened to plan for the development of a more physically fit soldier and to lower the rate of coronary problems.

Evaluation and Management Systems

This new program, the Health-Risk Appraisal Assessment, seeks answers to questions about life-style habits, such as smoking, diet, exercise, stress, and alcohol use. It also looks into the soldier's physiological status: weight, blood pressure, pulse rate, and cholesterol levels. The soldier receives a computer analysis of responses within minutes. The individualized responses highlight potential health risks while offering advice for life-style modifications and disease prevention.

The Army's "Wellness Check" will be phased in as part of all periodic physical examinations as well as for those turning 40. By adopting life-style changes and disease prevention, you and your soldiers will be able to avoid many of the causes for cardiovascular disease.

5

Promotion

Soldiers are recommended for promotion only after they develop the skills and abilities to perform the duties and assume the responsibility of the next higher grade. Those with great potential for leadership or increased technical skill in their fields are recognized. Generally, if soldiers do not do well in their present grades, they will not work well in the next higher grades.

Promotion is not a reward for honorable service. The Army promotion system has the following objectives.

- Fill authorized enlisted spaces with qualified soldiers.
- Provide for career progression and rank that is in line with potential.
- Recognize the best qualified soldier to attract and retain the highest caliber soldier for a career in the Army.
- Preclude promoting the soldier who is not productive or not best qualified.
- Provide an equitable system for all soldiers.

By using the standard promotion scoring forms with predetermined promotion point factors, corporals, specialists, and sergeants can generally measure how well they qualify for promotion. They can set precise goals with a self-improvement training program to increase their potential for promotion. Staff sergeants, sergeants first class, first sergeants, and master sergeants can judge their qualifications based on their relative qualifications when compared to other soldiers in their MOS.

The Army promotes soldiers who are qualified and who will accept Army-wide assignments. Selection eligibility criteria besides those outlined in Chapter 7, AR 600-200, are prohibited. For example, a commander may not require a soldier to be as-

Promotion

signed to his unit for a certain number of months as a prerequisite for promotional consideration.

AUTHORITY TO PROMOTE

The commanders below may promote, subject to authority and responsibility by higher commanders.

SPC and below. Unit commanders may advance or promote assigned soldiers and those of Reserve components. They may advance eligible attached soldiers to grades PV2, PFC, and SP, subject to concurrence of the assigned commander.

SGT and SSG. Field grade commanders of any unit authorized a commander in grade of lieutenant colonel or higher may promote soldiers assigned to units that are attached or assigned or on TDY or attached (for military justice and administration) to their command or installation.

SFC and above. Headquarters, Department of the Army.

Hospitalized soldiers. Commanders of medical facilities may promote hospitalized soldiers to SSG and below.

Students. Commandants and commanders of training installations and activities.

Posthumous promotion. Headquarters, Department of the Army.

ADVANCEMENT TO PRIVATE E-2 AND PRIVATE FIRST CLASS

Active Army personnel are advanced to the rank of private E-2 when they have completed six months of active federal service, unless it is stopped by the commander. ARNG and USAR personnel on initial active duty training are advanced to private E-2 when they complete six months of service from the day of entry, unless it is stopped by the commander.

To recognize outstanding performance, local commanders may advance soldiers to private E-2 who have at least four but less than six months' active service. The number of soldiers who may be given accelerated promotion to private E-2 is restricted by HQDA.

When a soldier has six months' active federal service but is not promotable for the reasons listed in paragraph 7-6, AR 600-200, or has been reduced to private E-1, he or she may be advanced to private E-2 on the date the promotable status is regained.

Advancement to private first class is not mandatory. Under normal conditions, unit commanders may, without constraint, advance soldiers who qualify with twelve

One of a drill sergeant's duties is to inspect and instruct soldiers. *U.S. Army photo*

months' time in service and four months' time in grade.

To recognize outstanding performance, unit commanders may advance soldiers who qualify. Those who otherwise qualify must have a minimum of six months in service and two months' time in grade (which may be waived). The number who may receive accelerated promotion is restricted by HQDA.

CRITERIA FOR PROMOTION TO SPECIALIST OR CORPORAL

Normally commanders may, without constraint, advance soldiers who meet the following qualifications.

- Twenty-four months in service.
- Six months' time in grade, waiverable to three months.
- Security clearance appropriate for the MOS in which promoted; advancement may be based on granting an interim security clearance.

To recognize outstanding performance, commanders may advance soldiers on an accelerated basis, providing advancements do not cause more than 20 percent of the total number of assigned specialists and corporals to have less than twenty-four months' time in service, and providing soldiers meet the following qualifications.

- Twelve months in service.
- Three months' time in grade.

Promotion

- Security clearance required for the MOS in which advanced; may be based on an interim clearance.

Unused waivers that are computed at unit level (not consolidated) may be returned to higher command for redistribution, providing that computation of the higher command's strength will allow additional promotions. For example, suppose that four companies in a battalion have ten promotion authorizations but use only eight. Computation of battalion strength indicates twelve promotions would have been authorized if consolidated. Thus the two unused authorizations may be redistributed.

Commanders with zero waiver authorizations may promote any soldier with 18 or more months' time in grade. Commanders may use all waiver authorizations to promote soldiers with 18 or more months' time in grade. In such cases, any remaining soldier with 18 or more months' time in grade also may be promoted.

Promotion selection boards or SDT scores are not needed to promote to specialist or corporal. If a board is used, however, commanders must establish a recommended list based on DA Form 3356, *Board Member Appraisal*, and DA Form 3357, *Board Recommendation*.

Commanders are enjoined to ensure that promotions to grade specialist or corporal do not exceed the limitations announced by Headquarters, Department of the Army.

PROMOTION TO SERGEANT AND STAFF SERGEANT

Promotion to sergeant and staff sergeant is made against promotion point cutoff scores. Headquarters, Department of the Army, determines the needs of the Army by grade and MOS, and based on this need, the promotion point cutoff scores for primary and secondary zone promotions are announced authorizing commanders to promote the best qualified soldiers Army-wide in each MOS.

Normal requirements for promotion are set forth below. The promotion authority may waive no more than two of the requirements for soldiers who are otherwise highly qualified. The secondary zone provides incentives to those who strive for excellence and whose accomplishments, demonstrated capacity for leadership, and marked potential warrant promotion ahead of their peers. Soldiers recommended for promotion in the secondary zone must be outstanding. This waiver allows soldiers who show outstanding potential through performance to be considered for promotion.

Noncommissioned officers and commanders control or have a great influence over the points a soldier can attain for promotion. To begin with, NCOs are responsible for the points granted by the promotion board—200 maximum. If a soldier does well on his or her SDT (maximum 200 points), you can be sure some NCO was there, coaching and encouraging him or her. NCOs are responsible for taking soldiers through NCOES—another 30 points. If a soldier performs his or her duties in an outstanding manner, the good NCO leader may recommend him or her for the Army Achievement Medal or an Army Commendation Medal—another 15 or 20 points. Of the 200 points that can be given by the commander on the soldier's duty performance, the commander must rely heavily on the recommendations of NCOs. Finally, it is NCOs who teach soldiers how to shoot and how to stay in physical shape; if they have done their jobs well, the soldier could get another 100 points for military training.

So out of a possible maximum 1,000 points a soldier can earn for promotion, NCOs have a direct influence over more than 700 of them. A good NCO's influence is even more far-reaching when he or she encourages a subordinate to pursue civilian correspondence and extension courses.

Cutoff Scores

When a soldier's number of promotion points is known, many wonder why he or she cannot be promoted immediately if the cutoff is low enough. In the first place, soldiers may be selected for promotion three months before they have the required time in service.

Second, reports from the field reflecting the number of soldiers on promotion lists, their number of points, and their zones and MOSs arrive at HQDA about the middle of the month following the month the soldier appeared before the promotion board.

At this point, MOS and grade vacancies are computed. The total number of promotions for a particular grade (regardless of MOS) is determined by comparing the number of personnel projected to be in that grade against the number allowed in the Army budget for the month in which promotions are to be made. This projection includes losses, those promoted in and out of the grade, and reductions. Available promotions are distributed to MOSs based on the percentage of fill.

Promotions go to those MOSs with the greatest need first, raising the percentage of fill for all MOSs until the available promotions are exhausted. Secondary zone or waiver promotions are limited, so they go to MOSs with the greatest need after the primary zone promotions are distributed. At this time—which is one to two months after the soldier appears before the promotion board—the soldier's number of promotion points comes into the process. For example, if the vacancies and budget permit the promotion of 100 soldiers from the primary zone of a particular MOS, a promotion cutoff score is established by going down the scores until the 100 limit is reached. That is, if the top 100 sergeants in an MOS have 716 or more points, the cutoff score would be 716. If the top 100 have 796 or more, the cutoff would be 796. If a cutoff for a particular MOS is high, that means that the available promotions went to soldiers in MOSs with a lower percentage of fill.

Time in Service and Time in Grade Requirements

The time in grade and time in service requirements for promotion to sergeant and staff sergeant are shown below.

SSG	10 months as SGT	(PZ) 84 months
		(SZ) 60 months
SGT	8 months as SPC or CPL	(PZ) 36 months
		(SZ) 24 months

In the above example, one-half the time in grade may be waived. Time in service may be waived for promotion in the secondary zone only: to sergeant, 12 months; to staff sergeant, 24 months. The promotion point cutoff score letter distributed to all commands by the U.S. Total Army Personnel Command provides guidance on the amount of time in service needed for promotion consideration and eligibility month.

Soldiers must be recommended or have concurrence in recommendation from their unit commander. If duty is under other than the unit commander to which assigned, the soldier's recommendation must be indorsed by the attached or administrative unit commander. Waivers are not granted.

Soldiers being considered for promotion to sergeant and staff sergeant must appear for selection board evaluation. Early appearance before a promotion selection board may be granted as outlined in paragraph 7-15d, AR 600-200.

Promotion

Soldiers may compete for promotion only in their career progression MOS. They must be fully qualified in the MOS in which recommended for promotion consideration. The commander's recommendation or approval affirms that the soldier is qualified in his career progression MOS at the next higher grade.

The goal of the personnel management system is that the soldier demonstrate qualifications for the next higher grade before competing for promotion. Until the SDT is completely implemented, soldiers may compete for promotion without waiver if they have successfully completed the appropriate on-the-job evaluation or NCO Education System requirement or have attained an MOS skill test GO Raw Score of 60 or higher as reported on the most recent SQT or SDT. Waivers may be granted for soldiers who meet any of the following criteria:

- Have successfully completed the appropriate OJE and NCOES requirements and have received a GO Raw Score of 59 or less.
- Have no SDT score, through no fault of their own.
- Have been involuntarily reclassified for other than inefficiency or misconduct and are not on a recommended list.

In addition, soldiers must be in the pay grade next below that of the promoted rank (no waiver granted); they must be physically qualified to perform duties of the MOS and grade to which promoted as outlined by AR 611-201; they must have appropriate security clearance or favorable security investigation required by the MOS in which promoted. Local position vacancies are not required for promotion.

Educational requirements for promotion to sergeant and staff sergeant are as follows:

- Completion of eighth grade or GED equivalent or higher education for promotion to sergeant.
- High school diploma, or GED equivalent, or associate or higher degree for promotion to staff sergeant.

School Requirements for NCO Promotions

The Army has changed the school requirements for promotion to some NCO grades. For example, now to become a sergeant or a staff sergeant, you must have completed the Primary Leadership Development Course. Formerly, only promotion to staff sergeant required completion of that course. Also, now promotion to sergeant first class requires completion of BNCOC. Promotion to master sergeant, sergeant major, and command sergeant major, however, remain the same: ANCOC, none, and USASMA, respectively.

Service Remaining Obligations

The service remaining obligation is three months for promotion to sergeant and twelve months for promotion to staff sergeant. Waivers are not granted. Service remaining obligation is computed from the first day of the authorized month of promotion. Exceptions are made for the following soldiers.

- Those whose active service exceeds the reenlistment ineligibility point established by Section II, Chapter 4, AR 600-200.
- Those whom HQDA will promote while missing, missing in action, captured, or detained.

- Those who are very seriously ill.
- Those who are 55 or older.
- Those who would lose entitlement or eligibility to reenlist in an MOS if they must extend their current term of service to meet the service obligation.

Establishing Date of Rank

Date of rank is based on total promotion points and is spread over the days of the preceding month. As an example, promotions made on 1 December will have date of rank spread over the calendar days of November.

THE PAPER WORK

Promotion Packets

The documents listed below are part of the promotion packet of a soldier.
- An approved recommendation for promotion and necessary waivers.
- The DA Form 3355 used for first board appearance and all later recomputations.
- If applicable, a copy of the approved request for reevaluation and the DA Form 3355 used.
- Each DA Form 3356 and DA Form 3357 used for the first board appearance and, if applicable, those used for each reevaluation.
- A copy of the approved Report of Promotion Board Proceedings for the soldier's first board appearance and, if applicable, each reevaluation.
- A copy of any document used to confirm the award of promotion points.
- If applicable, a copy of any document that allows the soldier's previously determined promotion score to be adjusted.

The promotion packet of a soldier who is on the recommended list is kept in the action-pending section of his military personnel records jacket until he is promoted. These documents are then given to the soldier. The counseling and promotion board documents of those who do not attain recommended list status are filed by the promotion authority for two years and then destroyed.

Recommended List

After completion of all promotion actions during the month, a recommended list is published. It lists all soldiers of the organization who have been selected, but not yet promoted. Names are listed by grade and zone in ascending MOS and descending promotion point score order. The list may be prepared by the promotion authority or may be a consolidation by a higher level authority.

Each soldier whose name is listed is given a copy of the list at the time of selection, reevaluation, and recomputation. A copy of the list is also retained in the files of the preparing organization for two years, and a copy of the most recent list is filed in the soldier's MPRJ on reassignment.

Soldiers are promoted from the current recommended list by three-character MOS. Promotions are made on the first calendar day of the month in which they are authorized. Promotion orders may be published with future effective dates.

Soldiers are eligible for promotion on the first day of the third month following date of selection: A soldier is recommended in January 1993; he becomes eligible for promotion on 1 April 1993.

PROMOTION POINT WORKSHEET

For use of this form, see AR 600-8-19, the proponent agency is ODCSPER

1. TYPE	2. DATE
☐ a. Initial ☐ b. Reevaluation ☐ c. Recomputation	

DATA REQUIRED BY THE PRIVACY ACT OF 1974

AUTHORITY: Title 5 USC, Section 301.
PRINCIPAL PURPOSE: To determine eligibility for promotion.
ROUTINE USES: Information may be referred to appropriate authorities to determine promotion eligibility and validity of points granted.
DISCLOSURE: Voluntary failure to furnish information requested may result in denial of promotion.

3. NAME	4. SSN	5. GRADE
6. CURRENT ORGANIZATION	7. SRB MOS	8. PMOS	9. RECOMMENDED GRADE/CPMOS

SECTION A - RECOMMENDATION

10. FROM (Commander)	11. THROUGH (Promotion Authority)	12. TO (PSC)

13. Under the provisions of AR 600-8-19, chapter 3 (Active Army); AR 140-158, chapter 3 (USAR); or NGR 600-200, chapter 6 (ARNG) (check one of the following):

   a. Recommend the above-named soldier for promotion/reevaluation to the grade indicated. *(Complete lines 13b (1) - (6) and send to the promotion authority.)*

   b. Request the following information be used in the next scheduled recomputation of promotion points. *(Complete lines 13(b)(2) - (6) and send to the PSC).*

(1) Waivers required *(maximum of two allowed)*	(2) Most recent individual assigned weapon qualification	
(a) Time in Service	(a) Expert	(d) DATE
(b) Time in Grade	(b) Sharpshooter	
(c) SQT score *(59 or below)*	(c) Marksman	
(3) Most recent Physical Fitness Test Scores *(Minimum score of 60 in each event.)*	(4) (a) SOLDIER'S CURRENT SQT SCORE	(4) (b) DATE
(a) Situps	(5) I certify (Must check one of the following on all recommendations):	
(b) Pushups	(a) That the soldier has taken an SQT during the most recent test period.	
(c) Two-Mile Run		
(d) Total (e) DATE	(b) That the soldier has not taken an SQT due to no fault of his/her own.	
14. REMARKS	(c) That the soldier failed to take an SQT during the most recent test period due to his/her own fault.	
	(6) PROMOTION POINTS AWARDED TO SOLDIER FOR DUTY PERFORMANCE *(Maximum 200 points)*	

15a. SIGNATURE BLOCK OF COMMANDER	15b. SIGNATURE OF COMMANDER	15c. DATE

16a. SIGNATURE BLOCK OF PROMOTION AUTHORITY	16b. SIGNATURE OF PROMOTION AUTHORITY	16c. CHECK ONE ☐ Approved ☐ Disapproved	16d. DATE

SECTION B - ADMINISTRATIVE POINTS

		POINTS GRANTED
1.	DUTY PERFORMANCE - MAXIMUM 200 POINTS. *(Enter points awarded by Commander for duty performance on promotion recommendation (See Section A, item (13b(6).)*	
2.	SKILL QUALIFICATION TEST (SQT) - MAXIMUM 200 POINTS	POINTS GRANTED
a.	Enter the soldier's latest SQT score from the Individual Soldier's Report *(ISR)*, or TSO data, if the score is 60 or higher ———————— x 2 =	
b.	Enter the number of promotion points granted under the no fault provision.	

DA FORM 3355, APR 91   DA FORM 3355, MAR 85 IS OBSOLETE

Note: SDT points are entered in lieu of SQT points in section B, part 2.

3. Awards and Decorations - *Maximum 50 Points*. List and multiply the number of awards received by the number of points authorized for the award as explained in the instructions.

	×		=			×		=			×		=	
	×		=			×		=			×		=	
	×		=			×		=			×		=	

Total Points Granted →

4. Military Education - *Maximum 150 Points*

5. Civilian Education - *Maximum 100 Points*

6. Military Training - *Maximum 100 Points*

a.	Marksmanship	
b.	Physical Fitness Test	
c.	Total Points →	

Total Points Granted →

7. I certify that the above administrative points shown have been accurately extracted from appropriate records and promotion points indicated are correct.

a. SIGNATURE OF RESPONSIBLE OFFICIAL	b. GRADE	c. DATE	d. SIGNATURE OF RECOMMENDED INDIVIDUAL

SECTION C - TOTALS

Note - *Only the fractional total promotion points in item 3 of this section will be rounded off to the nearest whole number.* A fraction of 5/10 or higher will be rounded up to the next higher whole number. A fraction of 4/10 or less will be rounded down to the next lowest whole number.

		GRANTED
1.	TOTAL ADMINISTRATIVE POINTS - MAXIMUM 800 POINTS (Total of items 1 through 6, Section B.)	
2.	TOTAL BOARD POINTS - MAXIMUM 200 POINTS	
3.	TOTAL PROMOTION POINTS - MAXIMUM 1,000 POINTS (Add items 1 and 2.)	

4. I certify that the total points shown have been accurately extracted from appropriate records and promotion list points indicated are correct.

a. SIGNATURE OF BOARD RECORDER	b. GRADE	c. DATE

5. I certify that the soldier has been recommended for promotion by a valid promotion board.

a. SIGNATURE BLOCK OF PROMOTION AUTHORITY	b. SIGNATURE	c. DATE BOARD PROCEEDINGS WERE APPROVED

6. STATEMENT (*Use only when a recommendation is disapproved, when a soldier is not selected by the board, or when the soldier cannot be added to the recommended list due to not attaining the minimum required points.*)

"I have been counseled on my promotion status and deficiencies."

a. SIGNATURE OF SOLDIER	b. DATE	c. TYPED OR PRINTED NAME OF COUNSELOR
		d. SIGNATURE OF COUNSELOR

PAGE 2, DA FORM 3355, APR 91

Promotion Point Worksheet (continued).

Promotion

A soldier's name on the secondary zone list for promotion to sergeant is transferred to the primary zone list on the first day of the month in which he completes 33 months of active service. He becomes eligible for promotion in the primary zone on the first day of the month in which he completed 36 months' active service.

A soldier's name on the secondary zone list for promotion to staff sergeant is transferred to the primary zone on the first day of the month in which he completes 81 months of active service. He becomes eligible for promotion in the primary zone on the first day of the month in which he completes 84 months of active service.

A soldier whose name is being transferred to the primary zone list continues to have secondary zone list status during the interim three reporting months. He also continues to compete against the secondary zone promotion point cutoff scores. When eligible to compete against primary zone promotion point cutoff scores, he will be eligible for promotion only from the primary zone list.

Promotion point cutoff scores announced for the primary zone are used to promote from that list only. The same is true of cutoff scores announced for the secondary zone.

Reevaluation

A soldier on the current recommended list for three months may ask to be reevaluated at that time and each three months thereafter if he or she is still promotable. A soldier reevaluated is not immediately eligible for promotion based on his new score. He will continue to be eligible for promotion based on the promotion point score he held immediately before reevaluation. Eligibility under the old score continues until the reevaluated score becomes effective. The new score becomes effective three months from the date of reevaluation because of the three-month reporting time.

After the request for reevaluation is approved, the soldier appears before the organization's next regularly scheduled promotion board. His promotion list status is then based on the number of points he attains. If he remains on the list, his original selection date is adjusted to the date the promotion authority approves the board report. This gives each soldier a chance to improve his total score. It also gives him a chance to *lower* his standing if he makes a poor showing before the board.

A soldier who asks to be reevaluated subjects himself to recomputation of total promotion points on DA Form 3355, plus those points attained because of the new board interview. Administrative points awarded a soldier are determined from his records as they existed before the approval of the local report of board proceedings.

Each soldier who asks to be reevaluated must understand clearly that the reevaluation will require him to compete equally with all other soldiers in the same grade and his placement on a recommended list is determined by the total promotion points (administrative plus board) he attains.

Requests for reevaluation are prepared in writing on DA Form 4187, *Personnel Action*, as outlined in paragraph 7-23c, AR 600-200. On approval of the board proceedings, *a soldier being reevaluated loses his recommended list status when he is not recommended for promotion by most of the voting members or the promotion score is below 550 if competing for promotion to staff sergeant or 450 if competing for promotion to sergeant.*

Loss of recommended list status through reevaluation does not, however, preclude promotion consideration by future boards. Such consideration, however, is not a vested right. Those being considered to regain recommended list status are subject to the provisions of Chapter 7, AR 600-200, and the recommendations of their commanders.

Removals

Soldiers may be removed from promotion lists for the following reasons.
- Failure to take the regular SDT due to their own fault.
- Failure to qualify, for cause, for the security clearance required for the MOS in which recommended. Those who fail to qualify for a security clearance through no adverse reason are reclassified and remain on the list in their new MOS.
- Failure to reenlist or extend to meet the service remaining obligation for promotion.
- When a bar to reenlistment is approved after the soldiers have been put on the list.
- Reclassification from the MOS in which their names appear on the list because of inefficiency or misconduct.
- Erroneous listing due to not meeting the criteria for promotion listed in Chapter 7, AR 600-200.
- When a second SDT failure (GO Raw score of 59 or less) is achieved in the current PMOS.
- When, after six months in a weight-control program, an individual still exceeds the screening table weight and has not made satisfactory progress toward the maximum allowable weight.
- When, after 12 months in a weight-control program, a soldier still exceeds the body fat standard or maximum allowable weight, even if satisfactory progress toward the maximum allowable weight is achieved and even if the soldier is at or below the screening table weight.
- When reclassification training ends in failure to complete the course.
- When reduced in grade after being placed on the recommended list.

Promotion packets of soldiers who are removed from a recommended list are retained in the functional files of the promotion authority for two years.

A removal board is convened when required. It determines whether a soldier should be removed from a recommended list. The board will be constituted as for promotion boards (Paragraph 7-19, AR 600-200). Although the provisions of AR 15-5 do not apply to the operation of such boards, the soldier being considered for removal has certain rights.

- He may appear before the board in all open proceedings.
- He may challenge any member of the board for cause.
- He may request any reasonably available witness whose testimony he believes to be pertinent to his case.
- He may elect to remain silent, to make an unsworn statement, to make a sworn statement, or be verbally examined by the board.
- He may question any witness appearing before the board.
- He may present written affidavits and depositions of witnesses who are unable to appear in his behalf.

Failure on the part of a soldier to exercise his rights as stated above is not a bar to the board proceedings or its findings and recommendations. The promotion authority is the final approval or disapproval authority on the board's recommendations. This action is final.

A soldier removed from a list and later exonerated is reinstated to the current local recommended list as soon as possible, but not more than 10 days after being completely exonerated.

Promotion

Recomputation of Promotion Points

A soldier with valid recommended list status for promotion to sergeant and staff sergeant as of the end of the month before the scheduled recomputation has his promotion points recomputed during that time. Promotion points are recomputed twice yearly without local promotion board action (see Table 7-1, AR 600-200).

Commanders must ensure that all scores recomputed are completed by the end of the required month so that they will be reported in the following month's report of enlisted personnel eligible for promotion. If scores are not recomputed during the scheduled month for a valid reason (such as in-transit status), they are recomputed at the earliest date. This recomputed score is shown on the current recommended list as of the scheduled recomputation month.

Each soldier is given an opportunity to review recomputed scores for accuracy and completeness. Recomputed scores are shown in the unit's next published and approved list for promotion. Soldiers continue to be eligible for promotion based on their old promotion point score until the recomputed scores become effective. New scores become effective three months from the day of the scheduled recomputation month.

Recomputations are limited to items 1 through 7, DA Form 3355. Adjustment of Board Points (item 8) applies to soldiers who request reevaluation.

Points awarded are determined from the soldier's records as they were before the board proceedings were approved. The promotion authority or the MILPO may correct all known errors before the report of board proceedings is approved. Other than to correct computation errors, no changes are made in the promotion point standings after the board proceedings are approved unless the promotion authority concludes that the soldier was considered in error or was granted more administrative points than he was entitled to. In such cases, the soldier is suspended from the promotion list.

The individual should be advised of the suspension, and the promotion authority should promptly request from the major area commander permission to correct the recommended list standing. The MACOM may approve adjustment of the points following the guidelines of Chapter 7, AR 600-200. The promotion authority may promote in spite of this procedure when the unchallenged total point score equals or exceeds the qualifying promotion point score announced by Headquarters, Department of the Army.

For example, if a soldier has a total point score of 675, of which 650 points are unchallenged and determined to be the correct score, the soldier could be promoted if the announced promotion point cutoff score for his or her MOS is 650 or lower, regardless of the pending decision from the appropriate MACOM. As another example, a soldier has a total point score of 650, but his records show that he should have been granted 25 more points, and he really had a score of 675 at the time of the initial computation. The soldier could be promoted if the announced promotion cutoff score for this MOS is 650 or lower, pending decision from the appropriate MACOM.

ASSIGNMENTS AND HOW THEY AFFECT PROMOTIONS

Personnel on Temporary Duty

Commanders must ensure that soldiers are considered for promotion before they are placed on temporary duty, in isolated areas, or on special duty or assignment.

Promotion authorities must ensure that they are kept informed of duty performance of soldiers on temporary duty.

Reassignment Before Promotion

Command interest is needed to ensure that soldiers are not penalized when they are transferred from one organization to another before they are promoted. When a soldier is processing for transfer, the promotion packet and a copy of the current recommended list must be sealed in an envelope and filed in the action-pending section of the soldier's MPRJ. The gaining promotion authority should then put the soldier's name on his current recommended list on the reporting date as stated in the orders.

Newly assigned soldiers who are on a recommended list from a previous command are added to the current recommended list of the gaining command effective on the reporting date stated in reassignment orders.

If there is no promotion packet, a recommended list is not valid, and the soldier's name will not be placed on the recommended list of the gaining command. In such cases, the gaining command must take prompt action to request the missing documents from the soldier's former command.

No soldier who is on a recommended list should depart a unit (or be permitted to depart) until his or her promotion packet has been prepared and its presence in the MPRJ has been verified.

Reclassification of PMOS

A soldier on a recommended list who is voluntarily or involuntarily reclassified for other than inefficiency or misconduct may compete against the announced DA promotion point cutoff scores in the newly awarded MOS and be promoted in the new PMOS on the first day of the month following reclassification, if eligible. Promotion points granted for SQT in prior PMOS are recomputed effective the date of reclassification. The "no fault" provision in item 4, DA Form 3355, is used (Paragraph 7-28, AR 600-200).

SELECTION AND PROMOTION TO SENIOR NCO RANKS

Soldiers who are eligible for senior-grade promotions are given the opportunity to review their promotion packets well in advance of the promotion board's convening. Because the selection board uses your records to determine whether you will be selected, your review must be thorough.

At no cost, you may obtain copies of your Official Military Personnel File (OMPF) microfiche by writing to Commander, U.S. Army Enlisted Records and Evaluation Center, ATTN: PCRE-RF-I, Fort Benjamin Harrison, IN 46249. Be sure to include your Social Security number and sign your request. The OMPF consists of the *P-fiche* and the *S-fiche*. The P-fiche contains performance and commendatory and disciplinary data; the S-fiche contains service computation data (active duty, promotion, separation, and other documents) and administrative data (information not included in the service computation portion of the S-fiche).

Review these documents, particularly the P-fiche, very carefully. Be sure that all the documents contained on the fiche pertain to you. The promotion board should catch any discrepancies, but look for them and correct them at once.

Promotion

Also, it is vital that soldiers have the proper NCO Education System codes recorded in their files. Soldiers should verify this information through local personnel service centers, because only NCOs with correct codes will be considered for promotion.

All staff sergeants and sergeants first class in a zone of consideration for promotion should make sure the correct NCOES course selection or completion codes are posted on DA Form 2A, *Personnel Qualification Record*, Part 1 and DA Form 2-1, *PQR*, Part 2.

The codes are as follows: "2" to denote Primary Leadership Development Course graduation, "W" for Basic NCO Course graduation, "T" for Advanced NCO Course selection or "S" for graduation, and "F" for Sergeant Major Course selection or "A" for graduation. Graduation from the First Sergeant Course, denoted by a "K," is not an NCOES requirement.

Be certain that any commendatory information not on file in your OMPF is provided to your MILPO at the time you screen your promotion jacket.

Be certain your official military photograph is current, especially if there has been a change in your physical appearance since the last one was taken. Your record gives a promotion board one view of the kind of soldier you are, but your photo gives board members an idea of what you look like in uniform. An outdated photo or none at all will count against you.

While your local military personnel office (MILPO) is required to inform you when a new official DA full-length photograph is required, it is your responsibility to have it taken and to ensure it meets the standards of AR 670-1, *Wear and Appearance of Army Uniforms and Insignia*, and AR 672-5-1, *Military Awards*. Two copies of the photo must be submitted by you to the MILPO to update your records.

The Total Army Personnel Command (PERSCOM) in Alexandria, Virginia, announced in early 1990 that NCOs and officers must update their official photos every five years. New staff sergeants and command sergeants major are required to get an official photo taken within 60 days of pinning on their rank. All staff sergeants and above must have color full-length photos in their official files. Photos are reviewed by U.S. Army Enlisted Records and Evaluation Center board officials who select soldiers for promotions, assignments, and training. One copy of photos of promotable master sergeants and sergeants major is maintained on file at Headquarters, Department of the Army.

Eligibility

Eligibility for promotion to sergeant first class and above is based on date of rank. In addition, for first sergeant or master sergeant and above, cumulative enlisted service is also required.

The criteria for the primary and secondary zones of consideration for each grade are announced by Headquarters, Department of the Army, before each board. Soldiers may not decline consideration. The following general criteria must be met before the board convenes to qualify a soldier for inclusion in a zone of consideration.

• Meet the announced date of rank requirements and other criteria prescribed by HQDA in the letter of instruction and general guidance provided to each selection board.

• Have at least eight and ten years' cumulative enlisted service creditable in computing basic pay for promotion to first sergeant or master sergeant and above.

Be sure your official DA full-length color photograph is current. *U.S. Army photo by SFC Phil Prater.*

Promotion

- Be serving on active duty in an enlisted status on the convening date of the selection board.
- Have a high school diploma or GED equivalent or an associate or higher degree.
- Not be barred from reenlistment according to AR 601-280 or denied reenlistment through the qualitative screening process outlined in Chapter 4, AR 600-200.

Selection Boards

Selection boards consist of at least five members, including both officers and senior NCOs, although most members of these boards are officers. The president of each board is a general officer.

Soldiers may not appear in person before a selection board, either in their own behalf or on the part of another person. No written communications from third parties, including a soldier's chain of command or supervisor, are authorized. Communications from soldiers (or their chain of command or supervisor) within an announced secondary zone of consideration are not accepted.

A soldier within an announced primary zone may write the president of the board, inviting attention to any matter he or she feels is important in considering his or her records (send these letters to the address given in the letter that announces the zone of consideration). These letters may not contain any information on the character, conduct, or motives of any person or criticism of any other person. Such letters must be received before the convening date, and they will not be acknowledged, nor will they be a basis for promotion consideration. They are not included in the soldier's OMPF.

Security Requirements

For promotion to sergeant first class, a soldier must have the security clearance required for the MOS in which promoted. For first sergeant or master sergeant and above, the soldier must have a favorable National Agency Check (NAC) completed or have a final secret security clearance or higher.

Selections

Selections are based on impartial consideration of all eligible soldiers in the announced zone. Boards select the best qualified in each career management field. They recommend a specified number of soldiers by MOS from the zones of consideration who are the best qualified to meet the needs of the Army. The total number that may be selected in each MOS is the projected number the Army needs to maintain its authorized by-grade strength at any given time. (Soldiers who are considered in the secondary zone face much stiffer competition than those considered in the primary zone.)

Soldiers who are not selected for promotion are not provided specific reasons for their not having been selected. Board members do not record their reasons, nor do they give any reasons for selecting or not selecting a soldier. Selections are based on relative qualifications and the projected need in each career management field.

Acceptance

Unless a soldier declines promotion, it is accepted as of the effective date of the announcing order. Letters of declination must be sent through command channels to the MILPO not later than 30 days after the effective date of the promotion given in the

Be sure your official DA full-length color photograph is current. *U.S. Army photo by SFC Phil Prater.*

Promotion

orders. Soldiers who decline promotion will be considered by the next regularly constituted board, providing they are otherwise eligible.

Soldiers promoted to sergeant first class and above incur a two-year service obligation. This obligation begins from the effective date of the promotion before voluntary nondisability retirement. The two-year service obligation does not apply to those separated for any reason other than voluntary nondisability retirement. Also, soldiers applying for retirement may request a remaining service obligation waiver. If granted, the soldier retires in grade.

Enlisted Standby Advisory Board (STAB)

This board considers the following records:
- From a primary and secondary zone not reviewed by a regular board.
- From a primary zone that were not properly constituted because of a major material error when reviewed by a regular board. The Deputy Chief of Staff for Personnel or designee will approve cases for referral to an STAB upon declaring invalid, in whole or in part, an adverse NCO Evaluation Report or academic evaluation report that was reviewed by a promotion board, providing that with the absence of this report, or portions thereof, there is a reasonable chance the soldier would have been recommended for promotion. PersCom determines whether a major material error (except for those just described) existed in a soldier's official military personnel file when it was reviewed by a promotion board. An error is major when, had it not existed, the soldier would clearly have been more competitive and his or her qualifications appear to have been increased to equal that of others who were selected. Sometimes the error is longstanding and, once corrected, qualifies the soldier for reconsideration based on the criteria of several boards.
- Of those recommended soldiers on whom derogatory information has developed that may warrant removal from a recommended list.

Only soldiers who were not selected from a primary zone of consideration will be reconsidered for promotion. Soldiers who were considered in a secondary zone are not reconsidered.

Reconsideration is granted for a wide variety of reasons (Paragraph 7-44d, AR 600-200), including invalidation of an adverse NCOER, misfiling of adverse information (such as Article 15 or court-martial), filing of court-martial orders in the performance fiche of the OMPF when the findings were "not guilty."

The above should reinforce the point made earlier in this section that *you should review your promotion packet carefully before it is sent before the board.*

Removal from a Recommended List

Commanders may recommend that a soldier's name be removed from a DA recommended list at any time. The recommendation for removal must be fully documented and justified. HQDA makes the final decision on the removal based on the results and recommendation of the DA Standby Enlisted Advisory Board.

Removal may be recommended for a number of reasons.
- Failure to make progress in the weight-control program.
- As a result of reprimand, admonition, censure, and other nonpunitive measures, including for substandard duty performance over a period of time.
- For misconduct.

Before forwarding a recommendation for removal, the initiator must send it in writing to the soldier. All documents must be included. The soldier must be allowed to respond to the proposed action and may submit a rebuttal within 15 days after receipt of the written notice. The commander initiating the removal may extend this time only for unusual circumstances beyond the soldier's control. A soldier who elects not to rebut must send a signed statement that he or she has reviewed the proposed action and elects not to submit a rebuttal.

Removal from a DA promotion recommended list has far-reaching, long-lasting effects on the soldier. The probability for subsequent selection for promotion, once a soldier has been removed from a list, is extremely limited.

FROCKING

Frocking is a venerable Navy tradition that has only recently been accepted by the Army for enlisted personnel. Basically, when a soldier is frocked, he or she assumes the insignia of a higher grade so that his or her title is commensurate with the duty position, although no pay or allowances are authorized in the higher grade.

The practice is said to have originated in the nineteenth century. When a ship lost an officer, the vacancy was filled with a midshipman who had passed the examination for lieutenant. He was appointed acting lieutenant and no longer wore the short coat of a midshipman, but assumed the frock coat of an officer. The Army has frocked general officers—a brigadier general, for example, who has been selected for promotion to major general and has been assigned to a major general's position in a new command—when such an action is in the best interest of the Army.

Sergeants first class (promotable) to first sergeants, master sergeants (promotable), and command sergeants major (designate) may be frocked.

Frocking of First Sergeants

Sergeants first class (promotable) who are assigned to an authorized first sergeant position may be frocked. Commanders in the position of full colonel or above may authorize and approve frocking. Priority goes to filling vacant first sergeant positions. They will not be approved to provide an interim fill for a first sergeant position, will not be done until the individual actually assumes first sergeant duties, and do not result in changing ID cards or official records.

Personnel who have been frocked and subsequently reassigned before promotion revert to their former grade. Frocked soldiers subsequently promoted to E-8 and reassigned retain the rank of first sergeant or are laterally appointed to master sergeant.

Frocking of Master Sergeants

Master sergeants (promotable) and command sergeants major (designate) who are assigned or branch cleared by PersCom to authorized CSM positions may be frocked. Commanding General, PersCom is the approving authority for frocking to CSM. Frocked CSM may serve as presidents of enlisted promotion boards. Frocking is not approved to provide interim fill for a CSM position, and priority for filling a CSM position is to assign a serving CSM or E-9 CSM (D). Orders announcing frocking are not published, nor are ID cards or official records changed to reflect frocking.

On the effective date of frocking the soldier is presented with DA Form 4873, *Certificate of Appointment to Command Sergeant Major.* Personnel who have been frocked and subsequently reassigned prior to promotion revert to their former grade.

Promotion

REDUCTIONS IN GRADE

Reduction Authority

The commanders below may administratively reduce the grade of assigned soldiers.
- Specialist or corporal and below. Company, troop, battery, and separate detachment commanders.
- Sergeant and staff sergeant. Field grade commanders of any organization authorized a lieutenant colonel or higher grade commander. For separate detachments, companies, or battalions, reduction authority is the next senior headquarters within the chain of command authorized a lieutenant colonel or higher grade commander.
- Sergeant first class and above. Commanders of organizations authorized a colonel or higher grade commander (an officer exercising special courts-martial authority). For separate detachments, companies, or battalions, reduction authority is the next senior headquarters within the chain of command authorized a colonel or higher grade commander.

Erroneous Enlistment Grades

Soldiers who were approved by higher grades than entitled when they enlisted or reenlisted in the Regular Army or Army Reserve will be reduced to the one to which then entitled. These grades are prescribed in AR 601-210, AR 601-280, AR 140-11, or AR 140-158.

Misconduct

For reductions imposed by court-martial, see Chapter 8 on military justice, or the Manual for Courts-Martial 1984. Sergeants first class and above cannot be reduced under the provision of Article 15, UCMJ.

Inefficiency

Inefficiency is defined as "demonstration of characteristics which show that the person cannot perform the duties and responsibilities of the grade and MOS" (AR 600-200). It may also include any act or conduct that clearly shows that the soldier lacks those abilities and qualities required and expected of a person of that grade and experience. Commanders may consider misconduct, including conviction by civil court, as bearing on efficiency.

A soldier may be reduced under the authority of Chapter 8, AR 600-200, for long-standing unpaid personal debts that he or she has not made a reasonable attempt to pay.

An assigned soldier who has served in the same unit for at least 90 days may be reduced one grade for inefficiency. The reduction authority for the grade or a higher commander who has authority may reduce the soldier. The commander starting the reduction action will present documents showing the soldier's inefficiency to the reduction authority.

The documents should establish a pattern of inefficiency rather than identify a specific incident. Reduction for inefficiency is never to be used to reduce soldiers for actions for which they have been acquitted because of court-martial, in lieu of Article 15, UCMJ, or for a single act of misconduct.

The commander reducing a soldier will inform him or her, in writing, of the action contemplated and the reasons. The soldier must acknowledge receipt of the letter, by endorsement, and may submit any pertinent matters in rebuttal. Sergeants and above may request to appear before a reduction board. If appearance is declined, it must be done in writing and will be considered as acceptance of the reduction action.

A reduction board, when required, must be convened within 30 days after the individual is notified in writing. This does not apply to specialists and corporals and below.

Reduction Boards

When required, reduction boards are convened to determine whether an enlisted soldier's grade should be reduced. The convening authority must ensure that the following conditions exist.
* The board consists of officers and enlisted personnel of mature judgment and senior in grade to the person being considered for reduction.
* For inefficiency cases, at least one member must be thoroughly familiar with the soldier's field of specialization.
* The board must consist of at least three voting members.
* The board must consist of unbiased members.
* The board has an officer or senior enlisted member (or both) of the same sex as the soldier being considered for reduction.
* The composition of the board is fully representative of the ethnic population of the soldiers under its jurisdiction.
* No soldier with direct knowledge of the case is appointed to the board.

A soldier who is to appear before the board will be given at least 15 working days' written notice before the date of the hearing so that the soldier or his counsel has time to prepare the case.

If the soldier requests a military counsel, one will be appointed by the supporting judge advocate. The soldier may also obtain civilian counsel at his own expense.

The convening authority may approve or disapprove any portion of the recommendation of the board, but his action cannot increase the severity of the board's recommendation. If he approves a recommended reduction, he may direct it. When the board recommends a reduction and the convening authority approves it, the soldier will be reduced without regard to any action taken to appeal the reduction.

The soldier has the following rights.
* He may decline, in writing, to appear before the board.
* He may have a military counsel of his own choosing, if reasonably available, or he may employ a civilian counsel at his own expense, or both.
* He may appear in person, with or without counsel, at all open proceedings of the board.
* If the soldier appears before the board without counsel, the president must counsel him on the action being contemplated, the effect of such action on his future in the Army, and his right to request counsel.
* He may challenge any member of the board for cause.
* He may request any reasonably available witness whose testimony he believes to be pertinent to his case. When requested, he must tell the nature of the information the witness will provide.
* He may submit to the board written affidavits and depositions of witnesses who are unable to appear before the board.
* He may employ the provisions of Article 31, UCMJ (prohibition against compul-

Promotion

sory self-incrimination), or submit himself to an examination by the board.
- He or his counsel may question any witness appearing before the board.

Failure of the soldier to exercise his rights is not a bar to the board proceedings or its findings and recommendations.

Appeals

Appeals from reduction for misconduct are governed by Article 15, UCMJ; Paragraph 135, MCM, 1984; and AR 27-10.

Appeals based on reduction for failure to complete training will not be accepted.

Appeals from staff sergeants and below based on reduction for inefficiency or conviction by civil court are allowed. They must be submitted in writing within 30 workdays from the date of reduction. The officer having general court-martial jurisdiction, or the next higher authority, may approve, disapprove, or change the reduction if he determines that the reduction was without sufficient basis, should be changed, or was proper. His action is final.

Written appeals from sergeants first class and above based on reduction for inefficiency or conviction by civil court must also be submitted within 30 days of the date of reduction. A copy of all correspondence and the appeal are furnished the authority next above the officer who reduced the soldier. This officer, if a general, will take final action on the appeal. If not reviewed at the appellate level by a general officer, the file is then sent to the first general officer in the chain of command next above the officer who acted on the appeal for final review and action. This authority personally reviews the file, including action taken on the appeal, and makes final corrections where indicated.

Authority to take final action on an appeal in the case of any soldier, regardless of grade, may not be delegated.

Other Reasons for Reductions

When a separation authority determines that a soldier is to be discharged from the service under other than honorable conditions, he will be reduced to the lowest enlisted grade. Board action is not required for such reductions.

Soldiers appointed to a higher grade on entering or while attending a service or civilian school and who fail to complete the course successfully may be reduced as follows.
- Officer candidates may be reduced by school commandant to grades based on entry or to grades considered appropriate.
- Fixed-wing and rotary-wing aviator pilot trainees may be reduced by the school commandant to the grade held on entry or to a grade considered appropriate.
- Other students may be reduced by school commandants or appointment authorities to grades in line with their abilities, but not below private E-2 or any grade held on entry.

Restoration to Former Grades

Grade restoration may result from setting aside, mitigation, or suspension of nonjudicial punishment, when a court-martial sentence is set aside or disapproved, when a conviction by a civil court is reversed, or when officers taking final appeal or review action after reduction direct that the soldier be restored to his former grade or any intermediate grade, on determining that reduction was without sufficient basis.

Records Check

All enlisted soldiers must keep tabs on their official records. Soldiers can check their official records at any time because of the new push-button phone service at the Enlisted Records and Evaluation Center, Fort Benjamin Harrison, Indiana. This interactive voice response system allows callers to check on NCO Evaluation Reports, official photographs, security clearances, and other important information. Any soldier who has a push-button touch-tone phone can use the system. When a caller dials DSN 699-3714 or commercial 317-542-3714, a computer-generated voice welcomes the caller and asks for a Social Security number. Once the number is accepted, the caller is offered several types of information. This system is especially helpful to staff sergeants and senior NCOs who need to check their records before a promotion board or school selection board convenes. It is effective, efficient, and quick.

6

Personal Affairs

> The higher one goes up the flagpole, the more the tail hangs out for all to see.
>
> —Gen. Creighton W. Abrams

Keeping your personal and family affairs in order at all times is important to your welfare now and in the future. You owe it to your spouse, children, and parents to put your personal affairs in order so that they will know what to do and what to expect, if it becomes necessary for them to go on without you.*

At the very least, you should do the following.

• Prepare a will, or if you have an old one, update it.

• Make certain that your Record of Emergency Data, DD Form 93, maintained by your MILPO, is current at all times.

• Maintain a permanent file of all records and documents pertaining to your military service.

• Prepare a personal affairs record and keep it up-to-date.

• Keep your important documents in a safe place, and tell your next of kin where they are.

• Let the members of your family know what you are doing for their future protection.

---

*See Chapter 9, "Your Legal Survival Kit," in Tomes, *The Servicemember's Legal Guide, 2nd Edition* (Stackpole Books, 1992).

• Inform your family of the government benefits they will be entitled to if you die, and tell them how to get casualty assistance from the Survivor Assistance Officer.

LEGAL ASSISTANCE

Most Army installations have legal assistance officers who are licensed attorneys and whose job it is to act as your legal advisor and consultant. A legal assistance officer will advise you on such matters as a will, a power of attorney, divorce and separation actions, estates, tax problems, and other civil legal matters. The legal assistance officer can also provide you a very useful "legal check-up," which is designed to identify any potential legal problems that you may have.

This officer is not normally permitted to represent you before a civil court or to give you advice in matters of a criminal nature. Neither may he or she advise you about court-martial investigations or charges (a military counsel appointed by the judge advocate will assist you in such cases). If your problem requires the services of a civilian lawyer, the legal assistance officer can refer you, through cooperating bar associations, to civilian legal advisors or legal aid bureaus ready to assist you.

YOUR WILL

Your legal assistance officer or a private attorney can provide you assistance in preparing your will. Do not try to prepare it yourself; it is too important a document to be left to the preparation of anyone untrained in law. To fulfill its purpose, your will must meet strict legal requirements, and only a lawyer can ensure that it does.

The importance of having a will cannot be overemphasized. A will is as important for soldiers without dependents as it is for those with them. You may not consider that you "own" very much, but not having a will could cause many legal complications after your death. If you were to die without a will—*intestate*—your estate would be distributed according to the descent and distribution laws of your state of legal residence or in the case of real property located in another state the laws of that state.

When you make out your will, decide on the person you will name to handle your affairs following your death. Pick someone who you know can do the job well.

If you are married, both you and your spouse should have wills, even if each will makes the same distribution of property and assets. It is particularly important to have a will if you have minor children so that their interests can be protected through a guardianship of your choice in the event both you and your spouse die.

Once you have made your will, review it periodically to keep it up-to-date. As circumstances change, you may want to change it to be sure that it still expresses your desires about the distribution of your property and assets.

Keep your will in a safe place. The safest place to keep it (and other important papers) is in a safe deposit box at your bank. It is not a bad idea to send a copy of your will together with a statement as to the location of the original to the principal beneficiary or the person named in the will as the executor.

POWER OF ATTORNEY

A power of attorney is a legal document by which you give another person the power to act as your agent, either for some particular purpose or for the transaction of your business in general.

Personal Affairs

A power of attorney may be very useful, especially while you are overseas. In the wrong hands, however, it can ruin you because the agent who holds such a power has, within the limits granted by it, full authority to deal with your property without consulting you. *Grant it only to someone you can trust* and then only when you must.

You may never need a power of attorney, or if you do need one, it may only be required to perform certain acts and no others—a limited or special power of attorney. It is also wise to limit the time of its operation. Always consult a legal assistance officer or a lawyer before assigning a power of attorney, and cancel it as soon as it is no longer required. Notify your dependents or next of kin whether or not you have granted anyone a power of attorney.

PERSONAL AFFAIRS RECORD

The simplest way to keep your survivors informed about the arrangements you have made for them is to prepare a record of your personal affairs. As a minimum, be sure that they know the location of the following items.
- Your birth certificate and those of all members of your immediate family.
- Your marriage certificate.
- Divorce papers or previous spouse's death certificate, if applicable.
- Your life insurance policies.

Rent a safe-deposit box at your bank, and keep all of your important papers—stocks and bonds, will, insurance policies, and so forth—in it. You may rent one in your name only or in the name of two persons as joint tenants or in the name of two persons with another being an "appointed deputy." If you put the original of your will in a safe-deposit box, be sure that your spouse or your executor has access to it. If you die and no one has access to the box, a court order must be obtained to open it.

Having a personal affairs record becomes increasingly important the older you get. It is a necessity for the married soldier because it serves as a vital source of information for his family should he die, depart suddenly on a tour of temporary duty, or be assigned to an unaccompanied overseas tour of duty.

Be realistic, though. An unmarried 19-year-old private will not have the same requirement for such a record as a 39-year-old sergeant major with a family and personal property. Keep that in mind when advising your soldiers on this matter. While renting a safe-deposit box is an excellent idea when you've settled down somewhere to live permanently, the Army family constantly on the move may find that keeping its vital records close to hand is more convenient.

Your personal affairs record can be as detailed as you think it needs to be, but make sure it includes at least the following information.
- Your insurance policy numbers and their amounts. Include automobile and home owner's policies, if you have them.
- Your previous years' tax records.
- Copies of the titles and bills of sale for your automobile.
- Information on your bank accounts (savings, checking, certificates of deposit, savings bonds, and so on). If you are married, and you're a person who believes in keeping secret caches of "mad money" around, be sure this money is recorded somewhere in case you die. Your spouse may be surprised (in more ways than one) to find out about it, but knowing your family will have those few extra dollars in reserve is worth the possibility you'll be found out and have to share the money while you're still alive.

- A list of all the allotments being taken out of your pay.
- Information regarding any veterans benefits to which you may be entitled, such as disability compensation or GI Bill benefits.

If you are married, be sure someone in your family knows how to pay your household bills, when they are due, and where to find them. A military family should be like a military unit in that every member backs up every other member. If you handle checking and your spouse handles savings, make sure either of you can deal with both in a pinch.

MILITARY RECORDS

Keep a permanent file of all records pertaining to your military service. Keep copies of orders, discharge certificate, awards, citations, letters of appreciation and commendation, medical and dental records, leave and earnings statements, and other information about your military history, even old efficiency reports.

Information from these records is frequently needed throughout your active service career and afterward, when you apply to the Department of Veterans Affairs for certain benefits.

Emergency Data

Your DD Form 93, *Record of Emergency Data*, must be accurate and up-to-date at all times. This record tells your MILPO where your next of kin can be located immediately in case of an emergency. It gives the name of the person you want to receive your pay if you are missing in action as well as other information of benefit to your dependents.

BANK ACCOUNTS

You should have some of your money in a checking account or a savings account, preferably both. If you are married, you and your spouse should decide who is going to keep the accounts, and you should divide up the responsibility accordingly; make them joint accounts so that if anything happens to you your family will have ready access to the funds held by your bank.

Current regulations require all new enlistees to have guaranteed direct deposit to a financial institution. Even for "old timers" it is a good idea to have your military pay deposited directly into a checking account. Checking accounts are a fast, easy, and safe way to transact business. With a guaranteed direct deposit from the U.S. Army Finance Center, you do not have to bother with anything but picking up your leave and earnings statement on payday.

There are many different kinds of banking and checking accounts, so study them carefully before you decide on the ones that are best for you. Any bank officer will be happy to explain them to you. Once you find a bank that satisfies your needs, stick with it.

INSURANCE PROGRAMS

You must have insurance: life, automobile, homeowner's or renter's, mortgage, even medical insurance. You are particularly insurable if you are still relatively young and you have school-age children who depend upon you.

It is beyond the scope of this book to discuss all the things to look for when you are shopping for various kinds of insurance. What kind of insurance to get and how much of it you may need depend strictly upon your individual or family situation. *Shop around.* There are numerous good individual and group insurance plans available; there are some pretty bad ones available as well (and plenty of unscrupulous insurance agents willing to take your money from you).

Consider the AUSA and NCOA health and life insurance programs, as well as the Armed Forces Relief and Benefit Association and the Armed Forces Cooperative Insurance Association insurance programs for yourself and your family. The NCOA offers a full range of insurance coverages: auto, homeowner's/renter's, mortgage, life and health, CHAMPUS aid health insurance, and even a dental program.

And do not forget that while you are on active duty you have the Servicemen's Group Life Insurance (SGLI), which offers coverages in multiples of $5,000 up to a maximum of $100,000, for very low premiums. The maximum you will pay per month is $8, and that entitles you to $100,000 worth of coverage. And when you leave the service, your SGLI is convertible to Veterans Group Life Insurance (VGLI). Remember, however, that you can convert only the amount of SGLI in force at the time of your separation or retirement, and that your VGLI policy runs for only five years after discharge.

YOUR PERSONAL PROPERTY

Legal ownership of various forms of family property is a matter many people take for granted, and most states allow joint ownership of such investment properties as stocks, bonds, and real estate. But if you do not understand the law, legal complications in estate settlement can cause you or your heirs a lot of trouble.

While joint ownership can have certain advantages in establishing an automatic and known passage of ownership upon the death of one owner, it can also have certain disadvantages. For example, tax exemptions extended to servicemembers in some states may cover only that portion of the property held by the servicemembers or may not extend to the property at all, requiring payment of state or county taxes on the spouse's share or on the entire value. This is particularly true in the case of automobile personal property taxes required in some states.

Inquire into the applicable federal and state laws regarding ownership of family property, and take actions that put your estate in the most favorable ownership positions.

In the event of your death, your immediate personal effects will be forwarded at government expense to the person entitled to their custody. This does not give the recipient legal title to them, but they should be retained for disposition under the law. Try not to keep any books, letters, or photographs in your possession that if transmitted to your next of kin along with your other personal effects might cause them embarrassment or emotional upset.

If you own real estate in your name and it is not paid for, show on your personal affairs record whether there is a mortgage or a deed of trust against it, along with the name of the person or organization to whom you are indebted. Also include information about taxes and insurance on the property. Record the type and the cost of any permanent improvements. If you have mortgage insurance, record the number of your policy and its location and who is to be notified in case of your death.

Transfer of automobile ownership is sometimes complicated because of varying state laws. Remember that joint titling may make you or your spouse subject to personal property taxes—active duty personnel are generally exempt from payment of personal property taxes, so adding your spouse's name to an automobile title can cost you a lot of money.

INCOME TAXES

Military pay in general is subject to income tax. You do not pay tax on subsistence, quarters, and uniform allowances. Dislocation allowance, however, is taxable.

Any nonmilitary earnings, including the pay received while employed during off-duty hours (and this includes proceeds from gambling), and the income of any of your dependents are taxable.

Your military pay is excluded from federal income tax for service in any area that the President of the United States designates by Executive Order to be a combat zone. Vietnam was the last area so designated. Whenever this exclusion applies, all military pay received by enlisted personnel and warrant officers while on active duty in such a zone is excluded.

Effective with the enactment of Public Law 94-455 in 1976, soldiers who claim legal residence in states that have a personal income tax must pay their state taxes. Deductions from military pay are made automatically, just as they are for federal income taxes. The Soldiers' and Sailors' Civil Relief Act, however, assures that a state in which a soldier is stationed, but not the member's legal residence, cannot tax service pay. Legal residence is established when a soldier executes DD Form 2058, *State of Legal Residence Certificate.*

The following states do not withhold income tax from the pay of military personnel: Alaska, Connecticut, Florida, Illinois, Michigan, Montana, Nevada, New Hampshire, South Dakota, Tennessee, Texas, Vermont, Washington, and Wyoming. Soldiers claiming legal residence in foreign countries or U.S. territories are also exempt from paying state income taxes.

The following states do not require military personnel claiming them as their legal residence to pay income taxes *providing they are not stationed there:* California, Idaho, Missouri, New York, and West Virginia.

Appendix K, "State Tax Withholding," to AR 37-104-3 contains specific information relative to each state for which withholding tax applies, including computation rates for individual taxation.

PERSONAL CONDUCT

A noncommissioned officer's personal conduct should be above reproach at all times. This does not mean that a slip automatically spells disaster. Everyone deserves a second chance, if there is the possibility thereby of reform. Keep this in mind when your subordinates err. While there is no excuse for improper conduct by senior noncommissioned officers, you should never take it upon yourself to judge your fellow soldiers or establish yourself as an expert on morals and ethics.

Borrowing and Lending

> Neither a borrower, nor a lender be;
> For loan oft loses both itself and friend,
> And borrowing dulls the edge of husbandry.
>
> —William Shakespeare

	YOUR CHAIN OF COMMAND	PERSONNEL NCO OR OFFICER	RE-ENLISTMENT NCO	JUDGE ADVOCATE	INSPECTOR GENERAL	FINANCE OFFICER	CHAPLAIN	HOUSING OFFICER	TRANSPORTATION OFFICER	AMERICAN RED CROSS	ARMY COMMUNITY SERVICES	ARMY EMERGENCY RELIEF	EDUCATION OFFICER/ADVISOR
APPEALS	1	2		2	2		2						
ASSIGNMENT, REASSIGNMENT, MOS & PROFICIENCY PAY	1	1				2							
REENLISTMENT	1		1										
PERSONNEL MATTERS: PROMOTION, REDUCTION, DISCHARGE, RETIREMENT	1	1	2	2									
VETERANS' BENEFITS													
COMPLAINTS (REQUESTS FOR ASSISTANCE)	1	2	2	2	2	2	2	2	2	2	2	2	
DEBTS AND CIVILIAN CREDITORS	1	1		2		2	2				2		
DEPENDENTS' SCHOOLS	1	1									2		
FAMILY AND RELIGIOUS AFFAIRS	1	2					1			2	2		
TRAVEL OF DEPENDENTS, SHIPMENT OF POV AND HOUSEHOLD GOODS	1	2				2			1		2		
MEDICAL SERVICE (INDIVIDUAL & DEPENDENTS)	1	1											
PAY, ALLOWANCES AND INCENTIVE PAY	1	2				1							
LEAVES AND PASSES	1	2											
INSURANCE, ALL TYPES (SGLI & COMMERCIAL)	1	1				2							
LEGAL ASSISTANCE, INCLUDING U.S. AND FOREIGN LAW, WILLS AND POWERS OF ATTORNEY	1			1									
MILITARY EDUCATION	1	2	2										
NON-MILITARY EDUCATION	1	2											2
PX, COMMISSARY, QM SALES STORE	1				2								
GOVERNMENT QUARTERS, OFF POST HOUSING	1	2						1					
REGISTRATION/OPERATION OF PRIVATELY OWNED VEHICLE (POV), REGISTRATION OF FIREARMS	1												
ENTRY INTO USA, PASSPORT, VISA, NATURALIZATION, IMMIGRATION, BIRTH CERTIFICATE (Children born in foreign country)	1	2		1							2		
HOME CONDITIONS AND EMERGENCY LEAVE	1	2					2			2	2	2	
EMERGENCY FINANCIAL ASSISTANCE	1	2				1				2	2	2	
POSTAL SERVICE	1												
DRUG AND ALCOHOL REHABILITATION PROGRAM	1						2				1		

Guide for obtaining information and assistance. This chart shows some of the staff officers and support agencies who can help soldiers with advice and assistance in their personal affairs. In all cases, personnel should first contact the right person in their chain of command for guidance: immediate supervisors, squad leaders, first sergeants, or unit commanders. Number one (1) above indicates primary or key contacts; number two (2) indicates other contacts, as applicable. *Courtesy* Soldiers *Magazine*

Parents probably have quoted lines like those above to their children from time immemorial, but like all proverbs, this one is conditional.

If you are old-fashioned and thrifty and you pay cash or do without, you are to be commended. But if you should someday decide that you want credit to make some large purchase, without a good credit record you will have difficulty obtaining a loan. Having *no* credit record can count against you as heavily as a *bad* record.

Lending is bad business for a noncommissioned officer. Never lend money to other soldiers for interest. Be careful about lending money to *anyone* based only on a verbal agreement, no matter how much is involved. Of course, if a friend or coworker asks for a small sum occasionally, to tide him over on a heavy date or to buy lunch, give it to him if you can afford to. But never telegraph through the outfit that you are an "easy touch," because if you do, every freeloader in the unit will hit you up for small loans, which they will seldom repay. Young soldiers are particularly vulnerable to this sort of thing. Guard against it yourself and advise your subordinates to do the same. Be alert for soldiers who are habitual borrowers. They're heading for financial troubles, and if they are your subordinates, soon their troubles will be yours.

You can lose friends by lending them money. You can also lose them by *not* lending them money. If a friend is really in trouble and you can help with a big loan, then what are friends for? But have him back it up by signing a promissory note. This note is merely insurance against the unexpected, not an indication of distrust; his note will enable you to claim any unpaid debt against his estate, should he die. Never charge a friend interest on small loans, even if he or she offers to pay you some. If your friend cannot pay you back all at once, be sure to give him receipts for each payment he does make. This will help you both later on if there is any disagreement about how much has been paid and how much remains to be paid.

Gambling

Gambling is illegal in most places, and noncommissioned officers should *never* gamble with subordinates, no matter what the circumstances. The penny-ante poker game, however, is virtually an institution in the Army, and it is not at all uncommon for a group of NCOs to form poker clubs and have poker parties in quarters. When the stakes in these games are low, the participants are all known to each other, and the reason for having the games is merely to enjoy the excitement of playing in the company of good friends, play if you like and enjoy the occasions.

But when soldiers serve on unaccompanied tours in overseas areas, the "friendly" poker games sometimes take on a more businesslike aspect, and if you drop in on one expecting small stakes and friendly conversations, you are likely to be very disappointed.

Gambling can be as addictive and as ruinous to some people as alcohol and drugs are to others. When you acquire financial responsibility for other people—your family—they must always come first. Don't allow what can be an innocent and pleasant pastime to develop into a compulsion that will wreck your family. Never allow sharks—card, pool, loan, or otherwise—to operate in your unit.

Adultery

Adultery does occur in the Army, and it is not restricted to any particular rank. Perhaps this situation exists because married soldiers often must spend long periods of time away from their families. (We are concerned here with adultery committed by soldiers, not their nonmilitary spouses.) The best advice you can receive in regard to this subject and the best you can give someone else about it is this: *Don't do it.*

At some time in your career, though, if you marry while you are in the Army, you will find yourself on an unaccompanied tour, without your spouse. The temptations to err are particularly strong in some overseas areas where alcohol and sex are readily available, the idle hours are long, and diversions are few. Precisely how a person deals with this problem depends on the individual. Cold showers will not help, but perhaps the chaplain can. Keeping up an active correspondence with your spouse is a good way to maintain a link that will help you to endure long separations. Go easy on the booze. Enough alcohol will convert a saint into a lecher. Concentrate on your military duty, and cultivate your hobbies.

Should you succumb—and many good soldiers do—you will have to live with your indiscretion. You probably can manage it, providing adultery does not become a habit with you; it does with some. If you continue to do it, your spouse will find out eventually. Repeated unfaithfulness becomes general knowledge in a small, tightly knit military community. Your soldiers will lose respect for you, and some of them may try to use their knowledge as leverage to get you to give them special consideration. (This may not be blackmail in the legal sense, but that word is as good as any to describe it.) Your superiors will give you frosty looks and dirty details, and eventually someone in the chain of command will tell you to straighten up, or else. And some dark night, the aggrieved spouse may teach you a lesson that you never wanted to learn.

Adultery hurts everyone—you, your partner, everyone. But adultery is particularly hard on the innocent parties, betrayed wives and husbands, friends, parents, and especially children.

A single person who enters into an adulterous relationship with a married man or woman is not much better off than the married person who is unfaithful. The single person's career (and life) can be as easily ruined by adultery as that of a married person.

Lying

Society would crumble if it were not for the accepted social lie—telling people that you are feeling fine when you do not—because we all know that nobody wants to listen to someone else's personal problems. And nobody in his right mind tells everyone just exactly what he thinks of them. Military life is no different from civilian life in this regard, and soldiers bite their tongues and force their faces into smiles just as often as civilians. The covering up of emotions and strong personal opinions is not lying in the strict sense of the word. But falsifying reports is.

Never lie to cover up mistakes, whether yours or those of your subordinates. Lying to a superior is conduct that may very well lead to your undoing. Once a superior loses faith in you because of a lie discovered, no matter how small that lie may be, you may never be able to recover that confidence. And once you get away with a lie, it sometimes becomes necessary to tell more and more of them to cover up the initial one, until you create a tissue of lies that sooner or later will tear and expose the truth.

Indebtedness

Our whole economy depends on personal indebtedness, and most of us are always in debt for something: homes, cars, credit card services, and so on. As a noncommissioned officer, you will, from time to time, counsel your soldiers on their indebtedness, and if you are a good leader, you will help them overcome a vicious cycle.

The good NCO pays his debts. Keep tight control on your own budget, and do not allow yourself to fall behind on your credit payments. This will require restraint and self-denial at times, but you are a member of a profession where those qualities are developed early. Just carry them over into your personal financial situation. A letter of indebtedness from a creditor will certainly harm your career, as well as damage your reputation in the business world and make it harder for you to get credit when you really need it.

Self-Perception

You are what you think you are. Much of what you think you are is based upon what others tell you you are. Thus, the Corps of Noncommissioned Officers *is* what NCOs *think* it is.

Sergeants have never been exactly humble. Captain Francis Grose "advised" the sergeants of the British Army of 1782: "Into whatever company you are admitted, you must be careful to impress everyone with an idea of your own consequence, and to make people believe, that the sergeants are the only useful and intelligent men in the corps." Captain Grose was actually satirizing the attitude he found prevalent among some of the British NCOs of his day. Captain Grose's sergeants were in the habit of inflating their egos and boosting their sense of self-importance by bragging about how indispensible they were. These men, and those who think like them today, are right, but for the wrong reasons.

NCOs have always been important people. You share a vital quality with the NCOs of the Roman legions—called, appropriately enough, "principales"—in that they also were professionals doing important work and doing it well. They were rightfully proud of themselves and the role they played in making the Roman army a superb fighting machine.

In units in which the noncommissioned officers are highly motivated, mission-oriented, and supportive of one another, things *click*. In units in which the NCOs are interested only in themselves, officers' careers get ruined, young soldiers quit the Army in disgust, and things go *clunk*. May you always serve in units that click, but should you have the misfortune to be assigned to one in which they clunk, *turn things around*. Don't wait for the officers to catch on, clue them in. And so for your fellow NCOs, tell them, *follow me!*

One person on his own can accomplish little, if that is what he thinks. If soldiers in wartime stopped to think how insignificant they were, no battles could ever be won. If you need occasional reassurance about this, pick up any citation for the award of the Medal of Honor and read it. The U.S. Army is brimming with heroes, and you are one of them. You are a hero because you rise to the occasion and you do what has to be done. You do not hem and haw and try to find ways to get out of doing things. You do not look back. You take the consequences as they come, and you get the job done.

Without you, there could be no Army. The quality of the Army depends on you. Never let there be any mistake that you are the finest.

DECIDING WHERE TO LIVE

Generally, if you are married, you have an option to decide whether you want to live on post or off. Depending upon the unit to which you are assigned, as well as some

Personal Affairs

other factors, even single soldiers sometimes have a choice between living in the troop billets or renting accommodations off post.

If you are assigned to an area where cost-of-living allowances and station housing allowances are authorized, you may find it to your advantage to forego taking occupancy of government quarters and move into rental housing off the post. In some instances, especially if your spouse is working, you may come out ahead on your budget if you take all your allowances and rent an apartment or a house.

If you decide to rent, check your lease very carefully, and never rent anywhere until you have checked with the local housing referral office first. Some renters offer leases with a clause stating that, if you must break your lease before it expires because of receipt of reassignment orders, you will not have to forfeit your security deposit; others do not. Be sure you understand this qualification before you sign. It's too late afterward.

Military families sometimes rent local housing while waiting for government quarters to become available. If you should ever find yourself in that position, you might want to consider renting an apartment on a month-by-month basis. Should you sign a lease for a specified period of time and then have to break it because a set of quarters unexpectedly becomes available, you may have to forfeit your deposit (usually an amount equal to a month's rent).

In some states, landlords are required to pay tenants interest on security deposits. But if you damage the landlord's property in any way, your deposit can be withheld to pay for repairs.

Renting an apartment gives to the single soldier a degree of independence and privacy that is not available in the barracks, and for this reason, many soldiers want to move off post.

Whether a single soldier can move off post depends on several things:

• Your company commander's policy. It is strictly up to the commanding officer of your unit whether you can move off post. Some commanders are very liberal in granting this privilege; it depends upon your unit's mission. You will find that commanders of headquarters and garrison-type units can be more liberal than those of tactical or combat support units.

• The amount and quality of troop housing available. Some small, specialized units have trouble finding adequate troop housing, especially at overcrowded installations in metropolitan areas where expansion for new housing is limited. On posts where there is sufficient troop housing available, however, commanders sometimes prefer to fill the billets up first before allowing lower-ranking single personnel to move off post.

• Nonabuse of the privilege. Should you be authorized to make the move, your commander will revoke your permission to live off post as soon as you start coming to work late, running up debts, or causing disturbances among the local population.

Be sure that you can afford to live off post. Your military pay combined with your housing and subsistence allowances may be enough, depending on the geographical area, but just enough and no more. If supporting yourself in an apartment leaves you flat broke at the end of the month, you are better off living in the barracks. Remember that setting up housekeeping requires linen, dinnerware, and a host of tiny expenses that you never think about when all these things are provided to you by the government. It is possible to go in debt just setting up an apartment.

Some soldiers find it a good idea to team up with two or three friends and rent a place by splitting all the costs. This is an excellent idea if your companions can be trusted to pay their share, take care of the communal areas, and respect your privacy and personal property. If you pick the wrong person as an apartment or house mate, however, you will lose all the benefits of independent living, so be very careful.

Another thing to consider is transportation. You will be required to show up for work, and you must be available anytime in case of military emergency. Therefore, you should own a car, or your partner should (and if your partner has the car and gets transferred, you are in a bind). Access to public transportation should be a consideration in choosing where to move.

ARMY COMMUNITY SERVICES (ACS) AND ARMY EMERGENCY RELIEF (AER)

The ACS is an official Department of the Army organization established to provide information, aid, guidance, and referral services to military personnel and their families. ACS activities are monitored by the Army Adjutant General.

The ACS provides a wide variety of services:
- Referrals for handicapped dependents.
- Family counseling services.
- Financial planning services.
- Lending services to provide bedding, linen, and housewares to military families until they can get settled at a new post.
- Volunteer services providing transportation to dependents when required.
- Child abuse information and referral.
- An emergency food locker from which families may draw food supplies when particularly destitute.

The Army Emergency Relief operates as a part of the Army Community Services. AER provides badly needed financial assistance in the form of cash loans to soldiers and their dependents. A local AER officer can authorize interest-free cash loans of up to $750 on his own authority. Loans of up to $1,000 can be authorized telephonically by the command deputy chief of staff for personnel, but loans in excess of $1,000 must be approved by Headquarters, AER.

AER loans may be approved for the following purposes.
- Defray living expenses because of nonreceipt of military pay (debt relief loan).
- Defray travel expenses.
- Help pay rents, security deposits, and utilities (debt relief loan).
- Help pay "essential POV expenses" (in cases in which a soldier must have a car to transport a chronically ill or handicapped dependent to a remote medical facility, as an example).
- Pay funeral expenses above and beyond those allowed by the government.
- Pay grants to the widows and orphans of deceased service personnel, in some cases.
- Provide cash for food when it is not available from the ACS food locker.
- Provide money to help defray emergency travel expenses.
- Provide money to replace lost funds (such as when a family loses cash while in transit).

Soldiers must apply for AER loans through their unit commanders by filling out DA Form 1103, Application for AER Financial Assistance. The soldier must document his or her expenses or financial situation (AER officials will verify this information independently, however), and an allotment must be executed before the AER will disburse any money. Although each soldier's commanding officer recommends approval or disapproval on each application, final approving authority resides with the AER officer. Requests for assistance must originate with the soldier's unit commander because this way the personal financial troubles of individual soldiers are identified and the commander is then able to monitor these problems and assist the soldier in solving them.

Each year, the AER disburses millions of dollars to help soldiers and their families. The only source for these funds is cash donations by individuals solicited annually during Army-wide fund-raising drives. Contribute generously because AER is one of the best examples of how the Army takes care of its own.

THE ARMY FAMILY ACTION PLAN

The Army has come a long way from the days, and not too long ago at that, when its attitude toward its families was summed up in an old adage: "If the Army wanted you to have a wife, you'd have been issued one." Today, more than half the active Army force is married. This figure breaks down into nearly 30 percent of the Army's first-term soldiers and nearly 80 percent of its career enlisted leaders.

Since Vietnam, and especially in the past few years, the Army's leaders have come to realize a greater responsibility to Army families. A new philosophy was specified by former Army Chief of Staff, General John A. Wickham, Jr., on 15 August 1983.

> A partnership exists between the Army and Army families. The Army's unique missions, concept of service and lifestyle of its members—all affect the nature of this partnership. Towards the goal of building a strong partnership, the Army remains committed to assuring adequate support to families in order to promote wellness; to develop a sense of community; and to strengthen the mutually reinforcing bonds between the Army and its families.

So was born the Family Action Plan (AFAP). The current plan includes more than 100 issues grouped into four major themes: relocation, medical, family support and role identity, and education and youth. The specific problem areas range from development of videos for overseas orientation programs, developing family member support groups at installations and units, and attempting to correct medical staff shortages, to providing English-as-a-second language instruction for family members whose native language is other than English.

As an NCO, whether or not you now have a family or plan to have one, your understanding and full support of the Army Family Action Plan is essential to its success. As former Sergeant Major of the Army Julius W. Gates said, one purpose of the AFAP is to give good soldiers a reason to stay in the Army. "Our rockets can't fly, our tanks can't fire without our most precious resource—our soldiers. We have to give them a reason to stay. We have to treat them with dignity and respect," he said.

Following are brief definitions of the critical elements of the plan's philosophy. Read them carefully and remember, their applications are much more far-reaching than to just the Army Family Action Plan itself—they are essential ingredients to the cohesion that makes an institution like the Army work.

Partnership. Partnership has to exist between the Army as an institution and the individuals who are part of it: soldiers, civilians, and family members. Partnership is a cohesion of the Army and family members based on mutual understanding of the mission and commitment to each other. It is a reciprocal relationship, based on moral and ethical responsibilities and statutory and regulatory requirements. Partnership between its members makes the Army an institution, not just a job or a workplace.

Wellness. Wellness is the concern for developing those strengths, skills, aptitudes, and attitudes that contribute to the wholeness and health in body, mind, and spirit. Wellness is achieved by concentrating now, and in the future, on what is working well and by drawing on the characteristics of the Army's many healthy families and transmitting those characteristics to the people who need assistance.

Sense of community. Sense of community is the center of the partnership with all members offered the challenge and opportunity to work together for the common good. It means each member of the Army community has a special responsibility to make the institution a better place in which to live and work.

Partnership, wellness, sense of community—all are important to military community residents and officials. The following are a few of the many examples that illustrate the value of the AFAP.

• In 1988, child care was among the top five AFAP priorities, at a time when nearly half of all Army spouses worked outside the home. Quality child care is still a top priority to the increasing numbers of spouses who work. In 1989 and 1990, AFAP initiatives brought about increased appropriated fund support for child care, fees for child care based on family income, better trained and higher paid care givers and more of them, parent advisory boards, and an ongoing five-year study of the demand for child care.

• Since relocation assistance and sponsorship are paramount, AFAP helped get increased allowances for transportation of household goods, especially for junior enlisted soldiers. In April 1990 an automated relocation assistance system began providing housing and other relocation information about areas in the United States and abroad.

• Because of the AFAP, reservists got a break in commissaries. Instead of being able to shop only when on active duty, they now may shop during a specified number of days during the year.

Since the first AFAP conference was held in 1983, more than 20 laws have been passed or amended to resolve more than 100 quality-of-life issues for the Army family. The 11th annual conference is scheduled for 1993.

7

Contemporary Problems

> As the soldiers of today are representative of the society from whence they come, they are also reflective of its ills—the educational short-comings, the expanding drug culture, the throw-away world, the buy-now-pay-later-live-in-debt economy—and they present motivational challenges which were not common only a few years ago.
>
> Former SMA William A. Connelly,
> USASMA Keynote Address, 12 June 1978

Today the Army is under much external scrutiny and criticism over whether the volunteer system is working. Everyone with an opinion seems convinced one way or the other, and it is difficult even for soldiers to know which view is right. The quality of the modern volunteer soldier is seen by many as directly related to the incidence of drug abuse and racial tension in the Army, and the higher the statistics are in these areas, the louder the Army's critics claim that the volunteer soldier emanates from the dregs of American society.

As a noncommissioned officer, you must be aware of these problems and know how to deal with them. The lives of your soldiers may very well depend upon how well you handle substance abuse and instances of racial or sexual discrimination among your subordinates. Ultimately, your success or failure in coping with these issues rests on how sincere you are in your desire to be a *good* noncommissioned officer. The good NCO, the good soldier, backs up or stands beside his or her comrades, regardless of the color of their skin, their sex, or their ethnic background.

COUNSELING

One of the best ways to help others is to learn the basics of counseling techniques. Counseling is the art of communicating with the intention of influencing a person's attitude or behavior. It may be conducted either formally or informally almost anywhere, but is usually conducted in private. The topics can range widely from family or financial problems to deciding on additional schooling.

The first step toward being a good counselor is to be available. This means much more than merely establishing an "open door" policy and then sitting back and waiting for the soldiers to flock into your office. A good leader is available whenever a soldier requires assistance.

When counseling, you should do three things.

• Provide encouragement and support for change in the person being counseled.

• Provide information in the form of knowledge and sources of knowledge that will help the soldier improve.

• Play a reinforcing role or an evaluating role in that you reinforce the soldier's expressions of feelings or present ideas that will tend to help improve performance or solve problems. (Guide discussion away from ideas that are not related to the problem at hand.)

You must be observant, able to communicate, and flexible in your use of counseling techniques. You should be able to see the person you are counseling, as well as listen to him, because observation of the soldier's actions during the course of the counseling session will tell you whether the individual understands what you are saying and whether he or she accepts what you are saying. If a soldier with a problem calls you at home (or from home), do what you can over the telephone, but set up a face-to-face counseling session at the earliest possible time if you have any doubt that your long-distance counseling is having the desired effect.

You must express yourself clearly and concisely, and you must address the problems under discussion directly. Speak in terms that the soldier can understand. Listen to what the soldier is telling you. The soldier has come to see you to discuss his or her personal problem, *not yours*. And even if you have had a similar problem and you handled it well, your solution may not work for another person.

Be specific when you counsel, especially when you counsel soldiers on their performance. Counseling for good performance is an excellent way to motivate your soldiers. But when you must counsel poor performers, zero in on specific examples of what they are doing that is wrong. If they have positive performance points, use them to motivate the individuals to improve their weak points.

Remember this: Many soldiers who wind up involuntarily separated from the service or punished under the UCMJ might have been saved if only their direct supervisors had taken the time to listen to their problems and tried to help them.

Types of Counseling

FM 22-101, *Military Counseling*, identifies five basic types of counseling that leaders will perform in the course of their duties. Each type of counseling requires a different approach—directive, nondirective, or a combination—to effectively address the needs of the individual being counseled.

• Reception and integration counseling helps acquaint soldiers with their new assignments and informs them of the unit standards. So that a soldier knows what to expect from his new assignment, this counseling must begin as soon as possible after

Contemporary Problems 129

An NCO inspects a recruit. *U.S. Army photo*

a soldier's assignment. Formal orientations, sponsors, and in-processing assistance are integral parts of reception and integration counseling.

• Performance counseling assists in improving the job performance of an individual or a unit. It can also be used to maintain a level of performance that already exists.

• Personal counseling is designed to help soldiers solve their personal problems. These problems include anything that threatens an individual soldier's well-being. In personal counseling, it is essential to stress that the soldier must solve the problem himself and that you will assist by helping him or her recognize the source of the problem and develop a strategy for dealing with it. Then it is important to encourage the soldier to implement his strategy. A good leader will not attempt to handle a soldier's serious personal problems alone. Professional counselors are available to help. *A good leader recognizes his or her own limitations.*

• Disciplinary counseling is necessitated by failure of an individual to follow established regulations, policies, or procedures.

• Professional growth and guidance counseling deals with such issues as reenlistment, career development, professional development, and educational goals.

Recognizing Soldiers with Problems

Some people are very reluctant to turn to others and seek advice or help. Therefore, you must know your soldiers well enough to recognize when they may need

assistance. Here are some of the more common signals.
- A good performer begins to turn in work consistently below standards.
- A normally attentive person suddenly begins to display a lack of care and concentration in his or her work.
- A soldier begins to drink heavily.
- An individual becomes involved in deliberate acts of misconduct or refuses to follow instructions.
- A soldier lingers after a meeting to talk, posing such leading questions as, "What if a person has a problem?" or, "I have this friend who has a problem."
- A person who normally gets along well with others begins to display aggressive, uncooperative conduct with his or her co-workers.
- A person begins to borrow money from others (especially if the sums are not repaid promptly).
- A soldier displays any sudden, drastic change of personality, as when a normally happy, enthusiastic person turns moody and uncommunicative.

Preparing for the Counseling Session

When preparing for an interview, you should consider advance notification, allotment of time, your plan of action for the conduct of the interview, the physical setting, and the general atmosphere.

Although it will not always work out this way, try to notify the soldier in advance of the time for the interview. This will give the individual time to think about the problem and to be prepared to discuss it with you. Allow sufficient time for the interview so that neither of you will feel rushed.

Conduct the interview in private and try to select an area that is comfortable physically and will not be subjected to disturbing distractions, such as people passing by, ringing telephones, other conversations, or equipment noises. But privacy is absolutely essential. A counseling interview must always be conducted in an atmosphere of strict confidentiality.

Conducting the Interview

The opening few minutes are the most critical phase of the counseling interview because it is during this time that the stage is set and the atmosphere created for the rest of the session. Accordingly, establish an easy relationship with the soldier at the very beginning. If you detect tension, try to relieve it by demonstrating to the individual that he or she is accepted in your presence, that you consider his or her views important, and that you are not forcing the individual to discuss them with you. Explain the reason for the interview at once, and draw the soldier into the discussion as soon as possible.

Try to guide the conversation as inconspicuously as possible. Brief questions are sometimes helpful in drawing the individual back to the topic under discussion. But sometimes it is necessary to let the soldier talk on for a while to get things out in the open and build confidence. When the person being interviewed begins to repeat himself or babble, bring the conversation back on to course.

Do not allow emotional displays to dissuade you from your objective, especially if it is to encourage self-improvement in the individual. If tears begin to flow, offer him (men sometimes cry under emotional stress) or her a tissue and proceed with the interview.

Contemporary Problems

Allowing a person to express pent up emotions sometimes solves most of the problem right away.

Give the individual a means of "saving face." Do not push the person into a position from which there is no retreat without embarrassment. As assault upon the individual's personal integrity, for instance, drastically reduces motivation. And under no circumstances should you allow yourself to be trapped into an argument with the person you are counseling.

The questions you ask during counseling sessions should be adapted to the purpose of the sessions: No set of questions will do for every kind of interview. The questions of Who, What, Where, When, Why are very valuable because they fit many situations. Questions that elicit "yes-no" responses should be used sparingly and be followed up with other questions designed to get more detailed and useful information from the person you are interviewing.

The influence you use to motivate a soldier may take many forms, and during a counseling session, you may find it necessary to use all of them: mapping alternatives, recommending, advising, persuading, urging, commanding, and even threatening.

When it is apparent that the purpose of the interview has been accomplished, end it, and dismiss the soldier in as graceful a manner as you can. Terminate the interview when all points have been covered and the individual has had ample time to understand, but no session should last more than an hour. If there is a need for further counseling, schedule it for another time. Remember, little can be accomplished if you are both exhausted.

If you are required to take any further official action after the interview is closed, such as submit a report to a higher authority, be sure to tell the interviewee. In every case, follow up on the counseling to make sure that the problem really has been solved.

SEXUAL DISCRIMINATION

> . . . our force will be weakened if one class of soldiers attempts to give special protection to another class. The female driver of the truck must deliver the ammunition to the guns. The female mechanic must go to the broken vehicle. The female medic must go to the wounded soldier.
>
> Former SMA William A. Connelly, "Women in the Army"

No matter what your opinion may be concerning whether women should serve in combat MOSs, whether they should be allowed to have children on active duty, or whether they will make good leaders, the fact is that women are just as intelligent and just as brave as men. Those are the two basic prerequisites for being a soldier, and with the proper training and motivation, brave and intelligent people do become good soldiers.

People continue the debate about whether women can function in combat, but current Army policy is to exclude women from serving in combat arms MOSs. So unless or until that policy changes, discussions about women as infantry soldiers are pointless. Similarly, to say that one wants to see the role of women in the Army curtailed because one does not wish to see them killed in war is also moot. It should be horrible to think of *anyone* being killed in war. But should war come tomorrow, many, many female soldiers could die along with their male comrades, and should war ever reach our own shores, American men, women *and* children will die indiscriminately.

Your duty as a noncommissioned officer is not to die in combat, but to stay alive in combat and help to win. To do this, you must use the people at your disposal, and some of them will be women soldiers. Train your soldiers well and lead them well and they will not let you down.

The Female NCO

For a woman to be a noncommissioned officer in the Army requires an extra measure of moral courage, self-reliance, and personal confidence. No woman who aspires to wear a noncommissioned officer's chevrons should think that because the Army's leadership favors the integration of women into the total Army force that her progression up through the ranks will be easy. It will not be. To succeed, the Army woman must have the patience of Job and the wisdom of Solomon.

Some males do not want women around because they do not understand them. Some men feel vaguely threatened by women who are clearly their equals, or by women who presume to be. Underneath their tough exteriors, many men have very delicate egos that bruise easily. While most do not like to be outdone by other men, it is even harder for some to have their weaknesses revealed before women. If a man happens to be outshot by a female soldier on the rifle range, or if he falls out of a run while a woman keeps up the pace, his male comrades may not let him forget it (his discomfort, after all, helps them overcome their own self-doubts).

The aim of the female NCO is to be a good soldier and derive her sense of self-fulfillment from rendering honorable and faithful service to her country. She should always strive to be the best at what she does, but she should never do less than she knows she can for fear of bruising some man's ego. Those she works with will expect her to carry her own weight, and when she leads men, they will expect her to be capable of making decisions for them and carrying her full share of responsibility.

In the crucible of shared hardship and danger, social conventions and prejudices have a tendency to boil away, and what is left behind is a relationship between the members of a unit that goes deeper than friendship, and it includes men as well as women.

Heretofore, this phenomenon has been most closely observed in exclusively male institutions—such as small infantry units in combat—but it is as real in mixed peacetime military units as it is among male line units in war. This bonding or "fellow feeling" grows up among any group of people who work well together. It is a basic ingredient of what in the military is called *esprit*, and it makes you feel proud of yourself, your companions, and your unit. You do not have to be shot at to appreciate it, and sex has absolutely nothing to do with it.

Sometimes the female NCO's job is made even tougher because when picked for a responsible position she is often in the spotlight. If a woman fails, men who are looking for evidence that women cannot "make it" in the Army will say, "See! I always knew women don't have what it takes!" And when a woman succeeds spectacularly in a difficult position, those same men will shrug her off as an "exception."

You cannot win with some people, and it is not worth the effort to try. Always put your mission first, your troops' welfare second, and yourself last. And remember that even the best teams sometimes lose. Do not worry about what people will think if you make a mistake. If you fail, learn from it and start again. Troops get to know who the good leaders are very quickly, and if you qualify, your troops will be loyal to you through thick and thin.

And many men who in theory resist the idea of women in the Army change their minds very quickly once they serve with them, much the same way our prejudices regarding people of other cultures dispel when we get to know them better.

The good leader looks at his or her troops as soldiers, not as blacks or whites, men or women. He or she knows that some soldiers do better at certain tasks than others, some are stronger than others, some more intelligent. The good leader capitalizes on the strong points of each soldier according to his or her abilities and talents.

Also understand that as a woman yourself, you can probably see right through other women who use their sex to their own advantage. You will probably be far less susceptible to staged tears and vague complaints than most men are. It will not take you very long at all to find out which women in your new outfit are like that. Counsel them with firmness and understanding. Many female soldiers will confide things to you that they never would to a man, so be very careful never to betray a confidence.

You will probably meet people who have the idea that a woman would only go into the Army to get a husband or because she is "strange." Some soldiers' wives are very uneasy with the thought of their husbands spending a lot of time with other women under primitive field conditions, and the uneasiness is compounded if these wives view Army women as a crowd of man-hungry females. Some people will ask you why you are in the Army in the first place, and even if they spare you the insult of saying so outright, you can be sure that some (but not all, by any means) think you are too incompetent to "get a man" in civilian life. Tell those people that you love your country as much as any man and that you believe you are just as able to serve your country. Tell them that if they think they are good enough, they might be able to enlist.

In short, the qualities of a good NCO apply equally to women as to men. Learn the principles and adopt the qualities as your own, and your troops will be proud to call you "Sergeant."

Fraternization

To fraternize, according to Webster's, is "to associate in a brotherly manner; be on friendly terms." What the Army means by the word is any improper relationship between persons of different ranks; it is improper if it meets one of the following criteria.

- Causes actual or perceived partiality or favoritism.
- Involves the improper use of rank or position for personal gain.
- Would have a clearly predictable, adverse impact on discipline, authority, or morale.

Usually, fraternization is thought of as occurring between officers of different ranks and enlisted personnel. Under Article 134 of the Uniform Code of Military Justice, if an officer or warrant officer's fraternizing meets any of the elements of proof listed there, criminal charges may be brought to bear. When a soldier has direct command or supervisory authority over others or has the capability to influence personnel or disciplinary actions, assignments, or other benefits or privileges, the superior must exercise the utmost restraint in social, commercial, or duty relationships with lower-ranking persons.

The main example of an improper relationship is the sexual one. NCOs simply should not have sexual affairs with lower-ranking soldiers, period. If you do, expect the trouble you deserve for committing such a willful and stupid act. Falling in love is different. If that happens, get married and get transferred, or one of you get out of the Army.

Another example of improper fraternization is the NCO who likes to have the troops come over to his quarters or his home for drinks and then allows those troops to act familiarly with him on the job.

There are other examples—the communications center shift supervisor who, for whatever reason, extends to a subordinate privileges that are excluded from others; the sergeant major who runs a business off post and uses his position to solicit customers among the troops—but the thing to remember about any relationship with subordinates is, if it's undignified or clouds your judgment, get out of it, fast.

One final thought on this topic: Generally what people perceive is what they believe. If you give anyone any reason whatsoever to doubt your intentions, no matter how innocent you may be, they will think the worst of you. So if you are the type who clowns around with young ladies or young men and you have to call one of them into your office for a little closed-door counseling, what do you think the troops will say is going on behind those doors?

Sexual Harassment

Two feature articles about sexual harassment were published in recent years in *Soldiers* magazine, one in November 1988, the other in May 1992. Each added the balance necessary to make all readers—male and female NCOs, officers, junior enlisted soldiers, and Army civilians—understand that sexual harassment is counterproductive: That is, it impairs Army members' ability to work professionally and contribute to the Army mission.

Sexual harassment, whether committed by a male (70 percent of the cases, according to one report) or by a female (the other 30 percent, according to the same report), often is judged as criminal conduct. Offenders may be severely punished and see their Army careers ruined. To help you avoid offending or being victimized, here condensed, edited, and reprinted with permission, is official Army policy as published in *Soldiers* magazine.

> You know the story. A supervisor says you'll get that promotion if you promise to rendezvous for a drink—and more. Or a co-worker brushes by you time and again. Or you endure off-color comments said just loud enough for you to hear, or suggestive leers, and on and on. Meanwhile, all you want is to be left alone to do your job.
>
> You're not alone. The Army leadership wants you to be able to do your job, too. Every day, someone in the Army is getting counseled, reprimanded, or court-martialed for sexual harassment. Just ask the sergeant first class who says he was only joking around with a couple of his female soldiers in Saudi Arabia. Although he had 17 years of exemplary service, his behavior during Operations Desert Shield and Desert Storm earned him a reduction to private and a bad conduct discharge (BCD).
>
> "To the Army, sexual harassment is unacceptable behavior," said retired LTC James M. Murphy, formerly the chief of the Army's Equal Opportunity Branch in the Office of the Deputy Chief of Staff for Personnel. "It's a violation of our professional ethic. Gender should not be an issue. A soldier is a soldier (an Army civilian is an Army civilian), and we expect peers, subordinates, and superiors to recognize the contributions of that soldier (or Army civilian) to the nation's defense and readiness."
>
> In spite of Army policy and training, some soldiers and civilian workers disregard the rights of others to a workplace free of sexual harassment. Some harassers are blatant and criminal, such as the Army civilian manager at the Pentagon who was convicted in 1987 of promising a young employee a promotion in exchange for sexual favors. The more common form of sexual harassment, though, is more subtle—unwelcome comments, gestures, and physical contact. These types of "socializing" become sexual harassment when unwel-

come, when repeated, when deliberate, and when considered offensive to the victim.

A victim should first talk to the person doing the harassing and explain that the behavior is offensive and should not be repeated. If the behavior continues, report it. "If a male soldier asks a female soldier who's his peer to go out on a date, that's not sexual harassment. It's how he goes about it," said MAJ Roy Plumer, who in 1992 worked in the Leadership Division of the Army PERSCOM's Human Relations Directorate.

Here's one more example. In 1991, a staff sergeant at Fort Leonard Wood, Missouri, decided to stray from his peer group while serving as an instructor at that post. He sought sexual favors from five female trainees over a one-month period during their advanced individual training. Before his arrest, one of the women took him up on his offer. The brief affair and his string of propositions proved costly. At his court-martial, he was hit with a BCD, reduced to private, and sentenced to three months' confinement. His case was under review in 1992.

The Fort Leonard Wood staff sergeant wasn't charged with sexual harassment because such an infraction isn't listed in the Uniform Code of Military Justice. Instead, he was hit with seven counts of violating Article 92 of the UCMJ, "Personal Relations." He failed to obey a general order prohibiting permanent party soldiers on post from nonprofessional social relationships with trainees. Other common UCMJ violations (and the penalties) associated with sexual harassment are indecent assault (five years, dishonorable discharge), indecent language (six months, BCD), and cruelty or maltreatment (one year, dishonorable discharge). If either party is married, tack on adultery (one year, dishonorable discharge).

A sexual harassment victim may go through his or her chain of command (or civilian supervisor or more senior supervisor), local equal opportunity advisor, the chaplain, provost marshal, judge advocate general, and the inspector general. Sexual harassment falls under the Army's equal opportunity program, outlined in AR 600-20. Unit leaders have a continuing requirement to place equal opportunity classes on their training schedules. If everyone in the unit knows the deal, it can be quickly recognized and dealt with.

Such a policy might have helped the NCO in Saudi Arabia. According to court records, the NCO testified that a few weeks after he was sent to Saudi Arabia, he received letters from members of his section who had not yet deployed. One, he claimed, was sexual in nature. When the writer arrived, several disputed incidents of intimate touching occurred between them. Despite other aspects of the case and conflicting testimony, the NCO compromised himself.

Soldiers and civilians need to avoid senior-subordinate personal social relationships. They also need to take a look at how they perceive and treat others. Sexual harassment is learned behavior. And all soldiers can learn to treat others fairly—without regard to their sex.

RACIAL PREJUDICE

Of all the social problems that beset the Army today, racial prejudice is the most serious because it can destroy a unit's combat effectiveness. Therefore, the Defense Equal Opportunity Management Institute was established at Patrick Air Force Base, Florida. Graduates of the institute are trained to assist commanders in increasing unit effectiveness and efficiency through improved racial harmony and equal opportunity. These personnel are available to conduct race relations seminars and assist commanders and senior NCOs in averting potentially dangerous racial confrontations in their units. This training can be effective, and you should use their expertise.

But you cannot afford to call in an equal opportunity counselor to calm things down when a distraught soldier calls someone "nigger" or "honky bastard" in the barracks. Those soldiers are not going to take their problem to the counselor. They are going to settle it right then and there, and *you* will have a riot on your hands that might require the presence of the military police.

Racial discrimination is based on fear and misunderstanding, and the most effective way to counter it is through open communications. This does not necessarily mean that close contact between persons of different racial or ethnic backgrounds will dispel tension; sometimes, just the opposite happens. Racial or ethnic identity is very important to minority groups, and any action seen as an attempt to undermine this identity will meet resistance. Acceptance of one another rather than brotherly love is probably the best relationship you can achieve under most circumstances.

Find out for yourself what is going on among the troops. Do not call in Sergeant Washington or Sergeant Smedley or Sergeant Garcia for a briefing on what blacks, whites, or Hispanics in your outfit are doing, and don't send those NCOs out to be your ethnic point men. Talk to your people yourself, as individuals and in groups, formally and informally.

Not only must you be fair and impartial in your leadership decisions, but also you must be *obviously* fair and impartial; your soldiers must know why you are letting A do this and not B. The fairness and impartiality of your judgments and decisions is a critical ingredient in your effectiveness as a communicator. Frequently, your soldiers do not have the same facts you do, so they cannot see your decisions as clearly and objectively as you can.

Here are some rules derived from lessons learned through past successes and failures in the area of race relations.

• If you think you do not have racial tension in your unit, you are probably wrong. The potential for racial trouble exists in every unit.

• Get out and go among your troops, and find out for yourself what they are thinking.

• Make use of human relations seminars and equal opportunity counselors in your unit training program.

• Make programs and literature outlining the history and culture of minority groups available to all the personnel in your unit. Education is one of the best means of alleviating racial tensions.

• Never ignore a soldier's grievance. An imagined problem can undermine a soldier's morale just as effectively as a real one. Keep the soldier informed of the progress of his or her complaint.

• Squash rumors and misinterpretations *at once*. Better still, be open in your judgments and decisions so that everyone will know at the outset what the truth of any situation really is.

• Exercise fairness and impartiality at all times.

• Avoid using only minority leaders to deal with tensions between groups. They may be able to give you good advice, but nothing can substitute for your personal involvement in the problems that affect your subordinates.

• Try to ensure that recreational facilities are available to all minority groups. Wherever possible, try to integrate social activities as much as possible.

• You are going to encounter racially prejudiced soldiers no matter how hard you try to convince everyone that they should live together in harmony. Be open-minded and patient with these people, and listen to their opinions carefully. You may not be able to convince them to abandon their attitudes, but you *must* make them accept the rights of others. You first must get their confidence.

• The barracks are the most common breeding grounds for racial tensions. Ensure that there is adequate NCO supervision in the unit area at night. Work closely with your first sergeant on this and if you are a first sergeant, go out of your way to solicit the

Contemporary Problems

help and cooperation of your NCOs. The very presence of a senior noncommissioned officer in the company area after duty hours helps to dispel tensions.
• The 12th rule is to remember and practice the other 11.

SUBSTANCE ABUSE

As a noncommissioned leader, you will, at some time in your service, encounter persons who are dependent on or are abusers of alcohol and other drugs.* The harm done to soldiers and to the Army by the nonmedical use of alcohol and other drugs and the human misery caused by substance abuse are incalculable. The Army Alcohol and Drug Abuse Prevention and Control Program (ADAPCP) is a vigorous and effective program designed to prevent substance abuse, identify the abuser as early as possible, and restore him to duty. To be an effective leader, you must be aware of this program and support its objectives.

The beneficial effects of this program can be seen from the following statistics. In 1976, the Army estimated the cost avoidance to the Army of the successful rehabilitation of substance abusers was $72 million over the alternative of simply discharging them. In 1981, the cost avoidance was $111.3 million; in 1982, $111.4 million; and in 1983, $212.2 million. This is based on the estimate that it costs approximately $8,900 to assess and train a soldier.

Application and Objectives of the ADAPCP

Basically, the ADAPCP is a command program, decentralized, worldwide in its application, in which alcohol and other drug abuse and all related activities are addressed in a single program. The Deputy Chief of Staff for Personnel (DCSPER), Headquarters, Department of the Army, has General Staff responsibility for plans, policies, programs, budget formulation, and behavioral research pertaining to alcohol and other drug abuse in the Army. The Surgeon General supports the ADAPCP with resources, statistical data, technical assistance, and medical research.

The following personnel are eligible for treatment under the ADAPCP.
• Active duty military and civilian employees.
• Full-time members of the Army National Guard and U.S. Army Reserve and other Guard or Reserve personnel on active duty for training.
• Retired military.
• Foreign nationals, under certain conditions.
• Family members of those otherwise eligible, exclusive of dependents of foreign nationals.

The objectives of the ADAPCP are the following.
• Prevent alcohol and other drug abuse.
• Identify alcohol and other drug abusers as early as possible.
• Restore both military and civilian employee abusers to effective duty or identify rehabilitation failures for separation from government service.
• Provide for program evaluation and research.
• Ensure that effective awareness education is provided at all levels.
• Ensure that adequate resources and facilities are provided to accomplish the ADAPCP mission.

---

*A drug is defined as "any substance which by its chemical nature alters structure or function in the living organism" (AR 600-85). This definition includes alcohol, glue, and aerosols.

• Ensure that all personnel assigned to ADAPCP staffs are appropriately trained and experienced to accomplish effectively the ADAPCP mission.

• Achieve maximum productivity in job performance and reduced absenteeism and attrition among Department of the Army civilian employees by preventing and controlling abuse of alcohol and other drugs within the civilian workforce.

Commanders at all levels are responsible for the ADAPCP implementation and the accomplishment of its objectives, including evaluation of the program and its effects within their organizations. Commanders and supervisors play a vital role in providing the necessary support and motivation for personnel to recognize the advantages of obtaining assistance, and all levels of the chain of command are charged with the responsibility for taking prompt action to identify abusers, regardless of grade.

As a noncommissioned officer, you are much closer to those under your control than your unit commander. Not to identify drug or alcohol abuse among your soldiers, either because of ignorance on your part or from the mistaken belief that such abuse can be tolerated so long as it does not cause *immediate* embarrassment, is to indulge in wishful thinking that in the long run will harm the individual and his unit. Addicted personnel do not get better without treatment; many die. To some extent addicts can develop a multitude of serious problems—family, job, health, legal.

The ADAPCP rehabilitation efforts for both alcohol and other drug abusers are shortterm and are conducted in a military environment. Once identified as an abuser, a person who refuses to enroll in the program disobeys a direct order; and once enrolled, those persons who do not show response or who refuse to cooperate may be separated from the service or their employment with the government terminated.

Nevertheless, continued military service, permanent access to classified information, job security, or promotion opportunities are generally not denied any individual solely on the basis of past or present alcohol or other drug abuse rehabilitation or treatment. Soldiers are responsible for the acts they commit while under the influence of drugs or alcohol, and enrollment in the ADAPCP does not provide immunity from prosecution for crimes.

Any information furnished to an alcohol and drug control officer (ADCO) or any other member of the staff of a Community Counseling Center (CCC) in the course of a confidential inquiry for the purpose of obtaining guidance is kept in confidence. A briefing of commanders or immediate supervisors by ADAPCP counselors is not considered a breach of confidence. Except under specified circumstances, commanders are prohibited from releasing information that an individual is or has been an abuser of substances. Release under these conditions is restricted to medical personnel to the extent necessary to meet a medical emergency, to personnel conducting scientific research, and to persons acting under the order of a court to receive such information.

ADAPCP Participation and Efficiency Reports

Paragraph 2-16, AR 623-205, *Enlisted Evaluation Reporting System*, provides that a soldier's participation in the ADAPCP is not normally mentioned in an evaluation report. Rating officials may, however, make note of incidents of alcohol or drug abuse not derived from ADAPCP records.

Once a soldier has been identified in an efficiency report as having an alcohol- or drug-related problem, his or her voluntary entry into the ADAPCP or successful rehabilitation may be mentioned in subsequent reports as a factor to the rated soldier's credit.

Contemporary Problems

Alcohol Abuse

> "Wine is a good familiar creature, if it be well us'd."
>
> Shakespeare, *Othello*

AR 600-85 stipulates:

> The use of alcohol is legal and socially acceptable, but it should not become the purpose or focus of any military social activity. Abuse or excessive use of alcohol will not be condoned or accepted as part of any military tradition, ceremony, or event.

While the abuse of alcohol among soldiers appears to be declining, alcohol abuse is still a serious problem among soldiers of all grades. The Army has recently placed command emphasis on curtailing alcohol abuse by taking steps such as banning "happy hours" in military clubs and making installations comply with local drinking-age laws. Much, however, still remains to be done, especially in the area of improving soldiers' attitudes toward the ADAPCP.

One of the most common misconceptions about alcoholism is that the alcoholic is a bum who staggers around back alleys drinking cheap wine out of bottles wrapped in brown paper bags. Nothing could be farther from the truth. "Skid row" alcoholics are only an estimated 3 percent of the more than 16 million Americans who suffer from alcoholism. Most practicing alcoholics are people who hold responsible positions and show up for work generally on time and not too noticeably hung over. They succeed in covering up their illness because their co-workers do not understand the symptoms of alcoholism, and when they do begin to get the idea, they rationalize by telling themselves, "Well, George is one of the finest guys I know, sober," or "Well, it's not my business to mess in George's personal life."

As an NCO, it is your responsibility to take action when the welfare of your troops is jeopardized. Before taking any action, however, you must be positively certain that the individual concerned displays the symptoms of an abuser. Document these symptoms, seek professional advice, and inform the commander. The coolest judgment and the utmost discretion are called for at all times when planning an intervention. When you intervene, you must walk a fine line with extreme caution, as if you were navigating through a minefield.

Identification of the Abuser. The term "alcoholic" has a precise medical definition which you are not qualified to determine, so be very careful about using it. "Drinking problem" not only sounds nicer and is more readily accepted by most people than "alcoholism," it is probably closer to the truth in most cases. A person who is arrested for driving while under the influence with a blood alcohol content of 10 percent may not be an alcoholic at all, but drinking has certainly created a "problem" for that individual. Likewise, the soldier who gets drunk at a unit party and starts a fight in the barracks is definitely in trouble because of drinking. People who establish patterns of getting into trouble while drinking are definitely "problem drinkers" and should be referred to the ADAPCP.

The following indicators, if repeated *consistently*, should be the basis for counseling and referral up the chain of command to the ADAPCP.

• Failure to report for duty or tardiness.

- Unexpected absences from duty, including brief and sudden disappearances several times during the day. Many problem drinkers keep alcohol stored in their automobiles or other places where they can resort to a drink in secret as needed during the day.
- Signs of a hangover in the morning, such as extreme irritation early in the morning, bloodshot eyes, flushed face, shakiness, excessive perspiration, even slurred speech, staggered walking, and the smell of alcohol on the breath.
- Extended lunch hours, especially if the person returns obviously under the influence of alcohol. Often the problem drinker does not even return after lunch.
- Fighting—not only physical fighting, but also any marked inability to get along with other members in the unit.
- Accidents and deterioration in personal appearance.
- Deterioration in work performance, such as increasing inability to concentrate, forgetfulness, sloppiness, and poor judgment. Sometimes the problem drinker will go through phases consisting of very hard work alternating with periods of very poor work performance. It will probably be on the basis of the individual's poor work performance that you will intervene.
- Drunkenness at off-duty functions, such as gulping down drinks, extreme garrulousness, and irresponsible behavior. Watch out for the NCO who prefers to drink with subordinates, because he or she may only be looking for an appreciative audience. Frequently, problem drinkers try to compensate for their feelings of insecurity by drinking with inferiors.
- Blackouts while drinking. Blacking out while drinking is not the same thing as passing out. When a person blacks out, he experiences a total or partial loss of memory while continuing to function, sometimes with apparent normality. While in this condition—it may continue for minutes or even hours—the individual carries on conversations, travels about, dines, and so on. But upon sobering up, he cannot remember what he has done. Problem drinkers often "misplace" things when in a blacked-out state and cannot remember where they left them when they sober up later. Some of the fear and anxiety alcoholics experience during withdrawal is caused because they cannot remember what they did when they were drinking.
- Any unusual behavior, such as mild paranoia. The problem drinker frequently imagines that someone is "out to get" him. Be alert for "medical" excuses for absenteeism; frequently, heavy drinking does induce a form of gastritis, and the problem drinker may use this as an excuse to stay home and nurse a bad hangover. Be alert for the person who is constantly talking about drinking, or who consistently admits to drinking more than his peers. Also be aware that problem drinkers often have family and financial problems. Be alert to the person who is constantly chewing breath mints or keeps mouthwash handy in the duty area. He may only be fastidious, but he may really be trying to cover up the odor of alcohol on his breath. And sometimes the problem drinker has something stronger than mouthwash in that bottle he keeps in his desk or locker.

Intervention. Intervention and subsequent referral to the ADAPCP is a function of command, and you should never undertake to intervene on your own. You may, however, be the first person to identify the problem drinker, and before discussing the situation with your commander or supervisor, you must have your facts in order. If you feel that alcohol may be a problem with a subordinate, be careful to document each incident using dates, times, and places. Confronted with the facts, problem drinkers cannot justify their poor performance and behavior. Remember that the problem

Contemporary Problems

drinker who is in the denial stage can come up with the most ingenious justifications for his drinking, including blaming nearly everybody but himself.

Remember that advice on the tactics of confrontation may be obtained from the staff at your local Community Counseling Center. Remember also that it is the commander's prerogative to *order* anyone suspected of having a drinking problem to the Alcohol and Drug Abuse Control Officer for evaluation.

Involuntary referral to the ADAPCP usually meets considerable resistance on the part of the individual. This resistance generally does not take the form of outright disobedience to orders or downright refusal to cooperate with ADAPCP personnel, but the more passive form of denying that the problem exists.

The individual must be reassured that no stigma attaches to him or her because of referral to or subsequent enrollment in the ADAPCP. You must make every effort to ensure that, once enrolled, the individual has the opportunity to attend counseling sessions and to make up all missed sessions. You must maintain a close liaison with the individual's counselor, and as with all other aspects of your soldiers' affairs, you must convince the individual of your sincere interest in his or her rehabilitative progress.

You are a key person in the rehabilitation of soldiers with substance abuse problems. Seldom will you experience a feeling more deeply satisfying than the realization that you have been instrumental in saving someone's life.

Remember that prevention is the best cure. If you are involved in your unit's training, ensure that classes on alcohol and drug abuse prevention are scheduled regularly. Support the ADAPCP in every way you can, and remember that example is the best precept.

Drug Abuse

The history of drug abuse in the Army does not extend much farther back than the era of social turbulence of the 1960s, when the use of various kinds of drugs became widespread among certain segments of the American population at large, particularly the young.

AR 600-85 is clear that drug abuse among the NCO corps is not acceptable. Abusers ". . . have violated the special trust and confidence that the Army has placed in them." NCOs who buy, sell, distribute, or use illegal drugs will be processed for separation.

There is apparently a direct correlation between the availability of certain drugs and their use. For instance, some units may experience a higher incidence than others of hard drug use among personnel simply because those kinds of drugs are more available in given geographical areas than they are in others. Similarly, an increase or decrease in the use of specific drugs may be an indication that their availability fluctuates.

Drug Testing. Drug testing as a means of preventing drug abuse and identifying drug users has become commonplace in the armed forces. Urinalysis (testing of urine samples) is done without warning, without choice, and regardless of rank.

The services test for six types of drugs: marijuana, cocaine, heroin, PCP, amphetamines, and barbiturates. If a soldier tests positive for drugs, he or she could face a court-martial, non-judicial punishment, or administrative discharge. Another alternative is for the commanding officer to order the individual into a drug rehabilitation program. Any servicemember whose urine tests positive for drugs should seek legal counsel.

Effects of Drug Abuse. The effects of any given drug upon a user depend on a variety of factors: the dose used, the physical condition of the user, and the user's tolerance to the drug.

The effects may range from agitation and anxiety associated with moderate use of amphetamines to convulsions, respiratory arrest, and death resulting from cocaine overdose. Barbiturates, cocaine, and tranquilizers may produce effects similar to those produced by alcohol. Physical dependence may result from prolonged heavy use of barbiturates, opiates, and tranquilizers, and barbiturate and tranquilizer users may also experience withdrawal symptoms. Psychological dependence may develop as a result of amphetamine, cocaine, hallucinogen, or opiate use.

Many health problems may develop from drug abuse. Anyone who shares needles for intravenous drug use is at high risk for contracting acquired immune deficiency syndrome (AIDS), for which there is no cure. Problems frequently experienced by heroin users include skin infections, ulcers, abcesses, and hepatitis. Cocaine can cause long-term tissue damage; heavy-dose users often suffer from tissue damage in the nose when the drug is sniffed.

The Synergetic Effect of Drugs. "Synergism" comes from a Greek root meaning "working together"; when drugs are synergetic, their combined effect is greater than their individual action. In other words, they combine to multiply their overall effects on the abuser. This synergistic effect is most often seen with the use of minor tranquilizers such as Valium or Librium or barbiturate sedatives like Quaaludes taken with alcohol.

This practice is extremely dangerous; it appears that more women are prone to taking drugs this way than are men. It is particularly easy to overdose this way, and frequently people choose a combination of alcohol and tranquilizers as an easy way to commit suicide, but sometimes the results are worse than death, producing a coma-like state from which the victim never awakes.

Cross-tolerance is easily established with these drugs, causing the user to take larger and larger doses to get the same effects. Persons taking tranquilizers as medication may induce accidental stupor by drinking on top of them. This effect can be extremely dangerous if the individual is driving because the amount of alcohol in combination with tranquilizers needed to produce a highly euphoric state is very small.

AIDS

The devastating effects of AIDS are being felt in the military community as well as in the general population. Acquired immune deficiency syndrome (AIDS) handicaps the body's ability to resist infection by destroying part of its immune system. The HIV virus, AIDS' precursor, is spread through sexual contact, through contaminated hypodermic needles, by a mother to her unborn child, and by a blood donor to a blood recipient.

AIDS is of particular concern to the military for two primary reasons.

• Soldiers in combat may be called upon to make immediate blood donations, and it is essential that this blood supply be disease free.

• Servicemembers must be vaccinated against various diseases when they first enter the military and when stationed overseas. AIDS may make them vulnerable to these diseases by damaging their immune systems, and infected individuals could die from live-virus vaccinations.

A minimum of four hours of AIDS education each year is required for all Army troops. Soldiers must have blood drawn annually to test for the virus.

Mandatory Testing. Initially, blood tests for the HIV virus were given to all prospective recruits. In 1986 blood testing was extended to include all active duty personnel and reservists. Active duty personnel who test positive are retained as long as no sign of the disease itself arises but are not deployed overseas or assigned to deployable units. Those overseas when the virus is detected are transferred stateside.

Once diagnosed, infected individuals are monitored every six months. If they show symptoms of illness, they are usually granted medical discharges. AIDS is not mentioned on their discharge papers. The Department of Veterans Affairs is then responsible for their long-term health care.

Congress has barred the armed services from using information about AIDS as the basis for adverse personnel actions including courts-martial, nonjudicial punishments, involuntary separations, reductions in grade, denials of promotions, unfavorable entries in personnel records, and bars to enlistment.

DOD requires notification of individuals within the military community who are at risk of infection because of contact with a servicemember who has tested positive for the HIV virus. All of these individuals are offered HIV testing and counseling.*

Primary Concern. According to AUSA, the Army Medical Research and Development Command is deeply involved in AIDS research with emphasis on prevention, education, early diagnosis, and the development of an effective vaccine or preventative drugs.

The occurrence of sexually transmitted diseases has traditionally been two to three times higher in U.S. military troops than in their civilian counterparts (up to 100 times higher in wartime). HIV infection is a new threat, and AIDS is fatal 100 percent of the time. In this regard, the military is caught in the classic catch-22 scenario: Some foreign nations will view our military as the conduit that contaminates their populace. Some countries have already stipulated that American troops are not welcome unless certified to be free of HIV.

Health care costs to the military, already stretched because of CHAMPUS costs, will be staggering. Even if no new cases were to occur, the 10-year projection in 1989 dollars for the Department of Defense is nearly $2 billion. At the present incidence rate of new cases, the cost is projected to be up to $3 billion. And these amounts are based on only 60 percent of health care beneficiaries using the military health care system. Therefore, the potential 10-year cost approaches $5 billion!

Why do you, the Army NCO, need to know as much as you can learn about HIV and AIDS? Because the Army is the leading agent for infectious disease research for the DOD, and in this capacity the Army has two main concerns: tracking the epidemic worldwide and within the Army, and prevention. Prevention is your primary job as an NCO involved in the fight to stem the infection rate. You will help prevent the disease from spreading by educating yourself and your soldiers.

You should know, for example, that the overall incidence rate in the Army between 1985 and 1990 fell from one in 2,000 to one in 3,500, or 41 percent. But during the same period, according to AUSA's Institute of Land Warfare, the rate in some minority subgroups and some MOSs has remained stable or increased. According to the Army News Service in the Pentagon, African-American and Hispanic soldiers have rates of infection per 1,000 that are higher than those in white soldiers, and the rate in black

---

*From *Handbook for Military Families, 1989 Edition*, supplement to *Army Times/Air Force Times/Navy Times*, April 3, 1989, by permission of the Times Journal Co., Springfield, Virginia.

female soldiers exceeds the rate in white male soldiers. Overall, the Army in 1990 predicted an HIV infection rate of 220 soldiers each year. That is down from earlier predictions of 600 new cases per year, according to the Walter Reed Army Institute of Research in Washington, D.C.

HIV infection (AIDS) burst upon the scene a dozen years ago. Because it is a sexually transmitted disease that infects blood—a vital military resource in times of peace and war—and because it kills its victims, it will impact on all aspects of the military. The Army has developed a comprehensive approach to address military concerns: surveillance of infection rates (intelligence) around the world and in the military; behavioral research to develop more effective means of education to change behavior; and biological research to develop a quick and easy field test, and a vaccine or drug to prevent the disease from occurring despite exposure. The Army's success—and your effort as an NCO in the fight against the disease—will influence the success of the Army in the future.

Sources
AMA Handbook on Drug Abuse. American Medical Association: Chicago, 1987.
    AR 600-85, *Alcohol and Drug Abuse Prevention Program.*
AR 623-205, *Enlisted Evaluation Reporting System.*
DA Pamphlet 600-17, *A Commander's Supervisor's and Physician's Guide to Alcohol Abuse and Alcoholism.*
Worldwide Survey of Nonmedical Drug Use and Alcohol Use among Military Personnel: 1986. Research Triangle Park, NC: Research Triangle Institute.
Facts about Drugs. Booklet available for $3 from Health Communications, Inc., 3201 SW 15th St., Deerfield Beach, FL 33442.
Soldiers Report III, DAPE-HRL, 21 November 1984.
Tramont, Edmund C. *AIDS and Its Impact on Medical Readiness.* The Association of the United States Army Institute of Land Warfare, November 1990.

8

The Uniform Code of Military Justice

The military justice system is firmly based upon the Constitution of the United States and international law, including the law of war. The specific provisions of the Constitution relating to military jurisdiction are found in the powers granted to Congress, in the authority vested in the President, and in a provision of the Fifth Amendment. The basic documents pertaining to the administration of the military justice system are the *Manual for Courts-Martial*, United States 1984 (with change), and AR 27-10, *Military Justice*.

A fact of military life is that, despite the availability of information on the subject and the effort of commanders to keep their soldiers informed, many individuals simply do not know very much about the military justice system or their rights under that system. But it is the noncommissioned officer's business to know nonjudicial punishment thoroughly—as thoroughly as any commander—and, inasmuch as it is the noncommissioned officer who first becomes aware of the offenses referred to commanders for punishment, it would be very good to consider that "prevention is the best cure."

NONJUDICIAL PUNISHMENT

Article 15 of the Uniform Code of Military Justice provides commanding officers the authority and procedures to impose disciplinary punishments for minor offenses without the intervention of a court-martial. These disciplinary punishments may be either in addition to or in lieu of admonition or reprimand. Unless the accused is embarked on a vessel, Article 15 punishment may not be imposed if the accused demands trial by court-martial.

Article 15 is intended to benefit both the military service and the individual servicemembers. From the soldier's perspective, Article 15 punishments are limited and generally less severe than court-martial punishments. *Unlike a special or general court-martial, Article 15 is not considered a federal conviction for a criminal offense.*

For commanders, Article 15 is intended to provide a swift, efficient, and relatively easy method for punishing those committing minor offenses, maintaining discipline, and deterring future offenses by encouraging positive behavioral changes. Under Article 15, commanders have a wide latitude of punishments that may be imposed ranging from oral reprimand to reduction in pay grade, fines, restriction, extra duty, or a combination of these.

Article 15 is the most likely contact you will have with the military justice system.

It is a very serious mistake to disregard the effect of an Article 15 on a serviceperson's career. The original copy of DA Form 2627, *Record of Proceedings under Article 15, UCMJ*, may be filed in the Official Military Personnel File Performance Portion filed permanently at the USAERC.

Records of Article 15 punishments can be used in a wide variety of personnel decisions, including assignments, promotions, and reenlistment. A record of Articles 15 can also lead to an involuntary administrative discharge.

Remember that Article 15 is not a legal process, and beyond the restraints imposed on a commander's exercise of Article 15 authority by the *Manual for Courts-Martial*, he or she is virtually unrestrained by legal process. For example, rules of evidence do not apply, and providing defense counsel at the hearing is not mandatory.

Nevertheless, the accused does have some protection against the possible arbitrary and capricious use of Article 15. In addition to the right to demand trial in lieu of Article 15 punishment, the accused has the right to consult with counsel to decide whether to accept the punishment; if the accused accepts Article 15 and considers the punishment too harsh, he or she may appeal it. Other rights include the right to remain silent, to fully present his or her case in the presence of the imposing commander, to call witnesses, to present evidence, to be accompanied by a spokesperson, to request an open hearing, and to examine available evidence.

Generally, any offense committed more than two years before imposition of punishment under Article 15 is not punishable.

Authority to Impose Article 15

Any commanding officer is authorized to exercise the disciplinary powers conferred by Article 15. A *commanding officer* is any commissioned or warrant officer who by virtue of rank and assignment exercises primary command authority over a military organization or prescribed territorial area that under pertinent official directives is recognized as a command.

Delegation of Authority under Article 15. The authority Article 15 gives to a commanding officer is an attribute of command and, except as indicated, may not be delegated.

• Any commanding officer authorized to exercise general court-martial jurisdiction and any general officer in command may delegate powers under Article 15 to a commissioned officer actually exercising the function of deputy or assistant commander.

• Authority delegated may be exercised only when the officer to whom such authority has been delegated is imposing punishment on a person junior to him in rank or when acting on an appeal or taking other action with respect to punishment imposed under Article 15 and is senior in rank both to the person being punished and the officer who imposed the punishment.

Limitation of Authority by Subordinates. Any commanding officer having disciplinary authority under Article 15 may limit or withhold the exercise by his or her subordinate commanders of the disciplinary authority they possess under Article 15. For example, limitations on the powers of subordinate commanders to exercise Article 15 authority over certain categories of military personnel, offenses, or individual cases may be reserved by a superior commander. A superior authority may limit or withhold any power that a subordinate might otherwise have under Article 15 authority.

Persons upon Whom Nonjudicial Punishment May Be Imposed

Punishment may be imposed under Article 15 by a commanding officer upon commissioned and warrant officers and other military personnel, except that punishment may not be imposed under Article 15 upon cadets of the United States Military Academy.

Nonjudicial punishment may not be imposed upon an individual by a commanding officer after the person ceases to be of his command by reason of transfer or otherwise. This rule is so even if Article 15 proceedings have been instituted, so long as the proceedings have not resulted in the imposition of punishment before the time of the individual's change in status. The commander who has instituted the proceedings may, in the case of such a change in status, forward the record of proceedings to the gaining commander for appropriate disposition. (As a matter of policy, nonjudicial punishment is not imposed by an Army officer upon a member of another branch of the service.)

Several minor offenses arising out of substantially the same transaction are not made the basis of separate actions under Article 15, and *normally* a person will not be tried by court-martial or punished under Article 15 for the same act or acts over which the civil authorities have exercised jurisdiction.

Purposes of Nonjudicial Punishment

A commanding officer is expected to use nonpunitive measures to the maximum extent possible in furthering the efficiency of his or her command without resorting to the imposition of nonjudicial punishment.

Resort to nonjudicial punishment is proper in all cases of minor offenses in which administrative measures are considered inadequate or inappropriate unless it is clear that nonjudicial punishment is not sufficient to meet the ends of justice and that more stringent measures must be taken. Nonjudicial punishment may be imposed in appropriate cases for the following purposes.

- Correct, educate, and reform offenders who have shown that they cannot benefit by less stringent measures.
- Preserve, in appropriate cases, an offender's record of service from unnecessary stigmatization by record of court-martial conviction.
- Further military efficiency by disposing of minor offenses in a manner requiring less time and personnel than trial by court-martial.

Generally, the term *minor offenses* includes misconduct not involving any greater degree of criminality than is involved in the average offense tried by summary court-martial.

Nonpunitive measures usually deal with misconduct resulting from simple neglect, forgetfulness, laziness, inattention to instructions, sloppy habits, immaturity, difficulty in adjusting to disciplined military life, and similar deficiencies. These measures are primarily tools for teaching proper standards of conduct and performance and do not constitute punishment. Included are denial of pass or other privileges, counseling, administrative reduction in grade, extra training, bar to reenlistment, and MOS reclassification. Certain commanders have the authority, apart from any under Article 15, to reduce enlisted persons administratively for inefficiency or other reasons. These two separate and distinct kinds of authority should not be confused.

A written administrative admonition or reprimand should contain a statement indicating that it has been imposed merely as an administrative measure and *not* as punishment under Article 15. On the other hand, admonitions and reprimands that are imposed as punishment under Article 15 should be clearly stated to have been imposed as punishment under that article.

Commanding officers also have the authority to impose restraints or restrictions upon a soldier for administrative purposes, such as to ensure the soldier's presence within the command. This authority exists apart from the authority to impose restriction as nonjudicial punishment. These nonpunitive measures may also include, subject to any applicable regulation, administrative withholding of privileges.

Extra training or instruction is one of the most effective nonpunitive measures available to a commander. It is used when a soldier's duty performance has been substandard or deficient. For example, a soldier who fails to maintain proper attire may be required to attend classes on the wearing of the uniform and stand inspection until the deficiency is corrected. The training or instruction must, however, relate to the deficiency observed and must be oriented to correct that particular shortcoming. Extra training or instruction may also be conducted after duty hours. Usually, it is initiated and conducted by noncommissioned officers.

Summarized Proceedings

If, after a preliminary inquiry, a commander determines that the punishment for an offense should not exceed extra duty or restriction for 14 days, oral reprimand or admonition, or any combination of these punishments, then Summarized Proceedings under Article 15 may be used. The record of these proceedings is recorded on DA Form 2627-1. Generally Summarized Proceedings are conducted as they are for more serious cases prosecuted under nonjudicial punishment except that the individual normally is allowed only 24 hours to decide whether to demand trial by court-martial and to gather matters in defense, extenuation, and/or mitigation. Because of the limited nature of the punishments imposed under these proceedings, the soldier has *no right* to consult with legally qualified counsel nor the right to a spokesperson.

Nature of Punishments

Nonjudicial punishments include the following actions.

• *Admonition and reprimand.* An admonition or reprimand may be imposed in lieu of or combined with Article 15 punishments.

• *Restriction.* The least severe form of deprivation of liberty, restriction involves moral rather than physical restraint. The severity of this type of restraint is dependent not only upon its duration, but also upon the geographical limits specified when the punishment is imposed. A soldier undergoing restriction may be required to report to a

Maximum Punishments for Enlisted Members under Article 15*

Note: The maximum punishment imposable by any commander under Summarized Procedures cannot exceed extra duty for 14 days, restriction for 14 days, oral reprimand, or any combination thereof.

Punishment	Imposed by Company Grade Officers	Imposed by Field Grade or General Officers
Admonition/Reprimand	Yes	Yes
and		
Extra Duties[1]	14 days	45 days
and		
Restriction	14 days	60 days
or		
Correctional Custody[2] (PVT1 to PFC)	7 days	30 days
or		
Restricted Diet Confinement (PVT1 to PFC attached or embarked on a vessel)	3 days	3 days
and		
Reduction: (PVT1 to SPC or CPL) (SGT and SSG)	one grade	One grade or more / One grade in peacetime[4]
and		
Forfeiture[3]	7 days' pay	Half of one month's pay for 2 months

[1] Combinations of extra duties and restriction cannot exceed the maximum allowed for extra duty.
[2] Subject to limitations imposed by superior authority, and presence of adequate facilities. If punishment includes reduction to private first class or below, reduction must be unsuspended.
[3] Amount of forfeiture is computed at the reduced grade, even if suspended, if reduction is part of punishment.
[4] Only if imposed by a field grade commander of a unit authorized a commander who is a lieutenant colonel or higher.

designated place at specified times if it is considered reasonably necessary to ensure that the punishment is being properly executed. For example, a person undergoing restriction on a weekend may be required to report to the unit charge of quarters every hour during the day. Unless otherwise specified by the commander imposing this form of punishment, a person in restriction may be required to perform any military duty.

- *Arrest in quarters.* Arrest in quarters as punishment under Article 15 may be imposed only upon commissioned officers and warrant officers and then only by an officer exercising general court-martial jurisdiction or by a general officer in command. As with restriction, the restraint is enforced by a moral obligation rather than by physical means, and an officer undergoing this punishment may also be required to perform those duties prescribed by the officer imposing the punishment.
- *Correctional custody.* This physical restraint of a person during duty or nonduty hours, or both, imposed as a punishment under Article 15 may include extra duties, fatigue duties, or hard labor but is not imposed on specialists and corporals and above.
- *Confinement on bread and water or diminished rations.* This punishment may be imposed only upon an enlisted person attached to or embarked in a vessel. Specialists and corporals and above are not placed in confinement on bread and water or diminished rations.
- *Extra duties.* This form of punishment involves the performance of duties in addition to those normally assigned to the person undergoing the punishment. Extra duties may include fatigue duties. In general, extra duties may not be assigned a specialist or corporal or above that would demean his or her position as a noncommissioned officer or specialist.
- *Reduction in grade.* This form of punishment involves these considerations.
  - Promotion authority. The grade from which a soldier is reduced must be within the promotion authority of the imposing commander or the officer to whom authority to punish under Article 15 has been delegated. See Chapter 5 for reduction authorities.
  - Lateral appointments or reductions of corporal to specialist are not authorized. An NCO may be reduced to a lower pay grade provided the lower grade is authorized in his primary MOS.
  - Date of rank. When a soldier is reduced in grade as a result of an unsuspended reduction, the date of rank in the grade to which reduced is the date the punishment of reduction was imposed. If the reduction is suspended either on or after the date the reduction is imposed or is set aside or mitigated to forfeiture, the date of rank in the grade held before the punishment remains unchanged. If a suspension is vacated, the date of rank in the grade to which reduced is the date the punishment was *originally* imposed, regardless of the date the punishment was suspended or vacated.
  - Entitlement to pay. When a soldier is restored to a higher pay grade because of a suspension or when a reduction is mitigated to a forfeiture, entitlement to pay at the higher grade is effective on the date of the suspension or mitigation. This situation is true even though an earlier date of rank is assigned. If a reduction is set aside and all rights are restored, the soldier concerned will be entitled to pay as though the reduction had never been imposed.
  - Senior Noncommissioned Officers. Senior NCOs (sergeant first class and above) may not be reduced under the authority of Article 15.
- *Forfeiture of pay.* This loss of entitlement to the pay forfeited is permanent. *Pay* as used in this context refers only to basic pay of the individual plus any foreign duty pay. Forfeitures imposed by a company grade commander may not be applied for more

Forfeitures of Pay Authorized under Article 15

Maximum monthly authorized forfeitures of pay under Article 15, UCMJ, may be computed using the applicable formula below:

1. Upon enlisted persons

$$\frac{(\text{Monthly Basic Pay}^{1,2}) + (\text{Foreign Pay}^{1,3})}{2} = \text{Maximum forfeiture per month if imposed by major or above.}$$

$$\frac{(\text{Monthly Basic Pay}^{1,2}) + (\text{Foreign Pay}^{1,3})}{30} \times 7 = \text{Maximum forfeiture if imposed by captain or below.}$$

2. Upon commissioned and warrant officers when imposed by an officer with general court-martial jurisdiction or by a general officer in command:

$$\frac{(\text{Monthly Basic Pay}^2)}{2} = \text{Maximum authorized forfeiture per month.}$$

---

[1] Amount of forfeiture is computed at the reduced grade, even if suspended, if reduction is part of the punishment imposed.
[2] At the time punishment is imposed.
[3] If applicable.

---

than one month, while those imposed by a field grade commander may not be applied for more than two months. If a forfeiture has been imposed in addition to a suspended or unsuspended reduction, the amount will be limited to the amount authorized for the reduced grade. The maximum forfeiture of pay to which a soldier is subject during a given month, because of one or more actions under Article 15, is one-half of his pay per month. Article 15 forfeitures cannot deprive a soldier of more than two-thirds of his or her pay per month.

Combination and Apportionment

Except that no two or more punishments involving deprivation of liberty may be combined in the same nonjudicial punishment to run either consecutively or concurrently, other punishments authorized under Article 15 may be combined. Restriction and extra duty may be combined in any manner to run for a period not in excess of the maximum duration imposable for extra duty by the imposing commander. Once begun, deprivation of liberty punishments runs continuously, except where interrupted because of the fault of the soldier or because the soldier is physically incapacitated.

Suspension, Mitigation, Remission, and Setting Aside

Suspension. The purpose of suspending punishment is to grant a deserving soldier a probational period during which the individual may show that he or she deserves a remission of the suspended portion of his or her nonjudicial punishment. If, because of further misconduct within this period, it is determined that remission of the suspended punishment is not warranted, the suspension may be vacated and the suspended portion of the punishment executed.

Mitigation. Mitigation means a reduction in either the quantity or quality of a punishment, its general nature remaining the same. For example, if a punishment of correctional custody for 20 days is reduced to correctional custody for 10 days or to restriction for 20 days, each action would constitute mitigation; the first lessens the quantity and the second lessens the quality, with both mitigated punishments remaining of the same general nature, that is, a deprivation of liberty. Mitigation is appropriate when it is determined that the offender has, by his or her subsequent good conduct, merited a reduction in the severity of punishment, or when it is determined that the punishment imposed was disproportionate to the offense or the offender. See Paragraph 3-18, AR 27-10, for details.

Remission. Remission can cancel any portion of the *unexecuted* punishment. Remission is appropriate under the same circumstances as mitigation.

Setting Aside and Restoration. Under this action, the punishment or any part or amount thereof, whether *executed or unexecuted*, is set aside, and any property, privileges, or rights affected by the portion of the punishment set aside are restored. The basis for this action is ordinarily a determination that, under all the circumstances of the case, the punishment has resulted in a clear injustice.

Notification and Explanation of Rights

The imposing commander must ensure that the soldier is notified of the commander's intention to dispose of the matter under Article 15. The soldier will also be notified of the maximum punishment that the commander could impose, and he or she will be provided a copy of DA Form 2627, *Record of Proceedings under Article 15, UCMJ*, with items 1 and 2 completed, including the date and signature of the imposing commander.

The imposing commander may delegate notification authority to another officer, warrant officer, or NCO (sergeant first class and above), providing that person outranks the person being notified. If an NCO is selected, that person should normally be the unit first sergeant or another NCO who is the senior enlisted person in the command in which the accused is serving.

The accused will return the DA Form 2627 to the commander for annotation, and it will subsequently be given back to him for retention when all proceedings have been completed.

The soldier must be given a "reasonable time" to consult with counsel, including time off from duty, if necessary, to decide whether to demand trial. The amount of time granted is determined after considering factors such as the complexity of the case and the availability of counsel, but *normally*, 48 hours is considered a reasonable decision period.

Before deciding to demand trial, the accused is not entitled to be informed of the type or amount of punishment he or she will receive if nonjudicial punishment is imposed. The imposing commander will inform the soldier of the maximum punishment allowable under Article 15 and the maximum allowable for the offense if the case proceeds to a trial by court-martial and conviction for the offense(s).

Right to Demand Trial

Army personnel attached to or embarked in a vessel may not demand trial by

The Uniform Code of Military Justice

court-martial in lieu of nonjudicial punishment. Any other soldier will be advised of this right. The demand for trial may be made at any time before imposition of punishment. The soldier will be told that if trial is demanded, it could be by summary, special, or general court-martial. The soldier will also be told that he or she may object to trial by summary court-martial and that at a special or general court-martial he or she would be entitled to be represented by qualified military counsel or by civilian counsel obtained at no government expense.

Appeals

Only one appeal is permitted under Article 15 proceedings. An appeal not made within a "reasonable time" may be rejected as untimely by the superior authority. The definition of what constitutes a "reasonable time" varies according to the situation. Generally, an appeal, including all documentary matters, submitted *more than five calendar* days (including weekends and holidays) after punishment is imposed will be presumed to be untimely. If, at the time of imposition of punishment the soldier indicates a desire not to appeal, the superior authority may reject a subsequent election to appeal, even if it is made within the five-day period.

The authority next superior to the commanding officer acts on an appeal if the punished soldier is still of that command at the time of the appeal. If the commander has acted under a delegation of authority, the appeal will not be acted on by the authority next superior to the delegating officer.

Appeals are made on DA Form 2627 or DA Form 2627-1 and forwarded through the imposing commander or successor-in-command to the superior authority. The superior must act on the appeal unless otherwise directed by competent authority. A soldier is not required to state the reasons for the appeal but he or she may present evidence or arguments proving innocence or why the sentence should be mitigated or suspended.

Unless an appeal is voluntarily withdrawn, it must be forwarded to the appropriate superior authority. An officer forwarding the appeal may attach any matter in rebuttal of the assertions made by the member. The imposing commander must also make available to the soldier reasonable assistance in preparing the appeal. The imposing commander may take any action on an appeal that the superior authority may make. If he suspends, mitigates, remits, or sets aside any part of the punishment, the appellant will be advised and asked to state whether he or she wishes to withdraw the appeal.

A superior authority must act on an appeal expeditiously, but if necessary and desirable, he may conduct an independent inquiry into the case. While a superior must refer an appeal from certain punishments to a judge advocate for consideration and advice before taking action, he or she may refer an appeal in any case. In acting, the superior authority may exercise the same powers with respect to the punishment as may be exercised by the imposing commander, but he cannot change a filing determination. A timely appeal does not terminate because a soldier is discharged from the service but will be processed to completion.

Announcement of Punishment

The punishment may be announced at the next unit formation after punishment is imposed or, if appealed, after the decision. It also may be posted on the unit bulletin board. The purpose of announcing the results is to avert the perception of unfairness of punishment and to deter similar misconduct by others. Commanders, however, should avoid inconsistency or arbitrariness in posting these announcements. In deciding whether to announce punishment in the case of sergeants and above, the commander should consider the nature of the offense, the individual's military record and duty position, the deterrent effect, the effect on unit morale or mission, the effect on the victim, and the effect on the leadership effectiveness of the individual concerned.

Records of Punishment

DA Forms 2627 are prepared in an original and five copies. What happens to those copies, especially the original, is of the utmost importance to soldiers who receive punishment under nonjudicial proceedings.

Original. For active duty officers and warrant officers, the original copy is forwarded to Headquarters, Department of the Army, by the individual's servicing military personnel office (MILPO); for enlisted personnel, to U.S. Army Enlisted Records & Evaluation Center, Fort Benjamin Harrison, Indiana. The decision on where in the punished soldier's official military personnel file (OMPF) this copy will be placed is determined by the imposing commander at the time punishment is imposed and is final. The imposing commander will decide if it is to be filed in the performance fiche or the restricted fiche of the individual's OMPF.

The *performance fiche* is that portion of the OMPF that is routinely used by career managers and selection boards for the purpose of assignment, promotion, and schooling selection. The soldier who has a copy of DA Form 2627 placed into this portion of his file can forget about promotion for a long, long time thereafter.

The *restricted fiche* is that portion of the OMPF that contains information *not viewed* by career managers or selection boards without *express written* approval by the Commander, Military Personnel Center, his delegate, or the selection board proponent.

Copy One. For those Articles 15 filed in the performance fiche of the OMPF, Copy One is placed into the permanent section of the military personnel records jacket (MPRJ) unless the original is transferred from the performance to the restricted fiche, at which time it is destroyed. Otherwise, it is kept in the unit personnel files and destroyed two years from the date of punishment or on the soldier's transfer, whichever occurs first.

Copies two through four are used variously as prescribed by AR 27-10, depending on whether forfeiture of pay is involved and whether the punished soldier appeals. Copy five is given to the individual.

Transfer or Removal of Records

Staff sergeants and above and commissioned and warrant officers may request the transfer of a record of nonjudicial punishment from the performance to the restricted fiche of their OMPF. To support such a request, the individual must submit substantive evidence that the purpose of the Article 15 has been served and that transfer of the record is in the best interests of the Army. The request must be made in writing to the Department of the Army Suitability Evaluation Board: President, DA Suitability Evaluation Board, HQDA (DAPE-MPC-E), Washington, DC 20310.

Requests should be submitted within three years of the date an individual is promoted to staff sergeant or three years from the date of imposition of punishment or action on appeal, whichever occurs later. The officer who directed the filing of the record in the OMPF may provide a statement to the soldier in support of a request for transfer to the restricted fiche.

The Uniform Code of Military Justice

Soldiers may also apply to the Army Board for Correction of Military Records (ABCMR) for the correction of military records by the Secretary of the Army. AR 15-185, *Army Board for Correction of Military Records*, contains policies and procedures for making such applications. Requests should be sent to the ABCMR to correct an error or remove an injustice only after other available means of administrative appeal have been exhausted.

COURTS-MARTIAL

Courts-martial are the agencies through which Army magistrates try personnel accused of violations of the so-called "punitive articles" of the Uniform Code of Military Justice (see Part IV). These are articles 77 through 134 of the UCMJ and they are designed to provide for punishment of three broad groups of crimes and offenses:
* Those crimes common to both the military and the civilian law, such as murder, rape, arson, burglary, larceny, sodomy, and frauds against the United States.
* Those crimes and offenses peculiar to the military services, such as desertion, disobedience, misbehavior before the enemy, and sleeping on post.
* General offenses that are prosecuted under Article 133 (Conduct Unbecoming an Officer and a Gentlemen) and 134 (the so-called "General Article"), which covers "all disorders and neglects to the prejudice of good order and discipline in the armed forces, all conduct of a nature to bring discredit upon the armed forces, and crimes and offenses not capital."

During peacetime, courts-martial may impose sentences ranging from simple forfeiture of pay to confinement and forfeiture of all pay and allowances and death (see Appendix 12, MCM, for the Maximum Punishment Chart). During time of war, a general court-martial may impose any penalty authorized by law, including death.

Composition of Courts-Martial

General courts-martial consist of a military judge and not less than five members or of a military judge alone. *Special courts-martial* consist of not less than three members or, if so detailed, a military judge and not less than three members or a military judge alone. The military judge is not a member of the court. In any case to which a military judge has been detailed, the accused, knowing the identity of the judge and after consulting with counsel, may request, in writing, trial by the military judge alone. If the military judge approves, he alone constitutes the general or special court-martial. *Summary courts-martial* consist of one commissioned officer.

Any commissioned officer on active duty with the armed forces is eligible to serve on courts-martial. Any warrant officer on active duty with the armed forces is eligible to serve on general and special courts-martial for the trial of any person other than a commissioned officer.

Any enlisted person on active duty with the armed forces who is not a member of the same unit as the accused is eligible to serve on general and special courts-martial for the trial of any enlisted person who has personally requested in writing before assembly that enlisted members serve on the court. If an enlisted person requests in writing that enlisted members serve on the general or special court-martial that will try his or her case, then the total membership of that court must include at least one-third enlisted persons unless sufficient eligible enlisted personnel cannot be obtained because of physical conditions or military emergency. If these members cannot be found, the court may be assembled and the trial held without them, but the convening authority must make a detailed written statement, to be appended to the record, stating why they could not be obtained.

When it can be avoided, no member of an armed force may be tried by a court-martial any member of which is junior to him or her in grade or relative rank.

Convening Authorities

General courts-martial may be convened by the President of the United States, the Secretary of the Army, the commander of a territorial department, army group, army, army corps, division, separate brigade, or corresponding unit, or any other commander designated by the Secretary of the Army or empowered by the President to convene such courts-martial (Article 22, UCMJ). It is unlawful for any commander who is an accuser to convene a general court-martial for the trial of the person so accused.

Special courts-martial may be convened by any person who may convene a general court-martial or the commanding officer of a district, garrison, fort, camp, station, or other place where members of the Army are on duty. The commander of a brigade, regiment, detached battalion, or corresponding unit of the Army or any other commander of any separate or detached command or group of detached units placed under a single commander for this purpose, or any commander when empowered to do so by the Secretary of the Army (Article 23, UCMJ) may convene special courts-martial. A subordinate commander may exercise the power to convene special courts-martial unless a competent superior reserves that power and so notifies the subordinate.

Summary courts-martial may be convened by any person who may also convene a general or special court-martial and the commander of a detached company or other detachment of the Army and any other officer empowered by the Secretary of the Army to convene such a court-martial.

If the convening authority of a summary court or the summary court officer is also the accuser of the person or persons to be tried, it is discretionary with the convening authority whether to forward the charges to superior authority with a recommendation that the court-martial be convened by the latter, but the fact that the convening authority or the summary court officer is the accuser in a case does not invalidate the trial.

When only one commissioned officer is present with a command or detachment, that officer is the summary court-martial authority of that command or detachment and hears and determines all summary court cases. Summary courts-martial may, however, be convened in any case by superior competent authority when considered desirable to do so (Article 24, UCMJ).

Jurisdiction and Punishments

General courts-martial have jurisdiction to try any persons subject to the Uniform Code of Military Justice for any offense made punishable by that code, under such limitations as the President may prescribe. In addition, they have the power to try any person who, by the law of war, is subject to trial by tribunal for any crime or offense against the law of war and for any crime or offense against the law of the territory occupied in wartime.

A general court-martial composed only of a military judge does not have jurisdiction to try any person for any offense for which the death penalty may be adjudged unless the case has been previously referred to trial as a noncapital case.

The Uniform Code of Military Justice

General courts-martial have the power, within certain limitations, to impose any punishment not forbidden by the UCMJ, but the death penalty can be adjudged only when specifically authorized.

Special courts-martial may, under such limitations as the President may prescribe, adjudge any punishment not forbidden by the UCMJ except death, dishonorable discharge, dismissal, confinement for more than six months, hard labor without confinement for more than three months, forfeiture of pay exceeding two-thirds pay per month, or forfeiture of pay for more than six months.

Special courts-martial may confer bad conduct discharges providing that a military judge is assigned to the trial (except in cases in which a judge cannot be detailed because of physical restrictions or military emergency), qualified counsel is detailed to represent the accused, and a complete verbatim record of the proceedings and testimony is made.

Summary courts-martial have the power to try persons subject to the UCMJ except commissioned officers, warrant officers, cadets, aviation cadets, and midshipmen for any noncapital offense made punishable by the code. No person with respect to whom summary courts-martial have jurisdiction may be brought to trial before a summary court if he or she objects thereto. This rule applies even though the person may also have refused punishment under Article 15 (see below) and demanded trial by court-martial. If objection to trial by summary court-martial is made by an accused, trial may be ordered by special or general court-martial, as may be appropriate.

Summary courts-martial may adjudge any punishment not forbidden by the UCMJ except death, dismissal, dishonorable or bad-conduct discharge, confinement for more than one month, hard labor without confinement for more than 45 days, restriction to certain specified limits for more than two months, or forfeiture of more than two-thirds of one month's pay; in the case of enlisted persons who are sergeants or above, summary courts may not adjudge confinement, hard labor without confinement, or reduction except to the next inferior rank.

Officers of the Court

The *military judge* presides over each open session of the court. Before the court closes to vote on the sentence, the military judge must give appropriate instructions, including the maximum authorized punishment that it may impose.

The *president of the court* is the senior person in rank among the members of a court-martial detailed to a general or special court. The senior member present at a trial, however, whether or not he is the senior member detailed to the court, is president of the court for that particular case. In special courts without a military judge, the president is responsible for the fair and orderly conduct of the proceedings in accordance with law.

The *members of courts-martial* hear the evidence, determine the guilt or innocence of the accused, and if guilty, adjudge a proper sentence. Each member has an equal voice and vote with the other members, the senior member having no greater rights in voting or balloting than any other member, officer or enlisted.

No member of a general or special court-martial may be absent from the court during the trial except for physical disability, as a result of a challenge, or by order of the convening authority. When less than the minimum number of members required is present, the court may not proceed. When an enlisted person requests participation of enlisted members in a trial by general or special court-martial, the court may not proceed with the trial unless at least one-third of the members actually sitting at all sessions are enlisted members or the convening authority has directed that the court assemble without enlisted members.

The *trial counsel* prosecutes in the name of the United States and, under the direction of the court, prepares the record of the proceedings.

The *defense counsel* performs such duties as usually are performed by the counsel for a defendant before a civilian court in a criminal case. The accused has the right to be represented in his or her defense before a general or special court-martial by civilian counsel if provided by him; the accused may ask that any person be defense counsel, if that person is reasonably available.

Challenges

The military judge and members of a general or special court-martial may be challenged by the accused or the trial counsel for cause stated to the court. The military judge, or, if none, the court determines the relevancy and validity of challenges for cause and may not receive a challenge to more than one person at a time. Challenges by the trial counsel are ordinarily presented and decided before those by the accused are offered.

Each accused and the trial counsel is entitled to one preemptory challenge, but the military judge may not be challenged, except by cause. In other words, the accused may challenge any member of the court to sit on his trial without offering any reasons for the challenge.

Appeals

At the close of a trial or as soon thereafter as possible, if the accused is found guilty, the defense counsel should prepare a recommendation for clemency setting forth any matters as to clemency he or she desires to have considered by the members of the court of the reviewing authority. The members of the court who are willing to do so sign the recommendation and it is appended to the record of trial.

If the accused is convicted, the defense counsel advises him or her of appellate rights.

The Court of Military Review. Article 66 of the UCMJ provides that each judge advocate general shall establish a court of military review. In reviewing court-martial cases, the court may sit in panels or as a whole. Appellate military judges who are assigned to a court of military review may be commissioned officers or civilians, each of whom must be a member of a bar of a federal court or of the highest court of a state.

The judge advocate general refers to a court of military review the record in every case of trial by court-martial in which the sentence, as approved, extends to death, dismissal of a commissioned officer, cadet, or midshipman, dishonorable or bad-conduct discharge, or confinement for one year or more.

In a case referred to it, the court of military review may act only with respect to the findings and sentence as approved by the convening authority. If the court sets aside the findings and sentence, it may, except where the setting aside is based on lack of sufficient evidence, order a rehearing. If it sets aside the findings and sentence and does not order a rehearing, it orders that the charges be dismissed.

The Court of Military Appeals. The U.S. Court of Military Appeals, established under Article I of the Constitution and located, for administrative purposes, only in the De-

The Uniform Code of Military Justice

partment of Defense, consists of three judges appointed from civil life by the President by and with the advice and consent of the Senate for a term of 15 years.

The Court of Military Appeals, located in Washington, D.C., reviews the record in all the following cases.

- Those in which the sentence, as affirmed by a court of military review, extends to death.
- Those reviewed by a court of military review that the judge advocate general orders sent to the Court of Military Appeals for review.
- Those reviewed by a court of military review in which, upon petition of the accused and on good cause shown, the Court of Military Appeals has granted a review.

The accused has 60 days from the time when he or she is notified of the decision of a board of review to petition the court for review.

The appeals system now also has an appeal to the U.S. Supreme Court.

Remission and Suspension of Sentences

The Secretary of the Army and, when so designated by the Secretary, any under secretary, assistant secretary, judge advocate general, or commanding officer may remit (lessen the severity of a sentence) or suspend any amount of the unexecuted part of any sentence, including all uncollected forfeitures other than a sentence approved by the President.

The Secretary of the Army may, for good cause, substitute an administrative form of discharge for a discharge or dismissal executed in accordance with the sentence of a court-martial.

The convening authority may suspend the execution of any sentence, except a death sentence.

Effective Dates of Sentences

Whenever a sentence as lawfully adjudged and approved includes a forfeiture of pay or allowances in addition to confinement not suspended or deferred, the forfeiture applies to pay or allowances becoming due on or after the date the sentence is approved by the convening authority. No forfeiture may extend to any pay or allowances accrued before that date.

Any period of confinement included in a sentence of a court-martial begins to run from the date of sentencing by the court-martial, but periods during which the sentence to confinement is suspended or deferred are excluded in computing the service of the term of confinement.

All other sentences of courts-martial are effective on the date ordered executed.

Reductions in grade are effective on the date the sentence is approved. But if the sentence is set aside or disapproved, or, as finally approved, does not include a dishonorable or bad-conduct discharge, confinement, or hard labor without confinement, the rights and privileges of which the accused was deprived because of that reduction are restored, and the accused is entitled to the pay and allowances to which he or she would have been entitled for the period the reduction was in effect, if the accused had not been so reduced.

Who May Prefer Charges

Charges are initiated by anyone bringing to the attention of the military authorities information concerning an offense suspected to have been committed by a person subject to the UCMJ. This information may be received from anyone, whether subject to the UCMJ or not.

Any person subject to the UCMJ may prefer charges, even if he or she is under charges, in arrest, or in confinement. In many cases, if the commander who exercises immediate jurisdiction over the accused under Article 15 is not empowered to convene courts-martial, he or she actually prefers the charges.

Action by Immediate Commander

Upon receipt of information that an offense has been committed, the commander exercising immediate jurisdiction over the accused under Article 15, UCMJ, must make or cause to be made a preliminary inquiry into the charges in order to permit an intelligent disposition of them. This inquiry is usually informal.

Based on the outcome of the preliminary inquiry, a commander may decide that all or some of the charges do not warrant further action, and those charges may be dismissed. The commander may also decide, based upon the preliminary investigation, that the offenses committed warrant punishment under Article 15, UCMJ. Unless competent authority has directed otherwise, a commander may thus impose punishment under Article 15, whether or not the offenses were originally charged, or the commander may punish minor offenses substantiated in the preliminary investigation under Article 15 and refer the more serious charges to higher authority for trial by courts-martial.

Preparation of Charge Sheets

Rule 307 and Appendix 4, MCM, contain specific instructions on the preparation of charge sheets, together with specimen forms for charges and specifications under the punitive articles of the Uniform Code of Military Justice. If your commander should ask you to draft specifications and charges, do not deviate from the examples provided. If you're not a legal clerk, it's important to get help from your JAG officer.

Forwarding of Charges. If trial by court-martial is believed to be appropriate for any offenses remaining after a preliminary investigation and/or action under the provisions of Article 15, these charges should be forwarded through the chain of command to the officer exercising summary court-martial authority over the command of which the accused is a member.

Before forwarding the charges, the accused's immediate commander must inform him or her of the charges being brought and complete and sign the certificate to that effect on the charge sheet.

Subject to jurisdictional limitations and at the discretion of the convening authority, charges against an accused, if tried at all, ordinarily are tried at a single trial by the lowest court that has the power to adjudge an appropriate and adequate punishment. The fact that, upon conviction of a particular offense, the Table of Maximum Punishments (Paragraph 127c, MCM) may authorize a punishment in excess of that which can be adjudged by a summary or special court-martial does not in itself preclude reference of such an offense to a summary or special court-martial for trial.

When trial by special or general court-martial is deemed appropriate and the summary court officer is not also empowered to convene such a court for the trial of the case, the charges together with necessary allied papers are forwarded to the officer

The Uniform Code of Military Justice

exercising the appropriate kind of court-martial jurisdiction. If, however, the forwarding officer is also an accuser, the court must be convened by a competent authority superior in rank or command.

At each stage of referral, the authority having jurisdiction over the accused may dispose of the case by acting on the charges or return the case to lower authority for appropriate action.

NCO Responsibilities

If you should be appointed to serve on a general or special court-martial as a member of the court, your duties and responsibilities will be very carefully explained to you before the court convenes and as the trial proceeds. If a soldier should seek your advice regarding what he or she should do in the event charges are brought against the individual, *advise the person concerned to seek assistance from an officer of the Judge Advocate General's Corps.*

Unless you are a legal clerk, your acquaintance with the military justice system will probably be only a superficial one. Your closest contact with the military justice system will come through your commander's exercise of judicial authority under Article 15 of the UCMJ, and you should be intimately familiar with every aspect of that part of the system. *But you are neither an expert in military law nor a lawyer*, and you should never take upon yourself the duties of counsel.

The *Manual for Courts-Martial* is an important text that every soldier should know well enough to understand what it contains and how to use it to answer questions on the military justice system. Do not, however, use that acquaintance to practice law.

Sources

AR 27-10, *Military Justice*, 1989.
FM 27-1, *Legal Guide for Commanders*, 1987.
FM 27-14, *Legal Guide for Soldiers*, 1986.
Manual for Courts-Martial, 1984.
Tomes, Lt. Col. Jonathan P., U.S. Army. *The Servicemember's Legal Guide, 2nd Edition*. Stackpole Books: Harrisburg, PA, 1992.

9

Courtesy, Etiquette, and Customs

COURTESY

Military courtesy is the respect shown to superiors by subordinates and the mutual respect demonstrated between senior and subordinate personnel. It is basic to military discipline and founded upon respect for and loyalty to properly constituted authority. Every feature of military life has its effect on military discipline and courtesy.

Saluting

The salute is a formal demonstration of courtesy between soldiers. It is both recognition of military rank and authority and a greeting exchanged between members of a unique professional organization with special rules and codes of conduct. Precisely how to salute is defined in FM 21-13, and whom to salute is defined in AR 600-25. But the best rule to follow when rendering either the hand salute or when saluting under arms is "When in doubt, whip it out." The salute is a universally recognized form of greeting, and no soldier should feel embarrassment because he or she may have saluted someone who is not strictly entitled to it by Army regulations.

All Army personnel in uniform are required to salute when they meet and recognize persons entitled to the salute. Salutes are exchanged between officers (commissioned and warrant) and between officers (commissioned and warrant) and enlisted personnel. Salutes are exchanged with personnel of the U.S. Army, Navy, Air Force,

Courtesy, Etiquette, and Customs

Marine Corps, and Coast Guard entitled to the salute. It is customary to salute officers of friendly foreign nations when recognized as such.

Civilians may be saluted by persons in uniform when appropriate, but the uniform hat or cap should not be raised as a form of salutation.

Salutes are not required to be given or returned if either the senior or subordinate or both are in civilian attire.

Military personnel under arms give the salute prescribed for the weapon with which they are armed, whether or not that weapon ordinarily is prescribed as part of their equipment.

The practice of saluting officers in official vehicles (recognized individually by rank or identifying vehicle plates or flags) is appropriate and should be observed. Salutes are not required to be given by or to personnel who are driving or riding in privately owned vehicles except by gate guards, who render salutes to recognized officers in vehicles unless their duties are of such nature as to make the salute impractical. When military personnel are driving moving vehicles, they should not initiate a salute. Salutes are not required in public areas, such as theaters, outdoor athletic facilities, or other situations when the act would be manifestly inappropriate or impractical.

Accompanying the hand salute with an appropriate greeting, such as "Good morning, sir," or "Good morning, ma'am," is encouraged. Personnel do not salute indoors except when reporting to a superior officer.

The salute is given when the person approaching or being approached is recognized as being authorized a salute, usually between thirty and six paces. The officer is obliged to return the salute. Do not be upset if occasionally you do not recognize a superior in time to salute. Apologize when you are corrected for this oversight.

Never turn and go another direction to avoid saluting someone.

If a superior remains in your area, but does not engage in conversation, he is saluted only once, upon the initial greeting; should a superior engage you in conversation, however, then you must salute when he finishes talking to you and departs your area.

Always salute with precision and enthusiasm. Never salute with anything in your hands or mouth. Never duck your head when you salute, but always keep your chin up and your back straight. Do not mumble a greeting, but speak out clearly, in a normal tone of voice, but use only enough volume to make yourself heard. You should not greet people in the same tone of voice you use when shouting out commands on the drill field.

You do not have to salute when you are in any of the following situations:

- A prisoner.
- At work; the officer or NCO in charge does the saluting for everyone.
- Indoors, except when reporting or on duty as a guard.
- Carrying articles with both hands or otherwise so occupied that to salute would be manifestly impractical.
- It is inappropriate to do so, such as when assisting a superior who is injured or in some sort of difficulty; a military policeman would not salute an officer whom he is apprehending.
- In ranks; the officer or NCO in charge will salute for the whole formation. If you are in ranks and an officer is inspecting, come to attention when he comes up to you.
- Engaged in athletics or sports.
- In places of public assembly or conveyance.
- Maneuvering against a hostile armed force or participating in field training exercises.

"Outdoors" may actually be indoors, such as in buildings used for drill halls, gymnasiums, and other roofed structures commonly used for drilling and exercising. Theater marquees and covered walkways open on both sides are considered outdoors and it is appropriate to salute when underneath them. Local commanders, however, may prescribe that specific outdoor areas such as walkways, building entrances, and large courtyards are not appropriate for saluting.

Reporting. A junior always gives the hand salute when reporting to a senior. Sometimes, however, the distinctions tend to blur, especially when on a large staff where there are many senior officers. If you are reporting to your company commander, you must salute and formally report. If you are told to report to a senior officer on the staff and discuss the details of a paper with him, whether you salute depends on the protocol considered acceptable on the particular staff (which is a reflection of the commander's wishes) and the frequency with which you visit.

When reporting to a commander, a salute is always given at the report and again when dismissed. When reporting indoors and without arms, first remove your hat and then knock on the commander's door. When given permission to enter, advance to within about two paces from the commander's desk, halt, salute, and make your report: "Sir (or Ma'am), Sergeant Onagainoffagain reporting as directed," or "Sir (or Ma'am), Sergeant Onagainoffagain has the first sergeant's permission to speak to the company commander." Hold the salute until it is returned. After stating your business, salute again, about face when it is returned, and exit the room.

When reporting while under arms, the hat is never removed. If carrying a rifle, enter with the weapon at the trail and give the rifle salute at *order arms*. Otherwise, give the hand salute. Outdoors, a soldier may approach an officer with the weapon at either *trail* or *right shoulder arms* and execute the rifle salute at *order* or *right shoulder arms*.

Saluting in Vehicles. Drivers of vehicles salute only when the vehicle is stopped and the engine is switched off. When a number of troops are riding in a vehicle, the senior member salutes for the whole group.

Saluting in Groups. Individuals in formations never salute except at the command *present arms*. The officer or NCO in charge does the saluting for the entire body of troops. If the troops are not at *attention* when it becomes necessary to salute a senior, the person in charge calls them to *attention* before saluting.

A soldier in formation, not standing at *attention*, comes to the position of *attention* when spoken to by a senior.

When a group not in formation is approached by a superior, the first person seeing him calls *attention*, and all come to *attention* and salute, unless they are at work or engaged in organized athletics.

Saluting on Guard. In garrison, guards armed with the rifle halt and face in the direction of the music (when the National Anthem or "To the Color" is played), person, or colors to be saluted and present arms. During the hours for challenging, the first salute is given when the officer has been recognized and advanced.

A sentinel armed with the pistol gives the hand salute, except when challenging, and then the weapon is held at the *raise pistol* position and kept there until the challenged party departs.

If the officer to whom a sentinel may be talking salutes a senior, the sentinel also salutes. Wherever he is posted, indoors or outdoors, a guard or a sentinel salutes all officers, except when saluting would interfere with the performance of his duties.

Courtesy, Etiquette, and Customs

Forms of Address

The title "sir" or "ma'am" should be used on all occasions when addressing an officer or civilian. For a detailed discussion on the use of these titles, see the section dealing with etiquette further on in this chapter.

Privates and privates first class are addressed as "private." Corporals and specialists are called "corporal" and "specialist," respectively. Sergeants through the rank of master sergeant are referred to as "sergeant," except first sergeants, who are called by their title or "top," but *never* "sergeant"! Likewise, sergeants major and command sergeants major (including the Sergeant Major of the Army) are called "sergeant major."

Uncovering

A soldier under arms should remove his or her hat only when in the following situations:
- Seated as a member of or in attendance at a court or board.
- Entering a place of divine worship.
- Indoors when not on duty.
- In attendance at an official reception.

When in uniform outdoors, except when attending divine worship, personnel in uniform always wear their hats.

Reporting for Pay

Answer "here" when your name is called, salute the pay officer, sign the payroll list, count your money, and leave without saluting again. The pay officer is not obliged to return your salute.

Courtesies Given Indoors

When an officer enters a barracks, or other indoor place where soldiers are not at work, it is customary for the first person seeing the officer to call the other occupants of the room to *attention*. All then stand and uncover, if unarmed, and *remain at attention* until he or she departs.

When an officer not directly involved in the ongoing work enters a workplace, it is not necessary for those who are working to stand up, although when a soldier is spoken to by an officer, he should stand if he is not at work.

When attending indoor ceremonies, stand at attention.

Courtesies Outdoors

When walking outdoors, the junior always accompanies the senior on the left. The same is true when riding in a vehicle with a senior (except when inspecting troops). When entering a vehicle or a small boat, the junior goes first, followed by others, in inverse order of rank, the senior person getting in last. When dismounting, the senior gets out first and the junior last.

When courtesies are given outdoors during ceremonies, the hand salute is given when in uniform, or the right hand is placed over the heart when in civilian clothes (at indoor ceremonies, stand at *attention*). When ceremonies (except military funerals) are being conducted, moving vehicles should be brought to a halt. On buses and trucks, only the senior occupant dismounts and gives the appropriate courtesy. Passengers and drivers in all other types of vehicles must dismount and give the appropriate courtesy. Women (military or civilian) never remove their headdresses during ceremonies.

Flags

The flag of the United States, national color, and national standard are not dipped by way of salute or compliment. An exception to this is the rule followed by naval vessels when, upon receiving a salute of this type from a vessel registered by a nation formally recognized by the United States, the compliment must be returned.

The organizational color or standard may be dipped in salute in all military ceremonies while the National Anthem, "To the Color," or a foreign national anthem is being played, and when giving honors to the organizational commander, an individual of higher grade including foreign dignitaries of higher grade, but not otherwise.

The U.S. Army flag is considered an organizational color and is also dipped when the National Anthem, "To the Color," or a foreign national anthem is being played. It is also dipped when giving honors to the Chief of Staff of the U.S. Army, his direct representative, or an individual of higher grade, including a foreign dignitary of equivalent or higher grade, but in no other case.

"Flag" is a general descriptive term for a cloth device with a distinguishing color or design, which has a special meaning or serves as a signal. The flag of the United States, the white flag of truce, and weather flags are examples.

In the military service, the color is a flag of a dismounted unit; an ensign is a national flag; a pennant is a small triangular flag usually flown for identification of a unit; a standard is a flag of a mounted unit; and a guidon is a swallow-tailed flag carried by Army units for identification, especially in drills and ceremonies.

The Flag of the United States. The flag of the United States is displayed at all Army installations. No more than one national flag is flown at any one time. The flag of the United States represents the Union—the 50 stars on a field of blue. The field is always to the left of the observer because it is the "field of honor," that is, on the right, the sword arm side.

The flag of the United States should never be used as part of a costume or dress or on a vehicle or float unless it is attached as to a staff, nor should it ever be displayed as drapery. Bunting—strips of cloth in the colors of the flag—is used for draping and decoration in general. No lettering or any other kind of object should ever be placed on the United States flag, and its use in any form of advertising is discouraged.

Soiled, torn, or weathered flags should be burned.

On Army installations, there are three different sizes of U.S. flags flown.

• Post Flag. This flag is flown in fair weather, except on those occasions when the garrison flag is prescribed. Its dimensions are 19 feet fly by 10 feet hoist.

• Garrison Flag. This flag is flown only on holidays and important occasions. Its dimensions are 38 feet fly by 20 feet hoist.

• Storm Flag. This flag is flown in lieu of the post flag in inclement weather. It is also used to drape caskets at a military funeral. Its dimensions are 9¼ feet fly by 5 feet hoist.

When the U.S. flag and the flags of other nations are flown from staffs, the U.S. flag is always displayed at the right end of the line. It is hoisted first and lowered last. In a group of flags consisting of state, society, or city flags, the U.S. flag should be placed in the center of the arrangement at the highest point.

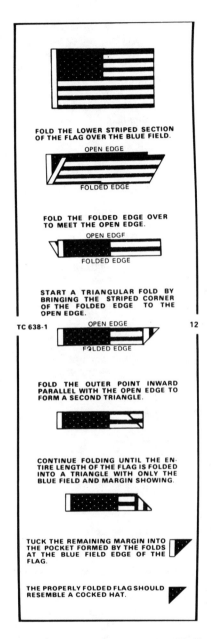

When folding the U.S. flag, it is important to fold it in the traditional manner as shown.

In an auditorium or on a platform, if the U.S. flag is displayed on the platform or the stage, it is to the speaker's right. If not displayed on the stage or platform, the U.S. flag is placed on the right of the audience. The other flags are displayed on the side to the opposite of the national flag. If the flag is displayed against the wall behind the speaker, it is above and behind the speaker's stand.

Whenever displayed with another flag in a crossed staff arrangement against the wall, the United States flag is placed to the right (the observer's left), and its staff is placed in front of the staff of the other flag.

Cannon Salutes

Salutes with cannon (towed, self-propelled, or tank-mounted) are fired with a commissioned officer present and directing the firing. They are not fired between retreat and reveille, on Sundays, or on national holidays (except Memorial and Independence days) unless, in the opinion of the officer directing the honors, international courtesy or the occasion requires an exception. They are given at the first available opportunity thereafter, if still appropriate.

The salute to the Union consists of one gun for each state. The national salute and the salute to a national flag are 21 guns each. The flag of the United States, national color, or national standard is always displayed at the time of firing a salute except for salutes given on the day of interment of the president, ex-president, or president-elect, when they are fired after the lowering of the flag.

Saluting Stations

The following installations are Department of the Army saluting stations designated to return salutes of foreign vessels of war in the ports and territorial waters of the United States.
- Fort Hamilton, Brooklyn, New York.
- Fort Lewis, Tacoma, Washington.
- Fort Monroe, Hampton Roads, Virginia.
- Fort Ord, Monterey, California.
- Presidio of San Francisco, California.

The Pledge of Allegiance to the Flag

The Pledge of Allegiance is not recited in military formations or in military ceremonies.

The following list prescribes the correct posture for military personnel.
- When in uniform outdoors, stand at *attention*, remain silent, face the flag, and give the hand salute.
- When in uniform indoors, stand at *attention*, remain silent, and face the flag. The hand salute is not given. Where the participants are primarily civilians or in civilian attire, reciting the pledge is optional for those in uniform.
- When in civilian attire, recite the pledge while standing at *attention*, facing the flag with the right hand over the heart. Men should remove headdress with the right hand and hold it over the left shoulder, the hand being over the heart.

Reveille and Retreat

Installation commanders set the time of sounding reveille and retreat.

Courtesy, Etiquette, and Customs

Reveille. At every installation garrisoned by troops other than caretaking detachments, the flag is hoisted at the sound of the first note of reveille.

Retreat. At the last note of retreat, a gun is fired if the ceremony is on a military installation, at which time the band, drum and bugle corps, or bugler plays the national anthem or sounds "To the Color," and the flag is lowered. The lowering of the flag is regulated so as to be completed at the last note of the music. The same respect is observed by all military personnel whether the national anthem is played or "To the Color" is sounded.

Flag Detail

Generally, a flag detail consists of one NCOIC, two halyard pullers, and two to eight flag handlers. The purpose of the flag handlers is to ensure correct folding and unfolding of the flag and to ensure that the flag does not touch the ground. Two flag handlers are needed when raising or lowering the storm flag; six handlers, for the post flag; and eight handlers, for the garrison flag.

Members of the flag detail are equipped according to local standing operating procedure and letter of instructions.

During the ceremony, the NCOIC inconspicuously gives the necessary commands or directives to ensure proper performance by the flag detail. On windy days, the NCOIC may assist the flag handlers to secure or fold the flag.

Raising the Flag for Reveille

The NCOIC forms the detail in a column of twos at double interval between files. He then secures the flag from the storage area and positions himself between the files and on line with the last two men. He then marches the detail to the flagpole.

The detail is halted in column, facing the flagpole on the downwind side. It is halted so that the flagpole is centered between the halyard pullers. The NCOIC commands *post*. On this command, the halyard pullers immediately move to the flagpole and ensure that the halyards are free of the pole. The flag handlers face to the center. The NCOIC then directs *unfold the flag*. On this directive, the two flag handlers nearest the NCOIC begin to carefully unfold the flag lengthwise, passing the freed end to the other handlers. When the two handlers nearest the flagpole have firmly secured the flag, the other handlers move away from the flagpole until the flag is fully extended. The flag is not unfolded widthwise. The flag handlers hold the flag waist high with their forearms horizontal to the ground.

At the appropriate time, the NCOIC directs *attach the flag*. On this directive, all flag handlers take one side step toward the flagpole. The two handlers nearest the flagpole immediately attach the top of the flag to the halyard. The halyard pullers raise the flag until the bottom of the flag can be attached. When raising larger flags, the NCOIC may command *side step, march*, and *halt* while the halyard pullers raise the halyard until the lower portion of the flag is attached.

At the first note of the music, the reveille gun is fired, and the halyard pullers rapidly raise the flag. The NCOIC salutes. As the flag is raised from the handlers' hands, they face the flagpole and salute. Reveille lasts 20 seconds. At the last note of the music, the NCOIC commands *order, arms* for himself and the flag handlers while the pullers secure the halyards. The NCOIC then positions himself between the halyard pullers, executes an *about face*, and commands *ready, face*. The detail faces in the appropriate direction to depart the flag pole. The NCOIC then marches the detail from the site.

Lowering the Flag for Retreat

The detail is marched and positioned at the flagpole in the same manner as when raising the flag. On the command *post*, the halyard pullers free the halyards, untangle them, ensure that they are free from the pole, and then temporarily resecure them. The flag handlers do not face to the center. The NCOIC then commands *parade, rest*.

At the cannon shot or at the last note of Retreat, each halyard puller immediately frees the halyards. The NCOIC commands himself and the flag handlers to *attention* and *present arms*. At the first note of "To The Color," the flag is lowered slowly and with dignity.

The call "To The Color" lasts about 40 seconds. As the flag is lowered to within reach, the two flag handlers farthest away from the flag terminate their salute, move forward rapidly, secure the flag, and move back from the flagpole. As the flag passes each handler, he terminates his salute and assists in securing the flag. The NCOIC terminates his salute at the last note of the music. Once the flag is detached, it is then folded. After securing the halyard, the handlers assist in the folding. After the flag has been folded properly and received by the NCOIC, the detail is marched to the storage site. Once the flag has been folded (cocked hat), it is treated as a cased color and not saluted by persons meeting the flag detail.

ETIQUETTE

Etiquette is merely the set of rules or forms for manners and ceremonies established as acceptable or required in professional or official life. As a professional noncommissioned officer, you are required to know these rules as they pertain to official social events conducted within the military community. Remember that the guides set forth in this section are not meant to be taken as commandments. In some situations, you may find it wholly proper and acceptable to depart from some of the normal rules of etiquette. Etiquette and courtesy go hand-in-hand, and if you take courtesy to others as your guiding principle, no matter what the situation, you can never go wrong.

Proper Speech

The ability to express yourself clearly, concisely, and in correct English is a priceless asset that you should cultivate. You should make every effort to develop and maintain good speech habits. As an NCO, you must be able to express yourself clearly and effectively.

Good speech begins with a good vocabulary and an understanding of the rules of grammar and pronunciation. To be constantly misusing and mispronouncing words in front of your soldiers will undermine your authority and cause you to lose their respect. A good speaker is listened to, and his message is understood. Being able to converse in an interesting, intelligent, and entertaining manner is a social asset that will reflect most favorably upon you in the eyes of your friends, your superiors, and your hosts. Never discuss your personal or business affairs at social gatherings. Never gossip, criticize others, boast, or engage in arguments. Maintain a broad interest in current events, movies, television, and so on, so that you may contribute to the conversation intelligently when those topics are brought up.

Special Courtesies to Women

At all formal social occasions, the man is expected to take the initiative. This is

Courtesy, Etiquette, and Customs

accepted procedure, and its extension to all sorts of social occasions is still quite proper. A lady does not escort a gentleman, nor is she expected to take the initiative in opening doors or taking off her escort's coat. No woman should feel in any way demeaned or insulted by gallant conduct on the part of a man. The social courtesies described here were not evolved nor are they practiced to be condescending to ladies.

Telephone Etiquette

Most soldiers have more contact with the public on the telephone than anywhere else. This is particularly true of the soldier who serves on a major military staff. It is essential that proper telephone courtesy is observed at *all* times because not to do so is to give everyone who calls a bad impression of you and your unit.

Basically, you should identify your unit or office first and then give your rank and name. Do not bury the caller under a deluge of acronyms or a long recitation of your chain of command. If you are in the "A" Company orderly room, answer, "Alpha Company orderly room, Specialist Cragg speaking, sir." Do not shout into the telephone or speak as if you were giving a command on the drill field. Speak clearly, in your normal tone of voice. If you are the first sergeant of Alpha Company, do not simply bellow your rank into the telephone, but give the caller the same courtesy you demand of your troops when they answer the telephone.

The use of the word "sir" is appropriate. Some object to this practice, pointing out that you never know the sex of the caller when you answer the telephone. "Sir" is a title of respect, and should the caller prove to be a woman, you will give her the same courtesy as you would any male caller and call her "ma'am."

Pay attention to the caller's own rank, title, and name, and use them, wherever appropriate, during the conversation. If the person being called is not in, offer to take a message or refer the caller to another party who may be able to help. Listen patiently and politely. Many people who ask for information do not know what they want, and sometimes you have to help them phrase their own questions. Above all, speak distinctly and with confidence. Some people answer the telephone as if they do not really know who they are, and this bad habit gives a very bad first impression of the organization they represent.

When calling someone else, always give your rank and name first: "This is Sergeant Major Purdom calling for Colonel Schweitzer." If you should get discourteous or bewildered people on the other end of the line, bear with them. It does no good for you to lose your patience. Always try to place official calls to avoid the lunch hour. You may find it necessary to dispense with a lunch hour and work straight through the day, but others may not.

Try not to tie up the telephone with long-winded personal conversations. There is a great temptation, and everyone gives in to it at times, to misuse DSN if it is available.

Should you dial a wrong number, *never* just hang up without saying anything. The proper procedure is to excuse yourself for the interruption and then check the number you have dialed. Never ask, "What number is this?" but "Have I reached 979-9383?"

Never let a telephone ring and ring because you happen to be talking to someone on another line. No military telephone should be left unattended during duty hours, and if one rings more than five times without being answered, someone is remiss. Do not assume that your subordinates will answer the telephone for you. If a phone is not answered by the fourth ring, pick it up yourself. Normally, sergeants major do not "take calls" for lower-ranking personnel, but if a sergeant major is put in this circumstance, he or she should do it gracefully and without complaint. If there is a problem keeping

Table of Honors

Grade, title, or office	Number of Guns Arrival	Number of Guns Departure	Ruffles & flourishes	Music
President	21	21	4	National anthem or "Hail to the Chief," as appropriate
Ex-President or President-elect	21	21	4	National anthem
Sovereign or Chief of State of a foreign country or member of a reigning royal family	21	21	4	National anthem of foreign country
Vice President	19	—	4	"Hail Columbia"
Speaker of the House of Representatives	19	—	4	March
American or foreign ambassador, or high commissioner while in country to which accredited	19	—	4	National anthem of United States or official's country
Premier or prime minister	19	—	4	National anthem of official's country
Secretary of Defense	19	19	4	March
Cabinet member, President pro tempore of Senate, governor of a state, or Chief Justice of the United States	19	—	4	March
Deputy Secretary of Defense	19	19	4	March
Secretary of Army	19	19	4	March
Secretary of the Navy or the Air Force	19	19	4	March
Director of Defense Research and Engineering	19	19	4	March
Chairman, Joint Chiefs of Staff	19	19	4	General's or admiral's march
Chief of Staff, U.S. Army; Chief of Naval Operations; Chief of Staff, USAF; or Commandant of the Marine Corps	19	19	4	General's or admiral's march

General of the Army, Fleet Admiral, or General of the Air Force	19	19	4	General's or admiral's march
Chairman of a Committee of Congress	17	—	4	March
Assistant Secretaries of Defense and General Counsel of the Department of Defense	17	17	4	March
Governor of a Territory of foreign possession within the limits of his jurisdiction	17	—	4	March
Under Secretary of the Army	17	17	4	March
Under Secretary of the Navy or the Air Force	17	17	4	March
Generals, admirals	17	17	4	General's or admiral's march
Assistant Secretaries of the Army	17	17	4	March
Assistant Secretaries of the Navy or the Air Force	17	17	4	March
American ambassadors having returned to the United States on official business	17	—	4	March
American envoys, American ambassadors having returned to the United States but not on official business, or ministers and foreign envoys or ministers accredited to the United States	15	—	3	March
Lieutenant general or vice admiral	15	—	3	General's or admiral's march
Major general or rear admiral (upper half)	13	—	2	General's or admiral's march
American ministers resident and ministers resident accredited to the United States	13	—	2	March
American charges d'affaires and charges d'affaires accredited to the United States	11	—	1	March
Brigadier general or commodore (lower half)	11	—	1	General's or admiral's march
Consuls general accredited to the United States	11	—	—	March

your receptionist in the office, deal with the receptionist, but don't take it out on the caller.

Tobacco Use

The Department of Defense is making a concerted effort to discourage smoking among the members of the armed forces. This is in response to the high cost of treating diseases caused by smoking. Within the Army, non-smoking offices and workplaces are now the rule. Smoking must be confined to designated areas. For soldiers, the risks of smoking in a tactical environment are enormous. One smoker could place his entire unit in jeopardy.

During off-duty hours, it is your choice to smoke or not, but if you smoke, you are responsible for being careful and considerate of those who do not. Observe "No Smoking" signs when posted, and never be insulted if a person asks you not to smoke in his or her presence. Never smoke in an automobile if there are nonsmokers present. While it is permissible to smoke out-of-doors, such as at sporting events, it is never done at ceremonies such as military reviews or funerals. Do not smoke while wearing gloves.

If you are not sure whether it is appropriate to light up, ask permission first. Never smoke when going through a reception line, and never carry a lighted cigarette with you into the dining room or onto the dance floor. If there are ashtrays provided and your hosts smoke during dinner, then you may smoke. Always use ashtrays, and never put ashes into cups or saucers or allow the ashes to fall on the floor or the table cloth at the dinner table.

If you are a smoker, remember that tobacco smoke is very distasteful to many people; it permeates hair and clothing and is carried home.

Generally, the smoking of pipes or cigars is not appropriate at official affairs unless permission is granted first. If you are a cigar or pipe smoker, be mindful that it is extremely discourteous to talk to someone with your pipe or cigar in your mouth. Try not to chew the end of your cigar into a slimy mass, and if you cannot help doing so, be discreet about removing the pieces from your mouth. If you must use your hands to gesture while you talk, keep your cigar or pipe in the ashtray or in the hand not being used at the moment.

As for snuff or "chew," this habit is totally inappropriate in any social setting. In the office, be considerate of those who find it offensive.

Receptions

Receptions are generally held in honor of someone, and the occasion may vary, but the rules of etiquette are the same, whether the reception is being held informally in a private home or on post following a ceremony.

If there is no reception or receiving line, seek the host or hostess, and pay your respects as soon as you enter the room. Try to chat with as many of the guests as you possibly can. It is very discourteous to associate only with your own friends or others known to you. Move from group to group, and should you become engaged in a long conversation with someone, especially a lady, invite that person to accompany you.

Make your departure brief and timely, but remember that it is inappropriate to leave a reception or dinner party before the guest of honor or senior person departs. It is also important to remember that when escorting a lady, should she make a move to depart before you are ready, you must conform to her wishes and prepare to leave. When taking your departure, simply say goodbye to the hosts and the guests and leave. If you

Courtesy, Etiquette, and Customs

are the host, you should always offer to see your guests to the door, unless they insist otherwise.

When invited to attend military receptions, you should consider attendance obligatory, and if you should need to absent yourself, do so only for those reasons that would require you to be absent from any military formation. Even if a military reception is being held for social reasons, it is still an official function.

Always face the people in the line and shake hands warmly and firmly. *Never carry anything in your hands when going through the receiving line.*

Conversations at receptions should be light and short. Move about, meet, and try to talk to as many different people as you can. When you desire to leave one group or person to greet friends, simply excuse yourself and leave. The length of time you should remain at a reception depends upon its size. At large receptions, plan to spend a minimum of 45 minutes; at smaller receptions, you may stay longer. Before leaving small receptions, pay your respects to the guests of honor, if any, and thank the host.

The House Guest

Many times during your career you will be invited to stay with people when you are traveling. You should always be appreciative when others open their homes to you in strange places, and you should do your best to be a courteous guest during your stay. The main point to remember is that when staying with someone else you should conform to the habits of that household—keep the same meal hours and go to bed and arise at the same times they do.

Unless you are specifically invited to stay for a certain number of days, make your stay as short as possible. Be sure to acquaint your host with your departure plans, and leave on time. If you dine with the family, be punctual at mealtimes.

Keep your room always neat, make your bed every day, and be sure that the bathroom is tidy after you use it. If you are the host, never let your guest take public transportation, but drive him or her to the terminal. Similarly, if guests are arriving in town via public transportation, you should make arrangements to pick them up.

Acknowledging Courtesies

When someone extends to you a social courtesy, you should reciprocate whenever possible. Of course, this is not always possible. Seniors, for instance, fully realize that a young couple or a bachelor cannot afford to host as elaborate an affair as they can themselves, nor would they expect as much. But you should remember that acknowledgment is due, and the method is not as important as the acknowledgment itself.

A card or flowers acknowledging a courtesy is always appropriate, whether or not you plan to reciprocate. Flowers are an especially appropriate way to thank your hostess if you have been her house guest, *and if you can afford them.* But a card will do just as well and is less expensive than a bouquet. It is the intent of the gift and not its price that determines its value to the recipient.

The Formal Dinner Party

As a noncommissioned officer whose sights should be set on eventual promotion to sergeant major, you will from time to time be assigned overseas or to other areas where formal entertaining frequently takes place, and you should expect invitations to formal dinner parties. It would be very embarrassing to you and your companion were you to arrive at the commanding general's quarters (or some foreign embassy) totally unprepared for the etiquette of a formal dinner party. If you can master the intricacies of the formal dinner party, you can handle anything.

As a noncommissioned officer, you should be able to fit into whatever company you happen to find yourself. You should know, however, what is proper to the occasion. At a formal embassy dinner, you do not use the same dining habits as you would in eating C rations in the field or sharing a pizza with buddies in the barracks. In some parts of the world, it is customary to eat the main courses at a meal with your fingers, and smacking the lips, sucking the teeth, and using toothpicks are not considered bad manners in the Far East. But if you use these techniques at dinners in the Western world, you will soon find yourself the object of ridicule.

Should you find yourself invited to a formal dinner party, consult with your command sergeant major on any questions regarding etiquette or protocol, and review the applicable chapters in *Service Etiquette*, by Swartz (U.S. Naval Institute Press), *Emily Post's Etiquette*, by Elizabeth Post (Funk and Wagnalls Co.), and USASMA Supplemental Reading I, *Protocol and Etiquette*.

The Formal Dining-In

The Dining-In is a formal military function held for the purpose of fostering cordiality, comradeship, and unit esprit. It is roughly comparable to a formal reception or dinner party in civilian life. Attendance at a formal Dining-In is mandatory for those concerned and is restricted to military personnel.

A Dining-In may be held exclusively by the officers of a unit, the noncommissioned officers, or in combination, to honor special guests or to commemorate a special occasion, such as unit organization day or a significant event in a unit's history. The Dining-In may also be held periodically, at the discretion of unit commanders and noncommissioned officers. During a Dining-In it is customary to honor those who have made outstanding contributions to the military service; a guest of honor is requested to address the assembly. Formal toasts are presented to dignitaries and chiefs of state.

The Dining-In is the American counterpart of the much older formal mess ceremony observed in the British Commonwealth and European armies. The American observance of the Dining-In was directly influenced by these customs and, in fact, is a transplant to this country. In earlier years the Dining-In was observed as a formal meal in the regimental mess with all present wearing the prescribed uniform. Protocol and etiquette were strictly observed at these affairs.

The revival of this tradition in today's Army should not be seen as a return to outmoded customs and traditions, but as paying the proper respect to an ancient and honorable custom of the military service that has always distinguished soldiers as members of an elite profession.

An Army is the sum of many small bodies of individuals who share a common set of values, principles, traditions, and perceptions of themselves and the world in which they live. One of the most important of these perceptions is *belonging*. The Dining-In reinforces this by providing an opportunity for soldiers to gather formally and focus attention on the common bonds of the service in an atmosphere of camaraderie. As a noncommissioned officer, you will attend formal Dinings-In and perhaps you will be called on to help organize them. But whatever your capacity, you will find the Dining-In a rewarding experience professionally and personally and one at which you should feel perfectly at ease.

"Black tie" is the appropriate dress for a Dining-In and should be specified on the

Courtesy, Etiquette, and Customs

invitations. Military personnel will wear a black bow tie with one of the four authorized uniforms: Army blue, Army blue mess, Army white, or Army white mess. Female soldiers will wear the equivalent uniforms. Miniature medals may be worn on the Army blue mess or the Army white mess; uniforms and ribbons, miniature or full-size medals may be worn on the blue or white uniforms.

Calling Cards and Social Calls

Calling cards (or visiting cards, as they are sometimes called) should be made by an engraver who is familiar with military calling cards. The cards should be engraved in black on plain white unglazed bristol board or thin white parchment. A very light cream color is also acceptable. The usual type style is *script* or *shaded roman*, but not ornate or with large letters. The customary size for visiting cards is 3½ inches by 2 inches. Never alter them in ink to correct changes in grade, position, or title. The following examples are correct: "Mrs. J. Piers Plowman," for a noncommissioned officer's wife's calling card; "CSM and Mrs. J. Piers Plowman," if a married couple prefer to use a joint card. And for an NCO's personal card:

J. B. Post
Command Sergeant Major
United States Army

Paying social calls upon local commanders is a tradition for officers newly arrived at a post, and the protocol on these occasions is well established. Junior noncommissioned officers should not be expected to make social calls, but very senior NCOs (sergeants major and command sergeants major) may occasionally be expected to do so.

A post or major command sergeant major may find it entirely appropriate to host social calls by newly arrived noncommissioned officers of the senior grades, although usually your first contact with these dignitaries will be through a visit to their office. Nevertheless, social calls among NCOs should be encouraged, wherever practical, as a means of fostering esprit among the members of the Noncommissioned Officer Corps. Upon arriving at a new post or duty assignment, check with your first sergeant or sergeant major to find out what the local procedures are governing formal social calls.

Etiquette in the Workplace

Good manners are never out of place, but there are some rules of courtesy you should observe scrupulously when you are on duty. Granted, as a young soldier—as a mechanic in a motor pool or a rifleman in an infantry squad—you will seldom have opportunities to deal with visitors to your "work" area. But as you rise in the ranks, you will at some time find yourself with a desk assigned to you in an office; you may even someday rate an office of your own, especially when you become a command sergeant major. As a senior NCO, you will find yourself assigned to staff duty at some time in your career, and if you are in personnel administration, you will spend your whole career behind a desk.

Never sit with your feet on your desk. Never sit at your desk reading non-job-related materials. The worst impression you can give a visitor is to be seen reading a novel with your feet propped up on the desk.

When a superior who is not your immediate supervisor enters your work area you are obliged to stand, if possible. But when anyone comes to see you, on business or just calling, you should stand when you greet that person. If you cannot stand—for example, if you are on the telephone—indicate by a nod of the head or a gesture with a free hand that the visitor should be seated. Never keep a person standing unless he or she is there to be disciplined.

If refreshments are available, such as coffee or tea, offer your visitor some. This may not always be appropriate, as when an NCO from another staff section drops by to deliver a report, but if the person is a friend or well known to you, make the offer a standard part of your greeting.

Never lean or sit on another person's desk while talking to him or her. If the person you are visiting is thoughtless enough not to offer you a seat, remain standing. To lean or sit on another person's desk presumes a degree of familiarity with that person that you should never display in public. Likewise, if you must, for some reason, sit at another person's desk, give up your seat as soon as he returns.

You should consider that a visit in person takes precedence over a telephone call. If you should happen to be on the telephone when a guest or visitor arrives, finish your conversation as quickly as possible or excuse yourself and call the other party back later.

Never spit in the wastepaper basket. Never deposit loose pieces of food such as unfinished fruit or sandwiches in the wastepaper basket.

It is best not to eat in the same place where you work. Many people believe that because of the pressures of work they must, and this is certainly true during exercises or actual military operations, but there are good reasons for not doing so under normal conditions. It is undignified for an NCO to eat at his desk. When at your place of duty, you should be working, not eating.

Give yourself a break. No matter how busy you think you may be, you can always find a few minutes to step outside your work area, find a quiet spot, and eat your lunch there. This practice will be good for your digestion and may help improve your overall attitude.

Be tolerant of your co-workers. In every work situation, certain people just do not get along, generally for the most frivolous reasons, but over a period of time, these minor dislikes can turn into deadly animosity. Set the example for others, and if you should encounter someone you dislike, suppress your intolerance. Allowing other people to annoy you is evidence of your own lack of self-discipline.

CUSTOMS

The customs of the service make up the unwritten "common law" of the Army. The customs of the service are rich in tradition, and knowing what they are and observing them should be second nature to every soldier.

Of course, times are changing. Today, hardly anyone remembers the ancient taboos against soldiers' carrying packages while in uniform or pushing baby carriages. But those customs that are still accepted should be observed, and the soldier who flouts them should be taken aside by the first NCO who spots him doing it and vigorously counselled about the importance of maintaining tradition and esprit in the Army.

Following are some of the customs observed in the Army today.

• Male personnel do not carry umbrellas. The thought behind this taboo is that it is too effeminate, and AR 670-1 does not authorize an umbrella as part of the male uniform.

• Never sit on another soldier's bed or bunk in the barracks without permission.

Courtesy, Etiquette, and Customs

- Never criticize a subordinate NCO in front of his or her troops.
- Never criticize the Army in front of civilians.
- Never accept gifts from subordinates.
- Never go over the heads of superiors.
- Never "pull rank" on another NCO (this action is very poor leadership).
- Never offer excuses. The by-line for any professional soldier who is caught short should be "No excuse, sir!"
- The commander's "desires" or "suggestions" should be acted upon as if they were orders (which they are, really, but politely phrased).
- Never "wear" a superior's rank by saying something like, "The colonel wants this done right away," when in fact the colonel has said no such thing and you are using his rank simply to awe people into doing something on the double.
- Never turn and walk the other way to avoid giving the hand salute.
- Never run indoors to avoid standing Reveille or Retreat.
- With the exception of on-the-spot corrections of uniform discrepancies or breaches of military courtesy and discipline, never give orders to another NCO's troops.
- Never appear in uniform while under the influence of alcohol.
- If you are a man, always show deference to women and children.

Remember these two responses to questions or orders from your superiors, and you will never go wrong: "I don't know, sir, but I'll find out," and "I'll do it or have it done."

Bugle Calls

These signals to the troops are transmitted on the bugle. Traditionally, Army bugle calls have been divided into four major categories.

- Alarm ("Fire," "To Horse").
- Formation ("Adjutant's Call," "Assembly").
- Service ("Church Call," "Fatigue," "First Sergeant's Call," "Mess Call," "Officer's Call," "Recall," "Retreat," "Reveille," "School Call," "Sick Call," "Taps," "Tattoo," "To the Color").
- Warning ("Boots and Saddles," "Drill Call," "First Call," "Guard Call," "Stable Call," "To Quarters").

The purpose of bugle calls is to order the activities of soldiers throughout the day. At most Army installations today, a few calls that are used are played from recordings on a public address system, although a live bugler is sometimes used to sound Retreat and Reveille.

Following are brief explanations of some of the more common calls, with traditional lyrics that soldiers have created to accompany the music.

First Call. This call is actually the first bugle call of the day, given as a warning that Reveille is to take place within a few minutes. It is very similar to the French *"Le Garde à vous."*

Mess Call. In former days, this call was affectionately dubbed "Soupy."

> Soup—y, soup—y, soup,
>   Without a single bean;
> Pork—y, pork—y, pork
>   Without a streak of lean;
> Coffee, coffee, coffee,
>   Without a bit of cream!
>   (or: The weakest ever seen!)

The tune has also been sung with these words: "Come and get your chow! Come and get it now!" This call is similar to the French *"Le Rappel."*

Reveille. The word is from the French *reveiller*, to arouse or awaken, originally from the Latin *evigilare*, to watch or to wake.

The custom of sounding some sort of call to signify the beginning of the day is very ancient. The British adopted the practice from the French and were calling it "revelly" as early as 1644.

Of course, "First Call" is actually the initial bugle call of the Army day, and if you are still in bed when "Reveille" is sounded, you are late. But "Reveille" has come into our vocabulary as the word for the bugle call that signifies to awake.

The traditional words to the call are:

> I can't get 'em up, I can't get 'em up,
>   I can't get 'em up in the morning;
> I can't get 'em up, I can't get 'em up,
>   I can't get 'em up at all;
> Corp'rals worse than the privates;
> Sergeants worse than the corporals;
> Lieutenants worse than the sergeants,
> And capt'ns the worst of all.

Taps. This call is the last bugle call of the military day. "Taps" is also traditionally played at all military funerals.

Originally, the U.S. Army used the French *"L'Extinction des feux"* ("Lights Out") to end the day. The music for "Taps" was written by Brigadier General Daniel Butterfield (1831-1901) in July 1862 at Harrison's Landing, Virginia, when he was a member of the Army of the Potomac during the Peninsular Campaign of the Civil War.

In 1932, the French adopted "Taps" for use in their own army.

Both the *American Heritage Dictionary of the English Language* and *Webster's New World Dictionary of the American Language* suggest the term comes from the "tap" of the drum, which was once used to signal "Tattoo."

Following are three versions of the words sometimes sung to accompany the music of this call:

I	II	III
Fades the light;	When your last	Day is done
And afar	Day is past,	Gone the sun
Goeth day,	From afar	From the lake
Cometh night;	Some bright star	From the hills
And a star	O'er your grave	From the sky;
Leadeth all,	Watch will keep	All is well
Speedeth all	While you sleep	Safely rest;
To their rest.	With the brave.	God is nigh.

Tattoo. This call is usually played at or very near 2100 hours, and it signifies that lights should be extinguished within 15 minutes. It is the longest bugle call in the U.S. Army—28 bars. The first eight bars are from the French *"L'Extinction des feux"* ("Lights Out"), and the following 20 bars are a British Army infantry tattoo.

Originally, this word appeared in English as "tap toe" or "tap-too." The *Oxford English Dictionary*'s earliest source is from 1644 A.D. and reads: "If anyone shall bee found tiplinge or drinkinge ... after ... the Tap-too beates, hee shall pay 2s 6d." Apparently in Dutch, at least as early as 1639 A.D., the colloquial expression "tap toe" meant to "shut up," possibly from "tap" meaning to tap a cask and "toe" meaning shut, therefore to put the bung into a beer keg. The commonly accepted origin of the military version is from the practice in seventeenth century armies of provost marshals' visiting the civilian inns and taverns at night, informing the proprietors when it was time for the troops to return to garrison—to "tap the bungs into the barrels" as it were. Eventually, the custom of the provosts' circulating among the taverns gave way to a party of drummers parading around a garrison at the same time each night, beating a signal to inform the soldiers that it was time for them to return to quarters. The first beat of the drum as the musicians fell in was known as "first post," and the final beat as "last post." "Last post" is sometimes used today as another name for a military obituary.

To the Color. This call is the bugle call played immediately after Retreat. The first note of "To the Color" signals that the flag is to be lowered. While this call is being sounded, military personnel in uniform give the appropriate salute. On many posts, the interval between the end of "Retreat" and the beginning of "To the Color" is used to fire a salute cannon. This call was adopted by the U.S. Army in 1835, replacing the cavalry "To the Standard."

Sources
Dining-In. Pamphlet available from Combat Studies Institute, U.S. Army Command and General Staff College, Fort Leavenworth, KS 66027.
Post, Elizabeth L. *Emily Post's Etiquette.* Funk & Wagnalls: New York, 1968.
Swartz, Oretha D. *Service Etiquette.* Naval Institute Press: Annapolis, MD, 1988.
USASMA Booklet: *Formal Dining-In Handbook.*
USASMA Supplemental Reading I: *Protocol and Etiquette.*

10

Uniforms and Insignia

WEARING THE UNIFORM

Your Army uniform is the outward evidence of your profession, your standing in that profession, and a prime indicator of the degree of respect with which you regard your service to the United States of America and the Army. The condition of your uniform and the way you wear it are also a reflection of your own self-respect.

One of the basic responsibilities of every noncommissioned officer is to know the composition of the Army uniforms and how to wear them properly. This rule is not to say that a good NCO will fly into a huff every time he or she spots a soldier whose personal appearance is less than recruiting-poster sharp, but no NCO should tolerate negligence when it comes to good grooming or ignorance when it comes to wearing the Army uniform.

There are soldiers—some of whom are relatively high-ranking—who pay little attention to their uniforms and personal appearance. Good NCOs will not let this fact bother them, but as in all other things, they will overcome these bad examples by setting the proper example themselves.

Recommending Changes to the Uniform

Changes to the Army uniform are approved by the Chief of Staff of the Army acting on the recommendations of the Army Uniform Board. AR 670-1 prescribes that major Army commanders thoroughly evaluate proposals to change or add to the uniform (accessories or related items) that are submitted through the Army Suggestion Program.

Uniforms and Insignia

Enlisted personnel may also submit recommendations for changes to the uniform through the enlisted chain of command up to the Sergeant Major of the Army. The SMA is a member of the Army Uniform Board. During the annual Major Command Sergeants Major Conference hosted by the SMA in Washington, significant items submitted for discussion are resolved at Department of the Army level. Often recommendations from enlisted personnel involving changes in the composition or wearing of uniform items are referred from the agenda of this annual meeting to the appropriate DA staff agency for comments and, if deemed appropriate, necessary action.

If the Sergeant Major of the Army, in his travels, hears enough complaints from enough soldiers about Army uniform policy or items of individual clothing or equipment, the word will get back to the Pentagon.

Classification of Service and Utility Field Uniforms

Class A Service Uniform. *For men:* Consists of the Army green coat and trousers, a short- or long-sleeved AG 415 shirt, a black four-in-hand tie (tied in a slip knot with the ends left hanging), and other accessories. *For women:* Consists of the appropriate Army green coat/jacket and skirt/slacks of the Army green uniform, Army classic uniform and the Army green pantsuit, a short- or long-sleeved AG 415 shirt, a black necktab, and other authorized accessories. The Army green maternity uniform (slacks or skirt) is also a Class A service uniform when the tunic is worn. The necktab will be worn with both the short- and long-sleeved maternity shirt when the tunic is worn.

Class B Service Uniform. *For men:* Consists of the same as for the Class A except the service coat is *not* worn. The black tie is required when wearing the long-sleeved AG 415 shirt and is optional with the short-sleeved shirt. *For women:* Consists of the same as for the Class A except the service coat/jacket and the maternity tunic are *not* worn. The black necktab is required when wearing the long-sleeved AG 415 shirt and the long-sleeved maternity shirt. It is optional with the short-sleeved version of both shirts. The AG 388 skirt and jacket and the dress and jacket uniforms are classified as Class B service uniforms.

A recent improvement in the fabric, fusible construction of the collar, pocket flaps, cuffs, and epaulets, and feedback from the field provided the necessary incentives to extend the wear of awards and decorations to include the Army green shirt (AG 415 and AG 428). Previously, only recruiters and those stationed in tropical climate areas were authorized to wear awards and decorations on Class B uniforms. Optional wear of awards and decorations includes the AG 428 polywool green shirt. All, some, or none of a soldier's awards and decorations, including miniature or full-size combat and special skill badges, may be worn. The following items are authorized for wear on Class B uniforms: marksmanship, identification, and foreign badges; regimental and infantry distinctive insignia; airborne background trimming; and service aiguillettes. Regimental insignia may be worn above the right breast pocket; however, distinctive unit insignia will not be worn on the epaulets. In addition, sew-on insignia, badges, patches of any type, and the combat leaders identification (green tabs) will not be worn. Ranger and Special Forces metal tab replicas, however, may be worn as group 4 special skill badges in the same way they are worn on the dress blue coat.

While this change in policy gives the soldiers the option of what they will wear on green shirts, commanders may require wear of awards and decorations for parades, reviews, inspections, funerals, and ceremonial or social events.

Class C Uniforms. These are utility, field, and other organizational uniforms, such as hospital duty and food service uniforms.

Occasions When the Uniform Is Required to Be Worn

The Army uniform is worn by all personnel when on duty unless Headquarters, Department of the Army (HQDA), has authorized the wearing of civilian clothes. The following general rules apply.

• Installation commanders may prescribe the uniforms to be worn in formations; duty uniforms are generally prescribed by local commanders or heads of agencies, activities, or installations.

• The wearing of combinations of uniform items not prescribed in AR 670-1 or other authorization documents is prohibited.

• Uniform items changed in design or material may continue to be worn as long as they are in serviceable condition unless specifically prohibited by Headquarters, Department of the Army.

Occasions When the Uniform May Not Be Worn

The wearing of the Army uniform is prohibited for all Army personnel under the following circumstances.

• In connection with the promotion of any political interests or when engaged in off-duty civilian employment.

• Except as authorized by competent authority, when participating in public speeches, interviews, picket lines, marches, rallies, or public demonstrations.

• When wearing the uniform would bring discredit upon the Army.

• When specifically prohibited by Army regulations.

Wearing of Headgear

The Army uniform is not complete unless the proper form of hat or cap is worn with it. Headgear is worn when outdoors, except by female officers when they are wearing the Army mess or evening dress uniforms.

Female personnel are not required to wear headgear when wearing the Army white or blue uniform to an evening social event. The appropriate headgear is, however, worn when wearing these uniforms on all other occasions.

Headgear is not required to be worn if it would interfere with the safe operation of military vehicles. The wearing of military headgear is not required when in privately owned or commercial vehicles.

Uniform Appearance

The word "uniform" as used in this context means "conforming to the same standard or rule." Although absolute uniformity of appearance by all soldiers at all times cannot reasonably be expected as long as armies are composed of so many various individuals, soldiers, when in uniform, should project a military image that leaves no doubt that they live by a common standard and are responsible to military order and discipline.

One important rule of uniformity is that, when worn, items of the uniform should be kept buttoned, zippered, and snapped, metallic devices (such as collar brass insignia) should be kept in proper luster, and shoes should be cleaned and shined.

Uniforms and Insignia 185

A soldier prepares for a field exercise with the help of an NCO. *U.S. Army photo*

Lapels and sleeves of coats and jackets for both male and female personnel should be roll pressed (without creasing). The AG-388 dress and jacket uniform and all skirts should also be without creases.

Trousers, slacks, and sleeves of shirts, blouses, and dresses other than the AG-388 dress should be creased.

Care and Maintenance of the Uniform

All solid brass items (belt buckles, belt-buckle tips, collar brass insignia) should be maintained in a high state of luster at all times; brass that is scratched and tarnished detracts from any soldier's overall military appearance. These items come coated with a lacquer, and if their surfaces are kept protected and gently rubbed clean with a soft clean cloth, they will keep their shine for a long time. But when the lacquer coating becomes scratched, dirt begins to accumulate in the scratches, and the item can only be kept shined by completely removing the lacquer surface.

The safest and most reliable method for removing the coating from brass items is to use Brasso polish applied with thumb and forefinger or a cloth. Once the lacquer coat is removed, the item must be shined regularly or it will tarnish quickly. Use one rag to take off the dirt and tarnish, and another to buff the item to a high shine (a wool blanket is excellent for this purpose). Some soldiers immerse the shined brass pieces in boiling water before drying and mounting them on their uniforms. This is supposed to remove any polish residue and keep the pieces in a high gloss for a longer period of time.

Never spit-shine leather items. Spit-shining does make shoes, boots, and equipment look sharp (and a good spit-shine can be maintained with little effort), but it dries out the leather, destroys its water-repellent capacity, and causes the item to become unserviceable much more quickly than if shoe polish is applied in the normal manner.

If you, however, purchase your own pair of leather boots or shoes and you want to spit-shine them to wear for special occasions or to keep them for inspection displays, here's how it's done: Kiwi shoe polish is the best brand for spit-shining. Some soldiers will remove all the old dye with soap and water and then start over, applying coat after coat of shoe polish. The important thing to remember is that you must have a smooth coat of polish on the leather surface for it to take a good shine. Apply the polish with the softest rag you can find. An old T-shirt is good for this purpose as is a cotton baby diaper, if you can find one.

Wet the cloth and wring it out thoroughly and wrap it tightly around the four fingers of one hand. Be sure there are no wrinkles on the polishing surface. When you have built up a solid coat of polish on the leather, it will shine easily with the application of small amounts of polish rubbed in with vigorous circular motions of the polishing rag. Be sparing with the use of water. Pour a little into the lid of the shoe polish can and use it occasionally. Judge how often to dip the rag into the water by the gloss of the shine.

The gloss you can put on leather this way is far superior to Corfram or even patent leather, and once you learn the knack of spit-shining, your shoes and boots will glisten like glass. Remember, though, eventually the leather will dry out and begin to crack, and once that happens your footgear will be good for only the trash can.

Wash shoes and boots with a mild soap using little water. Remove suds and wipe the insides clean with a dry clean cloth. Dry footgear slowly in a warm, dry place and stuff paper in the toes while the shoes and boots are still wet to keep the leather from shrinking out of shape. Rubbing saddle soap into them before they are completely dry will help soften the leather. Apply a light coat of shoe polish, brush with a soft-bristle brush, and buff with a soft rag.

Replace heels on shoes and boots after wear of $7/16$ of an inch or more.

Never starch cotton clothing, such as shirts, trousers, and socks; wash with soap or detergent and hot water. Untailored wool clothing, such as socks and glove inserts, may be washed in mild soap or detergent and lukewarm or cool water; stretch the items into shape while drying.

Pay attention to the removal of stains from your clothing. Pages 9–13 and Appendix D, FM 21-15, contain valuable information on stain removal techniques that each soldier can apply at home or in the barracks.

Never press dirty clothing, and be careful when you do press clothing that the iron is not too hot. Use a damp cloth between the iron and the fabric when pressing wool items, dampen the surface of cotton clothing before applying the iron, and observe the various fabric settings on the iron when pressing synthetic fabrics.

Never store dirty clothing. Never fold wet clothing or place wet clothing in a bag or a drawer. Brush, sun, and air-dry wool and cotton clothing before storing it so that it does not mildew in humid weather, and use naphthalene or mothballs to protect wool when it is to be stored for long periods in a closed space.

Frequent cleaning of uniform items will increase their longevity and maintain the neat soldierly appearance that the uniform is designed to project. Rotating items of clothing, such as shoes and boots, will contribute to their longer life. The initial investment made when buying extra sets of shoes and boots will be offset because fewer repairs and replacements will be needed, and the footgear will last much longer.

Uniforms and Insignia

Many soldiers, as an economy measure, make minor repairs to their clothing themselves. Chapter 2, FM 21-15, gives some good tips on how to go about making these repairs. But frequently, soldiers attempt to sew on shoulder sleeve insignia and insignia of grade by themselves. There is nothing wrong with this if it is done properly— it saves money and that is very important to lower-ranking enlisted soldiers. The problem is that most soldiers do not know how to perform that kind of sewing job properly, and their work often turns out amateurish and sloppy; before long, the stitches unravel, and the chevrons and patches curl up on the sleeve. The best advice to soldiers who want to look sharp is to have their insignia sewn on by a tailor and save money in some other way.

Fitting of Uniforms

Generally, uniforms are fitted at the time they are issued to soldiers; uniform items purchased in the Quartermaster Clothing Sales Store are fitted (or should be fitted) before they are taken off the premises. Personnel who purchase uniform items through the post exchange or from commercial sources should pay close attention to the proper fit of the items before wearing them. And some soldiers will gain or lose weight and, from laziness or excessive frugality, continue to wear improperly fitting uniform items.

An NCO should be able to tell at a glance whether a soldier (male or female) is wearing a properly fitted uniform.

Fitting instructions and alterations of uniforms are made in accordance with AR 700-84 and TM 10-227, *Fitting of Army Uniforms and Footwear*. The following is a summary of general fitting guidelines.

Black All-Weather Coat. For male personnel, the sleeve is half an inch longer than the service coat when worn under the black all-weather coat. The bottom of the coat reaches to a point 1½ inches below the midpoint of the knee. For female personnel, the length of the sleeves is the same as for males. The bottom of the coat reaches to a point one inch below the skirt hem but no less than 1½ inches below the crease in the back of the knee.

Uniform Coats and Jackets. For all personnel, the sleeve length is one inch below the bottom of the wristbone.

Trousers. Trousers are fitted and worn with the lower edge of the waistband at the top of the hipbone, plus or minus half an inch. The front crease of the trousers will reach the top of the instep and be cut on a diagonal line to reach a point approximately midway between the top of the heel and the top of the standard shoe in the back. They may have a slight break in the front.

Slacks. Slacks are fitted and worn so that the center of the waistband is at the natural waistline. The front crease of the slacks will reach the top of the instep and be cut on a diagonal line to reach a point approximately midway between the top of the heel and the top of the standard shoe in the back. They may have a slight break in the front.

Knee-length Skirts and Dresses. Skirt and dress lengths are not more than one inch above or two inches below the crease in the back of the knee.

Long-Sleeved Shirts. The sleeve length will extend to the center of the wristbone.

The Clothing Allowance System

The Army clothing allowance system consists of an initial issue of clothing and a subsequent clothing allowance.

An *initial clothing issue* is authorized for first termers and inductees, any individual who reenlists three months from the date of his or her last discharge or release, those personnel who do not receive a complete initial issue, retired personnel called back to active duty three months from date of their release or retirement (but only one such entitlement is authorized during any four consecutive years), and enlisted personnel enlisting from another service. The "initial issue" consists of the prescribed items and quantities of personal-type clothing and service uniforms with component items.

The *clothing allowances* are provided in order that each soldier may maintain the initial clothing issue. Monthly clothing allowances provide for the cost of replacement and purchase of new items or the purchase of additional clothing items, *not cleaning, laundering, and pressing*. The *basic allowance* begins on the soldier's 181st day of active duty and is paid each month for the remainder of the first three-year period. The *standard allowance* begins the day after the soldier completes 36 months' active duty. The clothing allowance accrues monthly and is paid annually during the month of the soldier's basic active service date. *Supplemental clothing allowances* may be issued when commanders determine that military duty clearly requires the issue of additional clothing to attain a military mission.

Items of clothing issued to soldiers should not be submitted to unauthorized alterations. AR 700-84 clearly enjoins commanders to discourage unauthorized alterations, such as form fitting, pegging, and tapering; items that have been so altered are not acceptable for turn-in, and soldiers who do alter their uniforms in these ways must replace the altered items at their own expense.

UNIFORMS

Temperate and Hot Weather Battle Dress

This uniform is authorized for year-round on-duty wear by all personnel when prescribed by the commander. These uniforms (BDUs) may not be worn for travel or off military installations except in transit between the soldier's quarters and duty station. This is not an all-purpose uniform, especially when other uniforms are more appropriate. The BDUs are utility, field, training, or combat uniforms.

Maternity Work Uniform

This uniform is authorized for year-round on-duty wear by pregnant soldiers when prescribed for wear by the commander. It is not intended as a travel uniform; however, it may be worn in transit between the individual's quarters and duty station.

Desert Battle Dress Uniform

The DBDU may be worn only when prescribed by the commander. This field uniform is not a travel uniform; however, it can be worn in transit between the soldier's quarters and duty station. The wear of the DBDU at public functions other than homecoming parades and activities directly related to the celebration of the return of soldiers from Southwest Asia is not authorized without an exception from the major command.

Cold Weather Uniform

The OG 108 cold weather uniform is designed for year-round wear by all personnel when issued as organizational clothing and prescribed by the commander. It is not

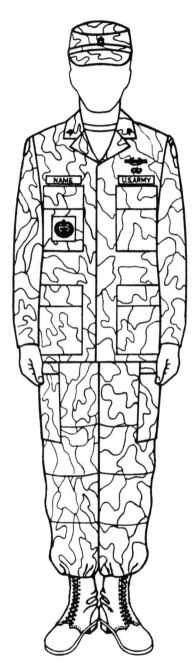

Temperate and hot weather BDU.

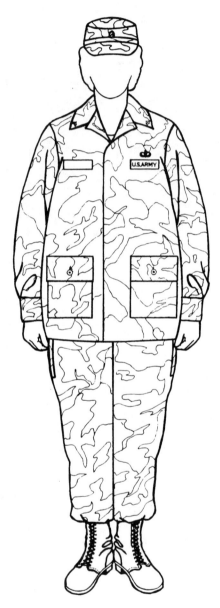
Maternity work uniform.

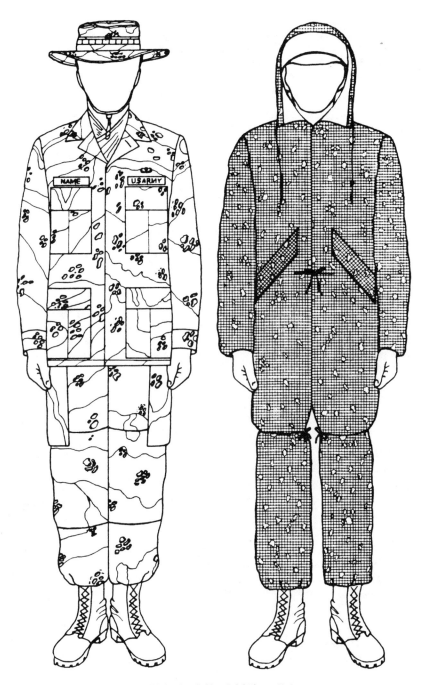

Desert DBU, daytime *(left)* and nighttime patterns.

authorized for travel or for wear off military installations except in transit. Components of this uniform may be worn with utility and other organizational uniforms as part of a cold weather ensemble when issued and prescribed by the commander.

Hospital Duty Uniform (Male)

This year-round duty uniform for all male soldiers in the Army Medical Specialist Corps and those in the medical, dental, or veterinary MOSs is worn in medical health care facilities as prescribed by the medical commander. It is not for travel except when worn in transit between quarters and duty station. The commander may, however, authorize the wear of this uniform in a civilian community when in support of civilian activities—even ceremonies and parades.

Hospital Duty and Maternity Uniform

This authorized year-round uniform is worn by Medical Specialist Corps personnel and enlisted women with medical, dental, or veterinary MOSs. It is not authorized for wear when in a travel status unless in transit between quarters and duty assignment.

Flight Uniform

This uniform is authorized for year-round wear when on duty in a flying or standby-awaiting-flight status. It is not worn for travel or off military installations except in transit between the soldier's quarters and duty station. Commanders may direct exceptions to wear policy.

Combat Vehicle Crewman Uniform

The CVC is a year-round duty uniform for combat vehicle crewmen when on duty or as directed by the commander. This uniform is not for travel.

Army Green Service Uniform (Male)

This uniform (Class A) and authorized variations (Class B) may be worn by all male personnel when on duty, off duty, or during travel. These uniforms are also acceptable for informal social functions after retreat, unless other uniforms are prescribed by the host.

Army Green Classic Service Uniform (Female)

This uniform is authorized for year-round wear by all female soldiers. The guidelines for wear are similar to those for male soldiers wearing the Army green service uniform.

Green Maternity Service Uniform

This uniform is authorized for year-round wear by pregnant soldiers when on or off duty or during travel. This uniform and its variations (Class B) may be worn for formal and informal social functions after retreat. Appropriate civilian maternity attire may be worn in lieu of this uniform for social functions.

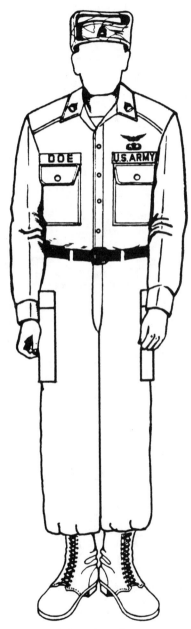

Cold weather uniform.

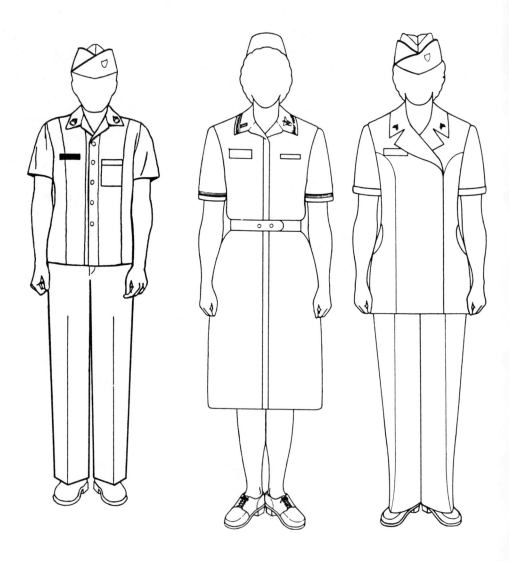

Hospital duty uniform, male *(left)* and female dress and pantsuit.

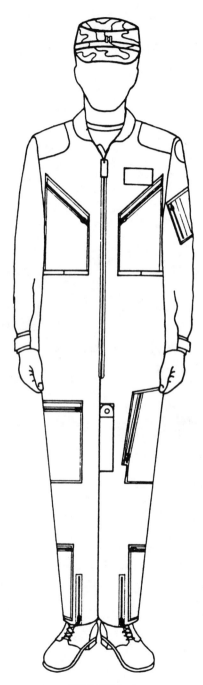

Flight uniform.

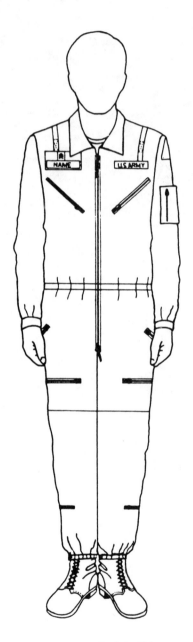

Combat vehicle crewman's uniform with Nomex cold weather jacket.

Army green uniform with garrison cap.

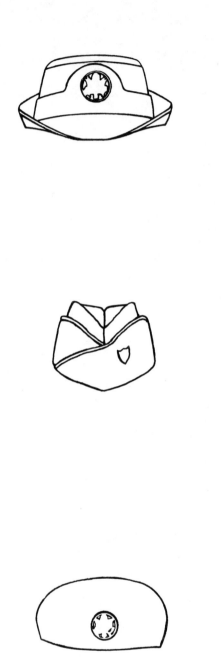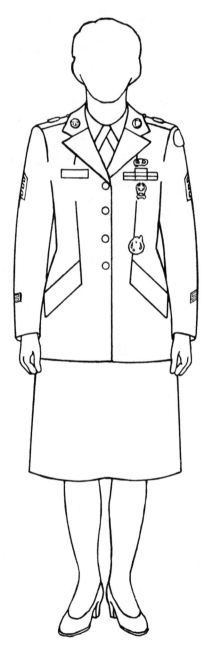

Army green classic ensemble with skirt. Army green service hat *(top)*, garrison cap *(center)*, and Army black service beret.

Army green maternity uniform, class A *(left)* and class B.

Army Blue Uniform (Male)

This uniform is authorized for optional wear by enlisted personnel. Although primarily a uniform for social functions of a general or official nature before or after retreat, it may be worn on duty if prescribed by the commander.

Army Blue Uniform (Female)

The guidelines for wear are similar to those for the blue uniform authorized for male soldiers.

Other Uniforms Authorized

- Army white uniform for both male and female soldiers.
- Food service uniform, including a maternity uniform.
- Army blue mess uniform.
- Army white mess uniform.

PERSONAL APPEARANCE

A vital ingredient of the Army's strength and military effectiveness is the pride and self-discipline that soldiers bring to their service. It is the responsibility of noncommissioned officers to assure that the military personnel under their supervision present a neat and soldierly appearance. It is the duty of each individual soldier to take pride in his or her appearance always.

Extreme or fad-style haircuts, such as punk, mohawk, multicolored, and so on, are not authorized. If dyes, tints, or bleaches are used, the artificial color must harmonize with the individual's complexion tone and not appear unnatural. Styles of hair and texture differ for the different ethnic groups, and these differences affect the length and/or bulk of hair as well as the style worn by each soldier.

Standards for Male Personnel

Many hairstyles are acceptable in the Army. So long as a soldier's hair is kept in a neat manner, the acceptability of the style should be judged solely by the criteria set forth in AR 670-1. Haircuts, without reference to style, should conform to the following standards.

- The hair on the top of the head should be neatly groomed. The length and/or bulk of the hair should not be excessive or present a ragged, unkempt, or extreme appearance. The hair should present a tapered appearance and, when combed, should not fall over the ears or eyebrows or touch the collar except for the closely cut hair at the back of the neck. The so-called "blockcut" fullness in the back is permitted in moderate degree, but in all cases, the bulk or length of hair should not interfere with the normal wear of all standard or adopted military headgear or protective masks.

- If the individual desires to wear sideburns, they should be neatly trimmed. The base should not be flared and it should be a clean-shaven, horizontal line. Sideburns should not extend downward beyond the lowest part of the exterior ear opening.

- A soldier's face should be clean shaven, except that Army regulations do permit mustaches. If you decide to grow a mustache, keep it neatly trimmed and tidy. No portion should be permitted to cover the upper lip line or extend beyond the crease of the upper and lower lips. Handlebar mustaches, goatees, and beards are not author-

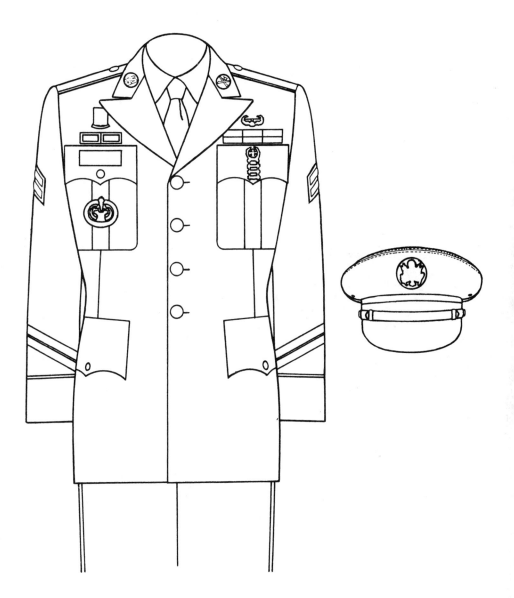

Army blue uniform with service cap.

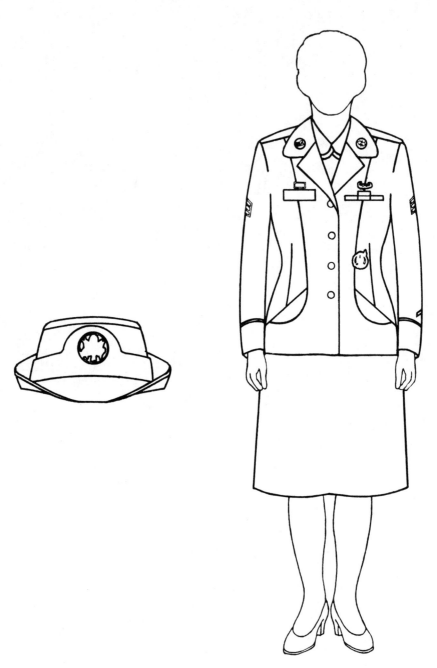

Army blue uniform with service cap.

A SOLDIER'S HAIR, SIDEBURNS, AND MUSTACHE ARE TO BE KEPT IN A NEAT MANNER AT ALL TIMES. (see AR 670-1 for guidelines.)

INSIGNIA OF BRANCH—Approximately 1″ above notch and centered on collar with the centerline of the insignia bisecting the notch and parallel to the inside edge of the collar.

DISTINCTIVE UNIT INSIGNIA (crest)—Centered between outside edge of button and shoulder seam.

SPECIAL SKILL BADGE—¼″ above ribbons.

SHOULDER SLEEVE INSIGNIA (Current Organization Patch)—½″ down from shoulder seam and centered.

SERVICE RIBBONS—⅛″ above pocket with or without ⅛″ space between rows and will be worn from wearer's right to left in order of precedence.

INSIGNIA OF GRADE (Stripes)—centered halfway between shoulder seam and elbow and centered on sleeve.

MARKSMANSHIP BADGE—centered between top of button hole and top of pocket.

IDENTIFICATION BADGE—centered on pocket between bottom of flap and bottom of pocket.

SERVICE STRIPES (Hash Marks)—4″ above bottom of sleeve and centered on the left sleeve (stripes run diagonally).

TROUSERS—will reach top of instep (may have a slight break in front), and cut diagonally to midpoint between top of heel and top of shoe at the rear.

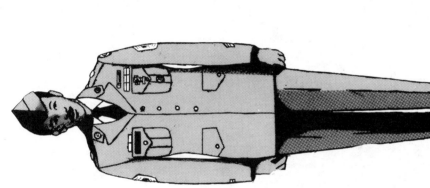

Army Green Uniform

GARRISON CAP—Worn with front vertical crease of cap centered on forehead in a straight line with nose. Cap will be slightly tilted to the right, but will not touch ear.

BLACK FOUR-IN-HAND TIE

US INSIGNIA—Approximately 1″ above notch and centered on collar with centerline of insignia bisecting the notch and parallel to the inside edge of the lapel.

SHOULDER SLEEVE INSIGNIA/FORMER WARTIME ORGANIZATION—½″ down from shoulder seam and centered.

UNIT AWARD EMBLEM—centered ⅛″ above pocket.

NAMEPLATE—on flap of pocket centered between top of button and top of pocket.

INSIGNIA OF GRADE—same as other side.

OVERSEA BARS (Hershey Bars)—4″ above and parallel to the bottom of the right sleeve and centered.

IDENTIFICATION TAGS (Dog Tags)—Worn when engaged in field training, when traveling in aircraft, and when outside CONUS.

BELT—1¼″ black web or woven elastic web with a black or brass tip. The tip will pass through the buckle to the wearer's left; the brass tip only will extend beyond the buckle.

BUCKLE—1¾″ x 2¼″ oval shaped, plain-faced, solid brass.

INSIGNIA OF BRANCH—Same as US Insignia.

DISTINCTIVE UNIT INSIGNIA (Crest)—Centered between outside of button and shoulder seam.

SPECIAL SKILL BADGE—¼" above ribbons.

SHOULDER SLEEVE INSIGNIA (current organization)—½" down from shoulder seam and centered.

SERVICE RIBBONS—Centered with bottom line positioned parallel to bottom edge of nameplate.

MARKSMANSHIP BADGE—Centered parallel to top edge of top button ¼" below service ribbons. (Slight adjustment to conform to individual figure differences authorized.)

IDENTIFICATION BADGE—Centered with top edge of badge parallel to top edge of third button from top.

SERVICE STRIPES (Hash marks)—4" above bottom of the left sleeve and centered (stripes run diagonally).

SOCKS—Optional plain black cotton or cotton nylon may be worn with black oxford shoes or Jodhpur boots, when worn with slacks.

SHOES—Black Oxford leather (nonpatent) with maximum of 3 eyelets, closed toe and heel (heel no higher than 2").

JEWELRY: EARRINGS—Screw-on or post-type on optional basis with service, dress, and mess uniforms only. NECKLACE: A purely religious medal on a chain is authorized as long as neither is exposed. A WRIST WATCH AND NOT MORE THAN TWO RINGS ARE AUTHORIZED.

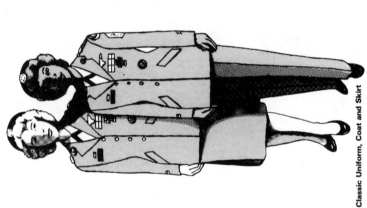

Classic Uniform, Coat and Skirt

Classic Uniform, Coat and Slacks

BERET—Worn tilted slightly to back of head with insignia centered on the forehead and not forward of forehead hairline (insignia will be placed ¾" from bottom edge of Beret front, parallel to floor and centered on eyelet).

US INSIGNIA—Bottom of disk centered approximately ⅝" up from notch with center line of insignia parallel to inside edge of lapel.

SHOULDER SLEEVE INSIGNIA—FORMER WARTIME ORGANIZATION—½" down from shoulder seam and centered.

UNIT AWARD EMBLEM—Centered with bottom edge ⅛" above top of nameplate.

INSIGNIA OF GRADE (STRIPES)—Centered halfway between shoulder seam and elbow and centered on sleeve.

NAMEPLATE—Centered 1-2" above top edge of top button.

OVERSEA SERVICE BARS (Hershey Bars)—4" above and parallel to the bottom of the right sleeve and centered.

SKIRT—Not more than 1" above or 2" below crease in back of knee.

STOCKINGS—Unpatterned/non-pastel materials of sheer or semi-sheer, with or without seams.

PUMPS—Black Service, untrimmed, closed toe heel, heel 1" to 3" and sole thickness ½" max.

IDENTIFICATION TAGS (Dog Tags)—Worn when engaged in field training, when traveling in aircraft, and when outside CONUS.

CAMOUFLAGE CAP—Straight on head so that cap band creates a straight line around the head parallel to the ground. (subdued insignia of grade ONLY and centered from top to bottom, right to left)

UNDERSHIRT—Army Brown is authorized.

SHOULDER SLEEVE INSIGNIA—Current Organization—½" down from shoulder seam and centered. (subdued only)

'US ARMY DISTINGUISHING INSIGNIA—Centered immediately above and parallel to top edge of pocket.

BLACK BOOTS—Clean and shined at all times (no patent leather).

SOCKS—ONLY Olive Green, shade 408, is authorized for wear with combat or organizational boots.

BLACK BUCKLE & BLACK TIPPED BELT ONLY COMBINATION AUTHORIZED.

Battle Dress Uniform (BDU)

HAIR—Neatly groomed and will not present an extreme, ragged, or unkempt appearance. Hair will not extend below bottom edge of collar, nor be cut to appear unfeminine. Styles will not interfere with the proper wearing of military headgear.

INSIGNIA OF GRADE—Subdued pin-on, or sew-on, will be centered on each collar bisecting the collar 1" from the point.

SHOULDER SLEEVE INSIGNIA—FORMER WARTIME ORGANIZATION—½" down from shoulder seam and centered (subdued only).

INSIGNIA NAMETAPE—Centered, immediately above and parallel to top of pocket.

ized. Where beard growth is prescribed by appropriate medical authority, as is sometimes necessary in the treatment of different types of skin disorders, the length required for medical treatment should be specified: "A neatly trimmed beard is authorized. The length will not exceed ¼ inch," for example. If you should have such a soldier under your authority, follow his medical progress closely and be sure he keeps his exemption slip handy at all times when in uniform.

• The wearing of wigs or hairpieces by male personnel while in uniform or on duty is prohibited by regulations, except to cover natural baldness or physical disfiguration caused by accident or medical procedure. When one is worn, it should conform to the standard haircut policy.

DA Poster 600-20 illustrates the various hairstyles, mustaches, and sideburns that are acceptable according to Army criteria. No style longer than the ones illustrated in the poster is permitted.

Standards for Female Personnel

The principle that soldiers should always maintain a neat and well-groomed personal appearance applies equally to men and to women, though the specific grooming standard for each reflects the traditional differences in appearance between the sexes.

Hair will be neatly groomed. The length and/or bulk of the hair should not be excessive or present a ragged, unkempt, or extreme appearance. Hair should not fall over the eyebrows or extend beyond the bottom edge of the collar. Ponytails, braids, and curlicues will not be worn hanging loose. Hair styles will not interfere with the proper wearing of military headgear or protective masks.

A hair net will not be worn unless it is required for health or safety reasons. If a commander requires its wear, it will be provided at no cost to the soldier. Wigs may be worn as long as the hairpiece is of a natural hair color and the style and length conform to appearance standards. Hair-holding ornaments (barrettes, pins, or clips), if used, must be transparent or match the hair color and should be inconspicuously placed.

Cosmetics shall be applied conservatively and in good taste. Exaggerated or faddish cosmetic styles are inappropriate with the uniform and shall not be worn. Lipstick may be worn with all uniforms. Extreme shades, however, such as purple, blue, white, and so on, will not be worn. Nail polish may be worn as long as it is conservative and complements the uniform. Only colorless nail polish may be worn with the field or utility uniforms.

Fingernail length shall be no longer than ¼ inch from the tip of the finger.

Wearing of Civilian Jewelry

The wearing of a personal wrist watch, identification wrist bracelet, and *not more than two rings* is authorized with the Army uniform as long as they are not prohibited for safety reasons and the style is conservative and in good taste. The wearing of a purely religious medal on a chain around the neck is authorized, provided that neither the medal nor the chain is exposed.

No jewelry, watchchains, or similar civilian items, *including pens or pencils*, should be allowed to appear exposed on the uniform. Exceptions are that a conservative tie tack or tie clasp may be worn with the black four-in-hand necktie, and a pen or pencil may appear exposed on the hospital duty and food service uniforms.

Female soldiers are authorized to wear screw-on or post-type earrings on an optional basis with the service, dress, or mess uniforms. Earrings may not be worn with Class C utility uniforms (utility, field, or organizational, including hospital duty and food

Uniforms and Insignia

service uniforms). Earrings will be small in diameter, 6 mm or ¼ inch; gold, silver, or white pearl; unadorned; and spherical. When worn, they will fit snugly against the ear and will be worn as a matched pair with only one in each ear lobe.

Fad devices, vogue medallions, personal talismans, or amulets are not authorized for wear in uniform.

Conservative civilian eyeglasses may be worn when prescribed. Oversize frames or frames with initials or other adornments are not authorized. Chains or ropes attached to the eyeglasses will not be worn while in uniform. Nonprescription conservative sunglasses may be worn in garrison except in formation. Conservative prescription sunglasses may be worn when prescribed by medical authority.

Wearing of Civilian Clothing

Civilian clothing is authorized for wear when off duty unless the wear is prohibited by the installation commander within CONUS or the major command overseas. When on duty in civilian clothes, soldiers will conform to the appearance standards of AR 670-1, unless specifically authorized for mission requirements.

Soldiers who are authorized to wear civilian clothing while on duty have been known to abuse the privilege by affecting longer hairstyles than authorized and generally fostering the impression that they are not even in the Army. Be alert for these people and deal with them firmly.

Identification Tags

More commonly known as "dog tags," identification tags are worn by all Army personnel when engaged in field training, when traveling in aircraft, and when outside the United States.

Identification tags have been used in the Army since 20 December 1906, when they were first prescribed by General Orders No. 204. Those early tags were round, about the size and thickness of a half dollar, and were issued free to enlisted men (at cost to officers).

Modern identity tags are made of noncorrosive metal and are worn around the neck, next to the skin, suspended on a beaded linked chain. The wearer's name, blood type, Social Security number, and religious preference (if any) are embossed in the metal.

When wearing identity tags in the field, many soldiers tape them or wrap them in plastic to prevent them from making undue noise and to prevent injury caused by falling on them; likewise, the chains are often threaded through rubber or plastic tubing to prevent chafing.

Security Badges

Security identification badges are worn in restricted areas as prescribed by local commanders. They are usually laminated plastic identification badges worn suspended from clips. They should never be worn outside the secure area for which they authorize an individual access. To prevent the possibility of losing them, some personnel suspend them from a chain worn about the neck and when in public, under their outer garments.

Nameplates

Nameplates are black laminated plastic measuring 1 inch by 3 inches by $1/16$ inch thick with a white border not to exceed $^1/_{32}$ inch in width. The lettering is white type, indented, ⅜ inch in height, and centered on the plate. Only last names are used. The finish may be gloss or nongloss. They are worn on the right side of the appropriate garments. See AR 670-1 for the precise placement on those uniforms. For male personnel, they are worn on the Army green 415 shirts, the coats of the Army green, white, and blue uniforms, and the hospital and food service uniforms. For females, they are worn on the green classic uniform, the Army green, blue, and white uniform jackets and the jackets of the Army green pantsuit and AG 388 uniforms, the AG 415 shirts, and hospital duty and food service pantsuits.

Nameplates are worn by all personnel on the black pullover sweater, centered on the black patch, except when also wearing a distinctive unit insignia. When a DUI is worn, the nameplate is worn half an inch above the bottom seam of the black patch with the DUI centered left-to-right, top-to-bottom above the nameplate. Female personnel may adjust positioning to conform to individual figure differences.

DISTINCTIVE UNIFORM ITEMS

The following uniform items are distinctive and should not be sold to or worn by unauthorized personnel: all Army headgear, badges (identification, marksmanship, combat, and special skill), buttons (uniform, U.S. Army, or Corps of Engineers), decorations, service medals, awards, tabs, service ribbons, and appurtenances, insignia of any design or color that have been adopted by the Department of the Army.

When turning in unserviceable uniforms, individuals should remove all distinctive items from them. Only those items listed above are considered distinctive. Therefore, it is proper that discharged personnel may wear any item of military clothing not specifically prohibited.

Headgear

The following items of headgear are authorized for Army personnel:

Item	*Female Version**
Beret, black (Ranger)	Beret, black, service
Beret, green (Special Forces)	
Beret, maroon (Airborne)	
Cap, baseball, black	
Cap, cold weather (AG 344)	
Cap, cold weather, utility (OG 107)	
Cap, food handlers, white, paper	
Cap, garrison, green (AG 344/434)	Cap, garrison (OG 108)
Cap, hot weather, utility (OG 106)	
Cap, service, blue	Hat, service, blue
Cap, service, green	Hat, service, green
Cap, service, white	Hat, service, white
Hat, camouflage, desert	
Hat, drill sergeant	
Hat, sun	
Helmet, flight	

---

*These are distinctively female items. Other items of headgear listed may be worn by female soldiers, as prescribed in AR 670-1.

Uniforms and Insignia

The garrison cap (sometimes called "overseas cap" and other names) is a soft, visorless cap with piping secured to the tip edge of the curtain. The service cap (sometimes called "flying saucer cap") is the visored, stiff-crown cap with chinstrap authorized for wear with specific dress uniforms. The white or blue service hat (commonly known as the "pot hat") is authorized for wear by female personnel with the dress blue or dress white uniforms.

Service Stripes

Service stripes are diagonal chevrons worn on the left sleeve of the prescribed uniform coat and in the prescribed manner (see below) that signify length of service. One stripe is authorized for each three years of active federal service, active reserve service, or combination thereof. Service need not have been continuous, and a tenth stripe is authorized after 29½ years.

Service stripes are worn by enlisted personnel of the U.S. Army, Army National Guard, and Army Reserve who have served honorably in either of the following:

• Active federal service as commissioned officers, warrant officers, or enlisted personnel in the Army, the Navy, the Air Force, or the Marines.

• Active Reserve service creditable for retirement as commissioned officers, warrant officers, or enlisted personnel in any Reserve component of the armed forces, including the Women's Army Auxiliary Corps for female personnel.

Service stripes worn by male personnel consist of a gold lace, gold bullion, or gold color rayon, diagonal stripe, $3/16$ inch wide and $1^{13}/16$ inches long on an olive green background that forms a $3/32$-inch border around the stripe and are worn on the Army green uniform, or a gold lace, gold bullion, gold color nylon, or gold color rayon, diagonal stripe, ½ inch wide and of variable length, on blue or white background that forms a $3/32$-inch border around the stripe and worn on the Army blue and white uniforms, respectively.

Service stripes worn by female personnel consist of a gold lace, gold bullion, or gold color rayon, diagonal stripe, ⅛ inch wide and 1¼ inches long on an olive green, blue, or white background that forms a $1/16$-inch border around the stripe and are worn on the Army green, blue, and white uniforms, respectively.

Service stripes are sometimes referred to as "hashmarks," which may have originated from the French *hacher*, meaning to engrave lines on or to chop up (the French Army used service stripes during the late 18th century, and General Washington, in adopting them for use by Continental troops, may have been imitating the French). Another supposition is that the term originated from the fact that, in order to earn a hashmark, a soldier must first consume a lot of Army hash.

Oversea Service Bars

Oversea service bars are gold lace, gold bullion, or gold color rayon bars, $3/16$ inch wide and $1^5/16$ inches long on an olive green background that forms a $3/32$-inch border around the bar, for male personnel. Female personnel wear a bar ⅛ inch wide and ⅞ inch long on an olive green background that forms a $1/16$-inch border around the bar.

The oversea service bar is worn centered on the outside bottom half of the right sleeve of the Army green uniform coat for male personnel and the Army green and Army green pantsuit uniform coats by female personnel.

One bar is authorized for wear for each period of six months' active federal service of the U.S. Army outside the continental limits of the United States:

• From 7 December 1941 until 2 September 1946, inclusive.

- In Korea from 27 June 1950 until 27 July 1954, inclusive; 1 April 1968 to 31 August 1973.
- In Vietnam from 1 July 1958 to 28 March 1973. Periods of TDY where credit was also given for hostile fire pay for one month may also be given credit for a month toward award of a bar.
- For each six months' service as a member of the U.S. Army in the Dominican Republic from 29 April 1965 to 21 September 1966, inclusive.
- In Laos from 1 January 1966 to 28 March 1973.
- In Cambodia, effective 1 January 1971.
- In Southwest Asia, effective 16 January 1991.

Service in World War II, Korea, Vietnam, the Dominican Republic, Laos, and Cambodia of periods of less than six months' duration, which otherwise meets the requirements for award of oversea service bars, may be combined to determine the total number of bars authorized.

Oversea service bars are frequently referred to as "hershey bars." The term seems to have originated during World War II and probably referred to both the appearance of the bars and the fact that for many personnel it was relatively easy to earn them—about as easy as going to the store to buy a candy bar.

Shoulder Sleeve Insignia—Current Organization

Full-color shoulder sleeve insignia of an individual's current organization are worn centered on the left sleeve ½ inch below the top of the shoulder seam on Army green coats for all personnel and the Army green pantsuit jacket for all female personnel. Subdued versions only are worn on the temperate and hot weather BDU, the OG 107 and 507 fatigues, OG 107 jungle fatigues (optional purchase), and the BDU and OG 107 field jackets by all personnel. They are not worn on the hospital duty and food service uniforms.

Only insignia approved by Headquarters, Department of the Army, are authorized to be worn. Any unit with an identifiable command structure, a valid justification in terms of unit mission, improvement of morale, and degree of unit permanency, with at least 500 military personnel assigned, may submit shoulder sleeve insignia designs for approval.

Individuals being transferred from one organization to another may continue to wear the insignia of their former unit until reporting for duty at the new organization. Organizational shoulder sleeve insignia are issued to individuals at the time they report to their new organizations.

Shoulder Sleeve Insignia—Former Wartime Service

At an individual's *option*, the shoulder sleeve insignia representing wartime service in a former organization may be worn on the right sleeve of all Army green uniform coats for all personnel and on the Army green pantsuit jacket for female personnel; a subdued version only may be worn on the field and work uniform coats and shirts.

Former wartime service shoulder sleeve insignia are authorized for individuals who served with U.S. Army organizations during the following periods:
- World War II, between 7 December 1941 and 2 September 1946, inclusive.
- In Korea, between 27 June 1950 and 27 July 1954, inclusive. Also from 1 April 1968 to 31 August 1973, those personnel who were awarded the Purple Heart, Combat Infantryman Badges, or Combat Medical Badges or who qualify for at least one service bar for service in hostile fire areas in Korea.

Uniforms and Insignia

- In Vietnam, from 1 July 1958 to 28 March 1973.
- In the Dominican Republic subsequent to 29 April 1965.
- In Grenada (including Green and Carriacou islands) between 24 October 1983 and 21 November 1983.
- In Panama (Operation Just Cause) 20 December 1989 to 31 January 1990.
- In Southwest Asia (Operation Desert Storm) 16 January to a date to be announced.

See AR 670-1 for further criteria.

Change 7 to AR 600-40, 31 October 1945, first authorized the optional wear on the right shoulder of the insignia of former wartime units.

Scarves

Scarves are the color of the branches of the service and are worn at the discretion of local commanders. They are bib-like and worn with the Army green and utility uniforms by male personnel, and with the Army green, green pantsuit, AG 388 green dress and jacket, AG 388 green skirt and jackets, classic and utility uniforms by female personnel.

When scarves are prescribed for wear, they are provided without cost to the individual.

Branch of Service — Colors and Scarves

Branch	Color	Scarf
Adjutant General	Dark blue & scarlet	Dark blue
Air Defense Artillery	Scarlet	Scarlet
Armor	Yellow	Yellow
Army Medical Specialist Corps	Maroon and white	Maroon
Army Nurse Corps	Maroon and white	Maroon
Aviation	Ultramarine blue & golden orange	Ultramarine blue
Branch Immaterial	Teal blue and white	Teal blue
Cavalry	Yellow	Yellow
Chaplains	Black	Black
Chemical Corps	Cobalt blue & golden yellow	Cobalt blue
Civil Affairs, USAR	Purple and white	Purple
Corps of Engineers	Scarlet and white	Scarlet
Dental Corps	Maroon and white	Maroon
Field Artillery	Scarlet	Scarlet
Finance Corps	Silver gray & golden yellow	Silver gray
Infantry	Light blue	Infantry blue
Inspector General	Dark and light blue	Dark blue
Judge Advocate General's Corps	Dark blue and white	Dark blue
Medical Corps	Maroon and white	Maroon
Medical Service Corps	Maroon and white	Maroon
Military Intelligence	Oriental blue & silver gray	Oriental blue
Military Police Corps	Green and yellow	Green
National Guard Bureau	Dark blue	Dark blue
Ordnance Corps	Crimson and yellow	Crimson
Quartermaster Corps	Buff	Buff
Signal Corps	Orange and white	Orange
Staff Specialist, USAR	Green	Green

Branch	Color	Scarf
Transportation Corps	Brick red & golden yellow	Brick red
Veterinary Corps	Maroon and white	Maroon
Warrant Officers	Brown	None

Note: The General Staff and the Sergeant Major of the United States Army have no color or scarf. Scarves are worn by the following personnel, without regard to branch:

Special Forces and Psychological Operations — Bottle Green
Supply, Supply & Service, Supply & Transportation & Support — Buff
Permanent Professors, Registrar, and Civilian Instructors of USMA — Scarlet
As Determined by Local Commanders — Camouflage

Combat Leader's Identification

The Combat Leader's Identification insignia is a green cloth loop, 1⅝ inches wide, worn in the middle of both shoulder loops of the Army green and cold weather coats. Personnel cease to wear them when reassigned from a command position or from an organization where these insignia are authorized to be worn.

The specific leaders in units authorized to wear the Combat Leader's Identification insignia are these: commanders; deputy commanders; platoon leaders; command sergeants major; first sergeants; platoon sergeants; section leaders (when designated in TOE); squad leaders and tank commanders; and rifle squad fire team leaders.

DISTINCTIVE UNIT INSIGNIA AND HERALDIC ITEMS

Distinctive unit insignia are made of metal or metal and enamel and are usually based on elements of the design of the coat of arms or historic badge approved for a specific unit. Sometimes erroneously referred to as "unit crests," distinctive unit insignia are subject to the approval of The Institute of Heraldry, U.S. Army, and, like shoulder sleeve insignia, are authorized for wear on the uniform as a means of promoting esprit de corps.

When authorized, these insignia are worn by all assigned personnel of an organization, except general officers. A complete set of insignia consists of three pieces: one for each shoulder loop and one for headgear (garrison, utility, cold weather caps, or berets). Approved designs are procured through the use of nonappropriated funds. The procurement of any distinctive unit insignia not approved by The Institute of Heraldry is prohibited.

Distinctive unit insignia are worn by male personnel on the Army green, white, and blue uniforms and the black pullover sweater. Female personnel wear them on the Army green, green pantsuit, classic, and the jacket of the AG 388 uniforms, the white and blue dress uniforms, and the black pullover sweater.

The distinctive unit insignia are worn on uniforms with shoulder loops, centered on the loops, an equal distance from the outside shoulder seam to the outside edge of the button, with the base of the insignia toward the outside shoulder seam, when insignia of grade are not worn. If insignia of grade are worn, the equal distance is measured from the outside edge of the insignia to the outside edge of the button. Enlisted personnel wear distinctive unit insignia centered on the left curtain of the garrison cap, one inch from the front crease, or centered on the stiffener of the beret.

When commanders authorize the wear of a special skill badge and a distinctive unit insignia, in addition to the mandatory insignia of grade, on the utility and cold

Uniforms and Insignia

weather caps, the distinctive unit insignia is worn above the insignia of grade or special skill badge with the base of the insignia toward the bill of the cap.

Heraldic items for Army organizations—distinctive unit insignia or shoulder sleeve insignia—reflect their history, tradition, ideals, and accomplishments. Coats of arms, historic badges, and distinctive insignia are designed so that each is distinctive to the organization for which they have been approved. They serve as identifying devices, an inspiration, and an incentive for unity of purpose. Designs of the coats of arms and historic badges are based on the lineages and battle honors of the organizations.

Regimental distinctive unit insignia are worn by all personnel affiliated with a regiment. The "crest" of the affiliated regiment is worn centered and 1/8 inch above the pocket seam or half an inch above unit and foreign awards, if worn, on the Army green, white, and blue uniforms. The DUI worn on the shoulder loops of the Army green, white, and blue (enlisted men only) coats and jackets is always the unit of assignment. If assigned and affiliated to the same regiment, then all three crests are the same.

Distinctive Items—Infantry

Infantry personnel are authorized to wear the following distinctive items.

• A shoulder cord of infantry blue formed by a series of interlocking square knots around a center cord. The cord is worn on the right shoulder of the Army green, blue, and white uniform coats and shirts, passed under the arm and through the shoulder loop and secured to the button on the shoulder loop. Officers and enlisted personnel who hold the Combat Infantryman Badge or the Expert Infantryman Badge or have completed the requisite training and period of service with an infantry unit of brigade or regiment size or smaller are authorized to wear the shoulder cord (see AR 670-1 for further details).

• An insignia disc, branch, and "U.S.," of infantry blue plastic, 1¼ inches in diameter. The disc is worn by enlisted personnel of the infantry, secured beneath the branch of the service and the U.S. insignia, with a ⅛-inch border around the insignia. It is authorized to be worn on the Army green, blue, and white uniforms. Discs are issued without cost to enlisted personnel. They are authorized to be worn upon completion of the advanced individual training program and assignment to an infantry TOE brigade, regiment, or smaller unit or to an infantry table of distribution unit.

• An insignia disc, service cap, of infantry blue plastic, 1¾ inches in diameter. This disc is worn secured beneath the insignia on the service cap. Criteria for wear are the same as those for the insignia disc.

Distinctive Items—Other than Infantry

Organizational Flash. This shield-shaped embroidered patch with a semicircular bottom approximately 2¼ inches long and 1⅞ inches wide is worn centered on the stiffener of the beret by personnel authorized to wear one of the organizational berets (Ranger, Special Forces, and Airborne).

Airborne Background Trimming. Background trimming is authorized for wear with the parachutist or air assault badge. When authorized, such background will be worn by all personnel of an airborne-designated organization who have been awarded one of the parachute badges or by personnel in an organization designated air assault who have been awarded the air assault badge. Only one background trimming is authorized to be worn. Generally, the trimming is an oval-shaped device of distinctive colors,

Distinctive items authorized infantry personnel. Note shoulder cord, scarf, and insignia discs (blue plastic) on service cap and collar brass.

1⅜ inches high and 2¼ inches wide, of embroidered cloth. The trimming is worn beneath any of the authorized parachutist/air assault badges.

Airborne Insignia. This white parachute and glider on a blue disk with a red border, approximately 2¼ inches in diameter, is worn by all personnel on jump status or by parachute-qualified personnel on special nonairborne duty (recruiting personnel or instructors). Enlisted personnel wear the insignia designed with the glider facing forward when it is worn centered on the left curtain of the garrison cap, one inch from the front crease.

Collar Brass Insignia

Collar brass insignia consist of "U.S." insignia and insignia of branch mounted on a one-inch-diameter disc of gold color metal worn on the prescribed uniform in a prescribed manner.

Male personnel wear these approximately one inch above the notch centered on the collar with the center line of the insignia parallel to the inside edge of the lapel on the Army green, white, and blue uniform coats.

Female personnel wear the bottom of the insignia disc so that it is placed approximately one inch above the notch centered on the collar with the center line of the insignia bisecting the notch and parallel to the inside edge of the lapel of the Army green pantsuit jacket, and green, blue, and white uniform coats. On the green classic uniform coat, they are centered on the collar approximately ⅝ inch up from the notch with the center line of the insignia parallel to the inside edge of the lapel.

 ADJUTANT GENERAL CORPS

 AIR DEFENSE ARTILLERY

 ARMOR

 BRANCH IMMATERIAL

 CAVALRY

 CHEMICAL CORPS

CORPS OF ENGINEERS

FIELD ARTILLERY

 FINANCE CORPS

 INFANTRY

INSPECTOR GENERAL

JUDGE ADVOCATE GENERAL

MEDICAL CORPS

MILITARY INTELLIGENCE

    MILITARY POLICE CORPS

ORDNANCE CORPS

QUARTERMASTER CORPS

SIGNAL CORPS

  THE SERGEANT MAJOR OF THE UNITED STATES ARMY

 TRANSPORTATION CORPS

Enlisted insignia of branch.

Note: Not shown are aviation branch, which is a propeller in a vertical position between two gold wings in a horizontal position, and special operations, which is two crossed arrows. The new public affairs insignia is depicted on page 216.

Public Affairs insignia of branch.

Basic trainees wear the "U.S." insignia on *both* collars in the same way as described above. Upon award of a basic MOS, the appropriate branch insignia is worn on the left collar.

The Sergeant Major of the Army wears SMA insignia in lieu of either insignia of branch or the "U.S." insignia.

ENLISTED INSIGNIA OF RANK

Enlisted insignia of rank come in three basic types: sew-on, pin-on, and shoulder mark type. The cloth sew-on sleeve insignia come in full-color; the metal pin-on collar insignia are either subdued metal or polished brass.

Noncommissioned officers, privates first class, and privates E-2 are identified by a system of chevrons and/or arcs. Privates E-1 have no insignia of rank. The Army specialist grade is identified by a spread-eagle device.

Full-Color Sew-On Insignia

Full-color sew-on insignia of grade are worn centered between the shoulder seam and the elbow on all uniform coats. Insignia with an Army green background are worn on the Army green coats for all personnel. Insignia with an Army blue or white background are worn with the Army blue or white uniforms.

Nonsubdued Pin-On Insignia

These insignia of grade are worn on the AG 415 shirt by personnel in the grade of specialist and below. They are worn by all soldiers on the hospital duty and food service uniforms, the black all-weather overcoat, the windbreaker, the AG 415 mater-

ARMY INSIGNIA OF RANK

Officer

- GENERAL OF THE ARMY
- GENERAL
- LIEUTENANT GENERAL
- MAJOR GENERAL
- BRIGADIER GENERAL
- COLONEL
- LIEUTENANT COLONEL (Silver)
- MAJOR (Gold)
- CAPTAIN
- FIRST LIEUTENANT (Silver)
- SECOND LIEUTENANT (Gold)

Enlisted

- SERGEANT MAJOR OF THE ARMY
- COMMAND SERGEANT MAJOR
- SERGEANT MAJOR
- FIRST SERGEANT
- MASTER SERGEANT
- SERGEANT FIRST CLASS
- STAFF SERGEANT
- SERGEANT
- CORPORAL
- SPECIALIST
- PRIVATE FIRST CLASS
- PRIVATE

Warrant Officers

- CHIEF WARRANT OFFICER (W4)
- CHIEF WARRANT OFFICER (W3)
- CHIEF WARRANT OFFICER (W2)
- WARRANT OFFICER (W1)

nity shirt, the AG 388 dress and jacket, and the AG 388 skirt and jacket. They are worn centered on both collars with the center line of the insignia bisecting the points of the collar and one inch from the collar point.

Subdued Insignia of Grade

These insignia are worn centered on both collars of the temperate camouflage uniform (old version of collar) with the center line of the insignia bisecting the points of the collar and positioned 1½ inches from the collar point. On modified temperate, hot weather camouflage, desert camouflage, durapress, hot weather noncamouflage uniforms, and cold weather coats, they are centered on both collars with the center line of the insignia bisecting the points of the collar and one inch from the collar point. Insignia may be pin-on or sew-on embroidered on subdued cloth backing. Pin-on and sew-on insignia of grade may not be mixed.

Shoulder Marks

Enlisted shoulder marks are black with replica insignia for grade embroidered ⅝ inch from the lower end of the shoulder mark. They come in two sizes, large (2⅛ inches wide at base and 4¼ inches long tapering to 1¾ inches at the top) for wear with the AG 415 shirt and small (2⅛ inches wide at base and 3½ inches long tapering to 1¾ inches at the top) for wear with the black pullover sweater. Shoulder marks are worn by all personnel corporal and above.

Sources
Romana Danysh and John K. Manon, *Army Lineage Series. Infantry. Part I: Regular Army.* Government Printing Office: Washington, DC, 1972, pp. 123–24.
AR 670-1, *Uniform and Insignia.*
AR 672-5-1, *Military Awards.*
AR 700-84, *Issue and Sale of Personal Clothing.*
FM 21-15, *Care and Use of Individual Clothing and Equipment.*

11

Awards and Decorations

The Army's awards and decorations program provides tangible recognition for acts of valor, exceptional service or achievement, special skills or qualifications, and acts of heroism not involving actual combat. It is the responsibility of any soldier having personal knowledge of an act, an achievement, or a service believed to warrant the award of a decoration to submit a formal recommendation into military command channels for consideration.

Under the above criteria, it is quite possible that a private may recommend a captain for a decoration, but usually the system works the other way around. As a noncommissioned officer representing a vital link in the chain of command, you must constantly be on the alert for service or acts on the part of subordinates that warrant the special recognition authorized under the awards and decorations program. But you must also be very careful not to abuse the system by recommending personnel who really do not deserve them.

The only consideration that should be used when deciding whether to recommend a soldier for a decoration is this one: *Does the person's act or service warrant a decoration?*

CRITERIA

The Army has established a "pyramid of honor" with its awards and decorations program that is designed to provide adequate recognition for every degree of heroism or meritorious act or service, from the Medal of Honor to the Army Achievement Medal.

In considering a soldier for a decoration, it is extremely important that that person's act or achievement be carefully measured against the decoration that best suits the act or achievement. An outstanding supply clerk, for example, would certainly deserve consideration for the Army Commendation Medal, but that same soldier would not qualify for the Legion of Merit.

Award recommendations must be factual and specific, and they must clearly demonstrate that the person being recommended deserves recognition. If your narrative does not support award of a decoration—if you use clichés and gobbledygook in place of straightforward and factual prose narrative writing—you will probably cheat a deserving soldier of a decoration.

TIME LIMITATION

The speed of recognition is essential for the purpose of maintaining morale. If a soldier deserves a decoration, it should be presented as soon as possible after the act or service. Awards for meritorious service should be anticipated, and your recommendation should be submitted through channels far enough in advance to ensure that the award is ready in time to be presented to the individual before departure.

Another reason for acting quickly on award recommendations is that the closer you are to the act or service for which an individual is being recommended, the fresher will be the details in your memory. In any event, each recommendation for an award of a military decoration must be entered into military channels within two years of the act, achievement, or service to be honored. No recommendation except the Purple Heart is awarded more than three years after the act or period of service to be honored (with the exception of lost recommendations or those circumstances covered in Paragraph 1-30, AR 672-5-1).

If a soldier under your supervision is deserving of an award recommendation, let him know about it. If the recommendation is not approved, at least the soldier will know you tried, and he will respect you for it. Most soldiers are not medal hunters, and you will find that they can accept the fact of disapproval of an award philosophically. This is especially true of junior officers and enlisted personnel; frequently, it is the much higher ranking, career-oriented soldier who feels "cheated" if his award recommendation is not approved. Such people should know better.

PRECEDENCE

Decorations, the Good Conduct Medal, and service medals are ranked in the following order of precedence when worn or displayed:

- U.S. military decorations
- U.S. unit awards
- U.S. nonmilitary decorations
- Good Conduct Medal
- Army Reserve Components Achievement Medal
- U.S. service medals and training ribbons
- U.S. Merchant Marine awards
- Foreign military decorations
- Foreign unit awards
- Non-U.S. service awards

U.S. military decorations, the Good Conduct Medal, and U.S. service medals are ranked in the following order of precedence when worn or displayed:

Awards and Decorations

    Medal of Honor
    Distinguished Service Cross
    Defense Distinguished Service Medal
    Distinguished Service Medal
    Silver Star
    Defense Superior Service Medal
    Legion of Merit
    Distinguished Flying Cross
    Soldier's Medal
    Bronze Star Medal
    Purple Heart
    Defense Meritorious Service Medal
    Meritorious Service Medal
    Air Medal
    Joint Service Commendation Medal
    Army Commendation Medal
    Joint Service Achievement Medal
    Army Achievement Medal
    Prisoner of War Medal
    Good Conduct Medal
    Army Reserve Components Achievement Medal

U.S. unit awards:
    Presidential Unit Citation
    Valorous Unit Award
    Joint Meritorious Unit Award
    Meritorious Unit Commendation
    Army Superior Unit Award

U.S. service medals:
    Army of Occupation Medal
    National Defense Service Medal
    Antarctica Service Medal
    Armed Forces Expeditionary Medal
    Vietnam Service Medal
    Southwest Asia Service Medal
    Humanitarian Service Medal
    Armed Forces Reserve Medal
    NCO Professional Development Ribbon
    Army Service Ribbon
    Overseas Service Ribbon
    Army Reserve Components Overseas Training Ribbon

Non-U.S. service medals:
    United Nations Medal
    Multinational Force and Observers Medal
    Republic of Vietnam Campaign Medal

WEARING OF MEDALS AND RIBBONS

All individual U.S. decorations and service medals (full-size medals, miniature medals, and ribbons) are worn above the left breast pocket or centered on the left side of the coat or jacket of the prescribed uniform (with the exception of the Medal of Honor,

Wearing of Service Ribbons Representing Decorations and Service Medals

	1		
2	3	4	5
6	7	8	9
10	11	12	13
14	15	16	17
18	19	20	21

1. Medal of Honor
2. Distinguished Service Cross
3. Distinguished Service Medal
4. Silver Star
5. Legion of Merit
6. Distinguished Flying Cross
7. Soldiers Medal
8. Bronze Star Medal
9. Purple Heart
10. Meritorious Service Medal
11. Air Medal
12. Army Commendation Medal
13. Army Achievement Medal
14. Good Conduct Medal
15. National Defense Service Medal
16. Armed Forces Expeditionary Medal
17. Vietnam Service Medal
18. Southwest Asia Service Medal
19. NCO Professional Development
20. Army Service Ribbon
21. Overseas Service Ribbon

which may be worn suspended around the neck). Decorations are worn with the highest displayed above and to the wearer's right of the others. A soldier authorized the Army Commendation Medal, the Good Conduct Medal, and the National Defense Service Medal would display them as follows (they would look this way to an observer):

        ARCOM   GCM   NDSM

Full-size decorations and service medals are worn on the Army blue, white, and green uniform when worn for social functions. They are worn in order of precedence from the wearer's right to left, in one or more lines, without overlapping within a line, with ⅛-inch space between lines. No line will contain fewer medals than the one above it. The Medal of Honor is worn with the neckband ribbon around the neck, outside the shirt collar and inside the coat collar, with the medal hanging over the necktie.

Miniature decorations and service medals are authorized for wear on the mess and evening mess uniforms only. They may be worn side-by-side or overlapped, but the overlap will not exceed 50 percent and will be equal for all. There are no miniature medals authorized for either the Medal of Honor or the Legion of Merit (degree of Chief Commander and Commander).

Service ribbons are worn in the order of precedence from the wearer's right to left in one or more lines either without a space between rows or with a ⅛-inch space. No row should contain more than four service ribbons. Male personnel are authorized to wear them on the Army green, white, and blue uniforms; female personnel may wear them on the AG 388 skirt and jacket, AG 388 dress and jacket, Army green pantsuit, Army green, classic, white, and blue uniforms.

Awards and Decorations 223

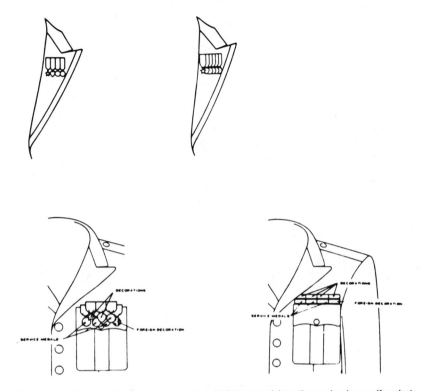

The top two illustrations show the proper placement of miniature medals on the evening dress uniform (note the overlapping in the figure on the right). The two lower illustrations show the placement of medals and ribbons on the Army green uniform.

Retired personnel and former soldiers may wear either full-size or miniature medals on appropriate civilian clothing on Veterans Day, Memorial Day, and Armed Forces Day, and at formal occasions of ceremony and social functions of a military nature.

Unauthorized Wearing of Decorations and Badges

Federal law prescribes stiff penalties for the unauthorized wearing of U.S. decorations, badges, appurtenances, and unit awards.

> Whoever knowingly wears . . . any decoration or medal authorized by Congress for the Armed Forces of the United States or any of the service medals or badges awarded to the members of such forces, or the ribbon, button, or rosette of any such badge, decoration or medal, or any colorable imitation thereof, except when authorized under regulations made pursuant to law, shall be fined not more than $250 or imprisoned not more than six months, or both.
> —62 Stat. 732, 25 June 1948, as amended 18 U.S.C. 704

An awards parade at Fort Monroe, Virginia.

The U.S. Code (18 U.S.C. 703) further prescribes:

> Whoever, within the jurisdiction of the United States, with intent to deceive or mislead, wears any naval, military, police, or other official uniform, decoration, or regalia of any foreign state, nation, or government with which the United States is at peace, or anything so nearly resembling the same as to be calculated to deceive, shall be fined not more than $250 or imprisoned not more than six months or both.

The Medal of Honor (MOH)

The Army and Air Force version of the Medal of Honor is the highest award for the risk of life "above and beyond the call of duty" involving actual conflict with an enemy; the Navy version can and has been awarded to noncombatants in peacetime, and Congress has similarly awarded special Medals to honor individual exploits during peacetime. Peacetime awards have included Captain Charles A. Lindbergh, General Billy Mitchell, and Admiral Richard E. Byrd.

The design of the Army Medal of Honor has undergone several changes since 1862. The one on which the present Medal is based was patented by General G. L. Gillespie on 22 November 1904. The Medal is designed in the form of a five-pointed star, made of silver and heavily electroplated in gold. In the center of the star appears the head of Minerva—the Roman goddess whose name is associated with wisdom and righteousness in war—surrounded by the words "United States of America." An open laurel wreath, enameled in green, encircles the star, and the oak leaves at the bases of the prongs of the star are likewise enameled. The Medal is suspended by a blue silk

Awards and Decorations

ribbon (the only U.S. decoration worn suspended from the neck), spangled with 13 white stars (representing the 13 original states), and attached to an eagle supported by a horizontal bar upon which is engraved the word "Valor."

The reverse of the Medal is plain so that the name of the recipient may be engraved thereon; the reverse of the bar is stamped "The Congress to."

On 21 December 1861, President Lincoln approved the Medal of Honor for enlisted men of the Navy and Marine Corps; a similar medal was established for the Army on 12 July 1862, further amended by legislation enacted on 3 March 1863 to include officers and making the provisions retroactive to the beginning of the war. The first Army Medals were awarded on 25 March 1863; the Navy Medals were first awarded on 3 April 1863.

The Medal of Honor is usually awarded by the President (but any "high official" may make the presentation) "in the name of the Congress of the United States," and for this reason, it is sometimes called the *Congressional* Medal of Honor.

Many Medal of Honor recipients are still alive, including soldiers from the Vietnam War, the Korean War, and World War II.

The Medal of Honor is awarded only to U.S. citizens, and only one Medal may be awarded to any one individual. The Army Medal may be awarded only to military personnel on active federal service.

Distinguished Service Cross (DSC)

Established by legislation on 9 July 1918 (as amended 25 July 1963), the Distinguished Service Cross evolved from the Certificate of Merit of 1847. This certificate was intended to be conferred only on private soldiers; NCOs received commissions for outstanding service and heroism; officers received brevet promotions.

The DSC is the second highest decoration for valor in war and is bestowed to recognize extraordinary heroism in connection with military operations in time of war. Unlike the Medal of Honor, however, the DSC may be awarded for heroism involving several acts over a short period of time that need not have been performed in actual conflict with an enemy, but must have involved extraordinary risk of life.

Authority to award the DSC is normally not delegated below Army (four-star) level, although such authority may be delegated in wartime to a brigadier general commanding a tactical unit in the position vacancy of a major general.

Successive awards are denoted by oak-leaf clusters.

Defense Distinguished Service Medal (DDSM)

Established by Executive Order 11545, 9 July 1970, the DDSM is awarded by the Secretary of Defense to any military service officer who, while assigned to joint staffs and other joint activities of the Department of Defense, distinguishes himself by exceptionally meritorious service in a position of unique and great responsibility. It is not awarded to any individual for a period of service for which a Distinguished Service Medal or similar decoration is awarded.

Subsequent awards are denoted by oak-leaf clusters.

Distinguished Service Medal (DSM)

Established by an act of Congress of 9 July 1918, the DSM is awarded to any person who, while serving in any capacity with the U.S. Army, has distinguished himself by exceptionally meritorious service in a duty of great responsibility. Awards may be made to persons other than members of the armed forces of the U.S. for wartime services only and then only under exceptional circumstances with the approval of the President.

The DSM is presented by the Chief of Staff of the Army; successive awards are denoted by oak-leaf clusters.

Silver Star (SS)

Established by an act of Congress of 9 July 1918 (as amended by an act of 25 July 1963), the Silver Star is the third-ranking U.S. decoration for heroism in wartime.

When first established, the SS was worn in the form of a small silver star, $3/16$ inch in diameter, upon the respective service medal and ribbon to indicate each separate citation for gallantry in action earned during the campaign for which the service medal was authorized. These stars were known as "citation stars."

The 8 August 1932 edition of AR 600-45 first authorized the Silver Star Medal and stated: "Those persons now authorized to wear citation stars may, at their option, continue to do so, or they may make application for the Silver Star and such oak-leaf clusters to which they may be entitled." Those authorized for certificates (for meritorious service and gallantry not in action) were requested to turn them in for award of the Purple Heart Medal.

The current version of the SS was designed by Bailey, Banks, and Biddle and is gilt bronze in the shape of a star 1¼ inches across. On the obverse is a laurel wreath within which is a silver star $3/16$ inch in diameter; on the reverse are inscribed the words "For Gallantry in Action."

The SS may be awarded by any commander who has the authority to award the DSC, and the SS, like the DSC, may be awarded for acts of heroism that take place over a period of time.

Successive awards are denoted by oak-leaf clusters.

Defense Superior Service Medal (DSSM)

Established by Executive Order 11904, 6 February 1976, the DDSM may be awarded by the Secretary of Defense to U.S. personnel who, in peace or wartime, while assigned to joint staffs and other joint activities of the Department of Defense, give superior meritorious service in a position of significant responsibility. It is not awarded to any individual for a period of service for which a Legion of Merit or similar decoration is awarded. Successive awards are denoted by an oak-leaf cluster.

Legion of Merit (LM)

Established by an act of Congress of 20 July 1942, the LM is awarded to any member of the armed forces of the U.S. or a friendly foreign country who distinguishes himself by outstanding meritorious conduct in the performance of outstanding services. The criteria for award of the LM during peacetime (or in situations not actually connected with war) apply to a lower range of positions than in time of war and require evidence of significant achievement.

Awards to foreign personnel are based on the relative rank or position of the recipient—called "degrees"—and are as follows: Chief Commander, for Chief of State

Awards and Decorations

or Head of Government; Commander, for the equivalent Chief of Staff or higher but not to Chief of State; Officer, to generals or flag officers below the equivalent of U.S. Chief of Staff; Colonels, in assignments equivalent to those normally held by general or flag officers in the U.S. Military Service; and Legionnaire, to all other eligibles. Awards of this decoration to U.S. military personnel are made without reference to degree.

Successive awards are denoted by oak-leaf clusters.

Distinguished Flying Cross (DFC)

Established by an act of Congress of 2 July 1926, the DFC may be awarded, in war or peace, to U.S. military personnel who distinguish themselves by heroism or extraordinary achievement while participating in aerial flight. Such awards are made only to recognize single acts of heroism or extraordinary achievement that are not sustained operational activities against an armed enemy. An act of heroism must be evidenced by voluntary action above and beyond the call of duty. Achievement awards must have resulted in an accomplishment so exceptional and outstanding as to clearly set the individual apart from other persons in similar circumstances.

Awards to foreign personnel serving with the U.S. armed forces may only be made in connection with actual wartime operations.

Successive awards are denoted by oak-leaf clusters.

Soldier's Medal (SM)

Established by an act of Congress of 2 July 1926, the SM is awarded to U.S. and foreign military personnel in recognition of heroism not involving actual conflict with an enemy. The performance must have involved personal hazard or danger and voluntary risk of life of approximately the same degree as that required for award of the Distinguished Flying Cross, but awards of the SM are not made solely on the basis of having saved a life.

Subsequent awards of this decoration are denoted by oak-leaf clusters.

Bronze Star Medal (BSM)

Originally established by Executive Order 9419 of 4 February 1944 (superseded by Executive Order 11046 of 26 August 1962), the BSM can be awarded to U.S. and foreign personnel, both military and civilian, for acts that display heroism, meritorious achievement, or service performed in connection with military operations against an armed force. A bronze V device is worn to denote awards for heroism, and successive awards are denoted by an oak-leaf cluster.

Purple Heart (PH)

Originally established by General George Washington on 7 August 1782 and revived by War Department General Orders 3, 1932, the PH is the oldest U.S. military decoration. The PH is awarded in the name of the President to any member of the armed forces or any civilian of the United States who, while serving under competent authority in any capacity with one of the U.S. armed services after 5 April 1917, has been wounded or killed or who has died or may die after being wounded.

A "wound" is defined as any injury (not necessarily one that breaks the skin) caused by an outside force or agent. Multiple injuries suffered at the same moment from the same agent are considered as one wound. Specific examples of injuries that would be authorized the award of the PH are those incurred while making a parachute landing from an aircraft that had been brought down by enemy fire or injuries received as the result of a vehicle accident caused by enemy fire (Paragraph 2-19b, AR 672-5-1).

The PH traces its lineage back to 7 August 1782, when General Washington established the Badge of Military Merit. The Badge of Military Merit was the first general military decoration established in the American Army.

Although there is some evidence that more may have been awarded, General Washington presented only three badges: Two were presented on 3 May 1783, one to Sergeant Elijah Churchill of the 2nd Regiment of Light Dragoons, and one to Sergeant William Brown of the 5th Connecticut Regiment, Continental Line; the third was presented to Sergeant Daniel Bissell of the 2nd Connecticut Regiment, Continental Line, on 10 June 1783.

The badge was allowed to lapse after the Revolution.

Recognition for wounds received in war was first given through the award of "wound chevrons" as prescribed by General Orders 6, 12 January 1918. A wound chevron was a small inverted chevron worn points down on the lower half of the right sleeve of the uniform coat by all officers and enlisted men who had received wounds in action. One chevron was authorized for each wound received.

AR 500-45, 8 August 1932, prescribed that "for acts or service prior to February 22, 1932," the PH could be awarded to those who had been awarded the meritorious service citation certificate (see Silver Star) and to those who were authorized to wear wound chevrons. Applications for award of the PH in lieu of wound chevrons and certificates were to be forwarded through proper channels.

The modern version of the medal bears the profile of George Washington and is engraved with the words "For Military Merit" on the reverse. Subsequent awards of the PH are denoted by oak-leaf clusters.

Defense Meritorious Service Medal (DMSM)

Established by Executive Order 12019 of 3 November 1977, the DMSM is awarded in the name of the Secretary of Defense to any member of the armed forces who, while serving in any joint activity of the Department of Defense on or after 3 November 1977 and for a period of 60 days or more, demonstrates incontestably exceptional service or achievement of a magnitude that clearly places him above his or her peers.

Subsequent awards of the DMSM are denoted by oak-leaf clusters.

Meritorious Service Medal (MSM)

Established by Executive Order 1144.8 on 16 January 1969, the MSM is awarded to any member of the armed forces of the United States who, while serving in a noncombat area after 16 January 1969, has distinguished himself by outstanding meritorious achievement or service. The achievement or service must have been comparable to that required for the Legion of Merit, but in a position of lesser, though considerable, responsibility. This decoration is the equivalent of the Bronze Star Medal for recognition of outstandingly meritorious noncombat achievement or service and takes precedence with, but after, the BSM when both are worn on the uniform. This decoration is not awarded to foreign personnel.

Subsequent awards are denoted by an oak-leaf cluster.

Awards and Decorations

Air Medal (AM)

Established by Executive Order 9242-A, 11 September 1942, the AM is awarded to any person who, while serving in any capacity in or with the Army, shall have distinguished himself by meritorious achievement while participating in aerial flight. Awards may be made in recognition of single acts of merit or heroism or for meritorious service. During the Vietnam War, personnel were frequently awarded Air Medals based in part on the number of combat-support missions flown. During his tour in the combat zone, the average Army aircrew member participated in hundreds of combat missions. Some veterans earned literally dozens of Air Medals in Vietnam. Thus, a system of denoting successive awards of the medal was devised using bronze arabic numerals instead of oak-leaf clusters. Therefore, an individual holding 15 awards of the AM wears the numeral "14" on the suspension ribbon and service ribbon.

Joint Service Commendation Medal (JSCM)

Established by Department of Defense Directive 1348.14, 17 May 1967, the JSCM is awarded to any member of the armed forces who distinguishes himself by meritorious achievement or service while serving in any joint assignment (see Paragraph 2-17b, AR 672-5-1, for a definition of "joint activities") after 1 January 1963. Awards made for acts or services involving direct participation in combat operations on or after 25 June 1963 may be denoted by the bronze V device.

The JSCM takes precedence with the Army Commendation Medal, but when both are worn, the JSCM is worn before the Army Commendation Medal. The JSCM is not awarded to any individual for a period of service for which another meritorious decoration has been awarded.

Subsequent awards of the JSCM are denoted by an oak-leaf cluster.

Army Commendation Medal (ARCOM)

Established by War Department Circular 377, 18 December 1945 (amended in DA General Orders 10, 1960), the ARCOM is awarded to any member of the armed forces who, while serving in any capacity with the Army after 6 December 1941, distinguishes himself by heroism, meritorious achievement, or meritorious service. The ARCOM may also be awarded to a member of the armed forces of a friendly foreign nation who, after 1 June 1962, distinguishes himself by an act of heroism, extraordinary achievement, or meritorious service that has been of mutual benefit to a friendly nation and the United States.

Awards of the ARCOM may be made for acts of valor performed under circumstances described above that are of lesser degree than those required for award of the Bronze Star Medal and may include acts that involve aerial flight. Awards may also be made for noncombat acts of heroism that do not meet the requirements for award of the Soldier's Medal.

To qualify for this decoration, the individual's achievement must have been of such magnitude that it clearly places him above his peers and must have been of the same degree as required for the award of the Meritorious Service Medal.

An award of this decoration for meritorious service normally will not be made for a period of service of less than six months, and the ARCOM is not authorized for award to general officers (Paragraph 2-18e, AR 672-5-1).

This decoration is primarily awarded to company-grade officers, warrant officers, and enlisted personnel.

Joint Service Achievement Medal (JSAM)

The Joint Service Achievement Medal is awarded to any member of the armed forces of the United States, below the grade of full colonel, who distinguishes himself or herself by meritorious achievement or service while serving in any joint activity after 3 August 1983. Military personnel on temporary duty to a joint activity for at least 60 days are also eligible.

The required achievement or service, while of lesser degree than that required for award of the Joint Service Commendation Medal, must have been accomplished with distinction. This decoration is not awarded for retirement.

The joint activities to which a soldier must be assigned to be eligible for this award include the Office of the Secretary of Defense, the Organization of the Joint Chiefs of Staff, the defense agencies (Defense Nuclear Agency, Defense Intelligence Agency, and so on), headquarters of unified and specified commands, and other activities designated in Paragraph 2-21, AR 672-5-1.

Second and subsequent awards are designated by oak-leaf clusters.

Army Achievement Medal (AAM)

The Army Achievement Medal is awarded to any member of the armed forces of the United States, or to any member of the armed forces of a friendly foreign nation who, while serving in any capacity with the Army in a noncombat area on or after 1 August 1981, distinguishes himself by meritorious service or achievement of a lesser degree than that required for award of the Army Commendation Medal.

The Army Achievement Medal is not awarded to general officers. Second and subsequent awards are designated by an oak-leaf cluster.

Prisoner of War Medal (POWM)

This award is authorized for all U.S. military personnel who were taken prisoner of war after 6 April 1917 during an armed conflict and who served honorably during the period of captivity.

Good Conduct Medal (GCM)

Established by Executive Order 8809, War Department Bulletin 17, 1941, and amended in 1943 (Executive Order 9323, War Department Bulletin 6, 1943) and 1953 (Executive Order 10444, Department of the Army Bulletin 4, 1953), the GCM is awarded to enlisted personnel for exemplary behavior, efficiency, and fidelity to active federal military service.

Generally, the qualifying period is three years of continuous active service completed on or after 26 August 1940. Exceptions are for those who are separated from the service by reason of physical disability incurred in the line of duty, who died or were killed before completing one year of service, or who separated after more than one year but less than three years (draftees). Those exceptions apply only to the first award.

Recommendations for award of the GCM originate with the individual's commander and are based on personal knowledge of the soldier's conduct, fidelity, and

DECORATIONS, SERVICE MEDALS, AND BADGES

U.S. ARMY AND DEPARTMENT OF DEFENSE MILITARY DECORATIONS

Medal of Honor (Army)

Distinguished Service Cross (Army)

Defense Distinguished Service Medal

Distinguished Service Medal (Army)

Silver Star

Defense Superior Service Medal

Legion of Merit

Distinguished Flying Cross

Soldier's Medal (Army)

Bronze Star Medal

Purple Heart

Defense Meritorious Service Medal

Meritorious Service Medal

Air Medal

Army Commendation Medal

Joint Service Commendation Medal

Joint Service Achievement Medal

Army Achievement Medal

OTHER U.S. ARMY AWARDS

Good Conduct
Medal (Army)

Army Reserve Components
Achievement Medal

PRE-VIETNAM U.S. MILITARY SERVICE MEDALS

World War II
Victory Medal

Korean
Service Medal

U.S. ARMY AND DEPARTMENT OF DEFENSE UNIT AWARDS

Presidential Unit Citation (Army)

Valorous Unit Award

Joint Meritorious Unit Award

Meritorious Unit Commendation (Army)

Army Superior Unit Award

U.S. MILITARY SERVICE MEDALS AND RIBBONS

National Defense Service Medal

Antarctica Service Medal

Armed Forces Expeditionary Medal

Vietnam Service Medal

Humanitarian Service Medal

Armed Forces Reserve Medal

U.S. ARMY SERVICE AND TRAINING RIBBONS

NCO
Professional Development
Ribbon

Army
Service Ribbon

Overseas
Service Ribbon
(Army)

Army Reserve Components
Overseas Training Ribbon

NON-U.S. SERVICE MEDALS

United Nations
Medal

Multinational Force
Observers Medal

Republic of Vietnam
Campaign Medal

U.S. ARMY BADGES AND TABS

Combat and Special Skill Badges

Combat Infantryman Badge
1st Award

Combat Medical Badge
1st Award

Combat Infantryman Badge
2nd Award

Combat Medical Badge
2nd Award

Combat Infantryman Badge
3rd Award

Combat Medical Badge
3rd Award

Expert Infantryman Badge

Expert Field Medical Badge

Master Astronaut Badge

Basic Astronaut Badge

Senior Astronaut Badge

Master Aviator Badge

Basic Aviator Badge

Senior Aviator Badge

Master Flight Surgeon Badge

Basic Flight Surgeon Badge

Senior Flight Surgeon Badge

Master Aircraft Crewman Badge

Basic Aircraft Crewman Badge

Senior Aircraft Crewman Badge

Master Parachutist Badge

Basic Parachutist Badge

Senior Parachutist Badge

Combat Parachutist Badge (1 Jump)

Combat Parachutist Badge (2 Jumps)

Combat Parachutist Badge (3 Jumps)

Combat Parachutist Badge (4 Jumps)

Combat Parachutist Badge (5 Jumps)

Air Assault Badge

Glider Badge

Pathfinder Badge

Special Forces Tab
(Metal Replica)

Ranger Tab
(Metal Replica)

Salvage Diver
Badge

Second Class Diver
Badge

First Class Diver
Badge

Master Diver
Badge

Scuba Diver
Badge

Master Explosive
Ordnance Disposal Badge

Basic Explosive
Ordnance Disposal Badge

Senior Explosive
Ordnance Disposal Badge

Nuclear Reactor Operator Badge (Basic)

Nuclear Reactor Operator Badge (Second Class)

Nuclear Reactor Operator Badge (First Class)

Nuclear Reactor Operator Badge (Shift Supervisor)

Parachute Rigger Badge

Driver and Mechanic Badge

Marksmanship Badges

Marksman

Sharpshooter

Expert

Identification Badges

Presidential Service

Vice-Presidential Service

Secretary of Defense

Joint Chiefs of Staff

**Guard,
Tomb of the Unknown Soldier**

Drill Sergeant

**U.S. Army Recruiter
(Active Army)**

**U.S. Army Recruiter
(Army National Guard)**

**U.S. Army Recruiter
(U.S. Army Reserve)**

Awards and Decorations

The Prisoner of War Medal.

efficiency. The soldier's record of service must indicate willing compliance with the demands of the military environment, loyalty and obedience to superiors, faithful support of the goals of the organization and the Army, and conduct in such an exemplary manner as to be distinguished from that rendered by the individual's comrades.

Isolated examples of nonjudicial punishment are not necessarily automatically disqualifying, but must be considered on the basis of the soldier's whole record; consideration as to the nature of the infraction, the circumstances under which it occurred, and when it occurred must be duly weighed by the individual's commander. Conviction by court-martial terminates a period of qualifying service; a new period begins following the completion of the sentence imposed by court-martial.

Successive awards of the GCM are identified by clasps, or bars ⅛ by 1⅜ inches, of bronze, silver, or gold, with loops (also called knots) that indicate each period of service for which the medal is authorized. The first award is the actual medal itself. Successive awards are indicated by clasps with loops as follows:

2d award:	Bronze, 2 loops
3d	Bronze, 3 loops
4th	Bronze, 4 loops
5th	Bronze, 5 loops
6th	Silver, 1 loop
7th	Silver, 2 loops
8th	Silver, 3 loops
9th	Silver, 4 loops
10th	Silver, 5 loops
11th	Gold, 1 loop
12th	Gold, 2 loops
13th	Gold, 3 loops
14th	Gold, 4 loops
15th	Gold, 5 loops

The Good Conduct Medal is worn just after the Prisoner of War Medal and just before all service medals.

Army Reserve Components Achievement Medal

Established by DA General Orders 30, 1971, this medal may be awarded upon recommendation of the unit commander for four years of honest and faithful service on or after 3 March 1972. Service must have been consecutive, in the grade of colonel or below, and in accordance with the standards of conduct, courage, and duty required by law and customs of the service of an active duty member of the same grade. The reverse of this medal is struck in two designs for award to personnel whose service has been primarily in the Army Reserve or primarily in the National Guard.

U.S. ARMY AND DEPARTMENT OF DEFENSE UNIT AWARDS

Unit awards are authorized in recognition of group heroism or meritorious service, usually during a war, as a means of promoting esprit de corps. They are of the following categories: unit decorations, infantry and medical streamers, campaign streamers, war service streamers, and campaign silver bands. Only personnel who were assigned to the unit during the period for which the unit award is made are entitled to wear an emblem signifying receipt of the decoration. Streamers and silver bands accrue to the unit only and are displayed on the guidon or color.

U.S. unit decorations, in order of precedence shown below, have been established to recognize outstanding heroism or exceptionally meritorious conduct in the performance of outstanding services. These awards may be worn permanently by those who served with the unit during the cited period. The Presidential Unit Citation (Army), the Valorous Unit Award, the Meritorious Unit Commendation, and the Army Superior Unit Award may be worn temporarily by those serving with the unit subsequent to the cited period.

Unit Award Emblems may be worn on the following uniforms:
• Male personnel: Army green, white, and blue.
• Female personnel: AG 388 skirt and jacket, AG 388 dress and jacket, Army green pantsuit, Army green, classic white and blue.

Unit Award Emblems are worn in the order of precedence from the wearer's right to left in lines of not more than three emblems per line, with up to ⅛-inch space between the lines. Male personnel wear them immediately above the right breast pocket; female personnel wear them centered on the right side of the uniform with the bottom edge ⅛ inch above the top edge of the nameplate.

Presidential Unit Citation

The Presidential Unit Citation is awarded to units of the armed forces of the United States and cobelligerent nations for extraordinary heroism in action against an armed enemy occurring on or after 7 December 1941. The unit must display such gallantry, determination, and esprit de corps in accomplishing its mission under extremely difficult and hazardous conditions as to set it apart from and above other units participating in the same campaign. The degree of heroism required is the same as that which would warrant award of a Distinguished Service Cross to an individual. Extended periods of combat duty or participation in a large number of operational missions, either ground or air, is not sufficient. Only on rare occasions will a unit larger than a battalion qualify for award of the decoration.

The Presidential Unit Emblem (Army) is a blue ribbon set in a gold-colored metal frame of laurel leaves. It is authorized for purchase and wear as a permanent part of the uniform by those individuals who served with the unit during the cited period. It may

Awards and Decorations

be worn temporarily by those persons serving in the unit subsequent to the cited period.

Valorous Unit Award

Criteria are the same as those for the Presidential Unit Citation except that the degree of valor required is that which would merit award of the Silver Star to an individual. The initial eligibility date is 3 August 1963. The emblem is a scarlet ribbon with the Silver Star color design superimposed in the center, set in a gold-colored metal frame with laurel leaves.

Joint Meritorious Unit Award

Awarded in the name of the Secretary of Defense to Joint Activities of the DOD for meritorious achievement or service, superior to that normally expected, during combat with an armed enemy of the United States, during a declared national emergency, or under extraordinary circumstances that involved the national interest.

Meritorious Unit Commendation

Awarded for at least six months of exceptionally meritorious conduct in support of military operations to service and support units of the armed forces of the United States and cobelligerent nations during the period 1 January 1944 through 15 September 1946, during the Korean War, and after 1 March 1961. The degree of achievement is that which would merit the award of the Legion of Merit to an individual. The emblem is a scarlet ribbon set in a gold-colored metal frame with laurel leaves.

Army Superior Unit Award

Awarded for outstanding meritorious performance of a difficult and challenging mission under extraordinary circumstances by a unit during peacetime. Peacetime is defined as any period during which wartime or combat awards are not authorized in the geographical area in which the mission was executed. The emblem is a scarlet ribbon with a vertical green stripe in the center on each side of which is a narrow yellow stripe, set in a gold-colored metal frame with laurel leaves.

SERVICE MEDALS DESCRIBED

Service or campaign medals denote honorable performance of military duty within specified limited dates in specified geographical areas. With the exception of the Humanitarian Service Medal, the Armed Forces Reserve Medal, the Army Reserve Component Achievement Medal, the Army Service Ribbon, and the NCO Professional Development Ribbon, they are awarded only for active federal military service.

Service medals are worn in order by the date when the person became eligible for the award, not by the date of entry in the records or the date upon which the award was established. For example, award of the National Defense Service Medal for the period subsequent to 1 January 1961 was not authorized until 1 April 1966, but personnel on active duty as of 1 January 1961 are entitled to wear the ribbon as of 1 January 1961.

Precedence among the following service medals is as follows: the Army of Occupation Medal, the National Defense Service Medal, the Antarctic Service Medal, the

Armed Forces Expeditionary Medal, the Vietnam Service Medal, the Humanitarian Service Medal, the Armed Forces Reserve Medal, the NCO Professional Development Ribbon, the Army Service Ribbon, the Overseas Service Ribbon, and the Army Reserve Components Overseas Training Ribbon.

Foreign military service medals are worn following authorized U.S. decorations. The Republic of Vietnam Campaign Medal is worn immediately following all foreign decorations, if any, otherwise immediately following all U.S. service awards and the United Nations Medal.

Not more than one service medal is awarded for service involving identical or overlapping periods of time, except that each of the following groups of service medals may be awarded to an individual provided he or she meets the criteria prescribed by Chapter 4, AR 672-5-1.

The service medals described hereafter will most likely be authorized at some future time for the readers of this *Guide*. Thus, the World War II and Korean War service medals are not discussed. For information concerning the criteria for the award of any service medal not listed below, see Chapter 4, Sections II and III, AR 672-5-1.

Army of Occupation Medal

Established by War Department General Orders 32, 1946, this medal is awarded for service for 30 consecutive days at a normal post of duty (as contrasted to inspector, visitor, courier, escort, passenger, temporary duty, or detached service) with the Army of Occupation of Berlin between 9 May 1945 and a terminal date to be announced.

This medal was previously authorized for post-WWII occupation duty in Germany, Austria, Italy, Japan, and Korea (see Paragraph 4-24, AR 672-5-1). Berlin service does not authorize the wearing of a clasp on either the service medal or the service ribbon.

National Defense Service Medal

Established by Executive Order 10448 (Department of the Army Bulletin 4, 1953) and amended by Executive Order 11265 (and DOD Directive 1348.17, 1 April 1966), this medal is awarded for honorable active service for any period from 27 June 1950 to 27 July 1954 or for the period from 1 January 1961 to 14 August 1974.

The NDSM was again authorized for wear when Secretary of Defense Dick Cheney announced that the medal could be worn by those who served honorably during the Persian Gulf hostilities. Inclusive dates are 2 August 1990 to a date to be announced later. (On 12 April 1991, a third campaign in Southwest Asia, Operation Provide Comfort, commenced.) Subsequent award of the NDSM is denoted by a service star on the medal or ribbon.

The medal is not authorized for any person on active duty for purposes other than for extended active duty. Guard and Reserve forces personnel on short tours of duty to fulfill training obligations, persons undergoing physical examinations, and persons called to temporary active duty to serve on boards, courts, commissions, and so forth, are not considered eligible.

Any member of the Guard or Reserve who, after 31 December 1960, becomes eligible for the award of the Armed Forces Expeditionary Medal or the Vietnam Service Medal is also eligible for award of the National Defense Service Medal; it may also be awarded to any Reserve components personnel who are ordered to federal active duty regardless of the duration of that duty (with the exceptions noted above).

The second award of this medal is denoted by a bronze service star.

Awards and Decorations

Antarctica Service Medal

Established by Public Law 86-600 (Department of the Army Bulletin 3, 1960) and promulgated in DOD Instruction 1348.9, 2 March 1973, this medal is awarded to any member of the armed forces who meets one of the following criteria.

- Is a member of a direct support or exploratory operation in Antarctica.
- Participates in or has participated in a foreign Antarctic expedition in coordination with a U.S. expedition while under the sponsorship and approval of a U.S. government authority.
- Participates in flights as a member of the crew of an aircraft flying to or from the Antarctic continent in support of operations there.
- Serves aboard a U.S. ship operating south of latitude 60 degrees south in support of U.S. programs in Antarctica.

Effective 1 June 1973, minimum time limits for the award are 30 days' duty at sea or ashore south of latitude 60 degrees south. Flight crews of aircraft providing logistics support from outside the Antarctica area receive one-day credit for flights in and out during any 24-hour period. Days need not be consecutive.

Personnel who remain on the Antarctic continent during the winter months are eligible to wear a clasp with the words "Wintered Over" on the suspension ribbon of the medal and a disc, $5/16$ inch in diameter, with an outline of the Antarctic continent inscribed thereon fastened to the bar ribbon. These appurtenances are awarded in bronze for the first winter, gold for the second, and silver for personnel who "winter over" three or more times. Not more than one clasp or disc is worn on the ribbon, and no person is authorized to receive more than one award of the medal.

Armed Forces Expeditionary Medal

Established by Executive Order 10977, dated 4 December 1961 (Department of the Army Bulletin 1, 1962), this medal is authorized for U.S. military operations, U.S. operations in direct support of the United Nations, and U.S. operations of assistance for friendly foreign nations.

Operations are defined as military actions or the carrying out of strategic, tactical, service, training, or administrative military missions and the process of carrying on combat, including movement, supply, attack, defense, and maneuvers needed to gain the objectives of any battle or campaign.

Designated areas and dates of service for eligibility are as follows:

U.S. Military Operation	Dates of Service
Berlin	14 Aug 61–1 Jun 63
Lebanon	1 Jul 58–1 Nov 58
Quemoy and Matus islands	23 Aug 58–1 Jun 63
Taiwan Straits	23 Aug 58–1 Jan 59
Cuba	24 Oct 62–1 Jun 63
Congo	23 Nov 64–27 Nov 64
Dominican Republic	28 Apr 65–21 Sep 66
Korea	1 Oct 66–30 Jun 74
Cambodia (EAGLE PULL)	11 Apr 75–13 Apr 75
Vietnam (FREQUENT WIND)	29 Apr 75–30 Apr 75
Mayaguez Operations	15 May 75
Grenada (OPERATION URGENT FURY)	23 Oct 83–21 Nov 83

(U.S. operations in direct support of the United Nations)

U.S. Military Operation	Dates of Service
Congo	14 Jul 60–1 Sep 62
(U.S. operations of assistance for a friendly foreign nation)	
Laos	19 Apr 61–7 Oct 62
Vietnam	1 Jul 58–3 Jul 65
Cambodia	29 Mar 73–15 Aug 73
Thailand (in direct support of Cambodian operations)	29 Mar 73–15 Aug 73
Lebanon	1 Jun 83–1 Dec 87
Libya (OPERATION ELDORADO CANYON)	12 Apr 86–17 Apr 86
Persian Gulf (since the Bridgeton incident)	24 July 87–
Panama (OPERATION JUST CAUSE)	20 Dec 89–31 Jan 90

Subsequent awards of this medal are denoted by bronze service stars. To be eligible for additional awards, service must have been in more than one of the areas and within the dates specified above. Two awards will not be made for service in the same designated area. Personnel who served in Vietnam before 3 July 1965 and then after 3 July 1965 are authorized *either* the Armed Forces Expeditionary Medal or the Vietnam Service Medal, but *both* service medals are *not* authorized for any period of Vietnam service.

Vietnam Service Medal

Established by Executive Order 11231 (DOD Directive 1348.15, 1 October 1965), the Vietnam Service Medal is awarded to all members of the armed forces who served in Vietnam and contiguous waters or airspace thereover after 3 July 1965 and through 28 March 1973. Members of the armed forces in Thailand, Laos, or Cambodia or the airspace thereover who during the same period served in direct support of operations in Vietnam are also eligible.

Personnel who qualified for the Armed Forces Expeditionary Medal for reason of service in Vietnam between 1 July 1958 and 3 July 1965 (inclusive) may be awarded the Vietnam Service Medal in lieu of the Armed Forces Expeditionary Medal upon request to the individual's unit personnel officer. If such a request is made and granted, the individual automatically loses entitlement to the Armed Forces Expeditionary Medal for any period of Vietnam service.

One bronze service star (or a combination of bronze and silver stars, as applicable) may be worn on the suspension ribbon and bar ribbon representing this medal. The authorized campaigns are as follows:

Vietnam Campaign	Inclusive Dates
Vietnam Advisory Campaign	25 Dec 65–30 Jun 66
Vietnam Defense Campaign	8 Mar 65–24 Dec 65
Vietnam Counteroffensive	25 Dec 65–30 Jun 66
Vietnam Counteroffensive, Phase II	1 Jul 66–31 May 67*
Vietnam Counteroffensive, Phase III	1 Jun 67–29 Jan 68
Tet Counteroffensive	30 Jan 68–1 Apr 68
Vietnam Counteroffensive, Phase IV	2 Apr 68–30 Jun 68

*An arrowhead is authorized for those personnel who participated in a landing in the vicinity of Katum, Republic of Vietnam, 0900–0907, 27 February 1967.

Awards and Decorations

Vietnam Counteroffensive, Phase V	1 Jul 68–1 Nov 68
Vietnam Counteroffensive, Phase VI	2 Nov 68–22 Feb 69
Tet 69 Counteroffensive	23 Feb 69–8 Jun 69
Vietnam Summer–Fall 1969	9 Jun 69–31 Oct 69
Vietnam Winter–Spring 1970	1 Nov 69–30 Apr 70
DA Sanctuary Counteroffensive	1 May 70–30 Jun 70
Vietnam Counteroffensive, Phase VII	1 Jul 70–30 Jun 71
Consolidation I	1 Jul 71–30 Nov 71
Consolidation II	1 Dec 71–29 Mar 72
Vietnam Cease-Fire	30 Mar 72–28 Jan 73

Southwest Asia Service Medal

Established by Executive Order on 13 March 1991, the Southwest Asia Service Medal (SWASM) is awarded to U.S. military personnel who served in the Persian Gulf area since 2 August 1990. According to official messages from PERSCOM dated June and October 1991 and March 1992, the SWASM is authorized for wear by soldiers who participated in the following campaigns: the Defense of Saudi Arabia campaign, 2 August 1990 to 16 January 1991; the Liberation of Kuwait campaign, 17 January 1991 to 11 April 1991; and the Southwest Asia Cease-Fire campaign, which commenced 12 April 1991 and will continue to the date of a presidential proclamation terminating the Persian Gulf conflict. Subsequent awards of the SWASM are denoted by service stars affixed to the medal.

Humanitarian Service Medal

Established by Executive Order 12019, 3 November 1977, and implemented by DOD Directive 1348.5, 23 June 1977, the Humanitarian Service Medal is authorized to be awarded to any armed forces personnel who directly participated in a Department of Defense-approved humanitarian act or operation, except when a by-name eligibility list is published.

The Southwest Asia Service Medal.

As a recent example, soldiers who served in Operation Provide Comfort between 5 April and 14 June 1991 are eligible to receive the Humanitarian Service Medal (HSM). In this example, award of the HSM was made to those soldiers on a by-name list provided in early 1992 to major Army commands.

No more than one award of this medal may be made for the same act or operation. Subsequent awards are designated by bronze numerals. Other operations for which award of the Humanitarian Service Medal have thus far been approved are listed in Appendix B, AR 672-5-1.

Armed Forces Reserve Medal

Honorable and satisfactory service is required in one or more of the Reserve components of the armed forces for a period of 10 years, not necessarily consecutive, provided such service was performed within a period of 12 consecutive years. Periods of service as a member of a Regular component are excluded from consideration. Required also is earning a minimum of 50 retirement points per year (AR 135-180). Individuals are advised to consult the unit instructor of their organization as to individual eligibility.

One 10-year device is authorized to be worn on the suspension and service ribbon to denote service for each 10-year period in addition to and under the same conditions as prescribed for the award of the medal. It is a bronze hour glass with a $5/16$-inch Roman numeral X superimposed.

NCO Professional Development Ribbon

Established by the Secretary of the Army 10 April 1981 and effective 1 August 1981, the NCO Professional Development Ribbon is awarded to members of the U.S. Army, Army National Guard, and Army Reserve for successful completion of designated NCO professional development course. The ribbon is awarded for five levels of professional development:

• Primary—primary NCO course, combat arms (PNCOC); primary leadership course (PLC); and primary technical courses (service schools—PTC).
• Basic—basic NCO course, combat arms (BNCOC) and basic technical courses (service schools—BTC).
• Advanced—advanced NCO courses (service schools—ANCOC).
• First sergeant's course.
• U.S. Army Sergeants Major Academy.

The colors of the ribbon, green, yellow, and flag blue, symbolize the significance of the role of the NCO corps in the Army.

Successive awards of the ribbon are designated by arabic numerals: 1, primary level; 2, basic level; 3, advanced level; 4, first sergeant's course; and 5, USASMA.

Army Service Ribbon

Established by the Secretary of the Army 10 April 1981 and effective 1 August 1981, the Army Service Ribbon is awarded to members of the U.S. Army, Army National Guard, and Army Reserve who have successfully completed initial entry training.

Officers receive the ribbon upon completion of their basic orientation or higher level course. Those officers assigned a specialty, special skill identifier, or MOS based on civilian or other-service acquired skills are eligible for the ribbon after completion of

Awards and Decorations

four months' honorable active service. Enlisted persons are eligible upon completion of initial MOS-producing courses. For those enlisted persons assigned an MOS based on civilian or other-service acquired skills, it is awarded after four months of honorable active service.

The ribbon's colors—scarlet, orange, golden yellow, emerald, and ultramarine blue—represent the completion of all initial training.

Overseas Service Ribbon

Established by the Secretary of the Army on 10 April 1981 and effective 1 August 1981, the Overseas Service Ribbon is awarded to all members of the U.S. Army, Army National Guard, and Army Reserve credited with a normal overseas tour completed in accordance with AR 614-30.

A soldier who has overseas service credited by another armed service is eligible for this ribbon.

The ribbon is not authorized for completion of an overseas tour of duty for which a service medal has been authorized. For example, if a soldier is credited with overseas tours for Vietnam, Alaska, Berlin, and Germany, he would be entitled to the Vietnam Service Medal, the Army of Occupation Medal (for Berlin service), and the Overseas Service Ribbon with the numeral "2" (for Alaska and Germany).

First and subsequent awards of the ribbon are designated by arabic numerals.

Army Reserve Components Overseas Training Ribbon

Established by the Secretary of the Army on 11 July 1984, the ribbon is awarded to members of the U.S. Army Reserve components for successful completion of annual training or active duty for training for a period of not less than 10 days on foreign soil. Numerals are used to denote second and subsequent awards.

NON-U.S. SERVICE MEDALS

United Nations Medal

Established by the United Nations Secretary-General 30 July 1959 and authorized for acceptance by U.S. personnel as announced in Department of Defense instruction 1348.10, 11 March 1964, this medal may be awarded to personnel who have been in the service of the United Nations for a period of not less than six months with one of the following units.

- United Nations Observation Group in Lebanon (UNOGIL).
- United Nations Truce Supervision Organization in Palestine (UNTSO).
- United Nations Military Observer Group in India and Pakistan (UNMOGIP).
- United Nations Security Forces, Hollandia (UNSFH).

Multinational Force and Observers Medal

Established by the Director General, Multinational Force and Observers, 24 March 1982, this medal was authorized for wear by eligible U.S. military personnel 28 July 1982. To qualify, a soldier must have served with the Multinational Force Observers at least 90 days after 3 August 1981. Subsequent awards for each completed six-month tour are indicated by an appropriate numeral, starting with numeral "1."

Republic of Vietnam Campaign Medal

Authorized for acceptance by Department of Defense Instructions 1348.17, 31 January 1974, by members of the armed forces who meet the following criteria.

• Have served in the Republic of Vietnam for six months during the period 1 March 1961 to 28 March 1973, inclusive.

• Have served outside the geographical limits of the Republic of Vietnam and contributed direct combat support to the Republic of Vietnam Armed Forces for six months. Such persons must meet the criteria established for the Armed Forces Expeditionary Medal (Vietnam) or the Vietnam Service Medal during the period of service required to qualify for the Republic of Vietnam Campaign Medal.

• Have served under the conditions listed above for less than six months and have been wounded by hostile forces, captured (but later escaped, were rescued, or were released), or killed in action or otherwise in the line of duty.

Personnel assigned to the Republic of Vietnam on 28 January 1973 must have served a minimum of 60 days in the Republic of Vietnam as of that date or completed a minimum of 60 days' service during the period 29 January 1973 to 28 March 1973, inclusive. Claims of eligibility for award of this medal for periods of service before 1 March 1961 or after 28 March 1973 must be forwarded to the Secretary of Defense for approval.

The Republic of Vietnam Campaign Medal with Device (1960) and the miniature medal are items of individual purchase. The ribbon Device (60-) is authorized for initial issue to eligible individuals.

Kuwait Liberation Medal

In early 1992, Deputy Secretary of Defense Donald J. Atwood accepted a Saudi Arabian offer to award the Kuwait Liberation Medal to U.S. military members who directly participated in Operation Desert Storm. To qualify, PERSCOM has stated, members must have served or flown into the war zone between 17 January 1991, the start of the air war, and 28 February 1991, when offensive operations ended. The war zone includes Iraq, Kuwait, Saudi Arabia, Oman, Bahrain, Qatar, the United Arab Emirates, the Persian Gulf, the Gulf of Oman, the Gulf of Aden, and part of the Arabian Sea.

U.S. ARMY BADGES AND TABS

Badges and tabs are appurtenances of the uniform. In the eyes of their wearers, several badges have a significance equal to or greater than all but the highest decorations. There is no established precedence with badges as there is with decorations and service medals or ribbons. The badges are of three types: combat and special skill badges, marksmanship badges and tabs, and identification badges. Badges are awarded in recognition of attaining a high standard of proficiency in certain military skills. Subdued combat and special skill badges and the Ranger and Special Forces tabs are authorized on field uniforms.

Combat and Special Skill Badges

These badges include the combat infantryman badges, expert infantryman badge, combat medical badges, expert field medical badge, Army astronaut badges, aviator, flight surgeon, and aircraft crewman badges, glider badge, parachutist badges, com-

Awards and Decorations

bat parachutist badges, pathfinder badge, air assault badge, Ranger tab, Special Forces tab, diver badges, driver and mechanic badge, explosive ordnance disposal badges, nuclear reactor operator badges, and the parachute rigger badge.

These badges are awarded to denote excellence in performance of duties under hazardous conditions and circumstances of extraordinary hardship as well as for special qualifications and successful completion of prescribed courses of training. (See AR 672-5-1 for details.)

Combat Infantryman Badges. Awarded to infantry personnel in the grade of colonel or below who, after 6 December 1941, satisfactorily perform duty while assigned or attached as a member of an infantry brigade, regiment, or smaller unit during any period such unit is engaged in active ground combat. Members of attached Ranger companies are also eligible, as well as officers of other branches who command similar size infantry units under similar circumstances for 30 consecutive days.

These badges are authorized for otherwise qualified Army members for service in Vietnam after 1 March 1961, in Laos from 19 April 1961 to 6 October 1962, and in Korea after 4 January 1969, in Grenada from 22 October 1983 to 21 November 1983, in Panama from 20 December 1989 to 31 January 1991, and in Southwest Asia from 17 January 1991 to 28 February 1991.

Expert Infantryman Badge. Awarded to infantry personnel of the active Army, ARNG, and USAR who satisfactorily complete prescribed proficiency tests.

Combat Medical Badges. Awarded to members of the Army Medical Department, the Naval Medical Department, or the Air Force Medical Service in the grade of colonel (Navy captain) or below who have satisfactorily performed medical duties while assigned or attached to a medical detachment of an infantry unit meeting the requirements for the combat infantryman badge.

Expert Field Medical Badge. Awarded to Army Medical Service personnel who satisfactorily complete prescribed proficiency tests.

Stars for Combat Infantryman and Combat Medical Badges. The second and succeeding awards of the combat infantryman and the combat medical badges, made to recognize participation and qualification in additional declared wars, are indicated by the addition of stars to the basic badges.

Only one award of the combat infantryman badge is authorized for service in Vietnam, Laos, the Dominican Republic, Korea (after 27 July 1954), Grenada, and Panama, regardless of whether an individual has served one or more tours in one or more of these areas.

Note that either, but not both, the combat infantryman badge or the combat medical badge may be awarded for the same period of service in Vietnam or Laos.

Army Astronaut Badges. An Army astronaut badge has been added to the authorized special skill badges. The requirements for award of this badge are not stated in the regulations, however.

These badges are awarded in three degrees: basic, senior, and master.

Army Aviation Badges. There are nine badges relating to Army aviation—three each for Army aviators, flight surgeons, and aircraft crewmen—in the degrees of basic,

senior, and master. The following publications will give information on these badges.
- AR 672-5-1, *Military Awards*.
- AR 600-105, *Aviation Service of Rated Army Officers*.

The master Army aviator badge, the senior Army aviator badge, and the Army aviator badge are awarded upon satisfactory completion of prescribed training and proficiency tests as outlined in AR 600-105.

The master flight surgeon badge, the senior flight surgeon badge, and the flight surgeon badge are awarded to Army Medical Corps officers who complete the training and other requirements prescribed by AR 600-105.

The master aircraft crewman badge, the senior aircraft crewman badge, and the aircraft crewman badge are authorized for award to enlisted personnel who meet the prescribed requirements. (See AR 672-5-1.)

Glider Badge. No longer awarded, but still authorized for wear by individuals who were previously awarded the badge.

Parachutist Badges. To be awarded the master parachutist badge, an individual must meet the following criteria: have participated in sixty-five jumps, twenty-five with combat equipment, four at night, and five mass tactical jumps; have graduated as jumpmaster or served as jumpmaster on one or more combat jumps or on thirty-three noncombat jumps; have been rated excellent in character and efficiency; and have served on jump status for not less than 36 months.

For the senior parachutist badge, an individual must meet the following criteria: have been rated excellent in character and efficiency with participation in thirty jumps, including fifteen jumps made with combat equipment, two night jumps, and two mass tactical jumps; have graduated from a jumpmaster course or served as jumpmaster on one or more combat jumps or fifteen noncombat jumps; and have served on jump status for not less than 24 months.

The parachutist badge is awarded for satisfactory completion of the course given by the Airborne Department of the Infantry School or while assigned or attached to an airborne unit or for participation in at least one combat jump.

Combat Parachutist Badges. Participation in a combat parachute jump entitles the individual to wear a bronze star, or stars, affixed to the parachutist badge.

Pathfinder Badge. Awarded upon successful completion of the Pathfinder course conducted at the Infantry School.

Air Assault Badge. Awarded to personnel who have satisfactorily completed either the Training and Doctrine Command (TRADOC) prescribed training course or the standard air assault course while assigned or attached to the 101st Air Assault Division since 1 April 1974.

Ranger Tab. Awarded to any person who successfully completes a Ranger course conducted by the Infantry School.*

Special Forces Tab. Awarded to any person who successfully completes the Special

---

***Note:** Highly qualified soldiers who have earned both the Ranger and the Special Forces tabs are authorized to wear both, according to a recent DA change.

Awards and Decorations

Forces Qualification Course conducted by the Special Forces School of the Special Warfare Center. This tab also may be awarded for former wartime service. See the regulation (AR 672-5) for details.*

Diver Badges. Awarded after satisfactory completion of prescribed proficiency tests (AR 611-75). Five badges are authorized for enlisted personnel.

Driver and Mechanic Badge. Awarded only to enlisted personnel to denote a high degree of skill in the operation and maintenance of motor vehicles.

Explosive Ordnance Disposal Badges. There are three badges under this heading, any of which may be awarded to officers: master explosive ordnance disposal badge, senior explosive ordnance disposal badge, and explosive ordnance disposal badge. They are awarded to individuals assigned to duties involving the removal and disposition of explosive ammunition under hazardous conditions.

Nuclear Reactor Operator Badges. The shift supervisor badge, the operator first class badge, the operator second class badge, and the operator basic badge were awarded upon completing the Nuclear Power Plant Operators Course or equivalent training and after operating nuclear power plants for specific periods. The reactor commander badge (same as the shift supervisor badge) was authorized for award to officers. These badges are no longer awarded but are still authorized for wear by individuals to whom they were previously awarded.

Parachute Rigger Badge. Awarded to any individual who successfully completes the Parachute Rigger course conducted by the U.S. Army Quartermaster School and who holds a Parachute Rigger MOS or skill identifier.

Physical Fitness Training Badge. Established by the Secretary of the Army on 25 June 1966, this badge is awarded to soldiers who obtain a minimum score of 290 on the Army Physical Readiness Test (APRT) and who meet the weight control requirements of AR 600-9. Once awarded, the badge may be retained as long as the individual achieves a minimum passing score on subsequent APRTs and continues to meet the weight requirements. The APRT scorecard (DA Form 705) will be used to document a soldier's entitlement. This badge is worn only on the left breast of the physical training uniform.

Marksmanship Badges and Tabs

These badges and tabs include basic marksmanship qualification badges, excellence in competition badges, distinguished designation badges, the United States distinguished international shooter badge, and the President's Hundred Tab.

Only members of the armed forces of the United States and civilian citizens of the United States are eligible for these qualification badges. Qualification badges for marksmanship are of three types: basic qualification, excellence in competition, and distinguished designation. Basic qualification badges (including expert, sharpshooter, and marksman badges) are awarded to those individuals who attain the qualification

---
*__Note:__ Highly qualified soldiers who have earned both the Ranger and the Special Forces tabs are authorized to wear both, according to a recent DA change.

score prescribed in the appropriate field manual for the weapon concerned. Excellence in competition badges are awarded to individuals in recognition of an eminent degree of achievement in firing the rifle or pistol. Distinguished designation badges are awarded to individuals in recognition of a preeminent degree of achievement in target practice firing with the military service rifle or pistol.

The distinguished international shooter badge is awarded to military or civilian personnel in recognition of an outstanding degree of achievement in international competition.

A President's Hundred Tab is awarded each person who qualifies among the top 100 contestants in the President's Match held annually at the National Rifle Matches.

Identification Badges

These badges include the Presidential service identification badge, the Vice-Presidential service identification badge, the Secretary of Defense identification badge, the Joint Chiefs of Staff identification badge, the Army Staff identification badge, the Guard, Tomb of the Unknown Soldier identification badge, the Army ROTC Nurse Cadet Program identification badge, the Drill Sergeant identification badge, the U.S. Army Recruiter badge, the U.S. Army Reserve Recruiter badge, the U.S. Army National Guard Recruiter badge, and the Career Counselor badge.

Presidential Service Identification Badge. The Presidential Service certificate and the Presidential Service badge were established by Executive Order 11174, 1 September 1964.

The Presidential Service certificate is awarded in the name of the President of the United States as public evidence of deserved honor and distinction to members of the armed forces who have been assigned to duty in the White House for at least one year after 20 January 1961. It is awarded to Army members by the Secretary of the Army upon recommendation of the Military Aide to the President.

The Presidential Service badge is issued to members of the armed forces who have been awarded the Presidential Service certificate. Once this badge is awarded, it may be worn as a permanent part of the uniform.

Vice-Presidential Service Identification Badge. The Vice-Presidential Service badge was established by Executive Order 11544, 8 July 1970. It may be awarded upon recommendation of the Military Assistant to the Vice President and may be worn as a permanent part of the uniform.

Secretary of Defense Identification Badge. Military personnel who have been assigned to duty and have served not less than one year after 13 January 1961 in the Office of the Secretary of Defense are eligible for this badge. Once awarded, it may be worn as a permanent part of the uniform. It also is authorized for temporary wear by personnel assigned to specified offices of the Secretary of Defense.

Joint Chiefs of Staff Identification Badge. This badge may be awarded to military personnel who have been assigned to duty and who have served not less than one year after 16 January 1961 in a position of responsibility under the direct cognizance of the Joint Chiefs of Staff. Once awarded, the badge may be worn as a permanent part of the uniform.

Awards and Decorations

Army Staff Identification Badge. This badge has been awarded by the Army since 1920 and is the oldest of the five types of identification badges now authorized for officers. It was instituted to give a permanent means of identification to those commissioned officers who had been selected for duty on the War Department General Staff, with recommendation for award based upon performance of duty. It has been continued under the present departmental organization.

The requirements for award of this badge include service of not less than one year between 1 August 1977 and 28 May 1985 as a commissioned officer, or between 22 August 1980 and 28 May 1985 as a warrant officer, while detailed to duty on the Army General Staff and assigned to permanent duty in a TDA position on the Army General Staff, to the Office of the Secretary of the Army, to the National Guard Bureau, or to the Office, Chief Army Reserve. Between 30 September 1979 and 28 May 1985, the badge could also be awarded to the Sergeant Major of the Army and to other senior staff NCOs (SGM E9) assigned to duty with the same staff units. Effective 28 May 1985, qualifying service must be on the Army General Staff or assigned to the Office of the Secretary of the Army. Once awarded, this badge may be worn as a permanent part of the uniform.

Guard, Tomb of the Unknown Soldier Identification Badge. (See AR 672-5-1.)

Army ROTC Nurse Cadet Program Identification Badge. (See AR 672-5-1.)

Drill Sergeant Identification Badge. (See AR 672-5-1.)

U.S. Army Recruiter Identification Badge. (See AR 672-5-1.)

Army National Guard Recruiter Identification Badge. (See AR 672-5-1.)

U.S. Army Reserve Recruiter Identification Badge. (See AR 672-5-1.)

Career Counselor Badge. (See AR 672-5-1.)

APPURTENANCES

Appurtenances are devices affixed to service or suspension ribbons or worn in place of medals or ribbons. They are worn to denote additional awards, participation in a specific event, or other distinguished characteristics of the award.

Service Ribbons

Service ribbons are identical to the suspension ribbon of the medals they represent and are mounted on bars equipped with attaching devices; they are issued for wear in place of medals. The service ribbon for the Medal of Honor is the same color as the neck band, showing five stars in the form of a letter *M*.

Miniature Medals

Miniature replicas of all medals except the Medal of Honor and the Legion of Merit in the Degrees of Chief Commander and Commander are authorized for wear on

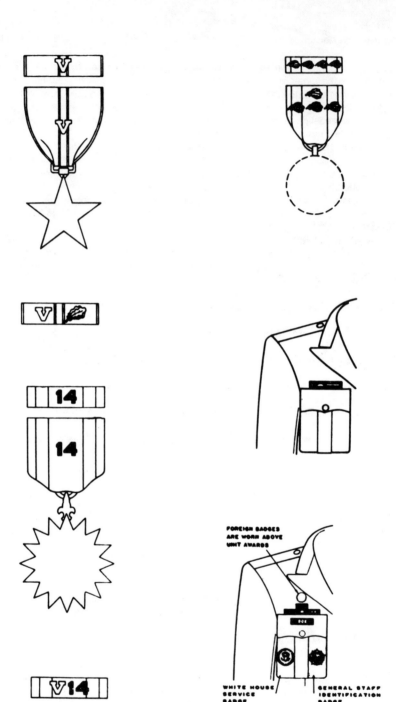

Wearing of appurtenances on medals and ribbons.

Awards and Decorations 247

specified uniforms in lieu of the issued medals. Miniatures of decorations are issued only to foreign nationals and with the award of the Distinguished Service Medal to U.S. personnel (award elements issued by the Secretary of Defense include miniature medals).

Oak-Leaf Cluster

A bronze or silver twig of four oak leaves with three acorns on the stem, $13/32$ inch long for the suspension ribbon and $5/16$ inch long for the service ribbon, is issued in lieu of a decoration for second or succeeding awards of decorations (other than the Air Medal) and service medals.

A silver oak-leaf cluster is issued to be worn in lieu of five bronze clusters. Oak-leaf clusters are not issued for the Legion of Merit awarded in degrees to foreign nationals. Five $1/16$-inch oak-leaf clusters, joined together in series of two, three, and four clusters, are authorized for optional purchase and wear on service ribbons.

Numerals

Arabic numerals $3/13$ inch high are issued in lieu of a medal or ribbon for second and succeeding awards of the Air Medal, the Humanitarian Service Medal, the Multinational Force and Observers Medal, the Army Reserve Components Overseas Training Ribbon, and the Overseas Service Ribbon. The numeral worn on the NCO Professional Development Ribbon denotes the highest completed level of NCO development. The numerals are worn centered on the suspension ribbon of the medal or the ribbon bar.

V Device

The V Device is a bronze block letter V, ¼ inch high with serifs at the top of the members (that is, the little strokes at the tops of the arms of the V that look like little rectangles). The V Device denotes awards of a medal for heroism and may be awarded with the Bronze Star Medal, the Air Medal, the Joint Service Commendation Medal (when the award is for acts or services involving direct participation in combat operations), and the Army Commendation Medal.

Clasps

Clasps are authorized to be worn on the Good Conduct Medal, the Army of Occupation Medal, and the Antarctic Service Medal.

Service Stars

The service star is a bronze or silver five-pointed star $3/16$ inch in diameter. Three-sixteenths-inch service stars joined together in a series of two, three, and four stars are authorized for optional purchase and wear on service ribbons. Service stars, signifying participation in a combat campaign, are authorized for wear on the Armed Forces Expeditionary Medal and the Vietnam Service Medal. (Note: Bronze and silver stars are worn on U.S. Navy decorations in the same manner as oak-leaf clusters are worn on Army and Air Force decorations.)

Arrowhead

The arrowhead is a bronze replica of an Indian arrowhead, ¼ inch high. It denotes participation in a combat parachute jump, combat glider landing, or amphibious assault landing, while assigned or attached as a member of an organized force carrying out an assigned tactical mission. It is worn on the service and suspension ribbons of the Vietnam Service Medal and the Armed Forces Expeditionary Medal.

Lapel Buttons

Lapel buttons are authorized for wear on the *left* lapel of civilian clothing only. They are available for service ribbons and other decorations and badges. Included in this category are the Army Lapel Button, which is awarded to any soldier (except retirees) who completed nine months' honorable active federal service after 1 April 1984, and the U.S. Army Retired Lapel Button.

FOREIGN INDIVIDUAL AWARDS

Decorations received from a foreign government in recognition of active field service in connection with combat operations or for outstanding or unusually meritorious performance may be accepted and worn upon approval of the Department of the Army. Without this approval, they become the property of the United States and must be deposited with the Department of the Army for use or disposal.

Qualification and special skill badges may be accepted if awarded in recognition of meeting the criteria, as established by the awarding foreign government, for the specific award. Commanders of major oversea commands reporting directly to Headquarters, Department of the Army, may approve acceptance, retention, and permanent wear of such badges.

Not more than one foreign badge may be worn at any one time. A foreign badge is worn on the right side above the U.S. and foreign unit awards. A foreign badge may not be worn unless at least one U.S. medal or service ribbon is worn at the same time. Foreign badges are authorized for wear only on service and dress uniforms. The German marksmanship award *(Schützenschur)* may be worn only by enlisted personnel, on the right side of the uniform with the upper portion attached under the center of the shoulder loop and the bottom portion attached under the lapel.

CERTIFICATES AND LETTERS

As a senior noncommissioned officer, you may write and sign letters of appreciation and commendation for other enlisted personnel. Frequently, soldiers will ask for these accolades, but you should be constantly alert to any circumstance that may authorize a letter of appreciation or commendation for a deserving individual. When writing these letters, you should give them your best effort and put as much into composing them as you would into the writing of a recommendation for a decoration. An important responsibility that you have as a noncommissioned officer is to see that your commander is aware of those deeds which deserve special recognition, and you should not be hesitant to recommend personnel for consideration. But do the commander a favor; prepare a draft citation or letter and offer it along with your verbal recommendations. The CO may sign the final product, but if the person being recommended is one of your soldiers, you should write the original draft—you know your soldiers better than the commander does.

Awards and Decorations

In short, certificates and letters may be nothing more than pats on the back. Nevertheless, they go a long way toward boosting the morale of most recipients, and their judicious use is a good way to recognize faithful and competent service.

Certificate of Achievement

Commanders may recognize periods of faithful service, acts, or achievements that do not meet the standards required for decorations by issuing to individual military personnel a Certificate of Achievement, DA Form 2442.

Certificates of Achievement are awarded under local criteria and may be used for awarding the Good Conduct Medal, for participation in the Department of the Army Suggestion Program, or to recognize meritorious acts or service. Only the original copy of DA Form 2442 is prepared; a memorandum is prepared stating that a certificate has been awarded and why, with copies to the individual's MPRJ.

The citation on these certificates is not written so that the act or service performed appears to warrant the award of a decoration. No distinguishing device is authorized for wear to indicate the receipt of a Certificate of Achievement.

Letters of Commendation and Appreciation

Acts or services that do not meet the criteria for decorations or a Certificate of Achievement may be recognized by written expressions of commendation or appreciation. These letters are typed on letterhead stationery and do not contain formalized printing, seals, or other distinguishing features that depart from normal letter form. Distribution of these letters is the same as for Certificate of Achievement memorandums.

12

Pay and Entitlements

The purpose of this chapter is to explain some basic facts about your Army pay and benefits and provide you a quick reference for questions that may come up in your day-to-day activities.

The soldier who enlists in the Army for the money is in the wrong business. Relatively substantial paychecks do not start coming until a soldier reaches the senior noncommissioned ranks with from 20 to 26 years of service.

If pay and benefits were the only inducement to a military career, then we would have no Army. Soldiers reenlist because they like the Army, and when the Army no longer offers young people the challenges and adventure of military life, they will not stay.

PAY

Military pay consists of basic pay, special and incentive pay, and allowances. Pay is computed on the basis of a 30-day month, and soldiers may elect to be paid once a month (at the end of the month) or twice a month (on the 15th and the 30th of each month).

In order to change your pay option, contact your local finance and accounting office to execute DA Form 3685, JUMPS—*Army Pay Elections*. Which option you select depends upon how you budget your money. Some soldiers find that they can get along quite well with one lump-sum pay at the end of the month; others prefer to get paid

JUMPS - ARMY PAY ELECTIONS
For use of this form, see AR 37-104-3; the proponent agency is USAFAC

PRIVACY ACT OF 1974 (5 USC 552a)
AUTHORITY: Title 37 USC, Section 101.
PRINCIPLE PURPOSE: To provide the service member a means of electing the manner in which he/she desires to receive pay and allowances.
ROUTINE USES: To establish account of the MMPF. Although disclosure of this information is voluntary, if the member does not provide it, input will automatically be established to receive all pay at end of month by "Check for Cash."

HOW DO YOU WANT TO BE PAID?   **Please check one item.**

☐ ONCE A MONTH (Complete A & B)   ☐ TWICE A MONTH (Complete C & D)   ☐ TOTAL ACCRUAL (Read E)

A   If you checked once a month, please check one item.
☐ ALL PAY END-OF-MONTH
☐ MID-MONTH PAY OF $ _____
   (Not to exceed ½ of total)
   ACCRUE BALANCE OF PAY (Read E)
☐ ACCRUE $ _____ EACH MONTH/
   BALANCE OF PAY END-OF-MONTH
   (Read E)

B   Please check one method of payment.
☐ SURE PAY/DIRECT DEPOSIT (Complete F)
☐ CHECK to address (Complete G)
☐ CHECK to me at my unit
☐ CASH

C   If you checked twice a month, please check one item.
☐ ½ OF PAY MID-MONTH
   BALANCE OF PAY END-OF-MONTH
☐ MID-MONTH PAY OF $ _____
   (Specify amount, not to exceed ½ of total)
   BALANCE OF PAY END-OF-MONTH
☐ ACCRUE $ _____ EACH MONTH
   MID-MONTH PAY OF $ _____
   (Not to exceed ½ of total)
   BALANCE OF PAY END-OF-MONTH (Read E)

D   Please check one method of payment for Mid-Month and one for End-Of-Month
(You can have only one check address)*

	MID-MONTH	END-OF-MONTH
CHECK to address (if SURE PAY/DIRECT DEPOSIT, Complete F) (All other address checks complete G)	☐	☐
CHECK to me at my unit	☐	☐
CASH	☐	☐

*YOU <u>CAN</u> <u>NOT</u> COMPLETE BOTH BLOCK F and G.

E   ALL AMOUNTS ACCRUED MAY BE WITHDRAWN AT ANY TIME UPON APPLICATION TO YOUR FINANCE OFFICER.

F   Please read the back of this form carefully before completing this block.

☐ SF 1199A Attached

☐ SF 1199A on File in my PFR

☐ Other (complete lines 1 thru 5 at right)

1. (Name of Financial Organization) _____
2. (Savings or Checking Account No.) _____
3. (Name of account holder) _____
4. (Street No., RR #, P.O. Box of the Financial Organization) _____
5. (City, State, Country of the Financial Organization) _____

G
1. (Name to be entered on check) _____
2. (Street No., RR #, P.O. BOX) _____
3. (City, State, Zip Code) _____

I HEREBY AUTHORIZE PAYMENT AS SPECIFIED ABOVE

_____ (Signature)   _____ (SSN)   _____ (Date)

_____ (Printed Name & Organization)

DA FORM 3685, OCT 86   EDITION OF DEC 82 IS OBSOLETE

twice a month. Read the pay elections form carefully before filling it out. Submit your options to the finance office as early in the month as possible to give the Finance Center enough time to process your request so that your new option will be reflected during the *next* pay period.

Report discrepancies in your pay *immediately*. To do so, you must know what you are authorized.

Leave and Earnings Statement (LES)

The Army recently adopted the Air Force's military pay system to pay Active and Reserve Component soldiers in an effort to improve the timeliness and accuracy of payment. The new LES is a computerized monthly statement of account for each soldier paid under the Joint Service Software (JSS) system, which is currently replacing JUMPS. The LES shows all entitlements earned, collections affected, and payments made during the period covered by the statement. In addition, this statement provides the soldier a complete record of transactions that affect his leave account for the period of the statement. It also serves as the official leave record.

Each finance and accounting office exerts every effort to assure that delivery of the LES is accomplished no later than by pertinent end-of-month payday. The FAO delivers the LES to the unit commander, who determines the best way to distribute them to the individuals concerned. In many units, though, personnel simply pick them up from their first sergeant or administrative office.

Study your LES very carefully. Should you discover any item you believe to be in error or should there be an entry recorded thereon that you do not understand, consult with your local finance office immediately. If, during a routine audit of your pay record, it should be discovered that you have been overpaid at some time in the past, the government will collect what is due.

Net Pay Advice

Under JSS a new form, called the Net Pay Advice (NPA), will be issued at mid-month. All Active Army soldiers will receive the NPA, even if they have not elected the mid-month pay option. The NPA will provide mid-month pay data for soldiers who have elected the mid-month pay option. It will provide administrative remarks for all soldiers, regardless of the pay option they have selected. Under JUMPS, administrative remarks appeared on the LES. Under JSS, only remarks affecting pay will appear on the LES.

Collections of Erroneous Payments

Local payments in excess of earned entitlements that are less than two months old upon computer update are affected immediately. If these payments are two or more months old, collection action is delayed for two months to allow time for unit commanders to arrange for prorated collection, if necessary, before computer collection action is initiated.

When an error is discovered, the Control, the Conversion Division, Department 20, U.S. Army Finance and Accounting Center, prepares an Adjustment Authorization and forwards the original to the individual's servicing finance and accounting office and suspends a copy for 60 days. A remark is then printed on the affected soldier's LES advising him to contact his servicing finance office. If at the end of the sixty days the

Pay and Entitlements

Finance Center has not received a rebuttal from the soldier's finance officer, collection action is taken under the statutory ⅓ rule.

If the indebted soldier's ETS falls within 90 days of the date of the Adjustment Authorization, an accelerated deduction—⅔ of the affected soldier's pay per month—is automatically initiated. This is the maximum amount that may be deducted from a soldier's pay unless he or she specifically authorizes a higher amount.

Overpayments identified by the Finance Center or the local finance office as a result of audit are processed as delayed collections to provide for 60 days to arrange for repayment.

A soldier's ETS date does not affect the automatic collection of indebtedness under the statutory ⅓ rule. The soldier's LES (one month before ETS month) is computed based on the statutory ⅓ rule, if applicable. Any remaining indebtedness is collected at ETS in accordance with the provisions of Chapter 7, Part Seven, *DOD Pay Manual*.

Wherever possible, the government collects indebtedness in a lump sum. In cases in which a lump-sum collection cannot be made and the indebtedness was incurred in good faith, however, collection is made in monthly installments in reasonable amounts over a period of time not greater than the anticipated period of the soldier's active duty. The term "reasonable amount" means an amount that would be judged by a prudent individual to be equitable to both the government and the soldier.

Soldiers may appeal the validity of a debt, the amount, or the rate of payment. If an enlisted soldier's appeal is denied, the Chief of Personnel Operations, Department of the Army, may consider his case for remission or cancellation of the indebtedness.

The amount deducted for any period normally will not exceed an amount equal to ⅔ of a soldier's pay, and monthly installments may be increased or decreased to reflect changes in pay.

Deductions are made only from basic pay, special pay (including reenlistment bonus), proficiency pay, and incentive pay for hazardous duty. When a proper monthly deduction cannot be established because of voluntary allotments, these allotments are administratively reduced or discontinued.

When indebtedness cannot be satisfied before separation, adjustments can be made by decreasing subsequent payments whatever their nature. Retirement pay, reserve duty training pay, lump sum leave payments, the subsistence and quarters allowance, and the reimbursement of the cost of travel of dependents and household goods are all available for setoff. *Travel allowances, however, are not.*

Advance Payments

An advance of pay is authorized upon permanent change of station to provide a soldier funds for expenses, such as transportation, temporary storage of household goods, packing and shipping costs, and securing new living quarters. Advance payments are limited to no more than one month's advance pay of basic pay less deductions or, if warranted, not more than three months' basic pay less deductions at the old station, en route, or within 60 days after reporting to a new station.

Requests for advance pay from enlisted personnel in pay grades E-1 through E-4 must be approved by their commander, and this approval must be indicated on the *Pay Inquiry Form* (DA Form 2142), together with a statement that the circumstances in the individual's case warrant advancing the amount requested and that advancing a lesser amount would result in hardship to the soldier or his family.

The DA Form 2142 must also include a statement that the enlisted person will have at least enough time left to serve on his or her current enlistment to completely repay the advance. If six or twelve months are allowed for repayment, for instance, the statement must show that the soldier has at least that much time to serve on his or her current enlistment beginning with the first of the month following the month in which the advance is made. Any extension of enlistment authorized by law is included in the computation of the requirement, and six or twelve months must remain for service subsequent to the date the advance of pay is made.

The commander's approval for an advance of pay is not required for enlisted personnel in the E-5 through E-9 pay grades, but advances are not made to senior grade personnel when it is apparent that the tour of duty (obligated service) will terminate before completion of the scheduled repayment of the advance.

Lump-Sum Payments

A lump-sum payment is made to pay bonuses and accrued leave paid on immediate reenlistments. These payments are made by cash or check through the use of a local payment. Lump-sum payments are always made in even dollar amounts. The maximum amount that may be paid is the gross amount of the enlistment minus the estimate of federal and, when applicable, state taxes. When the computation results in a new amount due in dollars and cents, the amount to be paid may either be the lesser full dollar amount or be rounded to the next higher dollar. Any monetary difference is paid or collected on the individual LES. The minimum amount that must be paid is $10. Where less than this amount due is paid, the remaining balance is included in the end-of-month payment.

Basic Pay

Basic pay is established by law and is that pay a soldier receives, based on grade and length of service, exclusive of any special or incentive pay or allowances.

Reserve Drill Pay

Reserve drill pay, like basic pay, is established by law. And like basic pay, Reserve drill pay is pay a soldier receives based on grade and length of service. Unlike monthly basic pay, however, Reserve drill pay is computed and paid for the number of days' service rendered. It is comparable to basic pay. For example, a Reserve sergeant first class with 16 years of service receives $65.02 a day. Multiplied by 30, the amount equals the monthly basic pay received by a Regular Army sergeant first class with 16 years of service.

Basic Allowance for Subsistence (BAS)

Upon entitlement to BAS (separate rations) a soldier's unit commander forwards to the finance officer a DA Form 4187, *Personnel Action* (see Chapter 8, DA Pamphlet 600-8), in duplicate, showing the effective date and hour of entitlement to BAS. When a soldier ceases to be entitled to BAS, the unit commander forwards to the finance officer a DA Form 4187 showing the date and hour of termination.

Officers receive $134.42 per month (FY 92). BAS rates for enlisted personnel are as follows.

Pay and Entitlements

	E-1 (less than 4 months)	All Other Enlisted
When on leave or authorized to mess separately	$5.92/day	$6.41/day
When rations in-kind are not available	$6.68/day	$7.23/day
When assigned to duty under emergency conditions where no messing facilities of the United States are available	$8.86/day	$9.59/day

Entitlement to BAS terminates automatically upon permanent change of station. Care should be taken during in-processing at a new duty station that entitlement is revalidated for personnel authorized separate rations.

Basic Allowance for Quarters (BAQ)

BAQ is paid at three different rates.
- Without dependents, full rate (paid to soldiers living off post).
- Without dependents, partial rate (paid to soldiers living in unit barracks).
- With dependents.

BAQ terminates for married personnel when they occupy government quarters or when dependency terminates. Dependency is verified by the local finance and accounting officer when the soldier submits DA Form 3298, *Authorization to Start and Stop BAQ Credit*. The documentary evidence that must be submitted to substantiate dependency includes the original or certified copy of a marriage certificate, the individual's signed statement (when called to active duty or active duty for training for 90 days or less), birth certificate, or a public church record of marriage issued over the signature of the custodian of the church or public records, and, if applicable, a divorce decree. Entitlements must be recertified upon permanent change of station.

BAQ Rates (1992)

Pay Grade	Without Dependents Full Rate	Without Dependents Partial Rate	With Dependents
E-9	418.20	18.60	551.10
E-8	384.30	15.30	507.90
E-7	327.90	12.00	471.90
E-6	296.70	9.90	436.20
E-5	273.60	8.70	392.10
E-4	238.20	8.10	341.10
E-3	233.70	7.80	317.40
E-2	190.20	7.20	302.10
E-1	168.90	6.90	302.10

Variable Housing Allowance (VHA)

The VHA was implemented to afford service personnel a tax-free amount of money for housing in addition to BAQ. The size of the allowance depends on the grade of the soldier and the size of his or her family. It is based on the typical housing costs for each rank in a certain area and biased toward meeting all the housing expenses for soldiers in high-cost areas.

MONTHLY BASIC PAY
(Effective 1 January 1992)

Years of Service

GRADE	Less than 2	2	3	4	6	8	10	12	14	16	18	20	22	26
COMMISSIONED OFFICERS														
O-10	6417.60	6643.50	6643.50	6643.50	6643.50	6898.20	6898.20	7280.40	7280.40	7801.20	7801.20	8323.50	8323.50	8733.30
O-9	5687.70	5836.50	5961.00	5961.00	5961.00	6112.50	6112.50	6366.90	6366.90	6898.20	6898.20	7280.40	7280.40	7801.20
O-8	5151.60	5306.10	5431.80	5431.80	5431.80	5836.50	5836.50	6112.50	6112.50	6366.90	6643.50	6898.20	7068.20	7068.30
O-7	4280.40	4571.40	4571.40	4571.40	4776.60	4776.60	5053.50	5053.50	5306.10	5836.50	6238.20	6238.20	6238.20	6238.20
O-6	3172.80	3485.70	3714.30	3714.30	3714.30	3714.30	3714.30	3714.30	3840.30	4447.50	4674.60	4776.60	5053.50	5480.70
O-5	2537.40	2979.30	3185.40	3185.40	3185.40	3185.40	3281.70	3458.40	3690.30	3966.60	4193.70	4320.90	4471.80	4471.80
O-4	2138.70	2604.60	2778.30	2778.30	2829.90	2954.70	3156.30	3333.60	3485.70	3638.70	3739.20	3739.20	3739.20	3739.20
O-3	1987.50	2222.40	2375.70	2628.60	2754.30	2853.00	3007.50	3156.30	3233.70	3233.70	3233.70	3233.70	3233.70	3233.70
O-2	1733.10	1892.70	2274.30	2350.50	2399.40	2399.40	2399.40	2399.40	2399.40	2399.40	2399.40	2399.40	2399.40	2399.40
O-1	1504.80	1566.30	1892.70	1892.70	1892.70	1892.70	1892.70	1892.70	1892.70	1892.70	1892.70	1892.70	1892.70	1892.70
OFFICERS WITH MORE THAN 4 YEARS' ACTIVE DUTY AS ENLISTED OR WARRANT OFFICER														
O-3E	0.00	0.00	0.00	0.00	2628.60	2754.30	3007.50	3156.30	3281.70	3281.70	3281.70	3281.70	3281.70	3281.70
O-2E	0.00	0.00	0.00	0.00	2350.50	2475.60	2604.60	2704.20	2778.30	2778.30	2778.30	2778.30	2778.30	2778.30
O-1E	0.00	0.00	0.00	1892.70	2022.30	2096.70	2172.60	2248.20	2350.50	2350.50	2350.50	2350.50	2350.50	2350.50
WARRANT OFFICERS														
W-5	0.00	0.00	0.00	0.00	0.00	0.00	0.00	0.00	0.00	0.00	0.00	3455.90	3587.10	3846.30
W-4	2025.00	2172.60	2172.60	2222.40	2323.20	2425.80	2527.50	2704.20	2829.90	2929.20	3007.50	3104.70	3208.50	3458.40
W-3	1840.50	1996.50	1996.50	2022.30	2045.70	2195.40	2323.20	2399.40	2475.60	2549.40	2628.60	2730.90	2829.90	2929.20
W-2	1611.90	1743.90	1743.90	1794.90	1892.70	1996.50	2072.10	2148.30	2222.40	2300.40	2375.70	2450.70	2549.40	2549.40
W-1	1342.80	1539.90	1539.90	1668.30	1743.90	1818.90	1892.70	1971.00	2045.70	2121.90	2195.40	2274.30	2274.30	2274.30
ENLISTED MEMBERS														
E-9	0.00	0.00	0.00	0.00	0.00	0.00	2355.90	2408.70	2463.30	2519.70	2576.10	2626.20	2763.90	3032.70
E-8	0.00	0.00	0.00	0.00	0.00	1975.50	2031.90	2085.60	2139.60	2196.30	2246.70	2301.90	2436.90	2708.40
E-7	1379.10	1488.90	1544.10	1598.10	1652.40	1705.20	1759.80	1814.70	1896.90	1950.60	2004.90	2031.00	2167.20	2436.90
E-6	1186.80	1293.30	1347.30	1404.60	1457.10	1509.60	1565.10	1645.80	1697.40	1752.30	1779.00	1779.00	1779.00	1779.00
E-5	1041.30	1133.40	1188.60	1240.20	1321.80	1375.50	1430.10	1482.60	1509.60	1509.60	1509.60	1509.60	1509.60	1509.60
E-4	971.10	1025.70	1086.00	1170.00	1216.20	1216.20	1216.20	1216.20	1216.20	1216.20	1216.20	1216.20	1216.20	1216.20
E-3	915.00	965.40	1003.80	1043.40	1043.40	1043.40	1043.40	1043.40	1043.40	1043.40	1043.40	1043.40	1043.40	1043.40
E-2	880.50	880.50	880.50	880.50	880.50	880.50	880.50	880.50	880.50	880.50	880.50	880.50	880.50	880.50
E-1	785.70	785.70	785.70	785.70	785.70	785.70	785.70	785.70	785.70	785.70	785.70	785.70	785.70	785.70

E-1 with less than 4 months—$726.60

ONE-DAY RESERVE DRILL RATES
(Effective 1 January 1992)

GRADE	Less than 2	2	3	4	6	8	10	12	14	16	18	20	22	26
COMMISSIONED OFFICERS														
O-10	213.92	221.45	221.45	221.45	221.45	229.94	229.94	242.68	242.68	260.04	260.04	277.45	277.45	294.74
O-9	189.59	194.55	198.70	198.70	198.70	203.75	203.75	212.23	212.23	229.94	229.94	242.68	242.68	260.04
O-8	171.72	176.87	181.06	181.06	181.06	194.55	194.55	203.75	203.75	212.23	221.45	229.94	235.61	235.61
O-7	142.68	152.38	152.38	152.38	159.22	159.22	168.45	168.45	176.87	194.55	207.94	207.94	207.94	207.94
O-6	105.76	116.19	123.81	123.81	123.81	123.81	123.81	123.81	128.01	148.25	155.82	159.22	168.45	182.69
O-5	84.58	99.31	106.18	106.18	106.18	106.18	109.39	115.28	123.01	132.22	139.79	144.03	149.06	149.06
O-4	71.29	86.82	92.61	92.61	94.33	98.49	105.21	111.12	116.19	121.29	124.64	124.64	124.64	124.64
O-3	66.25	74.08	79.19	87.62	91.81	95.10	100.25	105.21	107.79	107.79	107.79	107.79	107.79	107.79
O-2	57.77	63.09	75.81	78.35	79.98	79.98	79.98	79.98	79.98	79.98	79.98	79.98	79.98	79.98
O-1	50.16	52.21	63.09	63.09	63.09	63.09	63.09	63.09	63.09	63.09	63.09	63.09	63.09	63.09
COMMISSIONED OFFICERS WITH MORE THAN 4 YEARS' ACTIVE DUTY AS AN ENLISTED MEMBER														
O-3E	0.00	0.00	0.00	87.62	91.81	95.10	100.25	105.21	109.39	109.39	109.39	109.39	109.39	109.39
O-2E	0.00	0.00	0.00	78.35	79.98	82.52	86.82	90.14	92.61	92.61	92.61	92.61	92.61	92.61
O-1E	0.00	0.00	0.00	63.09	67.41	69.89	72.42	74.94	78.35	78.35	78.35	78.35	78.35	78.34
ENLISTED MEMBERS														
E-9	0.00	0.00	0.00	0.00	0.00	0.00	78.53	80.29	82.11	83.99	85.87	87.54	92.13	101.09
E-8	0.00	0.00	0.00	0.00	0.00	65.85	67.73	69.52	71.32	73.21	74.89	79.73	81.23	90.28
E-7	45.97	49.63	51.47	53.27	55.08	56.84	58.66	60.49	63.23	65.02	66.83	67.70	72.24	81.23
E-6	39.56	43.11	44.91	46.82	48.57	50.32	52.17	54.86	56.58	58.41	59.30	59.30	59.30	59.30
E-5	34.71	37.78	39.62	41.34	44.06	45.85	47.67	49.42	50.32	50.32	50.32	50.32	50.32	50.32
E-4	32.37	34.19	36.20	39.00	40.54	40.54	40.54	40.54	40.54	40.54	40.54	40.54	40.54	40.54
E-3	30.50	32.18	33.46	34.78	34.78	34.78	34.78	34.78	34.78	34.78	34.78	34.78	34.78	34.78
E-2	29.35	29.35	29.35	29.35	29.35	29.35	29.35	29.35	29.35	29.35	29.35	29.35	29.35	29.35
E-1	26.19	26.19	26.19	26.19	26.19	26.19	26.19	26.19	26.19	26.19	26.19	26.19	26.19	26.19

E-1 with less than 4 months—24.22

Family Separation Allowance

Two separation allowances are payable to eligible personnel to help meet additional family expenses during periods of separation:

• FSA I. This allowance is paid to a soldier who has dependents and is serving in an oversea location where dependents are not permitted and where government bachelor quarters are not available to help cover living expenses. The amount of this allowance is the same as the BAQ that a soldier *without dependents* would receive.

• FSA II. This allowance is paid to soldiers with dependents and in any grade who are involuntarily separated from their families because of PCS to a station where dependents are not authorized or temporary duty for a continuous period of more than 30 days away from their permanent duty station. FSA II is authorized in the amount of $30 per month.

Station Allowances

A list of areas where station allowances are authorized is in Chapter 4, Part Three, *DOD Pay Manual*, and Chapter 4, Part G, Volume 1, *Joint Travel Regulations*. These allowances are paid to offset the high cost of living in certain geographical areas (oversea and in the United States). They consist of Housing (HOUS) and Cost of Living (COLA) allowances. A Temporary Lodging Allowance (TLA) and Interim Housing Allowance (IHA) may also be paid in certain cases.

Clothing Maintenance Allowance

Clothing maintenance allowance is paid at two different rates:

• Basic, which covers replacement of unique military items that would normally require replacement during the first three years of service.

• Standard, which covers the replacement of unique military items after the first three years of service.

The rates also differ for males and females:

Male—
• Basic: $15.00.
• Standard: $21.60.

Female—
• Basic: $17.10.
• Standard: $24.30.

Female personnel are also authorized an initial cash allowance established by AR 700-84 for the purchase of undergarments, dress shoes, and stockings. Current regulations authorize a total payment of $126.07.

A soldier receives the clothing maintenance allowance annually, on the last day of the month in which the soldier's anniversary date of enlistment falls. These annual rates are as follows:

Male—
• Less than three years of service: $180.00.
• More than three years of service: $259.20.

Female—
• Less than three years of service: $205.20.
• More than three years of service: $291.60.

Pay and Entitlements

Civilian Clothing Allowance

When duty assignments require soldiers to wear civilian clothing, they receive lump-sum payments under the following circumstances:
- When both winter and summer civilian clothing ensembles are required: $1,087.
- When either winter or summer ensembles are required: $703.
- When in a TDY status from 16 to 30 days: $215.
- When in a TDY status over 30 days: $401.

Foreign Duty Pay

All enlisted personnel assigned to an area outside the contiguous 48 states and the District of Columbia where an "accompanied by dependents" tour of duty is not authorized have entitlement to foreign duty or "overseas pay." Chapter 6, Part One, *DOD Pay Manual*, lists the places where foreign duty pay is authorized (Paragraph 10606).

The following rates apply:
- Senior NCOs: $22.50 per month.
- SSG: $20 per month.
- SGT: $16 per month.
- CPL/SPC: $13 per month.
- PFC: $9 per month.
- PV1, PV2: $8 per month.

Hostile Fire Pay (HFP)

Hostile fire pay ($150) is paid to soldiers permanently assigned to units performing duty in designated hostile fire areas or to soldiers assigned to temporary duty in such areas. Hostile fire pay is authorized on a monthly basis or one-time basis, depending upon the soldier's period of exposure to enemy fire.

Diving Pay

Diving pay is authorized in amounts ranging from $110 per month (for scuba divers) to $300 per month (for Master Divers). To qualify for special pay for diving duty, a soldier must be a rated diver in accordance with AR 611-75 and be assigned to a TOE or TD position of MOS 00B or to a position that has been designated diving duty by the Assistant Chief of Staff for Force Development, Department of the Army.

Flight Pay

Flight pay for enlisted crewmembers ranges from $110 to $200 per month.

Demolition Pay

A soldier is entitled to receive incentive pay of $110 per month for demolition duty for any month or portion of a month in which he or she was assigned and performed duty in a primary duty assignment as outlined above.

Parachute Pay

Soldiers who have received a designation as a parachutist or parachute rigger or are undergoing training for such designations and who are required to engage in parachute jumping from an aircraft in aerial flight and actually perform the specified minimum jumps (see Table 2-3-3, *DOD Entitlements Manual*) are authorized $110 per month parachute duty pay. An additional $55 is authorized for parachutists who are assigned to positions requiring high altitude, low-opening (HALO) jump status.

Experimental Stress Pay

Experimental stress duty pay of $83 per month is authorized for all Army personnel who, on or after 1 July 1965, participate in thermal stress experiments or experimental pressure chamber duty.

Special Duty Assignment Pay

Special duty pay is authorized for enlisted members in designated specialties who are required to perform extremely demanding duties or duties demanding an unusual degree of responsibility. Qualifying jobs include career counselor, recruiter, and drill sergeant. Those eligible receive an additional monthly amount ranging from $55 to $275.

Special duty assignment pay replaced proficiency pay in October 1984. Proficiency pay is still paid to members who were entitled to it on 30 September 1984. A member may not receive both proficiency pay and special duty assignment pay.*

Enlistment Bonus

The enlistment bonus is an enlistment incentive offered to those enlisting in the Regular Army for duty in a specific MOS. The objective of the bonus is to increase the number of enlistments in MOSs that are critical and have inadequate first-term manning levels. Section A, Chapter 9, Part One, of the *DOD Pay Manual* gives basic conditions of entitlement, amount of the bonus, time of payment, and reduction and termination of the award.

Entitlement to the bonus accrues on successful completion of training and award of the designated MOS. Specific eligibility criteria are in Paragraph 9-5, AR 600-200. The bonus amount is prescribed by the Secretary of Defense but cannot exceed $8,000. The first installment may not exceed $5,000, and the remainder is paid in equal periodic installments, which may not be paid less frequently than once every three months.

Selective Reenlistment Bonus (SRB)

The SRB is a retention incentive paid to soldiers in certain selected MOSs who reenlist or voluntarily extend their enlistment for additional obligated service. The objective of the SRB is to increase the number of reenlistments or extensions in critical MOSs that do not have adequate retention levels to man the career force.

The SRB is established in three zones: Zone A consists of those reenlistments falling between twenty-one months and six years of active service; Zones B and C

---

*From *Handbook for Military Families, 1989 Edition*, supplement to *Army Times/Air Force Times/Navy Times*, April 3, 1989, by permission of the Times Journal Co., Springfield, Virginia.

Pay and Entitlements

consists of those reenlistments or extensions of enlistments falling between six and fourteen years of service.

Payments are based on multiples, not to exceed six, of a soldier's monthly basic pay at the time of discharge or release from active duty or the day before the beginning of extension, multiplied by years of additional obligated service.

The SRB is paid by installments. Up to 50 percent of the total bonus may be paid as the first installment with the remaining portion paid in equal annual amounts over the remainder of the reenlistment period.

A list of the MOSs designated for award of SRB and enlistment bonuses is in the DA Circular 611-series, *Announcement of Proficiency Pay/Selective Reenlistment Bonus/Enlistment Bonus/Comparable MOS for Bonus Recipients*. Periodic program changes are announced by Headquarters, Department of the Army.

Allotments

An allotment is a specified amount of money withheld from military pay, normally upon the soldier's authorization, for a specific purpose. Payment is made by government check mailed to the payee.

Allotments are made by filling out DD Form 2558, *Authorization to Start, Stop, or Change an Allotment for Active Duty or Retired Personnel*. These forms are prepared by the individual's military personnel office, unit personnel office, or finance office, and by the Army Emergency Relief and the American Red Cross. Preparation of allotment documents in the finance office, rather than in the personnel office, is intended to eliminate delays of one or more days. When there is a delay near the end of the processing month, the effective date of an allotment may be delayed a full month. Commanders may have the DD Form 2558 prepared in the unit personnel office, if it will conserve time and assure that there will be no delays in transmission to the finance office.

Individuals must sign DD Form 2558 in the presence of their commanding officer, personnel or disbursing officer, or one of their representatives who shall witness the signature. This requirement may be waived for senior NCOs and in cases of loan repayment allotments payable to the Army Emergency Relief, the Navy Relief Society, the Air Force Aid Society, and the American Red Cross.

The following types of allotments are available to soldiers. Allotments for any purpose other than those shown below are not authorized. For those types of allotments that are limited to a specific number, the soldier's personal finance record is examined by the finance officer to determine whether he or she already has the authorized number in effect. If so, the individual is advised, and the request for allotment is denied.

Repayment of Army Emergency Relief Loans (AER). These allotments are authorized in multiples. AER allotments are established for a definite term of not less than three months (although this provision may be waived in certain cases) in an amount of not less than $5 per month.

Combined Federal Campaign Contributions (CFC). This allotment is authorized to be in effect one at a time only. CFC allotments are made for a period of 12 months, beginning in January and ending in December. The allotment must be for at least $1 per month. Military personnel who execute the *Payroll Withholding Authorization for Voluntary Charitable Contributions* (a Civil Service form) may do so in lieu of DA Form 1341.

Payment to a Dependent (SPT-V). This kind of allotment is authorized in multiples. This voluntary allotment is paid to a soldier's dependent without regard to whether the

AUTHORIZATION TO START, STOP OR CHANGE AN ALLOTMENT FOR ACTIVE DUTY OR RETIRED PERSONNEL

CONTROL NO.

PREPARED BY

Privacy Act Statement

AUTHORITY: 37 U.S.C. 101 et seq; E.O. 9397, November 1943 (SSN).

PRINCIPAL PURPOSES: To permit starts, changes, or stops to allotments other than bond allotments. To maintain a record of allotments other than bond allotments and ensure starts, changes, and stops are in keeping with member's desires.

ROUTINE USES: Information may be released to computer service centers and other accounting services when such centers and services act as authorized agents of financial organizations specified by the member to receive allotments. Disclosure may be made to the Federal Reserve System when payment of allotment is made through the electronic fund transfer system to financial organizations. Records may also be disclosed to Congress; allottees; Secret Service; General Accounting Office; Federal, State and local courts; U.S. Treasury; and to the Department of Justice, in some cases for prosecution, civil litigation, or for investigative purposes.

DISCLOSURE: Voluntary; however, failure to provide the requested information as well as the SSN may result in the member not being able to start, change, or stop allotments.

TO BE COMPLETED BY ALLOTTER

1. ALLOTTER'S NAME (Last, First, Middle Initial) (Print or type)	2. SOCIAL SECURITY NUMBER	3. GRADE (AD only)
4. ALLOTTER'S MAILING ADDRESS (Street or Box Number, City, State, Zip Code)	5. EFFECTIVE DATE (YYMM)	6. ALLOTMENT AMOUNT (Per Month) $

7. ALLOTTEE'S NAME (First, Middle Initial, Last)	8. ALLOTMENT ACTION		
	a. START	b. STOP	c. CHANGE

9. CREDIT LINE (If applicable)	10. ALLOTMENT CLASS AUTHORIZED (X only one)
	C CHARITY / CFC (Note 2)
	D SUPPORT (Note 1)
	F CHARITY - EMERGENCY / ASSISTANCE FUND CONTRIBUTIONS
11. ALLOTTEE'S MAILING ADDRESS (Street or Box Number, City, State, Zip Code)	H REPAYMENT OF HOME LOAN (Note 2)
	I INSURANCE
	L REPAY SERVICE ORGANIZATION (Red Cross, etc.)
	N PAY PREMIUMS ON USGLI OR NSLI TO VA (Note 2)
	S PAYMENT TO FINANCIAL ORGANIZATION / VEAP (Note 3)
12. IF FOREIGN ADDRESS COMPLETE AS FOLLOWS (Province, Country)	T LIQUIDATION OF DEBTS TO U.S. OR DELINQUENT STATE / LOCAL INCOME / EMPLOYMENT TAXES
	X LOCALLY PAID ALLOTMENT
	OTHER (Specify)

13. REMARKS	
	14. ACCOUNT NUMBER / POLICY NUMBER
	15. TOTAL CLASS L AMOUNT $	16. TOTAL CLASS T AMOUNT $
17. SIGNATURE OF ALLOTTER	18. DATE (YYMMDD)

NOTE 1. Must be different address than allotter. Each dependent allotment must have a different credit line. Only one support allotment per dependent is allowed.

NOTE 2. May not be started after retirement.

NOTE 3. May not be started or changed after retirement.

DD Form 2558, MAR 90

Pay and Entitlements

soldier is already receiving BAQ. In addition, *involuntary* SPT-V allotments can be administratively established. Normally, the amount of these allotments is not permitted to exceed 80 percent of a soldier's pay. Not more than one SPT-V allotment may be made to the same person.

Payment to a Financial Institution for Credit to a Member's Account (FININ). Only two of these allotments are authorized to be in effect at any one time. FININ allotments are for payment to a financial organization for credit to the allotter's savings, checking, or trust accounts. The FININ allotment may be established for an indefinite term and for any amount the soldier designates, provided he or she has sufficient pay to satisfy the deduction of the allotment.

Payment for Indebtedness to the United States (FED). FED allotments are for the purpose of payment of delinquent federal, state, and local taxes and/or indebtedness to the United States. A separate allotment is required for each debt or overpayment to be repaid. FED allotments will not be established for a period of less than three months or for an amount of less than $5.

Payment of Home Loans (HOME). Only one HOME allotment is authorized to be in effect at any one time. This allotment is authorized for repayment of loans for the purchase of a home, mobile home, or house trailer. A HOME allotment is established for an indefinite term and for any amount designated provided the soldier's pay credit is sufficient to satisfy the deduction of the allotment.

Payment of Commercial Life Insurance Premiums (INS). These allotments are authorized in multiples. INS allotments must be made payable to a commercial life insurance firm. INS allotments are not authorized for payment of insurance on the life of a soldier's spouse or children except under a family group contract or for health, accident, or hospitalization insurance. INS allotments are established for an indefinite period and in the amount of the monthly premium as indicated by the number on DA Form 1341.

Repayment of American Red Cross Loans (REDCR). REDCR allotments are authorized in multiples. These allotments cannot be established in an amount of less than $5 per month.

Servicemen's Group Life Insurance (SGLI). Maximum coverage is $100,000, with an automatic deduction of $8 per month for premiums, unless the soldier declines coverage or requests a reduced amount of coverage. Coverage may be reduced in increments of $15,000.

Payment of Government Life Insurance Premium (NSLI). These allotments are not authorized in multiples and are exclusive of SGLI deductions.

Payment of Retired Serviceman's Family Protection Plan (RSFPP). Only one RSFPP allotment is authorized to be in effect at one time. These allotments apply only to retired members serving on active duty.

Educational Savings Allotment (EDSAV). This allotment is authorized to allow soldiers entering service after 13 December 1976 (except those who enlisted under the Delayed Entry Program before 1 January 1977) to participate in the Veterans Educational Assistance Program (VEAP). Only one such allotment is authorized. The EDSAV allotment is established with no discontinuance date. The soldier may stop it at any time after one year of participation. The amount of the monthly allotment will be not less than $25 or more than $100. Amounts between $25 and $100 must be in multiples of $5. The maximum amount allowable by a two-year enlistee is $2,400. When the maximum amount has been reached, the EDSAV will automatically stop.

Class X Allotments. A Class X allotment is paid locally and is authorized in emergency circumstances when other classes of allotments are impracticable. This instance applies overseas only. Class X allotments may be ordered by a commander as a standby allotment when adequate provision for the financial support of a soldier's dependents has not been made.

BENEFITS

Medical Care

The U.S. Army provides the finest emergency medical care of any comparable organization that has ever existed.

This statement does not mean that you always have a choice to exercise or not, as you want. Soldiers on active duty or active duty training are usually required to submit to any medical care that is considered necessary to protect or maintain the health of others, to preserve lives, or to alleviate unnecessary suffering. A commanding officer may, with the concurrence of the medical treatment facility commander, *order* the hospitalization or a medical examination for any member of his or her command.

For instance, the individual has no option when it comes to immunization. It is a military obligation, and an exception is granted only for medical or religious reasons (AR 40-562).

Dental Care

The Army strives to provide dental care that is among the best available anywhere. Active duty personnel may use this service without limitation. Full dental services are not available to dependents at most Army installations, but many dental services for family members are covered by the Delta Dental Plan, which is discussed later in this chapter.

CHAMPUS. The Civilian Health and Medical Program of the Uniformed Services (CHAMPUS) is a medical benefits program provided by the federal government to help pay for civilian medical care given to spouses and children of active duty uniformed services personnel, to retired personnel and their spouses and children, and to spouses and children of deceased active duty and deceased retired personnel.

CHAMPUS is provided by law (Title 10, United States Code, Chapter 55). It is operated in accordance with policies and procedures set forth in Department of Defense CHAMPUS Regulation 6010.8-R. Under CHAMPUS, authorized medical services and supplies are cost-shared by the government from money appropriated by the Congress to the Department of Defense for this purpose.

Although it is not a health insurance program, CHAMPUS is similar in many ways to health insurance provided by private employers to their employees. CHAMPUS does not involve any premium payments, but annual deductibles—$150 per individual, $300 per family—do apply to the program. Before a soldier's family may receive care covered by CHAMPUS, the soldier must first enroll his or her family members in DEERS, the Defense Entitlement Eligibility Reporting System. Local military personnel offices handle DEERS processing.

A valid ID card establishes proof of eligibility for CHAMPUS care (children 10 years of age and older must have their own ID cards to receive CHAMPUS benefits; children under 10 may receive benefits on their parent's ID). The following persons are eligible for medical benefits under CHAMPUS.

• The spouse or child of an active duty member of the uniformed services.

Pay and Entitlements

- A retiree.
- The spouse or child of a retiree.
- The spouse or child of a deceased active duty service member or deceased retiree.

The following persons *are not* eligible for medical benefits under CHAMPUS:

- Active duty servicemembers.
- Parents and parents-in-law (if they are dependent upon a servicemember, they may be eligible for care in a service medical facility).
- Foster children.
- Grandchildren.
- A disabled veteran (as determined by the VA) who is not entitled to retired, retainer, or equivalent pay.
- The spouse and children of a person serving on active duty called or ordered to active duty for a period of 30 days or less.

It is the intent of Congress that as many beneficiaries as possible obtain needed medical care from uniformed services medical facilities. Because of a shortage of physicians, inadequate facilities, and overcrowding, however, care is not always available from those facilities. Also, many families do not live near a military hospital. Therefore, Congress authorized medical benefits from civilian sources with the government sharing the cost.

A CHAMPUS beneficiary who lives within a certain radius, or "catchment" area, of a military medical facility must obtain a statement of nonavailability (DD Form 1251) before seeking *nonemergency* treatment from a civilian hospital. The geographical area is determined by zip code of the patient's residence and in some cases may extend 60 miles away from the nearest military facility. If you live within 35 miles of a military treatment facility, assume the nonavailability statement is required, but check with your health benefits advisor (HBA) to be sure. HBAs are located at all inpatient military treatment facilities.

Remember also that a patient must be admitted to the civilian hospital within 30 days of the date of the nonavailability statement. The statement is valid for readmission for the same condition for only 15 days after discharge from initial hospitalization.

If the medical provider from whom you receive services accepts CHAMPUS assignment, it agrees to accept the CHAMPUS allowable charge as its full fee for your care. The provider may ask you to pay your cost-share immediately, or it may wait until after CHAMPUS has paid the claim. Providers who accept assignment usually file the claims for you. Providers who do not accept assignment bill you for their normal charges. You arrange how to pay the bill. When you file the CHAMPUS claim, you will be paid the CHAMPUS share of the allowable charge, which means you pay your cost-share *and* any difference between the allowable charge and the actual bill.

Providers accept assignment voluntarily, so they can choose to accept on a case-by-case basis. *Shop around* for the nearest provider that accepts CHAMPUS assignments. Your nearest HBA will assist you, or you can write to CHAMPUS, Aurora, CO 80045.

A CHAMPUS beneficiary is responsible for the first $150 of CHAMPUS-determined reasonable costs/charges for covered *outpatient* services and supplies during any fiscal year (1 October through 30 September). The total deductible amount for two or more beneficiary members of the same family who submit claims during the same fiscal year is $300. *The beneficiary must pay 20 percent of allowable charges above the deductible* (25 percent if the beneficiary is a retired servicemember or the dependent of a retired servicemember).

Your Medical Benefits

Patients	Military Hospitals Inpatient & Outpatient	CHAMPUS General Medical Services Inpatient	CHAMPUS General Medical Services Outpatient	Program for the Handicapped
Active duty families	Yes, on a space available basis	Yes, but may need nonavailability statement	Yes	Yes
Retirees, their families, and survivors	Yes, on a space available basis	Yes, unless entitled to Medicare (Part A). May need nonavailability statement	Yes, unless entitled to Medicare (Part A)	No
Dependent parents, parents-in-law	Yes, on a space available basis	No	No	No

Your Costs*

Patients	Military Hospitals		CHAMPUS		
			General Medical Services		Program for the Handicapped
	Inpatient	Outpatient	Inpatient	Outpatient	
Active duty families	Small fee/day	No charge	Small fee/day or $25, whichever is more	After deductible, 20% of allowable charges	Depends on pay grade of service-member
Retirees, ** **their families, and survivors**	Small fee/day	No charge	25% of allowable charges	After deductible, 25% of allowable charges	
Dependent parents, parents-in-law	Small fee/day	No charge			

*Costs are likely to change over time. If unsure about charges, check with the HBA.
**Retired enlistees pay no charge for inpatient care at military hospitals.

For *inpatient* medical care, CHAMPUS pays 100 percent of the allowable charges, and the active duty family member pays $6.55 per day (this rate fluctuates) or $25, whichever is greater. CHAMPUS pays 75 percent of the allowable charges for all other beneficiaries.

A properly completed claim must be submitted on the appropriate CHAMPUS claim form before CHAMPUS can extend its benefits. There are different forms for the different categories of medical care. If there are two or more different categories of expenses, it is necessary to file two or more claims on separate forms.

A claim, together with documents, should be sent to the CHAMPUS provider for the state or country *in which the medical care is received*. Required documents consist of a nonavailability statement, deductible certificate (providing the outpatient deductible of $150 or family deductible of $300 has been satisfied by a previous claim or claims), itemized bills, and so forth.

Many civilian hospitals and doctors keep a supply of CHAMPUS claim forms. These forms can also be obtained from the nearest CHAMPUS advisor or health benefits advisor located at your local military medical facility, from a CHAMPUS provider, or from CHAMPUS, Aurora, CO 80045.

If a beneficiary receives treatment from an individual or institution that is not participating in the CHAMPUS, that provider bills the beneficiary or sponsor, and the beneficiary or sponsor files the CHAMPUS claim form with the CHAMPUS contractor. The CHAMPUS share of the reasonable charge is then sent to the beneficiary or sponsor. The beneficiary or the sponsor is responsible for settling the medical bills presented by the individual doctor or hospital.

If the provider participates in CHAMPUS, the claim form must be completed by the beneficiary and the provider. Benefits are then paid directly to the provider. *All claims must be submitted to the appropriate CHAMPUS provider not later than 31 December of the calendar year in which the covered service or supply was received.* When a beneficiary is receiving continuing medical care that can be expected to last more than 30 days, claims should be submitted at least every 30 days (or more often, if the provider wishes).

CHAMPUS also authorizes a program for the handicapped that provides financial assistance to *active duty members* for the care, training, and rehabilitation of a dependent who is seriously and physically handicapped or who is moderately or severely mentally disabled.

It is absolutely essential that retired personnel consider obtaining a CHAMPUS-supplementing health care program. The 25 percent of medical facility charges and professional fees that CHAMPUS does not pay may add up to a medical bill that could wipe out a retired soldier's entire life savings. If you have this coverage, remember that, even when CHAMPUS payment is involved, the other program usually has primary liability—responsibility for paying its benefits first—in a double-coverage situation. Check CHAMPUS Regulation DOD 6010.8-R for complete guidance.

Delta Dental Plan

The Uniform Services Active Duty Dependents Dental Plan, the Delta Dental Plan (DDP), is a voluntary dental insurance program that covers basic dental care for the spouses and children of active duty members of the uniformed services. No matter where the servicemember is stationed, dependents who live in the United States, the District of Columbia, Guam, Puerto Rico, or the U.S. Virgin Islands can be enrolled in the DDP. (Family members residing overseas with their military sponsors receive dental care through the Army's direct care system, not through DDP.)

Pay and Entitlements

DDP covers routine, basic dental care. Some services are completely covered, such as cleanings, fluoride treatments, routine X-rays, lab tests, sealants and space maintainers (for children under 14), and some emergency treatment. Other services are 80 percent covered, such as fillings, stainless steel crowns on baby teeth, and repairs to dentures. The plan also features a partial payment allowance toward some crowns for adults. DDP has no deductibles and no maximums on covered services, which is a benefit to families on tight budgets. If you have only one dependent, your monthly payroll deduction will be $4.57 ($54.84 a year). For two or more dependents it costs $9.14 monthly ($109.68 annually).

According to DDP literature, the yearly cost for coverage is less than most dentists charge for just two regular checkups. More than 100,000 dental offices across the nation participate in the plan. Participants take care of submitting claim forms and are paid directly by DDP. Most will not require you to pay up front for covered services (except your cost-share on services covered at 80 percent). Your family members can go to any licensed dentist they choose, but the fees of nonparticipating dentists may not be fully covered and you could be required to pay up front and file your own claims. Using a DDP-participating dentist can save you time, money, and paperwork.

The health benefits advisor in the CHAMPUS office at your installation can tell you more about DDP and has a current list of participating dental offices. The benefits advisor can also provide you with a copy of the *Summary Plan Description of Your Group Dental Plan*, a helpful booklet that explains the details and policies. To sign up, just go to your military personnel office. You are eligible if you have an extended active duty service commitment of at least 24 months or have been accepted for reenlistment. Your coverage will start on the first of the month *after* the deduction shows up on your LES.

Government Quarters

Whether you live in barracks or family housing, your quarters are your home. You hold them in trust for their future occupants, and although your Army home is to be used and enjoyed, occupancy carries responsibilities, too.

Bachelor accommodations for enlisted personnel range from the fairly austere communal living conditions offered junior enlisted personnel in troop units to the small but private and well-appointed quarters offered senior NCOs in bachelor enlisted quarters (BEQ). During the course of an Army career, you will see them all if you do not marry at a young age.

The newer troop billets are dormitory-style facilities with central air conditioning and heating; two-, three-, or four-man rooms; recreational facilities; and convenience facilities—almost self-contained dwellings. Do not take these facilities for granted. Less than a generation ago, the bulk of the Army's bachelor enlisted personnel were living in one- and two-story wooden World War II barracks that were hot in the summer, cold in the winter, a real effort to keep clean, and generally overcrowded—older soldiers remember very well living in large troop bays, double-bunked, with only a small wooden footlocker and a metal wall locker to use for the storage of their uniforms and personal clothing.

Family housing—where it is available—ranges in style from detached single-family housing units to high-rise apartment-style buildings accommodating scores of families. In some cases, the quarters you are assigned will be in excellent condition and will require little maintenance to keep them that way; others will cause you constant maintenance headaches. Although your neighbors may sometimes be irksome, they will often prove to be friends whom you will cherish for the rest of your life.

When reporting to some new duty stations, you will find pleasant family housing waiting for you; at other stations, you will have to wait weeks or even months to get any kind of quarters. In some areas, the waiting lists for government housing are so long that you might find it necessary to buy or rent off of the post. Your family housing officer will be of great assistance to you if you should decide to occupy off-post quarters. Each installation and each major overseas command has a different family housing situation, and if your military sponsor (see Chapter 13) does not apprise you of the local situation, inquire before leaving for your new assignment.

Because of your rank, you may very well find yourself either the senior occupant of a multiple dwelling or responsible for a number of families in a stairwell of such a dwelling. These assignments are necessary, and you should consider them as part of your obligation as a noncommissioned officer to the military community in which you live. You should discharge them with the same dedication and enthusiasm that you devote to your primary duties, but be prepared for many headaches, and expect that from time to time your patience will be severely tried.

Occupancy of family quarters carries the responsibility for doing "handyman work." The facilities engineer performs all maintenance and repairs other than those that are within the capabilities of the occupants. Emergency work or work beyond your individual capabilities can be obtained by making a service call or submitting a job order request to the installation repair and utilities office. Do not, however, expect the engineers to drop everything and run to your quarters, no matter how severe the emergency.

If you are fortunate enough to be assigned to a single-family dwelling, you will be expected to perform that type of self-help maintenance that is done by any prudent homeowner to conserve funds and preserve the premises, such as minor carpentry, maintenance of hardware (door hinges, etc.), touch-up and partial interior painting, caulking around doors and windows, repair of screens, repair of simple plumbing malfunctions (minor leaking, defective washers, simple drainage stoppages), and so forth. Accumulate a set of tools that you can use around the house or apartment for this minor maintenance work.

No matter where you live—family quarters or the barracks—you are expected to exercise individual initiative to preserve energy and utilities. Soldiers are among the most flagrant violators of good energy conservation, wasting water and electricity and fuel as if there were no tomorrow. Remind yourself and others to be conservation conscious.

Your quarters will be inspected by someone from the housing office before you are cleared to vacate your quarters. This inspection can be very rigorous. The specific details will be furnished to you by the housing officer. Some people prefer to hire a civilian contractor to do the work for them. You can avoid this unnecessary expense if you and your family take proper care of your quarters while you are living in them. For example, use rugs on the floors, keep the walls clean and in good repair, and keep your appliances clean.

DA Pamphlet 210-2, *Handbook for Family Housing Occupants*, is an excellent guide for you and your family. Get a copy, keep it at your quarters, and study it thoroughly.

Commissary and Post Exchange Services

The price you pay for a grocery item in the commissary is the same price the government pays for it: If an item is sold to the government for 85 cents, then that is its cost to you. Even the commissary surcharge—5 percent of the total bill—and tipping

Pay and Entitlements

do not add as much to the cost of an item as do the standard markups found on similar items in civilian retail outlets.

The price of meat and produce items is more involved, however. If the commissary buys $1,600 worth of beef, that price includes bone and fat. If the loss in trimming amounts to $800, that loss is passed on to the consumer. About $200 may be recovered by selling the waste parts to contractors, but the remaining $600 is recovered in the selling price of the cuts. The cost of produce is based on invoice cost. If a case of oranges costs the government $13.50 and there are 88 oranges in a case, customers will pay 15 cents an orange so that the commissary is reimbursed for the purchase price.

The commissary surcharge pays for operating supplies, equipment, utilities, facility alterations, and new construction.

Here are some tips that will help you to cut down on grocery expenses when commissary shopping.

- Avoid shopping as a team. Surprisingly, statistics show that families tend to spend nearly one-fourth more when both wife and husband shop together.
- Never shop when you are hungry. You buy more when your resistance is low.
- Cut out and save manufacturers coupons that come to you through the mail, in newspapers, and in magazines. But do not buy something simply because you have a coupon for it. Use coupons to buy those items you planned to buy anyway.
- Do not assume that items prominently displayed are automatically on sale.
- Buy in large quantities if you can save by doing it.
- Avoid precut meat items. You can save by cutting things like chicken yourself. A roll of luncheon meat is cheaper than packages of individually sliced cuts.
- Avoid snack items—they are expensive—and substitute fruits and vegetables instead.
- Do comparison shopping. Get to know the prices for specific items in the commissary as opposed to the civilian marketplace. When the local drug store or supermarket has a special sale, check it out. Sometimes you can buy certain items cheaper on sale than you can in the commissary.

The Post Exchange Service was designated the Army and Air Force Exchange Service in 1948. The Headquarters of the Army and Air Force Exchange Service (AAFES) is in Dallas, Texas.

What originally began as an outlet "To supply troops at reasonable prices with articles of ordinary use . . . not supplied by the Government . . . to afford them the means of rational recreation and amusement" (General Order 46, July 1895) has since become a multibillion dollar enterprise that spans the globe. Many post exchange stores are actually department stores designed for family shoppers, although single soldiers can buy all the necessities (and some of the luxuries) of barracks life. Some stores even permit personnel in uniform to be waited on first during certain hours of the day, such as the lunch hour.

Some of the items now approved for sale in CONUS exchanges are microwave ovens, a more extensive line of convenience grocery items, and higher priced men's and women's clothing. Price limitations have also been removed from cameras and projectors, power tools, small electrical appliances, and dinnerware. All sports and recreational equipment except ski equipment and accessories no longer have price limitations either.

Several hundred military exchanges are operated throughout the world by the Department of Defense. The Army and Air Force Exchange Service (AAFES), headquartered in Dallas and headed by a general officer, operates more than 250 outlets worldwide. Military shoppers and their dependents save an average of 20 percent compared with what they would spend if they bought the same items off post. At a minimum, AAFES customers save the state sales tax, which is not charged.

Identity Cards

Your DD Form 2A, *U.S. Armed Forces Identification Card* (green, active duty), is possibly the most important military document you possess; DD Form 1173, *Uniformed Services Identification and Privilege Card*, is equally important to military dependents. These cards identify the bearers as persons who are entitled to the wide range of entitlements, privileges, and benefits authorized for military personnel and their dependents.

All ID cards are the property of the U.S. government. They are not transferable. The individual (or sponsor) to whom the card is issued must turn in cards in the following circumstances.

• Expiration of the card.

• Change in eligibility status (such as change in grade or rank and changes caused by disciplinary action, discharge, death, retirement, reenlistment, age, marriage, or release to inactive duty of the sponsor).

• Replacement by another card.

• Request from competent authority.

• Demand of the installation commander, verifying activity, or issuing activity.

• Recovery of a lost card after a replacement has been issued.

• Request by the installation commander for temporary safekeeping while an individual is taking part in recreational and gymnastic activities.

• Official placement of a sponsor in a deserter status.

• Change in the status of a sponsor if it terminates or modifies the right to any benefit for which the card may be used.

A lost ID card must be reported promptly to military law enforcement authorities or to ID card issuing authorities. DA Form 428, *Application for Identification Card*, or DD Form 1172, *Application for Uniformed Services Identification and Privilege Card*, is used for this purpose. The form also becomes the application for a new card, provided the individual continues to be eligible to receive it. DA Form 428 or DD Form 1172 must contain a statement of the circumstances of the loss, what was done to recover the card, and the card number, if known.

Any commissioned or noncommissioned officer, military police, or civilian law enforcement officer who is performing his or her official duties may confiscate an ID card that is expired, mutilated, used fraudulently, or presented by a person not entitled to use it. Managers and employees of benefit and privilege activities may confiscate any expired or obviously altered ID card or document.

Military Identification Cards. DD Form 2A (green) is issued to the following:

• All military personnel on active duty for more than 30 days.

• Members of the Army National Guard and the U.S. Army Reserve serving on initial active duty for training or a special tour of active duty for training for more than 30 days.

• Cadets of the U.S. Military Academy.

Commissary Cards. Since 1 January 1990, National Guard and Reserve soldiers and their families have been required to present their Armed Forces Commissary Privilege

Pay and Entitlements

cards to enter and shop in commissaries. They also must show their military or family member ID cards.

Dependent ID Cards. DD Form 1173 is used throughout the Department of Defense to identify persons, other than active duty or retired military, who are eligible for benefits and privileges offered by the armed forces.

Dependent ID cards are authorized for issue to lawful spouses, unremarried former spouses married to the member or former member for a period of at least 20 years, during which period the member or former member performed at least 20 years of service, children (adopted, legitimized, stepchildren, wards), parents (in special cases), and surviving spouses of active duty members or retired members. See AR 640-3 for specific details.

Generally, DD Forms 1173 are replaced for the same reasons that govern replacement of military ID cards.

To verify eligibility for issue of a dependent ID card, sponsors must be prepared to show marriage certificates, birth certificates, death certificates (in the case of unremarried widows or widowers), or any other documentation prescribed by AR 640-3 required to establish dependency.

Abuse of Privileges. All DD Forms 2, DD Forms 1173, and other authorized identification documents issued to Army members and their dependents may be confiscated and overstamped for abuse of privileges in Army facilities. Suspension of medical benefits, however, is not authorized.

Abuse of privileges includes the following.
- Unauthorized resale of commodities bought in Army activities to unauthorized persons, whether or not to make a profit (customary personal gifts are permissible).
- Shoplifting.
- Unauthorized access to activities.
- Misuse of a privilege (such as allowing an unauthorized person to use an otherwise valid ID card to gain access to a facility).
- Issuing dishonored checks in Army facilities.

Penalties for abuse of privileges in an appropriated or nonappropriated fund facility are warning letter, temporary suspension of privileges, and indefinite suspension of privileges.

Leave

All members of the Army serving on active duty are entitled to leave with pay and allowances at the rate of 2½ calendar days for each month of active duty or active duty for training, including the following:
- Members of the Army serving in the active military service, including members of the Army National Guard and the Army Reserve serving on active duty for a period of 30 days or more.
- Members of the Army National Guard and Reserve who are serving on initial active duty for training or active duty for training for a period of 30 days or more and for which they are entitled to pay.
- Members of the Army National Guard who are serving on full-time training duty for a period of 30 days or more and for which they are entitled to pay.

The following circumstances do not qualify as periods of earned leave:
- AWOL.

- Confinement as a result of a sentence of court-martial; confinement for more than one day while awaiting court-martial (providing the court-martial results in a conviction).
- When in excess leave.
- Unauthorized absence as a result of detention by civil authorities.
- Absence due to misconduct.

The total accumulation of accrued leave (earned leave) at the end of a fiscal year (30 September) cannot exceed 60 days. Leave accumulated after that date is forfeited. The single exception to this policy applies to personnel who, after 1 January 1968, serve in a designated combat zone, who may accumulate up to 90 days' leave. Leave that begins in one fiscal year and is completed in another is apportioned to the fiscal year in which each portion falls.

Upon discharge and immediate reenlistment, separation at ETS, or retirement, soldiers are authorized to settle their leave accounts for a lump-sum cash payment at the rate of one day of basic pay for each day of earned leave, up to 60 days. Public Law 94-212, 9 February 1976, limited to a maximum of 60 days settlement for accrued leave during a military career.

The following types of leave are authorized:

- *Advance leave.* Leave granted before its actual accrual, based on a reasonable expectation that it will be earned by the soldier during the remaining period of active duty.
- *Annual leave.* Leave granted in execution of a command's leave program, chargeable to the soldier's leave account. Also called "ordinary leave," as distinguished from emergency leave and special leave.
- *Convalescent leave.* A period of authorized absence granted to soldiers under medical treatment that is prescribed for recuperation and convalescence for sickness or wounds. Also called "sick leave," convalescent leave is not chargeable.
- *Emergency leave.* Leave granted for a bona fide personal or family emergency requiring the soldier's presence. Emergency leave is chargeable.
- *Environmental and morale leave.* Leave granted in conjunction with an environmental and morale leave program established at overseas installations where adverse environmental conditions exist that offset the full benefit of annual leave programs. This leave is chargeable.
- *Excess leave.* This leave is in excess of accrued and/or advance leave, granted without pay and allowances.
- *Graduation leave.* A period of authorized absence granted, as a delay in reporting to the first permanent duty station, to graduates of the U.S. Military Academy who are appointed as commissioned officers. Not chargeable, providing it is taken within three months of graduation.
- *Leave awaiting orders.* This is an authorized absence, chargeable to accrued leave and in excess of maximum leave accrual, awaiting further orders and disposition in connection with disability separation proceedings under the provisions of AR 635-40.
- *Reenlistment leave.* This leave is granted to enlisted personnel as a result of reenlistment. May be either advance leave or leave accrued or a combination thereof; chargeable against the soldier's leave account.
- *Rest and recuperation—extensions of overseas tours.* This is a nonchargeable increment of R&R leave authorized enlisted soldiers in certain specialties who voluntarily extend their overseas tours. It is authorized in lieu of $50 per month special pay.

Pay and Entitlements

The tour extension must be for a period of at least 12 months. Options under this program include nonchargeable leaves of 15 or 30 days.

• *Rest and recuperation leave* (R&R). This leave is granted in conjunction with rest and recuperation programs established in those areas designated for hostile fire pay, when operational military considerations preclude the full execution of ordinary annual leave programs. R&R leave is chargeable.

• *Special leave.* This is leave accrual that is authorized in excess of 60 days at the end of a fiscal year for soldiers assigned to hostile fire/imminent danger areas or certain deployable ships, mobile units, or other duty.

• *Terminal leave.* This leave is granted in connection with separation, including retirement, upon the request of the individual.

When possible, soldiers should be encouraged to take at least one annual leave period of about 14 consecutive days or longer (Paragraph 2-3b, AR 630-5). Personnel who refuse to take leave when the opportunity is afforded them should be counseled and informed that such refusal may result in the loss of earned leave at a later date.

Leave is requested on Part I, DA Form 31, *Request and Authority for Leave*. Requests for leave must be processed through the individual's immediate supervisor, although this step may be waived where supervisory approval or disapproval is inappropriate. The approval authority (generally, the soldier's commanding officer) ascertains that the individual has sufficient leave accrued to cover the entire period of absence requested.

Requests for leave that encompass two or more periods of absence, during which the individual is not required to perform duty from the termination of one leave period to the commencement of another leave period, are not approved except under emergency conditions. For example, one leave ends at the beginning of a three-day weekend, and then another starts at the end of the weekend.

Leave and special pass cannot be combined; pass periods are not authorized to be used in succession through commencement of one immediately after return to duty from the other.

When a soldier on leave fails to return to his or her proper station or appointed place of duty by 2400 hours of the last day of authorized leave, he or she becomes AWOL, unless the unauthorized absence is excused by competent authority. To avoid AWOL, soldiers should be informed before departing on leave of their obligation to make every reasonable effort to return to duty by the appointed time or to inform their commander of the reason(s) for delay, so that the period of leave may be extended.

Personnel should be physically present when DA Form 31 is authenticated and when commencing and terminating leave. Commanders may, at their discretion, authorize telephonic confirmation of departure and return.

DA Forms 31 are prepared in "Original," "Organization," "Individual," and "Suspense" copies.

Pass

A pass is an authorized absence not chargeable as leave, granted for short periods to provide respite from the working environment or for other specific reasons, at the end of which the soldier is actually at his or her place of duty or in the location from which he or she regularly commutes to work. This provision includes both regular and special passes.

Regular passes are granted to deserving military personnel for those periods when they are not required to be physically present with their unit for the performance of assigned duties. Normally, regular passes are valid only during specified off-duty hours, not more than 72 hours, except for public holiday weekends and holiday periods which, by discretion of the President, are extended to the commencement of working hours on the next working day.

Special passes are granted for periods of three or four days (72 to 96 hours) to deserving personnel on special occasions or in special circumstances for the following reasons: as special recognition for exceptional performance of duty, such as Soldier of the Month or Year; to attend spiritual retreats or to observe other major religious events; to alleviate personal problems incident to military service; to vote; or as compensatory time off for long or arduous duty away from home station or for duty in an isolated location where normal pass is inadequate.

Passes may not be issued to soldiers so that two or more are effective in succession or used in a series, through reissue immediately after return to duty.

Extension of a pass is authorized provided the total absence does not exceed 72 hours for a regular pass, 72 hours for a special three-day pass, and 96 hours for a special four-day pass. Special passes will not be extended by combination with public holiday periods or other off-duty hours in cases in which the combined total will exceed the maximum limits of a three-day or four-day pass. Extensions beyond the authorized maximum are chargeable to leave (Paragraph 11-6, AR 630-5).

Pass forms are normally not required when granting passes to military personnel. A valid ID card normally is sufficient to identify a soldier on authorized absence not classified as leave. When a commander determines that it is desirable to control the authorized absence of personnel (other than leave or administrative absences), only DD Form 345, *Armed Forces Liberty Pass*, is authorized to be used.

Leave and pass may be taken in conjunction with temporary duty subject to the restrictions of Paragraph 11-9, AR 630-5, concerning combination of leave and pass.

PUBLIC HOLIDAYS

Public holidays are established by law and are observed except when military operations prevent observance. When the holiday falls on a Saturday, the preceding Friday will be considered a holiday; when it falls on a Sunday, the following Monday is a holiday. Following is a list of public holidays:

New Year's Day, 1 January.
Martin Luther King's Birthday, third Monday in January.
Washington's Birthday, third Monday in February.
Memorial Day, last Monday in May.
Independence Day, 4 July.
Labor Day, first Monday in September.
Columbus Day, second Monday in October.
Veterans' Day, 11 November.
Thanksgiving Day, fourth Thursday in November.
Christmas Day, 25 December.

13

Assignments

There are two old Army sayings that every soldier knows by heart: "Never volunteer," and "There are only two good posts in the Army: The one you just left and the one you want to go to." Add to these, "The grass is always greener on the other side of the fence" and "You can never go back," and you have some wisdom about the Army that some soldiers never learn.

The Army sends soldiers where it needs them, and *everyone* must take his or her turn.

The professional soldier never endures an assignment alone. The Army really is a great big family that shares its mutual experiences—the good times and bad times—and after a few tours, you will not go anywhere without meeting friends. The warm hearts and the friendly faces of comrades gone before have welcomed many a soldier to some foreign shore.

The following general policies and procedures apply to Army assignments. They are in addition to those prescribed by AR 614-6 and 614-30. (A more detailed listing is in Paragraph 1-4, AR 614-200, *Selection of Enlisted Soldiers for Training and Assignment*.)

• A soldier may make a second or later permanent change of station (PCS) in the same fiscal year only when authorized by AR 614-6 or approved by the Secretary of the Army.

• The needs of the Army are the main considerations in selecting individuals for reassignment. Consistent with these needs, an attempt is made to assign a soldier to his or her area of preference.

- Qualified volunteers are the *first* to be considered for all assignments. They must, however, have spent at least 12 months at their present duty station before being reassigned.
- Promotion of soldiers to 1SG/MSG or below cannot be the only reason for a PCS.
- Soldiers returning from overseas cannot be assigned involuntarily to another overseas area. They must serve in CONUS for one year. As an exception, soldiers assigned to Hawaii may be reassigned to another overseas area.
- Enlisted women are not assigned to battalions or similar size infantry, armor, cannon field artillery, combat engineer positions, or low altitude air defense artillery units.
- Personnel in the ranks of sergeant through master sergeant (except promotable master sergeants) are given either a home base or advanced assignment when selected for a short-tour area.
- PCS cannot be made within CONUS solely because of the passage of a set time.
- Assignments are not made on a nominative basis except as specifically authorized by AR 614-200.
- Soldiers who have physically, emotionally, or intellectually handicapped dependents may request that PersCom consider the condition when making assignment selections (see Procedure 4-28, DA Pam 600-8, for procedures involving the Exceptional Family Member Program).
- Before departure in compliance with assignment instructions, a soldier must take actions authorized in Chapter 3, AR 601-280, to meet any remaining service requirement.

PCS travel for all military personnel is made only because of military necessity. Commanders may approve reassignment of personnel within their commands and between major commands at the same installation, providing both concur and the move costs no more than $250.

CONUS commanders may approve reassignment of sergeants and below when the PCS involves a unit redeployment overseas or a CONUS unit relocation or when the soldier will have completed at least one year at the old duty station and will complete at least one year at the new one.

When reassigning personnel in accordance with the policies contained in the regulations specified above, commanders are enjoined always to use soldiers in accordance with the provisions of AR 600-200, which further directs that soldiers will be placed in positions that further their career progression and development (Paragraph 1-6c).

PERSONNEL ACTION REQUEST

DA Form 4187, *Personnel Action Request*, gives soldiers a way to communicate to the U.S. Total Army Personnel Command (PersCom) their personal choices for such things as assignments, schools, and special duty. This document is considered before making an assignment, but the needs of the Army always come first. Nevertheless, the request is given full consideration whenever possible. It is incumbent upon the individual soldier to check his/her field file (DA Form 2A and 2-1) approximately one month after submitting DA Form 4187 to ensure assignment requests are in the file.

THE ENLISTED PERSONNEL ASSIGNMENT SYSTEM

The primary goal of the enlisted personnel assignment system is to satisfy the

Assignments

personnel requirements of the Army. The secondary goals are as follows:
- Equalize desirable and undesirable assignments by reassigning the most eligible soldier from among those of similar MOSs and grade.
- Equalize the hardships of the military service.
- Meet the personal desires of the soldier.
- Assign each soldier so that he or she will have the greatest opportunities for professional development and promotion advancement.

Normally, the military personnel office (MILPO), in coordination with the unit, compares authorized and projected positions with current assigned strength and known or projected gains and losses to determine the requirements for assignments. Requisitions are then prepared for these requirements and submitted to Commanding General, Total Army Personnel Command (PersCom) in Alexandria, Virginia. On receipt, PersCom edits and validates the requisitions. It is the responsibility of the requisitioning unit not to over- or underrequisition and to resolve any discrepancy before submitting the validated requisition for processing.

Soldiers become available to be assigned against these requisitions for a variety of reasons. Soldiers who enlist in the Army are available for assignment on completion of training and award of an MOS. Others are available when they have done one of the following.
- Volunteered for reassignment.
- Completed an overseas tour of duty.
- Completed schooling or training.
- Completed a stabilized tour of duty.
- Completed normal time on station in the continental United States for a given MOS ("turnaround time" varies by MOS).

The Centralized Assignment Procedure III (CAP III) System is used to assign all soldiers except those completing Basic and Advanced Individual Training. This automated nomination/assignment procedure compares the requirements recorded on requisitions against selected qualification factors for each soldier. Some of the major qualifications considered are grade, MOS and skill level, area of preference, and Special Qualification Identifier (SQI). Other qualifications considered are the expiration term of service (ETS), the number of months since last PCS, the number of months since return from overseas, the soldier's availability month compared with requirement month on the requisition, and an Additional Skill Identifier (ASI). An ASI (expressed as the sixth and seventh characters of an MOS Code) identifies skills acquired through functional training or OJT in maintenance and operation of weapon or equipment systems or subsystems and other training not identified by MOS or SQI (see AR 611-201).

Each soldier is compared to each requisition and given a numeric score for every one for which he or she can be nominated. Once a soldier's record has been reviewed and awarded points for a qualitative match to each requisition, the system then selects that group of nominations that provides the best over requisition fill in terms of quantity and quality. The assignment preferences of the individual and the requirements of the positions receive maximum consideration within the primary goal of filling all the Army's requirements. The nomination process has three basic goals:
- Each valid requisition must have at least one soldier nominated to it, provided sufficient soldiers are available for assignment in the requisition MOS and grade.
- Requisitions are filled by relative priority. When a shortage of soldiers exists, the shortage is shared proportionately by all requisitioning activities according to priority.
- A soldier is nominated to an assignment for which he or she is well qualified.

The CAP III produces nominations to match the requisition. These nominations

PERSONNEL ACTION

For use of this form, see DA PAM 600-8 and AR 680-1; the proponent agency is MILPERCEN.

DATA REQUIRED BY THE PRIVACY ACT

Authority: Title 5, section 3012; Title 10, U.S.C. E.O. 9397. Principal Purpose: Use by service member in accordance with DA Pamphlet 600-8 when requesting a personnel action on his/her own behalf (Section III). Routine Uses: To initiate the processing of a personnel action being requested by the service member. Disclosure: Voluntary. Failure to provide Social Security Number may result in a delay or error in processing of the request for personnel action.

THRU: (Include ZIP Code)	TO: (Include ZIP Code)	FROM: (Include ZIP Code) COMMANDER

SECTION I - PERSONAL IDENTIFICATION

NAME (Last, first, MI)	GRADE OF RANK/PMOS (Enl only)	SOCIAL SECURITY NUMBER

SECTION II - DUTY STATUS CHANGE (Proc 9-1, DA Pam 600-8)

The above member's duty status is changed from _____

_____ to _____

_____ effective _____ hours, _____ 19 ___

SECTION III - REQUEST FOR PERSONNEL ACTION

I request the following action:

TYPE OF ACTION	Procedure	TYPE OF ACTION	Procedure
Service School (Enl only)		Reassignment Married Army Couples	
ROTC or Reserve Component Duty		Reclassification	
Volunteering For Oversea Service		Officer Candidate School	
Ranger Training		Asgmt of Pers with Exceptional Family Members	
Reasgmt Extreme Family Problems		Identification Card	
Exchange Reassignment (Enl only)		Identification Tags	
Airborne Training		Separate Rations	
Special Forces Training/Assignment		Leave - Excess/Advance/Outside CONUS	
On-the-Job Training (Enl only)		Change of Name/SSN/DOB	
Retesting in Army Personnel Tests		Other (Specify)	

SIGNATURE OF MEMBER (When required)	DATE

SECTION IV - REMARKS (Applies to Sections II, III, and V) (Continue on separate sheet)

SECTION V - CERTIFICATION/APPROVAL/DISAPPROVAL

I certify that the duty status change (Section II) or that the request for personnel action (Section III) contained herein -

☐ HAS BEEN VERIFIED ☐ RECOMMEND APPROVAL ☐ RECOMMEND DISAPPROVAL
☐ IS APPROVED ☐ IS DISAPPROVED

COMMANDER/AUTHORIZED REPRESENTATIVE	SIGNATURE	DATE

DA FORM 4187 DEC 82   EDITION OF FEB 81 WILL BE USED.   COPY 1

DA Form 4187 is the soldier's basic request form for any personnel action.

Assignments

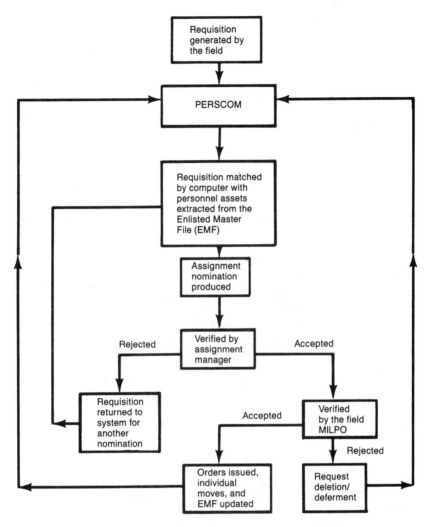

This flow chart illustrates the enlisted personnel assignment system.

are then passed to an assignment manager for verification. Based on a review of all available information, the assignment manager either accepts a soldier for the assignment or rejects all nominees and returns the requisition to the selection process for new nominations. If maintained by the Enlisted Personnel Management Directorate, PersCom, the career management individual files (CMIF) are also included in this review. A qualified individual may also be selected manually to match the requisition regardless of nomination by CAP III.

Assignment instructions are transmitted to both the losing and gaining command or installation by the automated digital network (AUTODIN). The losing commander then verifies the assignment. This step is the key in the process. Because of delays in reporting and errors in the data bases, the individuals selected may not qualify for the assignment. When assignment instructions are received by the losing commander's military personnel office, the soldier's qualifications and eligibility are verified. The MILPO interviews the soldier and reviews his or her records.

If the soldier is qualified and the assignment is in keeping with announced Department of the Army policy, the process is finished when the necessary orders for travel are issued. If the soldier does not qualify or cannot qualify in time to meet the requirement, a deletion or deferment request is submitted in accordance with Section V, Chapter 2, AR 614-200.

Homebase and Advance Assignment Program (HAAP)

A soldier is given a *homebase assignment* when he or she is projected to return to his or her previous permanent duty station after completing a short tour. An *advanced assignment* is given when a soldier is projected to be assigned to a duty station other than his or her previous permanent duty station after completing a short tour.

Eligible soldiers are given a home base or an advance assignment when selected for a dependent-restricted short-tour area. The Homebase and Advance Assignment Program (HAAP) minimizes family dislocation and reduces the expenditure of PCS funds. Only active Army sergeants through the ranks of first sergeant and master sergeant who are assigned to dependent-restricted 12-month short-tour areas are affected. HAAP assignments are not furnished to sergeants major, or first sergeants or master sergeants (promotable) except that consistent with the needs of the Army, the CSM/SGM Office, PersCom, honors individual preferences when issuing assignment instructions to personnel in these ranks returning to CONUS.

The following primary factors determine HAAP assignments.
- The needs of the Army.
- Professional development.
- Least-cost factors.
- Assignment choice.
- Regimental affiliation.

Requests for PCS or Deletion from Assignment

Chapter 3, AR 614-200, establishes specific policies governing individual requests submitted by soldiers for a PCS or deletion from assignment instructions. A soldier may submit a request for any of the following reasons.
- *Extreme family problem that is temporary* and can be resolved in one year.
- *Extreme family problem that is not expected to be resolved in one year.*
- *Sole surviving son or daughter.* The sole surviving son or daughter of a family that has suffered the loss of the father, the mother, or one or more sons or daughters in the military service will not be required to serve in combat. Soldiers who become sole surviving sons or daughters after their enlistment may request discharge under AR 635-200.

A soldier may waive entitlement to assignment limitations, whether entitlement was based on his or her own application or the request of his or her immediate family.
- *Assignment of married Army couples.* Army requirements and readiness goals are paramount when considering personnel for assignment. Married Army couples desiring joint assignment to establish common household (joint domicile) must request

Assignments

such assignment. The assignment desires of soldiers married to other soldiers are fully considered. There are two ways for married Army couples to apply for joint domicile assignment:

• By applying on a one-time basis to be continually considered for worldwide joint assignments. Thereafter, when one member is being considered for reassignment, the other will automatically be considered for assignment to the same location or area.

• By applying for joint domicile assignments each time consideration is desired. In this case, the spouse who has received assignment instructions must submit an application for joint domicile consideration.

Soldiers assigned to COHORT/NMS units are not assigned out of the unit for the purpose of establishing a joint domicile. The spouse of the soldier in the COHORT/NMS unit may request a joint domicile assignment in or near the location of the unit, provided the other criteria of AR 614-200 are met.

• *Exchange assignments.* For mutual convenience, CONUS-assigned soldiers may request an exchange assignment with a soldier within CONUS; a soldier assigned overseas may request an exchange assignment with a soldier within his or her same overseas command.

This policy applies only to exchange of current duty assignments. Only one of the soldiers can apply. Prior agreement between the two must be arranged on a person-to-person basis. Inquiries about the application cannot be made through official correspondence, nor will installation commanders be queried by personal letters. If a married Army couple who presently occupy a common household is separated because one member is granted an exchange assignment, the other member *may not* apply for reassignment to the same installation to reestablish a joint residence. Exchange assignments are not granted for soldiers who have received assignment instructions, and all travel time is charged as leave. The soldiers applying for exchange must be of the same grade, similarly qualified, and serving in the same MOS. All commanders concerned must concur in the proposed exchange assignment. They must establish a mutually agreeable date of assignment.

Procedures 3-18, DA Pam 600-8, contain detailed guidance for preparing and processing requests for an exchange assignment. The *Army Times* publishes lists of soldiers who desire to contact others to arrange for exchange assignments.

Assignment from duty requiring extensive TDY. Soldiers assigned to duties requiring extensive travel or family separation may, on completing three years in that duty, request reassignment. For this purpose, extensive travel/family separation is defined by AR 614-200 as "TDY away from the home station requiring travel or family separation for 4 or more days per week for not less than 22 weeks per year."

CAREER DEVELOPMENT PROGRAMS

A career development program is a system of intensive management of selected MOSs or career management fields (CMF). Career development programs are established to ensure that there are enough highly trained and experienced soldiers to fill positions that require unique or highly technical skills. To develop soldiers with the required proficiency, career fields within each program often require the following:

• Frequent movement from one job to another to gain required experience.
• An above average frequency of advanced training.
• Lengthy or frequent training periods.
• A combination of any of the above factors.

Unless otherwise stated in Chapter 7, AR 614-200, volunteers for a career development program should submit applications on DA Form 4187, using DA Pam 600-8 for detailed application procedures. In applying for career programs and related training, applicants should consider the prerequisites listed in DA Pam 351-4 for the appropriate course of instruction.

Chapter 7, AR 614-200, contains the minimum requirements (subject to change) for each career program. Attaining the prerequisites does not automatically ensure entry into a career program. The appropriate career management branch selects the best qualified soldiers for a career program.

Waivers are not granted for remaining service requirements for formal training. Waivers for other eligibility requirements or selection standards are considered unless otherwise stated in AR 614-200. Waivers cannot be implied. Each must be specifically requested. In the application for entry into the program or training requested, the applicant must include the reason for the waiver.

Career development programs include the following:
- Intelligence Career Program.
- Noncommissioned Officer Logistics Program (NCOLP).
- Explosive Ordnance Disposal (EOD) Career Program.
- Technical Escort (TE) Career Program.
- Personnel Specialty Career Program (PSCP).
- Army Bandsman Career Program (ABCP).
- Enlisted Club Management Career Program.

Assignment to Specific Organizations and Duty Positions

Chapter 8, AR 614-200, contains specific policies and procedures for nomination, evaluation, selection, and assignment of enlisted soldiers to the following.
- Presidential support activities.
- Drill Sergeant Program.
- Assignment as instructors at uniformed service schools.
- Assignment to international and overseas joint headquarters, U.S. Military Missions, Military Assistance Advisory Groups (MAAGs), and Joint U.S. Military Advisory Groups (JUSMAG).
- Assignment to certain organizations and agencies: Office of the Secretary of Defense and Office of the Joint Chiefs of Staff; U.S. Central Command; U.S. Readiness Command (USREDCOM) and Joint Deployment Agency; Defense Communications Agency; Defense Intelligence Agency; U.S. Army Element, Defense Nuclear Agency; HQDA, PersCom and HQ TRADOC; U.S. Military Academy, U.S. Army Command and General Staff College and U.S. Army War College; U.S. Disciplinary Barracks; First Battalion (Reinf), 3d Infantry (The Old Guard), Fort Myer, VA; U.S. Army Military District of Washington; U.S. Army, Berlin, and Berlin Brigade; U.S. Army Intelligence and Security Command; Office of the Assistant Chief of Staff for Intelligence; U.S. Army Correctional Activity; U.S. Army Courier Service; U.S. Army Service Center for the Armed Forces; U.S. Army Element, Armed Forces Police Detachment, Washington, D.C.; U.S. Army Criminal Investigation Command; and Defense Logistics Agency.
- Reserve Component or Reserve Officer Training Corps (ROTC) Duty.
- Armed Forces Examining and Entrance Stations (AFEES).
- Food inspection specialists.
- Selection and assignment of first sergeants.

This section will consider in detail only selection for assignments as drill sergeants and first sergeants.

Assignments

Drill Sergeant Program

The Drill Sergeant Program is designed to allow highly motivated, well-qualified professionals to serve as cadre at the following:

- U.S. Army Training Centers (USATC).
- TRADOC training centers at Fort Sill and Fort Bliss.
- U.S. Army Correction Activity, Fort Riley, Kansas.

Generally, active Army soldiers in the infantry, armor, field artillery, and engineer career management fields are selected for assignment. Soldiers from other career fields, however, including female soldiers, are also considered for selection and assignment.

To be eligible to enter the Drill Sergeant Program, all candidates must meet the following nonwaiverable prerequisites.

- If you are selected, you must pass the Army Physical Fitness Test (APFT) shortly after arrival at the duty station (AR 600-9). Volunteers must have successfully passed the APFT within the last six months and must furnish a copy of their physical test score cards with their applications. Weight limits are prescribed in AR 600-9. The minimum physical profile guide for selection is 222221.
- Have no speech impairment.
- Display good military bearing.

Drill sergeants inspect a field training area. Fulfilling a drill sergeant assignment can be career enhancing and personally rewarding. *U.S. Army photo*

- Have no record of emotional instability as determined by screening of health records.
- Be a high school graduate or possess the GED equivalent.
- Have demonstrated leadership ability during previous tours of duty.
- Have no record of disciplinary action or time lost during the current enlistment or in the last three years, whichever is longer.
- Have demonstrated the capability to perform in positions in increasing responsibilities as a senior NCO in the Army, as reflected in NCOERs, commanders' drill sergeant duty recommendations, and USAEEC Forms 10 or 10A.
- Have been placed consistently in the upper half of his or her peer group as demonstrated by MOS evaluation.
- Be serving in ranks sergeant through sergeant first class, if male, or in ranks specialist through sergeant first class, if female. Male sergeants may volunteer regardless of MOS. All sergeants must have a minimum of four years in service, must have completed PLDC, and be recommended by a commander in the rank of lieutenant colonel or higher.
- Not have received enlistment bonus or selective reenlistment bonus for current service obligation if PMOS is not among those authorized for drill sergeant positions.

Soldiers assigned to drill sergeant duty incur a 24-month obligation for drill sergeant duty after successful completion of drill sergeant school and a stabilized tour for 24 months with an option to extend an additional 6 to 12 months. The tour of duty for a drill sergeant does not exceed 36 months.

As an exception to AR 614-6, CG, PersCom, may grant a second PCS in the same fiscal year for personnel who volunteer for drill sergeant duties, fail to graduate from drill sergeant school, or are removed from the program, either voluntarily or involuntarily.

Applications should be submitted through channels on a DA Form 4187. See Procedure 3-34, DA Pamphlet 600-8.

Selection and Assignment of First Sergeants

> The soldier having acquired that degree of confidence of his officers as to be appointed first sergeant of the company, should consider the importance of his office; that the discipline of the company, the conduct of the men, their exactness in obeying orders, and the regularity of their manners, will in great measure depend on his vigilance.
>
> Stuben, *Regulations for the Order of the Troops of the United States,* approved by Congress, 29 March 1779

Only the most highly qualified and motivated senior soldiers are selected and assigned to first sergeant positions. Moreover, first sergeant duty assignments must be career enriching and serve as professional development experience for soldiers in career management fields where first sergeant opportunities are available.

Soldiers in grades SFC/PSG and MSG are assigned as first sergeants based on outstanding qualities of leadership, dedication to duty, integrity and moral character, professionalism, MOS proficiency, appearance and military bearing, physical fitness, and proven performance or potential for the first sergeant position.

Soldiers who meet the above requirements are eligible for award of SQI *M*. Installation or division commanders may approve and award SQI *M* to qualified soldiers.

Assignments

They may not award the first sergeant SQI to soldiers because of duty as a detachment sergeant. Positions must be authorized first sergeant positions.

CG, PersCom, conducts professional development reviews of soldiers and selects outstanding candidates for possible award of SQI *M.* When a soldier is identified by PersCom, efforts are made to assign him or her to a first sergeant position on his or her next PCS. Acceptance or rejection of selection is not a soldier's right.

Unit commanders may select eligible soldiers and recommend, if appropriate, award of SQI *M.* Recommendations are prepared on DA Form 4187 and forwarded through normal channels to the installation or division commanders.

Eligible soldiers may request award of SQI *M* through their immediate commander. The soldier's battalion (or equivalent level) commander reviews the request and sends it with recommendations through channels to the installation or division commander.

Attendance at the First Sergeant's Course at Fort Bliss, Texas, is not mandatory for award of the SQI *M* (see Chapter 3 for more information on the course), but successful completion of the course is an important indicator of first sergeant potential.

Selection priorities for assignment to authorized first sergeant positions are these:
- Master sergeants who possess the proper PMOS and have been awarded the SQI *M.*
- Master sergeants who do not possess the SQI *M*, but possess the proper PMOS and are considered by local commanders to have first sergeant potential.
- Master sergeants who possess the SQI *M* and a PMOS in the CMF appropriate to the type unit.
- Master sergeants who do not possess the SQI *M* but possess a PMOS in the CMF appropriate to the type unit and are considered by local commanders to have first sergeant potential.
- Master sergeants who possess the SQI *M*, but do not possess PMOS/CMF appropriate to the type unit.
- As an interim measure, until a master sergeant who meets one of the priorities listed above can be assigned, sergeants first class may be assigned first sergeant duty in accordance with the provisions of Paragraph 8-67d(6)(a)–(d). (For frocking of first sergeants, see Chapter 5.)

Soldiers are stabilized as first sergeants for at least 24 months, except for overseas areas, where stabilization will not involuntarily exceed normal tour length.

Repetitive assignments to first sergeant duty are based on these factors.
- The needs of the Army.
- The soldier's performance as a first sergeant.
- The soldier's desires and professional development needs.

OVERSEAS SERVICE

Many Americans work very hard all their lives, and then in their declining years, when they at last have the leisure and money to travel, they see the world. Soldiers not only see the world when they are young, but they also have the unique opportunity to live among foreign peoples for extended periods of time and learn about their cultures from first-hand experience.

There are two ways that you can approach your first overseas tour. You can go kicking and screaming and spend your time in some foreign country, isolated in the American community, never venturing very far outside the cocoon of familiar surroundings, counting the dreary days until you rotate, or you can approach foreign service as a thrilling adventure to be experienced to the fullest, and you can be a goodwill ambassador for the United States of America.

Running afoul of the law in a foreign country can be very dangerous. In countries where a Status of Forces Agreement (SOFA) exists between the United States government and the foreign government, soldiers may be tried for offenses under the laws of the country concerned. Such agreements exist with Japan, Korea, and the NATO countries. While the U.S. government pays a soldier's legal and court fees and guarantees his constitutional rights, sentences handed down by foreign judges can be very strict, and a "tour" in a foreign prison usually rates somewhere between "very bad" and "worse."

Most major overseas commands operate orientation programs for newly arrived personnel in the command. These courses attempt to expose soldiers to the culture in which they will be living in order to lessen the effect of "cultural shock" that some people experience the first time they encounter an alien society. When you receive overseas assignment instructions, it would be a very good idea for you and your spouse (if you have one) to study the language of the country to which you will be going. Some special assignments require extensive formal language training, but most Army installations do provide some language instruction for soldiers and their dependents who are bound overseas. German is the most frequently taught language. Learning the rudiments of a foreign language can be fun, and speaking a foreign language is a very valuable talent to have once you arrive at your overseas duty station.

Standards of living overseas vary depending on the country. Western Germany's standard of living is very high, and your money will not go far there; other countries are beset with substantial economic problems, and the standards of living in those places can sometimes be so low that only the very rich can afford luxuries that are considered common in the United States, but you won't be able to afford them at local prices.

As with everything else, what you get out of your situation is what you make of it. And remember that your overseas tour will not last forever; sooner or later you must leave to come home. Emotional attachments are very hard to break off, so be warned if you establish any kind of relationship with a foreign man or woman. What usually starts as a casual, fun-filled lark, a pleasant way to pass the time, frequently develops into a serious involvement. If it is not consummated by marriage, its termination can be an emotional trauma that will be very painful for both of you. A sad commentary on this subject is the thousands of illegitimate children American servicemen have abandoned in various foreign countries over the years.

Policies

The chief consideration in selecting a soldier for service overseas is that a valid authorization exists for his or her military qualifications. Equitable distribution is made, within a given MOS and grade, of oversea duty assignments, considering both desirable and undesirable locations. All reasonable efforts are made to minimize periods of forced separations and any adverse effects of oversea service encountered by soldiers and their families.

Between oversea tours, with the exception of Hawaii, soldiers are assigned in their sustaining base for at least 12 months on station. Consistent with Army needs, soldiers are retained as long as possible in the continental United States. Among individuals who have previous overseas service, those with the earliest date of return from overseas normally will be selected first. Subject to personnel requirements to short-tour areas, soldiers who have completed a normal overseas service tour in a short-tour area will not be assigned to another short-tour area on their next overseas assignment.

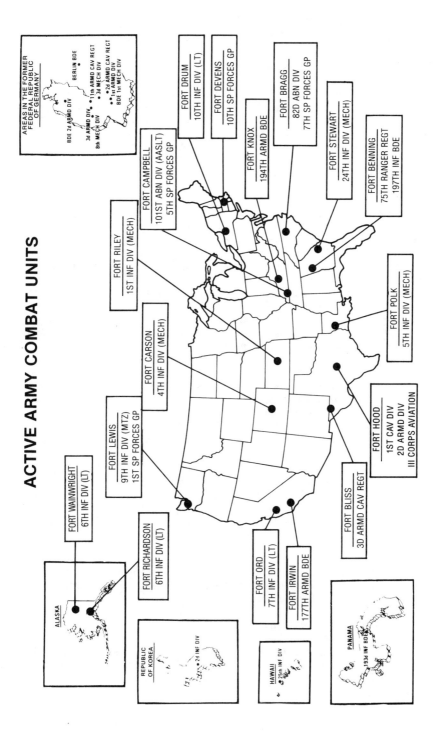

Volunteering

Permanent party enlisted personnel, except those participating in the New Manning System, may volunteer for overseas duty after six months of service in CONUS under the following conditions.

• They have not been alerted for overseas service.

• They are not assigned to units alerted for overseas movement; soldiers assigned to a unit alerted to move but who are not scheduled to deploy may, however, volunteer to do so.

• Reassignment will not be effected before twelve months on station are completed.

• Those serving in stabilized assignments based on enlistment options may waive their unfulfilled enlistment commitment. This waiver applies only if overseas assignment is to an area of choice.

• Personnel may volunteer for any area. Approval, however, is influenced by requirement for the MOS. Personnel who volunteer for a return long-tour assignment are checked to see whether their MOS is normally rotated in a short-to-short-tour sequence.

• Reassignment will not cause a soldier to have a second PCS in the same fiscal year, unless authorized by AR 614-6, or HQDA has granted authorization.

Applications for all grades are submitted on DA Form 4187, as outlined by Procedure 3-14, DA Pam 600-8.

Once submitted, a volunteer's application remains current until his or her next PCS, unless it is denied upon submission or withdrawn. Approval must be obtained from HQDA to withdraw a volunteer application.

If not selected within six months after applying, a volunteer may submit a new application for a different location.

Requests for intertheater transfers are shown on DA Form 2635, Enlisted Preference Statement. The MILPO sends the form to HQDA at least ten months before DEROS if currently in a long-tour area and five months if in a short-tour area.

Submitting a request for overseas service constitutes the following conditions: a waiver, if applicable, of indefinite retention in CONUS after required service is completed; a commitment to extend term of enlistment or to reenlist in order to have enough service to complete the prescribed tour for the area if the application is approved; or a waiver, if applicable, of an unfulfilled enlistment commitment.

Individuals who volunteer for foreign service are applied against requirements in the area of choice; otherwise, they are not ordered overseas until other people in the same grade and skill are considered.

Temporary Deferments

Because of the possible adverse effect on command operational readiness, granting of deferments for overseas service is strictly controlled and held to an absolute minimum. The needs of the service are the major determining factor in granting deferments.

Normally, once an application has been submitted, the soldier will be retained at the home station, pending a final decision. When a soldier requests deferment and it results in his or her having less remaining time in service than the length of the prescribed tour, the individual will continue on the oversea assignment. Unless he or she voluntarily reenlists or extends to be eligible to complete the prescribed tour, the individual must sign a counseling statement, which is a bar to reenlistment.

Assignments

Applications are initiated by the individual concerned on DA Form 4187 in accordance with Chapter 4, DA Pam 600-8-10.

Personnel for whom a deferment is authorized for 90 days or less are reassigned upon completion of deferment period in accordance with their original reassignment instructions, unless otherwise directed by HQDA. For those deferred in excess of 90 days, action concerning removal from the reassignment instructions or movement upon completion of deferment is as prescribed by HQDA.

Deferments and Deletions

The following conditions normally warrant deferments.

- A recent severe psychotic episode involving a spouse or child after a soldier receives assignment instructions.
- The soldier's children are being made wards of the court or are being placed in an orphanage or a foster home because of family separation. This separation must be because of military service and not because of neglect or misconduct on the part of the soldier.
- Adoption cases in which the home study (deciding whether a child is to be placed) has been completed and a child is scheduled to be placed in the soldier's home within 90 days.
- Illness of a family member (see Paragraph 6-5a(4), AR 614-30, for details).

Criteria for deletion are these.

- Terminal illness of a family member where death is anticipated within one year.
- The death of the soldier's spouse or child, after receipt of assignment instructions.
- Prolonged hospitalization of more than 90 days where the soldier's presence is deemed essential to resolve associated problems.
- Documented rape of the soldier's spouse or child within 90 days of the scheduled movement date, where the soldier's presence is deemed essential to resolve associated problems.
- Documented child abuse, where the soldier's presence is essential to resolve associated problems.
- Selection to attend the basic or advanced NCO courses or OCS, where attendance will delay overseas travel more than 90 days.
- Enrollment in the Drug and Alcohol Abuse Residential Rehabilitation Treatment Program.
- Pregnancy or related complications exceeding 90 days.

Eligibility for Overseas Service

Personnel are assigned to short-tour overseas assignments according to the following priorities.

- Volunteers who have completed a minimum of 12 months' time on station or are not otherwise stabilized.
- Personnel with no previous overseas service.
- Personnel in CONUS who have not previously served in a short-tour area and whose last overseas assignment was a "with dependents tour"; those whose last overseas tour was a "with dependents" tour in a long-tour area and who previously served a short tour; those whose last overseas tour was in a short-tour area and who

were in accompanied status; and those who have not previously served in a short-tour area and whose last assignment was an "all others" tour.
• Personnel in Hawaii after completion of a prescribed accompanied tour.
• Personnel in CONUS whose last overseas tour was in a short-tour area and who were in an unaccompanied area.
• Personnel in Hawaii after completion of a prescribed "all others" tour.

Personnel are assigned to long-tour overseas areas according to the following priorities.
• As in the first two conditions listed for short-tour overseas assignments.
• Personnel serving in CONUS whose last overseas tour was "with dependents" in a short-tour area.
• Personnel serving in CONUS whose last overseas tour was "all others" in a short-tour area; "all others" in a long-tour area; and "with dependents" in a long-tour area.
• Personnel in Hawaii after completion of a prescribed "with dependents" tour or an "all others" tour.

For regimentally affiliated combat arms soldiers, overseas tours are normally either all long or all short, depending on the out-of-CONUS location(s) of their regiment.

An overseas long tour of duty is one in which the length is equal to or greater than 36 months "with dependents" and 24 months "all others." A short tour is one in which the length is less than 36 months accompanied and 24 months "all others."

Curtailment of Tours

Overseas commanders may curtail overseas tours when military requirements so dictate. They may also disapprove curtailment requests.

When curtailments of more than 60 days are considered, commanders must recommend curtailments and request reassignment instructions from PersCom as early as possible, but not later than 45 days before the departure date. Curtailing a tour must not cause an emergency requisition to fill the vacated position.

Overseas commanders may, at any time, curtail the tour of a soldier who has discredited or embarrassed or may discredit or embarrass the United States or jeopardize the commander's mission. They may also curtail tours when family members are moved to the United States because of criminal activity, a health problem, or death in the immediate family living with the sponsor. In exceptional cases, the commander may waive advance HQDA coordination and attach the soldier to the nearest personnel assistance point for issue of PCS orders: potential defectors; extreme personal hardship; and expeditious removal of a soldier in the best interests of the service (for example, when a soldier causes an embarrassment to the command in its relationship with a foreign government).

Pregnant soldiers are not curtailed from their overseas tours solely because of their pregnancy. If noncombatant evacuation is ordered, however, pregnant soldiers who have reached the seventh month of pregnancy will be curtailed and evacuated. Such a curtailment does not, however, preclude the soldier being reassigned overseas again after completion of the pregnancy and discharge from inpatient status.

Extension of Tours

Acceptable members are encouraged to extend their overseas tours. Major overseas commanders may disapprove requests for extension. Table 9-2, AR 614-30, lists

Assignments

rules and approval authorities for extensions of overseas tours, but generally, a request for an extension must be approved no later than 10 months before DEROS.

Kinds of Overseas Tours

Personnel accompanied or joined by their dependents at government expense must have enough remaining service to serve the tour prescribed for those "with dependents" or 12 months after arrival of dependents, whichever is longer.

Army personnel married to each other and serving in the same overseas area serve tours in accordance with Table 7-3, AR 614-30. They must extend or reenlist, if necessary, to have enough time in service to serve the tour prescribed by the table before compliance with orders directing movement.

The "all others" tour is served by soldiers who meet the following criteria:
- Elect to serve overseas without their dependents.
- Are serving in an area where dependents are not permitted.
- Do not have dependents (this rule does not apply in areas where personnel who have no dependents must serve "with dependents" tours).
- Are divorced or legally separated and pay child support.

Tours normally will be the same for all personnel at the same station. Where there are personnel of more than one service, the service having the main interest (normally, the most personnel in the area) develops a recommended tour length that is coordinated with the other services. Tour length may vary within any given country or area, depending on the specific duty station. Appendix B, AR 614-30, lists overseas duty tours for military personnel.

RELOCATION ASSISTANCE

Sponsorship Program

The sponsorship program assists soldiers and their dependents in establishing themselves at a new duty station and assists and guides soldiers while they adjust to their new work environment.

A "sponsor" is an individual designated by name at a gaining organization to assist incoming members and their families in making a smooth transition into the unit and community environment. The act of sponsorship is the guided integration of new soldiers into the unit and the community. This act includes the exchange of correspondence between the incoming soldier and a sponsor before the new soldier's arrival and assistance and orientation after arrival. Sponsors should be in a grade equal to or higher than that of the incoming soldier, be the same sex, marital status, and MOS, be familiar with the surrounding area, and not have received assignment instructions.

Gaining commanders are required (Paragraph 3-7, AR 612-10) to appoint sponsors for incoming soldiers within five days after receiving DA Form 4787, *Reassignment Processing* (this rule does not apply when soldiers are assigned to Eighth U.S. Army units for 12-month unaccompanied tours).

Sponsors' duties are varied:
- Forward a welcoming letter to the incoming soldier. It should include the sponsor's duty address and telephone number and home address and home telephone number, as well, but this is not specifically required by the regulation.
- Try to provide information requested by incoming soldiers.
- Advise the incoming soldiers that they will be met at the point of arrival in the

area or at the aerial port of debarkation.
- Offer to assist in getting temporary housing (guest house or similar accommodations). The sponsor should contact the housing referral office for guidance and information. Sponsors are not required to contract for permanent or temporary housing; however, if the sponsor desires to provide this service and the incoming soldier agrees, the sponsor should seek legal advice about the commitments and liabilities involved.
- Accompany the incoming soldier after his or her arrival in the unit while he or she goes through in-processing.
- Acquaint the incoming soldier with the surrounding area and facilities.
- Introduce the incoming soldiers to their supervisors and immediate chain of command.

Gaining commanders are required to send incoming soldiers welcoming letters within 10 working days after they receive DA Form 4787. Informality and information sharing are the primary goals of these letters. This letter also responds to any request for specific information appearing in item 42 of DA Form 4787. The welcoming letter and its enclosures should as a minimum contain the gaining unit's address and telephone number and the following information.

- The projected availability of government and economy housing, including, when available, rent and utility costs, security deposit, and advance rent requirements if the incoming soldier is requesting dependent travel. This information is obtainable from the local housing officer.
- The location of the family housing referral office.
- Education facilities available for dependents in both the military and the civilian communities.
- The types of household goods that are essential, optional, or not required at an overseas location.
- The type of climate and recommended clothing.
- Local vehicle registration, safety, emission standards, and insurance requirements and, when available, typical insurance rates.
- The availability of military and civilian medical and dental care facilities.
- Community services and facilities that are available both on and off post.
- The host nation culture, customs, and lifestyle.
- Local firearms laws and restrictions.
- Problems they might have when shipping pets to the overseas command.

Commanders are also responsible for ensuring that sponsors are provided enough time from their duties to help new soldiers and arranging transportation for sponsors to meet new members arriving with their dependents at the point of arrival and bring them back to the unit (overseas only).

The incoming soldier should answer the sponsor's letter immediately and do the following:

- Inform the sponsors of their times, dates, and points of arrival (including flight numbers). Any changes to their itineraries should be reported to the sponsors immediately.
- Provide sponsors a unit mailing address and telephone number (commercial or DSN).
- Inform sponsors of expected departure dates from losing duty stations.
- If desired, provide sponsors leave addresses and telephone numbers.

Assignments

Orientation Program

Commanders and supervisors are responsible for conducting a thorough and timely orientation to start new arrivals off properly. These orientations should make the new soldier feel needed and wanted and instill in him or her the motivation to contribute to the unit's mission.

The orientation program should be informative and show a genuine interest in the welfare of the new arrival and give him or her a feeling of belonging and acceptance. The entire family should be included in orientations. Official, semi-official, and voluntary organizations should be requested to assist the entire family during the period of adjustment. The orientation should also aim at ensuring that the soldier's spouse understands the nature of the soldier's work environment and the opportunities available to the entire family group.

Transportation of Household Goods

Transportation of household goods at government expense is authorized for soldiers in accordance with the table below. Presently, command-sponsored soldiers to some overseas locations may ship only 25 percent of their household goods. For information on authorized weight limitations for other grades, see M8003, *Joint Federal Travel Regulations* (JFR).

PCS Weight Allowances (Pounds)

Pay Grade	With Dependents	Without Dependents
E-9	14,500	12,000
E-8	13,500	11,000
E-7	12,500	10,500
E-6	11,000	8,000
E-5	9,000	7,000
E-4 (over 2 years service)	8,000	7,000
E-4 (2 years service or less)	7,000	3,500
E-3	5,000	2,000
E-2, E-1	5,000	1,500

14

Transitions

THE DRAWDOWN

>Ours will be a smaller, more versatile and lethal Army that is more CONUS-based with the right force mix capable of responding to any contingency, quickly and decisively. Good leadership can better prepare soldiers and their families to understand and deal with the potential prospect of life outside or apart from the service when Congress makes the final decision on the size of our Army ... What the Army will ultimately look like is best left for the policy makers to speculate on. I'm not a policy maker and you are not policy makers. My job and that of every NCO is to work our "lane"—leading, training, and caring for soldiers and their families. Our job as NCOs is to ensure that whatever number of soldiers we ultimately end up with are physically fit, technically and tactically proficient; that they are trained and ready to defend our great nation, to do it quickly and decisively and with minimal loss to American lives.
>
>—SMA Richard A. Kidd, January 1992

As the *NCO Guide, 4th edition* was going to press, the Army was in the middle of a painful five-year force reduction and realignment. Bases were and still are being closed or consolidated. Good soldiers were exiting the service with voluntary separation benefits. Otherwise qualified officers and NCOs were and still are being involuntarily retired when they hit career retention control points that were abbreviated in 1992. Substandard soldiers were and still are being separated involuntarily, some with reduced benefits, others with nothing. Those who remain after the fog clears in 1995 or later must be in their "lane," as the sergeant major of the Army said. NCOs today must also be familiar with the policies and standards associated with the drawdown, not only so they understand it, but so they may help their peers and subordinates understand and deal with its effects. A solid education on this very complex issue is therefore critical.

Senior soldiers throughout the Army began providing the necessary "command information" about the drawdown—the nature of the changing threat, reduced budgets, and mandated force reductions—in 1992 when the Army Chief of Staff, GEN Gordon Sullivan, ordered senior field commanders and command sergeants major to get the word out through the Chain Teaching Program. He wanted all soldiers to know four things: The Army has a plan; the Army will continue to be trained and ready; the Army will continue to be a great place to serve; and there are programs in place for those who will leave.

Statistics released in 1992 showed a Total Army (Active, Guard, and Reserve) of 1,831,000 troops in FY 91 decreasing to 1,389,000 in FY 95. In mid-1992, however, Congress reduced the President's defense budget more than expected and thus created a situation that likely will cause deeper cuts. The Army's plan in 1992 was to reduce its force by 25 percent, but the cuts may end up being even deeper and cause more soldiers to retire or separate earlier.

The Army is shrinking through voluntary separations, retirements, accession (recruiting mission) reductions, and by managing involuntary separations as required. For enlisted soldiers, this means voluntary early transition programs (such as the valuable Army Career and Alumni Program, discussed later in this chapter), enhanced standards, tightened reenlistment standards, shorter career retention control points, voluntary separation options, and selective early release of sergeants major and command sergeants major. The idea is to retain a quality force and maintain the promotion flow while, according to the Army's 1992 plan, taking the enlisted force down from 603,000 in FY 91 to 452,000 in FY 95.

Tougher Standards

Soldiers who want to remain in service face tougher standards associated with the Weight Control Program, NCOES, reenlistment criteria, physical fitness, substance (drug and alcohol) abuse, the Qualitative Management Program, retention, and promotions.

Weight Control. Formerly, soldiers were considered for separation if they were overweight. Current policy requires commanders to initiate a bar to reenlistment or separation proceedings against overweight soldiers who fail to make satisfactory progress in the Weight Control Program. Also, soldiers who report overweight to NCOES schools will be denied enrollment and be removed from the DA selection list.

Local Bar to Reenlistment. Bars to reenlistment used to be reviewed after six and twelve months. Now they are reviewed after three and six months. After the second review either the bar is lifted or the soldier is processed for separation.

NCOES Misconduct. Soldiers formerly eliminated for cause from NCOES schools were subject to being reclassified to another MOS, removed from the promotion list, barred from reenlisting, or separated. This gave commanders more latitude when dealing with soldiers who were valuable to the organization. Now, soldiers removed for cause from an NCOES school must be barred or separated.

The APFT. The Army has always emphasized physical fitness, but never more than it does today. In the past, soldiers who repeatedly failed the Army Physical Fitness Test could be considered for separation. Now, soldiers who fail two consecutive APFTs are barred from reenlisting or are separated.

Drug Abuse. Formerly, policy required the separation of first-time abusers who were sergeants or above, and all second-time abusers. Currently, all first-time abusers with three or more years active federal service and all second-time abusers are separated.

Alcohol Abuse. Alcohol and Drug Abuse Prevention and Control Program (ADAPCP) failures were formerly considered for separation. Now, ADAPCP failures must be separated.

Qualitative Management Program. Sergeants with eleven or more years active federal service used to be considered as Qualitative Management Program (QMP) candidates. Now the cutoff is eight or more years.

Promotions. Currently, soldiers must graduate from the Primary Leadership Development Course to be eligible for promotion to sergeant. Graduation from the Basic and Advanced NCO Courses are required for promotion to staff sergeant and master sergeant, respectively. And graduation from the U.S. Army Sergeants Major Course is required for promotion to sergeant major.

Reenlistment and Retention. Qualified soldiers used to be able to re-up for two to six years. Now the reenlistment period is two to four years, except for soldiers serving in critical MOSs. The reenlistment "window" is now three to eight months before expiration term of service (ETS). Approval from Headquarters, Department of the Army is required if a soldier is within three months of ETS.

Waiver provisions for lost time and courts-martial have been eliminated for all soldiers. Waiver exceptions apply only in two situations. Initial-term soldiers may receive a one-time waiver from their battalion commanders for one to five days of lost time (AWOL). And soldiers promoted or selected for promotion since lost time (AWOL) or court-martial require no waiver.

Initial-term soldiers may no longer reenlist for retraining, except for sergeants or those soldiers with GT scores of 110 or higher. Mid-career soldiers, sergeants and staff sergeants with seven years of service or less, may reenlist for retraining or Regular Army; others, those with seven to ten years of service, must request to reenlist through PersCom. If PersCom denies the request, the soldier's commander may request an override. If the override is denied, soldiers with more than six years of service would be eligible for separation pay as defined below.

Soldiers on career status—those having 10 or more years service—have few options. Qualified staff sergeants with 15 or fewer years of service may re-up in the Regular Army or for retraining. Sergeants first class through sergeant major and all other soldiers with more than 15 years of service may only re-up Regular Army. If reenlistment is denied by PersCom, career soldiers are eligible for separation pay.

Retention Control. Retention control points have also been reduced in most rank categories. They now are as follows: specialist and corporal, 8 years (no change); promotable specialist and corporal, 8 years (effective 1 October 1992); sergeant, 13 years (no change); promotable sergeant, 15 years (effective 1 October 1993); staff sergeant, 20 years (no change); promotable staff sergeant, 22 years (effective 1 January 1992); sergeant first class, 22 years (effective 1 January 1992); promotable sergeant first class, 24 years (effective 1 January 1992); master sergeant, 24 years (effective 1 January 1992); and promotable master sergeant, 30 years (no change).

Selective Early Release Board (SERB). The SERB convened in January 1992 to consider up to 300 sergeants major and command sergeants major with 25 to 28 years of service for involuntary retirement. Data on Official Military Personnel Files, including information from the Restricted Fiche, was reviewed. Senior NCOs selected by the SERB faced mandatory retirement dates no later than 1 September 1992. Those eligible for SERB review could voluntarily submit retirement paperwork for retirement not later than 31 January 1993. Voluntary retirements had to be approved by 31 December 1991.

Transition Entitlements

Separation Pay. Soldiers in selected MOSs who are involuntarily separated may receive separation pay computed as follows: 10 percent times monthly basic pay, times 12, times years of service. A sergeant first class with 17 years of service who was involuntarily separated but eligible for separation pay would receive (in 1992 pay chart dollars and before taxes) a lump sum payment of $38,697.

Voluntary Separation Entitlements. Soldiers in selected MOSs had to decide whether to take the Voluntary Separation Incentive (VSI) or the Special Separation Benefit (SSB) when applying for voluntary separation payments offered in 1991 and 1992.

Under the VSI, a soldier would receive an annual payment of 2.5 percent times monthly basic pay, times 12, times years of service at separation. The annual payment would continue for twice the number of years' service the soldier had rendered. Under the VSI plan, former soldiers receive no transition benefits and must serve in the Ready Reserve as long as they receive VSI payments. As an example of its value, and based on the 1992 pay tables, VSI for a sergeant first class with 17 years of service would amount to $9,674 a year, before taxes, for 34 years, or a total of $328,916 (before taxes).

The SSB, on the other hand, provides the soldier with a lump-sum payment calculated as follows: 10 percent times monthly basic pay, times 12, times years of service, times 1.5. The SSB provides what is known as the "Cadillac bonus," a large, one-time cash payment. The VSI, however, is worth much more over the long term. Soldiers volunteering to leave the service had from 1 January to 29 February 1992 to apply for VSI or SSB and had to separate not later than 30 August 1992. The SSB is worth 50 percent more than separation pay, and soldiers who elected to take it remain eligible for transition benefits. A sergeant first class with 17 years of service who took the SSB would receive (in 1992 dollars) a lump-sum payment of $58,045, before taxes.

The VSI was the most valuable incentive offered. Oddly, though, the majority of soldiers taking a voluntary separation chose the SSB. Both voluntary separation packages were aimed at soldiers with at least six but not more than nineteen years of service. Soldiers selected for involuntary discharge, and those in certain critical MOSs, were not eligible for the voluntary separation incentives.

DISCHARGES

> With some Regret I quit the active Field,
> Where Glory full Reward for Life does yield.
>
> Farquhar, *The Recruiting Officer* (1706)

For whatever reason, sooner or later each soldier must quit the service. In this section, we will consider the various types of discharges, the operation of U.S. Army Transfer facilities, retirement, and veterans' rights.

Title 10, U.S. Code (Section 1168), provides that a discharge certificate will be provided for each enlisted member of the Army upon discharge from the service.

Honorable Discharge

An Honorable Discharge is given when an individual is separated from the military service with honor. An Honorable Discharge cannot be denied to a person solely on the basis of convictions by courts-martial or actions under Article 15 of the Uniform Code of Military Justice. Denial must be based on patterns of misbehavior and not isolated instances. An Honorable Discharge may be awarded when disqualifying entries in an individual's service record are outweighed by subsequent honorable and faithful service over a greater period of time during the current period of service.

Unless otherwise ineligible, a member may receive an Honorable Discharge if he or she has, during the current enlistment or extensions thereof, received a personal decoration or is separated by reason of disability incurred in the line of duty.

General Discharge

A General Discharge is issued to an individual whose character of service has been satisfactory but not sufficiently meritorious to warrant an Honorable Discharge. Such persons would have, for example, frequent punishments under Article 15 of the UCMJ or be classified as general troublemakers.

Other than Honorable Discharge

Discharges that fall within this category are given for reasons of misconduct, homosexuality, or security, or for the good of the service and are covered by AR 635-200. No person shall receive a discharge under other than honorable conditions unless afforded the right to present his case before an administrative discharge board with the advice of legal counsel.

Discharge at the Convenience of the Government

"Convenience" discharges carry with them either an Honorable or General Discharge certificate, at the discretion of the Secretary of the Army, and may be given in these instances.

- Discharge of aliens not lawfully admitted to the United States.

- Discharge of personnel who did not meet procurement or medical fitness standards.
- Discharge for failure to qualify medically for flight training.
- Inability to perform prescribed duties because of parenthood. This discharge applies to soldiers who are separated because of inability to perform prescribed duties, repeated absences, or nonavailability for worldwide assignment as a result of parenthood.
- Sole surviving sons or daughters.
- Lack of jurisdiction. This type of discharge applies to people who enlist fraudulently, enlist while underage, or are enlisted as a result of recruiter misconduct.
- Personality disorder. The condition must be a deeply ingrained maladaptive pattern of behavior of long duration diagnosed by a psychiatrist. This discharge does not apply to cases of combat exhaustion and other acute situational maladjustments.
- Concealment of arrest record.
- Failure to meet Army weight control standards.

Uncharacterized Separations

There are two types of uncharacterized separations, those given when a soldier is in entry-level status and those given because of void enlistments or inductions.

Dependency or Hardship Discharges

Dependency or hardship discharges are granted when it is determined that a servicemember's continued active duty will result in undue dependency or hardship upon either the soldier or his or her family or dependents.

Dependency exists when, because of death or disability of a member of the soldier's or his or her spouse's immediate family, family members become principally dependent upon the servicemember for care or support. *Family* in this context is defined as spouse, children, father, mother, brothers, sisters, only living blood relation, or persons who stand *in loco parentis* to the servicemember.

Hardship exists when instances not involving death or disability of a soldier's immediate family require separation to provide care or support by alleviating undue and genuine hardship. Cases that might fall into this category include unmarried servicewomen or sole parents. A "sole parent" is a person who is single by reason of never having been married.

Supporting evidence in these cases must be submitted in affidavit form and must include at least two affidavits by agencies or individuals (other than the family) that substantiate hardship or dependency.

Discharge for the Good of the Service

A soldier who has committed an offense or offenses, the punishment for any of which, under the UCMJ and the MCM, includes a Bad Conduct Discharge or a Dishonorable Discharge, may submit a request for discharge for the "good of the service" at any time after court-martial charges are preferred, regardless of whether charges are referred to a court-martial and regardless of the type of court-martial to which they may be referred. Requests may be submitted at any stage in the processing until final action on the case has been determined by the court-martial convening authority. Submission of a request does not prevent or suspend disciplinary proceedings.

Misconduct Discharges

Discharges for misconduct may include minor disciplinary infractions, a pattern of misconduct, commission of a serious offense, conviction by civil authorities, desertion, and absence without leave. Discharges granted for misconduct are not initiated instead of disciplinary action solely to spare an individual the harsher penalties that may be imposed under the Uniform Code of Military Justice. Before taking action because of minor disciplinary infractions or a pattern of misconduct, however, commanders must ensure that the individual has received adequate counseling and rehabilitation.

An under other than honorable conditions certificate is normally given for misconduct discharges.

Separation for Homosexuality

"Homosexual" means a person, regardless of sex, who engages in, desires to engage in, or intends to engage in homosexual acts. A "homosexual act" means bodily contact, actively undertaken or passively permitted, between members of the same sex for sexual satisfaction.

When the *sole basis* for separation is homosexuality, a discharge under other than honorable conditions may be issued if it is determined that the act was committed by using force, coercion, or intimidation, with a person under 16, with a subordinate in circumstances that violate the superior-subordinate relationship, openly in public view, for compensation, aboard a military vessel or aircraft, and if the conduct had or was likely to have had an adverse effect on discipline, good order, or morale. In all other cases, the type of discharge granted to a homosexual reflects the character of that person's military service.

TRANSFER POINTS AND FACILITIES

U.S. Army transfer facilities provide an informal, quiet atmosphere centrally located at a post where personnel being separated may be processed within acceptable time limits. Final disposition of records is made from transfer facilities, billeting is available for separating personnel, and a variety of counseling services is also provided.

AR 635-10 prescribes that oversea returnees, except retirees, be separated on the first workday after their arrival at the separation transfer point, when possible. Personnel being released from active duty discharged before ETS or the period for which ordered to active duty are separated by the third workday after approved separation. All others are separated on their scheduled separation dates, except for those individuals who elect to be separated on the last workday before a weekend or a holiday.

Medical Examination

There is no statutory requirement for members of the active Army, including U.S. Military Academy cadets and members of the Reserve or National Guard on active duty or active duty for training, to undergo a medical exam incidental to separation. It is Army policy, however, to accomplish a medical examination if a soldier is active Army and retiring after 20 or more years of active duty, being discharged or released and requests a medical examination, review of the soldier's health record by a physician or physician's assistant warrants, or an examination is required by AR 40-501, *Standards of Medical Fitness*.

Each person being processed for separation must prepare DA Form 664, *Service*

Member's Statement Concerning Compensation from the Department of Veterans Affairs. If a separating soldier wishes to apply for compensation from the VA, then VA Form 21-526e *(Veterans Application for Compensation or Pension at Separation from Service)* is prepared if he or she has undergone prolonged hospitalization or suffered wounds or injury or disease while on active service or had a physical defect when entering the Army that he or she feels was aggravated by military service.

Each soldier undergoing separation processing will have his or her medical records screened by a physician, regardless of whether a separation physical has been requested. As a responsible noncommissioned officer, advise your soldiers that a separation physical may be one of the *most important medical examinations* of their lives.

Separation physicals end in a personal interview with a doctor. That interview is the proper time to bring up *every single medical fact incident to military service.* This interview substantiates service connection should a soldier, after discharge, request disability compensation from the Department of Veterans Affairs based on military service.

Above all, each soldier being separated or retired from the service should *make a copy of his or her medical and dental records* and keep them after discharge. Transfer point personnel will assist in making the necessary reproduction service available for this purpose.

Preseparation Service Program

This program integrates the preseparation efforts of the education center, reenlistment NCO, in-service recruiters, and the military personnel office in a mandatory briefing format for honorably separating soldiers (not retirees) conducted not later than 90 days before separation. Spouses are encouraged to attend.

This program provides an opportunity to thank soldiers for their honorable service, give them and their spouses a realistic view of transition to civilian life early enough for them to plan for it, and apprise separatees of the benefits and opportunities available through participation in the Reserve and National Guard.

The counseling briefings are normally presented in classroom areas to groups of not more than 50 soldiers at a time. The sessions include discussion of civilian living expenses, documentation of education and training received in the service, civilian job research activities, VA benefits, college or vocational school benefits available, presentations by in-service and Reserve Components recruiters, and a military personnel office preprocessing orientation.

Orientations

Individual or group orientations are conducted at transfer facilities based upon the number of soldiers being processed. The purpose of these orientations is to apprise separating soldiers of their major rights, benefits, and obligations of personal interest. The services of civilian agencies available to soldiers after separation also are discussed. The talks are usually conducted by a senior NCO, and each participant receives a number of handouts consisting of relevant fact sheets and publications.

Records Interview and Check

This last-minute check of service records ensures that the information contained in them is correct. Soldiers who have received decorations presented shortly before reporting to the transfer activity should check to see that this fact has been posted to their records. If not, one should be sure to have copies of the award order with him to ensure that this information is posted.

At the close of this interview, the soldier's records are prepared for shipment to one of the following locations:
- Headquarters, Department of the Army, for officers and warrant officers.
- U.S. Army Enlisted Records and Evaluation Center, Fort Benjamin Harrison, Indiana, for retirees and those having no further service obligation.
- The Army Reserve for those who have a service obligation.

Career and Alumni Program

The Army Career and Alumni Program (ACAP) is a transition and job assistance initiative located at 62 military sites worldwide. Each ACAP site includes a Transition Assistance Office (TAO) and a Job Assistance Center (JAC), which are available for all active and Reserve Component soldiers, Army civilians, and military and civilian family members. The TAO provides eligible clients with transition advice and serves as a focal point for problems. The JAC provides clients with job search training, individual assistance and counseling, and a referral service.

Transition Assistance. The TAO synchronizes current pre-service transition services (those mandatory-attendance services mentioned earlier in this chapter) on an individual basis to help personnel leaving the Army and provides total quality management by offering the following:
- First step in the transition process.
- Individual transition plans.
- Awareness of available resources.
- Defense Outplacement Referral System.
- Federal and public sector job information.

Ideally, the TAO staff like to see you 180 days before your separation or retirement date, but if that is not possible you are eligible to be seen at the ACAP office until you are discharged from the Army.

Job Assistance. The JAC, which complements the TAO, conducts individual, small and large group workshops to accomplish the following.
- Target your second career.
- Prepare for interviews.
- Establish your goals.
- Find hidden markets for your skills. (Only about 20 percent of jobs available are advertised, according to one ACAP official.)
- Evaluate job offers.
- Build negotiating skills.
- Teach you to dress for success.
- Track job leads.
- Evaluate employment agencies, job fairs, and automated résumé services.
- Develop your résumé.
- Help with essential correspondence.

Like the TAO staff, the JAC staff encourages you to start the ACAP process 180 days prior to your discharge date. Commanders at every echelon are aware of the importance of allowing soldiers the required time to take advantage of the service. The

Army leadership supports the JAC and will continue to ensure commanders support it, too. Ultimately, the JAC strives to provide eligible clients with the skills to pursue and secure employment, but it is up to the client to apply what is learned during the assistance process.

Employment Network. The Army Employment Network (AEN) is an ACAP data base that contains information from employers who are committed to considering Army personnel for employment. The AEN provides the company name, location of all branches of the company, total number of personnel hired annually, the types of positions for which a company hires, points of contact, and in some cases a listing of currently available positions. The AEN also contains information from employment-related service providers who may have information on the job search process, including specific information about new careers and career requirements. The service providers may also have information about other organizations that can assist separating personnel, such as the National Education Association, the Noncommissioned Officers Association, and the National Association of Nurses.

The ACAP is linked to regional, federal Office of Personnel Management computers that list federal jobs, and is also tied to the Department of Labor and the Department of Veterans Affairs, which with the ACAP conduct a combined three-day job training seminar, three-hour training session, and six-hour training workshop. Clients choose the seminar, session, or workshop, depending on their needs and available time.

Civilians using a service similar to the ACAP would pay between $1,500 to $2,500 for the services provided, according to an ACAP official at the Fort Benjamin Harrison, Indiana, ACAP office. The official, whose office covers an eight-state regional area, said soldiers interested in the program should visit their local ACAP offices and pick up the brochure entitled "Client Bill of Rights." She said clients are told up front that they are presented to potential employers as "quality products who are leaders, drug-free, healthy, educated, and motivated." For more information about ACAP, call toll-free in the continental United States 800-445-2049. If you are stationed overseas, call DSN 221-0993. If you are an NCO, you should visit your local ACAP office and learn more about the program, then relate it to every soldier you supervise.

Getting Back In

It's a good idea to make up your mind early to stay in the Army as a career or get out. Of course, nothing is quite that easy, and there are as many good reasons for taking a discharge as there are for coming back into the service once you've left it. Remember this: The grade at which you come back in and whether or not you can come back at all depends largely upon how long you've been out and whether or not the Army has an MOS vacancy for you at the grade you want when you decide to return.

For example, if you are separated as a sergeant and enlist within 24 months of discharge, you may come back at the rank of sergeant, providing a vacancy exists in your former MOS at that pay grade; otherwise you will return as a specialist or corporal. But if you wait until 36 months to apply for enlistment, you come back as a private E-2. And a sergeant first class who enlists after 93 days following separation comes back in at a grade to be determined by Commander, U.S. Army Enlisted Eligibility Agency, but *at least one grade lower* than the pay grade in which separated.

Last, if you have a break in service and enlist at a lower grade than the one you held at discharge, you will be considerably behind your contemporaries who continued in the service and who will be enjoying the higher pay and increased responsibilities that would have been yours had you stayed on.

RETIREMENT

> My sword I give to him that shall succeed me in my pilgrimage, and my courage and skill to him that can get it.
>
> —John Bunyan

The important thing to remember is that, when a soldier puts the uniform into the closet for the last time, he or she does not have to stay in there with it. Those who do often do not last very long. One should begin early in one's career to think of retirement not as a thing that comes near the end of active life, but the point of departure between the end of one exciting and fulfilling career and the beginning of another. "Career transition" is a phrase that has become popular in recent years to replace "retirement."* Actually, a man or a woman of 45 or so has no more business thinking about an inactive retirement than he or she would have at the age of 25.

Making the Decision

Only you can make the decision to retire. If you are married, you will want to discuss the decision thoroughly with your spouse and family, but in the final analysis, it is you who must submit that application for retirement.

Read the literature on retirement procedures and veterans' benefits so that when you arrive at the transfer point for discharge, you will already know what to expect. Do not wait for someone else to tell you what your rights and benefits are. If you are to be retired at a post that does not have a transfer activity, your processing will be done at the local military personnel office, and to an extent, you will be on your own there unless the personnel officer has people as experienced in processing retirements as the commander of a transfer activity.

Submission and Withdrawal of Retirement Applications

Any soldier who has completed 19 or more years' service may apply for retirement. The request must be made within 12 months of the requested retirement date, except that the retirement approval authority is authorized to set a minimum time for submission, which cannot be less than two months before the desired retirement date. To be eligible, all service obligations incurred as a result of schooling, promotion (unless a waiver is granted), and duty tours (see AR 635-200) must be completed. Exceptions to this rule are those soldiers who have completed 30 years of service, are 55 years old or older, and have been selected to promotion to pay grades E-7, E-8, or E-9. The usual two-year lock-in does not apply to retirement applications on the part of these soldiers.

Retirement in lieu of permanent change of station orders is authorized providing the individual has nineteen years and six months or more of active federal service when notified of a PCS move. The retirement application must be completely proc-

---

*For information about planning your military retirement, see *Transition from Military to Civilian Life: How to Plan a Bright Future* Now *for You and Your Family,* Stackpole Books, 1984.

essed within 30 days of receipt of alert notification. The retirement date will not be later than six months from the date of notification or the first day of the month following the month in which twenty years of service is completed, whichever is later. Service obligations must be fulfilled not later than the approved retirement date.

Applications for retirement instead of PCS that are approved will not be withdrawn, nor will the retirement date be changed.

A retirement application cannot be withdrawn unless it is established that retaining the soldier concerned will be for the convenience or best interest of the government or will prevent an extreme hardship to either the soldier or his immediate family. The hardship must have been unforeseen at the time of the retirement application. Requests for withdrawal must be fully documented.

Terminal Leave

Deciding whether to take terminal leave may not be an easy decision. Whether to take it depends upon how much leave a soldier has accrued at the time of retirement, how much leave he or she may have previously cashed in for pay, and what plans the retiree may have for job-hunting activities, travel, or vacation.

Personnel taking terminal leave will be allowed to finish processing at the local transfer activity before departure on leave. On the day of retirement, a telephone call from the retiree, verifying his status and whereabouts, is all that is needed to finish outprocessing; the retiree's DD Form 214 will be sent to him via registered mail. Arrangements to pick up retired ID cards may be made at any military installation.

Retirement Processing

Most installations that have transfer activities conduct periodic retirement briefings that are open to all personnel, whether or not they are in receipt of retirement orders. It would be wise to attend such a briefing as soon as possible after you have made the decision to retire.

If everything has been done correctly, if you have done everything for which you are responsible, and if you have double-checked the things others are supposed to do for you, your final processing should move quickly and smoothly.

Allotments

Retirees are permitted to continue allotments that they had in effect while on active duty except for Combined Federal Campaign, deposits to the Uniformed Services Savings Deposit Program, and allotments to the VA for deposit to the Post-Vietnam Era Veterans Education Account. After retirement, the only allotments authorized to be established or changed are for purchase of savings bonds; payment of life insurance premiums in cases in which the primary insured is the retiree (only one allotment per insurance company); voluntary liquidation of debts to the government; support payments; contributions to the AER; and repayment of AER loans.

Requests to establish, discontinue, or change an authorized allotment after retirement may be submitted to Retired Pay Operations by letter over your signature. No specific form is required. Forms are provided, however, with USAFAC Pamphlet 20-194, *Retired Pay Information*, a copy of which should be forwarded to you by the Retired Pay Operations, U.S. Army Finance and Accounting Center, Indianapolis, Indiana.

This rule does not include automatic deductions under the SBP. (Also see Chapter 12, "Pay and Benefits.")

Ceremonies

Each soldier who retires from the U.S. Army is authorized to participate in a retirement review in honor of the occasion. These reviews are generally held on the last day of the month, and all personnel retiring from the service on that day at any specific post or installation are honored at the same special formation. You will be given the option to accept or decline a ceremony during your preretirement processing.

CHAMPUS Entitlement

The spouses and children of retired service personnel continue to remain eligible for CHAMPUS benefits as well as Uniformed Services Health Benefits.

Checks

If you do not already have your active duty paychecks going to a financial institution, consider doing so when you retire. The Direct Deposit system guarantees the deposit of your retirement check in the bank or credit union of your choice.

Discharge Certificates

Your DD Form 214, *Certificate of Release or Discharge from Active Duty*, is the most important of all the documents you will accumulate during your retirement processing; it is one of the most important documents you will ever receive during your military career. At the time of your retirement you will receive copies 1 (original) and 4 (carbon) of DD Form 214. *Be sure to make copies of these forms and protect the originals.* DO NOT LET THE ORIGINAL OUT OF YOUR POSSESSION!

Military Installation Privileges

Retired members, their dependents, and unmarried surviving spouses are authorized the use of various facilities on military installations when adequate facilities are available. This privilege includes commissary stores, post exchanges, clothing sales stores, laundry and dry-cleaning plants, military theaters, Army recreation services facilities, officer and NCO messes, and medical facilities.

Army regulations regarding exchange and commissary privileges for retired personnel apply overseas only to the extent agreed upon by the foreign governments concerned.

If traveling in an overseas area, it would be very wise to check beforehand to determine which privileges are available in that command for you and your dependents.

Mobilization Planning

All eligible retired Regular Army personnel are subject to recall to active duty during a time of national emergency.

At the announcement of mobilization, retired personnel will be ordered to active duty in their retired grade. Initially, current medical fitness retention standards will apply until such time as the Secretary of the Army directs the application of mobilization standards. Current plans call for retirees to report for active duty not later than M+10. Priority for assignment to active Army installations is within 300 miles of the retiree's place of residence, within the same state or, if insufficient assets versus requirements exist, then within the same CONUS Army area, and, finally, CONUS-wide assignment.

Pay

There are two ways of computing your retired pay.
- Retired pay based on length of service: basic monthly pay multiplied by 2½ percent times years of active service; up to 75 percent of basic pay.
- Retired pay based on disability: basic monthly pay multiplied by the percentage of disability.

Your paycheck will be mailed to you (or to your bank) on or before the last calendar day of each month. The Retired Pay Operations Office at Indianapolis will mail a computation form to you when your retired pay account is initially established.

Queries concerning retired pay should be submitted in writing to the following:
Commander, USAFAC
ATTN: Retired Pay Operations
Indianapolis, IN 46249

Telephone inquiries may be made by calling (toll free) 800-428-2290 (Indiana residents call collect 317-542-2900). Retired pay estimates may be obtained by submitting your anticipated retirement date, grade at retirement, date of rank, years of service for basic pay purposes, and years, months, and days of active service.

Retired Personnel Records

Military personnel records for retired personnel (less general officers) are on file at the U.S. Army Reserve Components Personnel and Administration Center, 9700 Page Boulevard, St. Louis, MO 63132. All inquiries requesting information from these records should be addressed to the Commander of the USARCPAC and must include as a minimum your full name, grade, Army service number, and Social Security number.

You should, however, make copies of all the important documents in your military personnel file at some point before you retire.

If you should consider that an error or injustice has occurred and desire to request a review of your case by the Army Board for Correction of Military Records, you should apply in writing on DD Form 149, *Application for Correction of Military or Naval Record*. The application should be addressed to the following:
Army Board for Correction of Military Records
Department of the Army
Washington, DC 20310

Forms and explanatory material may be obtained from The Adjutant General's Office, ATTN: DAAG-PSR, 2461 Eisenhower Avenue, Alexandria, VA 22331.

Finance records of retired personnel are maintained at the U.S. Army Finance and Accounting Center, Indianapolis, Indiana. Medical and dental records are maintained by the Department of Veterans Affairs.

Survivor Benefit Program (SBP)

The SBP allows retired personnel to provide an annuity to certain designated survivors. Various amounts and types of coverage may be elected, with the maximum being 55 percent of the amount of a member's retired pay at the time of death. These persons may be the widows or widowers, dependent children, or other persons with an insurable interest in a retired soldier.

A detailed description of the SBP is provided in AR 608-9. Most retirees must enroll in the program before retirement. An exception is those who are unmarried at the time and who later acquire a spouse and children. Declinations must be made in writing and, *if declination is not made by the time of retirement, enrollment in the plan is automatic, at full coverage*. Once enrolled in the SBP, you are in for life, unless you survive all your beneficiaries.

When making an election, a soldier chooses a base amount, ranging from a minimum of $300 to full retired pay or full pay for those drawing less than $300. The maximum a survivor can receive under SBP is 55 percent of the retired soldier's pension.

The cost of the plan for spouse only coverage is 2½ percent of the first $300 of the base amount and 10 percent of the remainder. If the base is $900, 2½ percent of the first $300 is $7.50 and 10 percent of the remaining $600 is $60, for a total cost to the retiree of $67.50. Cost for children is based on actuarial tables but is approximately ½ percent of the annuity payable when spouse and children coverage is taken and 3 percent of the annuity payable for children only coverage. Amounts withheld from retired pay for participation in the SBP are exempt from federal income tax.

Because the SBP and Social Security are both federal programs and the government pays part of the cost of both, SBP and Social Security survivor payments are integrated. SBP payments to a surviving spouse are offset by the amount of Social Security provided by the deceased retiree's active federal service after 31 December 1956. The offset does not start until the spouse reaches age 62.

SBP payments to a widow 62 or older without a dependent child are reduced by the amount of Social Security benefits to which he or she is entitled as a result of the deceased soldier's active duty earnings. The SBP payment, however, can be reduced no more than 40 percent.

Travel and Transportation Allowances

Retired Army personnel are authorized travel allowances from their last duty station to their home.

Shipment and storage of household goods incident to retirement is authorized on a one-time basis, subject to weight limitations and other controls. Specific information relative to shipment and storage of household goods is contained in DA Pamphlet 55-2, *Personal Property Shipping Information*. As an exception to this rule, personnel who are undergoing education or training at the time of retirement or who enroll in such training or education during the one-year period subsequent to retirement are entitled to shipment and storage of household goods for a period of one year after completion of education or training or two years after the date of termination of active duty, whichever is earlier.

Retired personnel are eligible for space available travel, category 4, within the continental limits of the United States on DOD-owned or -controlled aircraft. *Depen-*

Transitions

dents of retired personnel are not authorized space available travel on military aircraft flying within the continental limits of the United States and therefore may not accompany retired members on such flights.

Uniformed Services Health Benefits Program

Under the provisions of Chapter 55, Title 10, U.S. Code, retired members and their eligible dependents are authorized certain hospitalization and outpatient care in civilian medical facilities, as well as uniformed services facilities. Health care provided to retired personnel and their dependents in uniformed services medical facilities *is subject to the availability of space and facilities* and the capabilities of the professional staffs at those facilities. Retired members (but not their dependents) may also receive care in Department of Veterans Affairs facilities on a space-available basis. Dental care, except as a necessary adjunct to medical or surgical treatment of a condition other than dental, is not authorized from civilian sources.

Army personnel retired for length of service or those permanently or temporarily retired for physical disability are authorized the same treatment and care as active duty members.

Normally, eligible persons requesting care at a uniformed services medical facility will be expected to use the facility servicing the area in which they reside. In areas where facilities of two or more uniformed services are available, the appropriate officials of each service participate jointly in determining capabilities and establishing areas of responsibility for care.

United States Soldiers' and Airmen's Home

To some people, the "old soldier's home" is a joke, but the United States Soldiers' and Airmen's Home (USSAH) is no joke. You pay toward the maintenance of the home; it belongs to you.

Three categories of personnel are eligible for admission to the home.

• *Category I—More than 20 years' service.* This category includes every soldier, airman, or Regular warrant officer, male or female, of the Army or Air Force who has had some Regular service, who has served honorably for 20 years or more, and who is discharged from active duty in an enlisted or warrant officer grade.

• *Category II—Service-connected disability.* This category includes personnel who have some Regular enlisted or warrant service and who, by reason of disease, injury, or wounds received while in the military service, are incapable of earning a living. Disability must not have been as a result of misconduct and must have been incurred in the line of duty.

• *Category III—Nonservice-connected disability.* This category includes persons otherwise eligible—some Regular service in enlisted or warrant officer grades—who, by reason of wounds, sickness, old age, or other disability, are unable to earn a living.

Admission to the home is denied to any person convicted in a civil court of a felony or any other serious crime *after entry into the service of the United States.* This rule includes convictions of crimes after retirement or discharge from active duty. Personnel convicted of desertion or mutiny or alcoholics without proof of rehabilitation are not eligible for admission.

The home is supported by contributions of 50 cents per month from every active duty Regular Army or Air Force enlisted person and warrant officer.

In addition to active duty pay deductions, all fines levied by courts-martial and Articles 15 of the UCMJ are donated to the home, and since 1976, members have been charged a "user fee" for living there, which amounts to 25 percent of retired pay or Civil Service annuity, if based in any part on active military service. Twenty-five percent is the limit set upon such deductions by law; Social Security pensions are exempt from this assessment.

A fourth source of income for the home comes from a permanent fund. Although this money belongs to the home—none of it was appropriated from public funds—permission to use it must be obtained by submitting an appropriation through the Office of Management and Budget to the Congress of the United States.

Further information on admission criteria, administrative procedures for application for membership, and facilities available to the members may be obtained by writing to the following:

Board of Commissioners
United States Soldiers' and Airmen's Home
3700 North Capitol Street, NW
Washington, DC 20317

Department of Veterans Affairs (Disability Compensation)

If you believe that you have a condition that may entitle you to VA compensation, file your claim at the time of separation.

If the VA, upon reviewing your medical records, finds that you do have grounds for seeking compensation, an appointment for a physical exam will be made for you at the Department of Veterans Affairs hospital closest to your retirement home. Your claim will be processed based upon the examination results and, depending upon a variety of factors, may take up to six months to complete.

If your condition worsens after you receive compensation at a fixed rate of disability, you may apply for reconsideration (but similarly, should your condition improve, your rate of compensation may be decreased). Current rates of disability compensation for a single veteran with dependents (effective 1 December 1991) are as follows:

% of Disability	Compensation Rate
10	$ 83
20	157
30	240
40	342
50	487
60	614
70	776
80	897
90	1,010
100	1,680

In addition, specific rates up to $4,799 per month are paid when a veteran is adjudged to have suffered certain specific severe disabilities. These rates are decided on an individual basis. Beneficiaries can expect rates to change in 1993.

You cannot receive both VA compensation for disability and an Army retirement check. Therefore, the amount of your VA disability is deducted from your regular retirement check (which is issued by the U.S. Army Finance Center). Your monthly income will remain the same, except that part will be paid by the Department of the Army and part by the VA. For example, if you have been found eligible for a 30 percent disability compensation rating from the VA—$185—and you are also eligible for a retirement check from the Army of $1067.72, the Army will pay you $882.72 while the difference, $185, will be paid to you by the VA. *The VA check is exempt from state and federal income taxes.*

Wearing the Uniform, Military Titles and Signatures, Awards and Decorations

Wearing of the uniform by retired personnel is a privilege granted in recognition of faithful service to the country. Retired personnel may wear the uniform when such wear is considered appropriate. For ceremonial occasions, retired personnel may wear either the uniform reflecting their grade and branch on the date of their retirement or the uniform for personnel in the active Army of corresponding grade and branch. The two uniforms cannot, however, be mixed. Occasions of ceremony are legally interpreted as gatherings essentially of a military character at which the uniform is more appropriate than civilian clothing. Examples are military balls, parades, military weddings, military funerals, memorial services, and meetings or functions of associations formed for military purposes, the membership of which is composed largely or entirely of honorably discharged veterans or Reserve personnel.

Retired personnel wear the same uniform prescribed for active duty personnel. Retired personnel not on active duty may wear the uniform with decorations and awards. Shoulder sleeve insignia are not authorized for wear on the uniform by retired personnel except that the shoulder sleeve insignia of a former wartime unit may be worn on the right shoulder.

All retired personnel not on active duty are permitted to use their military titles socially and in connection with commercial enterprises. Such military titles must never be used in any manner that may bring discredit to the Army or in connection with commercial enterprises when such use, with or without the intent to mislead, gives rise to any appearance of sponsorship, sanction, endorsement, or approval by the Department of the Army or the Department of Defense.

Retired personnel who have not received the awards to which they are entitled or who desire replacement of items previously issued that were lost, destroyed, or unfit for use without fault or neglect on their part may obtain them upon written application.

Requests should be addressed to the Commander, U.S. Army Reserve Components Personnel and Administration Center, 9700 Page Boulevard, St. Louis, MO 63132. The application should include a statement or explanation of the circumstances surrounding the loss or nonissue of the items concerned. The original issue of all decorations and service medals is made without cost to the awardee. Replacements are made at cost. No money should be mailed for replacements until you are instructed to do so.

VETERANS' RIGHTS

The benefits discussed in this section are available to *all* veterans regardless of status. All VA benefits (with the exception of insurance and certain medical benefits) payable to veterans or their dependents require that the particular period of service upon which entitlement is based be terminated under conditions other than dishonorable. Honorable and general discharges qualify the veteran as eligible for benefits.

Dishonorable discharges and bad conduct discharges issued by general courts-martial are a bar to VA benefits. Other bad conduct discharges and discharges characterized as other than honorable may or may not qualify depending upon a special determination made by the VA, based on the facts of each case.

In order to prove your eligibility for VA benefits, you must remember to do these things.
- *Keep a complete copy of your medical records.*
- *Protect your DD Form 214, Discharge Certificate.* Keep the original in a safe place (some people keep it in a safe deposit box in a bank vault), and have copies made of it that you can use as needed. If you served more than one enlistment or tour of duty, keep all of your certificates.

Burial

Burial is available to any deceased veteran of wartime or peacetime service (other than for training) who was discharged under conditions other than dishonorable at all national cemeteries having available grave space, except Arlington Cemetery.

Payment of an amount not exceeding $150 as a plot or interment allowance, in addition to the $300 basic burial allowance, is authorized when the veteran is not buried in a national cemetery. Burial or plot allowances may be paid to the extent that they might be paid by the deceased's employer or by a state agency or political subdivision of a state.

Payment of an amount not to exceed $1,100 or the Federal Death Benefit, whichever is greater, is authorized as a burial allowance if a veteran dies as a result of service-connected disabilities.

Eligible veterans' dependents may receive a headstone or grave marker without charge and shipped to a designated consignee. The cost of placing the marker in a private cemetery must be born by the applicant. The VA may pay an amount not to exceed the average actual cost of a government headstone or marker as partial reimbursement for the cost incurred by the person acquiring a nongovernment headstone or marker for placement in a cemetery other than a national cemetery.

Conversion of SGLI to VGLI

Currently, maximum coverage under the Servicemen's Group Life Insurance (SGLI) is $100,000. Unless a soldier reduces the amount or declines coverage in writing, he or she automatically has the $100,000.

Coverage under the Veterans' Group Life Insurance (VGLI) is also $100,000. Those separated from the service on or after 1 December 1981 are eligible for this coverage. Under VGLI, however, a servicemember can get only as much coverage as he or she was receiving under SGLI at the time of separation.

A servicemember has 120 days after separation to apply for VGLI, with no health requirements. Beyond the 120 days, a soldier has one year to apply, but there are then some health requirements. During the 120 days after separation, the SGLI coverage continues without premiums.

After five years, the VGLI expires and is not renewable, but before it expires, it can be converted to an individual commercial policy at standard rates, without physical examination or other proof of good health. The Office of Servicemen's Group Life Insurance will notify you several months before your policy expires; at that time, a Conversion Notice and a list of participating insurance companies will be sent to you. Hundreds of companies participate in the Conversion Program.

Veterans Benefits Timetable

You Have (after separation from service)	Benefits	Where to Apply
Time varies	**GI Education:** The VA will pay you while you complete high school, go to college, or learn a trade, either on the job or in an apprenticeship program. Vocational and educational counseling is available.	Any VA office
10 years	**Veterans Educational Assistance Program:** The VA will provide financial assistance for the education and training of eligible participants under the voluntary contributory education program. Vocational and educational counseling is available upon request.	Any VA office
12 years, although extensions are possible under certain conditions	**Vocational Rehabilitation:** As part of a rehabilitation program, the VA will pay tuition, books, tools or other expenses and provide a monthly living allowance. Employment assistance is also available to help a rehabilitated veteran get a job. A seriously disabled veteran may be provided services and assistance to increase independence in daily living.	Any VA office
No time limit	**GI Loans:** The VA will guarantee your loan for the purchase of a home, manufactured home, or condominium.	Any VA office
No time limit	**Disability Compensation:** The VA pays compensation for disabilities incurred or aggravated during military service.	Any VA office
1 year from date of mailing of notice of initial determination	**Appeal to Board of Veterans Appeals:** Appellate review will be initiated by a notice of disagreement and completed by a substantive appeal after a statement of the case has been furnished.	VA office or hospital making the initial determination
No time limit	**Medical Care:** The VA provides hospital care covering the full range of medical services. Outpatient treatment is available for all service-connected conditions, or nonservice-connected conditions in certain cases. Alcohol and drug dependence treatment is available.	Any VA office
Time varies	**Burial Benefits:** The VA provides certain burial benefits, including interment in a national cemetery and partial reimbursement for burial expenses.	VA National Cemetery having grave space, any VA office
No time limit	**Readjustment Counseling:** General or psychological counseling is provided to assist in readjusting to civilian life.	Any Vet Center, VA office, or hospital
Within 90 days of separation	**One-Time Dental Treatment:** The VA provides one-time dental care for certain service-connected dental conditions.	Any VA office or hospital
No time limit	**Dental Treatment:** Treatment for veterans with dental disabilities resulting from combat wounds or service injuries and certain POWs and other service-connected disabled veterans.	Any VA office or hospital
1 year from date of notice of VA disability rating	**GI Insurance:** Low cost life insurance (up to $10,000) is available for veterans with service-connected disabilities. Veterans who are totally disabled may apply for a waiver of premiums on these policies.	Any VA office
120 days or 1 year beyond with evidence of insurability; or up to 1 year if totally disabled	**Veterans Group Life Insurance:** SGLI may be converted to a 5-year nonrenewable term policy. At the end of the 5-year term, VGLI may be converted to an individual policy with a participating insurance company.	Office of Servicemen's Group Life Insurance, 213 Washington St., Newark, NJ 07102, or any VA office
No time limit	**Employment:** Assistance is available in finding employment in private industry, in Federal service, and in local or state employment service.	Local or state employment service, U.S. Office of Personnel Management, Labor Department, any VA office
Limited time	**Unemployment Compensation:** The amount of benefit and payment period vary among States. Apply after separation.	State employment service
90 days	**Reemployment:** Apply to your former employer for employment.	Employer
30 days	**Selective Service:** Male veterans born in 1960 or later years must register.	At any U.S. Post Office; overseas at any U.S. Embassy or Consulate

Employment

Assistance in finding jobs is provided to veterans through state employment or job service local offices throughout the country. Local veterans' employment representatives provide functional supervision of job counseling, testing, and employment placement services. Priority referral to job openings and training opportunities is given to eligible veterans, with preferential treatment for disabled veterans. Additionally, the job service assists veterans who are seeking employment by providing information about job marts, OJT and apprenticeship training opportunities, and so on in cooperation with VA Regional Offices and Veterans Outreach Centers.

At the time of your retirement or separation, you will be asked to fill out Department of Labor form OVRR-2. Be sure to indicate as accurately as possible where you expect to live and seek employment after separation. You will be contacted by the state employment office serving your home area and given information concerning the assistance available to you by your state employment commission.

Veterans may seek employment with the federal government. A regular Army retiree, however, and this rule applies to enlisted soldiers as well as officers, cannot be hired in a federal government job until *six months* after separation. There are some exceptions, but they are very rare.

Veterans receive some breaks when applying for federal employment.

• A five-point preference is given to those who served during any war, in any campaign, in an expedition for which a campaign medal has been authorized, or for 180 consecutive days between 31 January 1955 and 15 October 1976.

• A 10-point preference is given to those who were awarded the Purple Heart, have a current service-connected disability, or are receiving compensation, disability retirement benefits, or pension from the VA.

• A veteran with a 30 percent or more disability may receive appointment without competitive examination with a right to be converted to career appointments and retention rights in reductions-in-force.

Education Benefits

See your Army Continuing Education Services (ACES) counselor for details on the GI Bill, the Veterans Education Assistance Program (VEAP), and other education benefit programs.

GI Loans

The purpose of VA GI loans is to buy a home, to buy a residential unit in certain condominium projects, to build a home, to repair, alter, or improve a home, to refinance an existing home loan, to buy a manufactured home (with or without a lot), to buy a lot for a manufactured home that you may already own, to improve a home through installation of a solar heating and/or cooling system or other weatherization improvements, to purchase and simultaneously improve a home with energy conserving measures, to refinance an existing VA loan to reduce the interest rate, to refinance a manufactured home loan in order to acquire a lot, and to simultaneously purchase and improve a home.

Eligibility requirements vary, based on period of service (except that all veterans, to be eligible, must have an other than dishonorable discharge certificate). Eligibility for Vietnam veterans requires active duty for 90 days or more, any part of which occurred after 4 August 1964 and before 8 May 1975. Post-Vietnam eligibility requires active duty for 181 continuous days or more, all of which must have occurred after 7 May

1975. Eligibility requirements for service that began after 7 September 1980 (enlisted) are completion of 24 months of continuous active duty or the full period (at least 181 days); completion of at least 181 days with a hardship discharge, discharge for the convenience of the government, or disability compensation; or discharge after less than 181 days for service-connected disability. Any veteran with a service-connected disability, regardless of the period of service involved, is eligible for a GI loan.

The loan terms are subject to negotiation between the veteran and the lender. The repayment period or maturity of GI home loans may be as long as 30 years and 32 days. Newly discharged veterans have Certificates of Eligibility mailed to their homes by the VA shortly after discharge. Other veterans may secure their certificates by sending VA Form 26-1880, *Request for Determination of Eligibility and Available Loan Guaranty Entitlement*, along with required supporting documents, to the VA Regional Office nearest them.

Active duty personnel may also take advantage of these loans.

Military Benefits

Honorably discharged veterans with a service-connected disability rated at 100 percent, their eligible dependents, and unmarried surviving spouses are entitled to unlimited exchange and commissary store privileges in the United States. Certification of disability will be given by the VA. Assistance in completing DD Form 1172 *(Application for Uniformed Services Identification and Privilege Card)* may be provided by the VA.

A death gratuity payable to surviving spouses and dependents consisting of a sum equal to six months' pay but not less than $800 nor more than $3,000 is authorized in the case of death in active service or death within 120 days thereafter from specified causes related to active service.

One-Time Dental Treatment

In addition to dental conditions that qualify for treatment because of service connection, veterans are entitled to one-time dental treatment without review of service records to establish service connection. This treatment must be applied for within 90 days of separation. *Do not* fail to take advantage of this *very important* benefit. Contact the local VA office, and you will be sent a copy of VA Form 10-10, *Application for Medical Benefits*.

Unemployment Compensation

The purpose of unemployment compensation for veterans is to provide a weekly income for a limited period of time to help them meet basic needs while searching for employment. The amount and duration of payments vary because they are governed by state laws. Benefits are paid from federal funds. Veterans should apply immediately after discharge at the nearest state employment service, *not* at the VA. A copy of DD Form 214 is needed to establish type of separation from the service.

VA Correspondence and Records

Keep a file of *every* paper the VA may send you. Your dealings with the VA will require patience and persistence; the degree of either required will depend to a large extent on how busy your local VA office is. Invariably, VA personnel are courteous, and they try to be helpful, but processing your claim may take months, and if you apply for GI Bill benefits, it may take some time to get your payments straightened out.

VA Medical Benefits

The Department of Veterans Affairs offers the whole spectrum of medical benefits to qualified veterans: alcohol treatment; blind aids and services; domiciliary care; drug treatment; hospitalization; care for dependents or survivors; nursing home care; outpatient dental treatment; outpatient medical treatment; and prosthetic appliances.

Eligibility criteria for hospitalization gives top priority to veterans needing hospitalization because of injuries or disease incurred or aggravated in line of duty in active service. Veterans who are receiving compensation or who would be eligible to receive compensation (except for retirement pay) who need treatment for some ailment and connected with their service are admitted as beds are available. Under certain circumstances, veterans who were not discharged or retired for disability or who are not receiving compensation and who apply for treatment of a nonservice-connected disability may be admitted to a VA hospital.

Any veteran with a service-connected disability may receive VA outpatient medical treatment. If your service-connected disability is rated at 50 percent or more, you may receive outpatient care for any medical condition.

Vocational Rehabilitation

Generally, a veteran is eligible for vocational rehabilitation twelve years following discharge or release from active service. A four-year extension is possible under certain circumstances, and further extension may be granted for veterans who are seriously disabled when it is determined by the VA to be necessary because of disability and need for vocational rehabilitation.

Eligible disabled veterans may get training up to a total of four years or its equivalent in part-time or combination of part-time and full-time training.

Eligibility for this training is determined by the VA.

Sources
AR 612-10, *Reassignment Processing and Army Sponsorship (and Orientation) Program.*
AR 614-30, *Overseas Service.*
AR 635-10, *Processing Personnel for Separation.*
AR 635-200, *Separations Enlisted Personnel.*
DA Pam 600-5, *Handbook on Retirement Services.*
DA Pam 600-8, *Management and Administrative Procedures.*
VA FS 1S-1, *Federal Benefits for Veterans and Dependents.*

Index

Abuse of privileges, 273
Acknowledgments, 175
Address, forms of, 165
Adultery, 120-21
Advanced NCO Courses (ANCOCs), 49-50
Advanced Skills Education Program (ASEP) 55-56
Advance pay, 253-54
AIDS, 142-44
Airborne insignia, 213-14
Airborne training, 62-63
Air Medal (AM), 229, 247
Alcohol abuse, 137-38
  identification, 139-40
  intervention, 140-41
  tougher new standards, 298
Alcohol and Drug Abuse Prevention and Control Program (ADAPCP), 137-41, 298
Alcohol and drug control officer (ADCO), 138, 141
Allotments, 261, 263-64, 307-8
Allowances
  BAQ, 255
  BAS, 254-55
  civilian clothing, 259
  clothing maintenance, 258
  Family Separation, 258
  station, 258
  travel and transportation, 310-11
  VHA, 255
Antarctic Service Medal, 233, 235, 247
Appeals
  courts-martial, 158-59
  evaluations and, 79-80
  punishment and, 153
  of reduction in grade, 111
Appurtenances, 245, 247-48
Armed Forces Cooperative Insurance Association, 117
Armed Forces Expeditionary Medal, 234-36, 240, 247, 248

Armed Forces Relief and Benefit Association, 117
Armed Forces Reserve Medal, 233, 234, 238
Army Achievement Medal (AAM), 93, 230
Army Board for Correction of Military Records (ABCMR), 155
Army Career and Alumni Program, 297, 304-5
Army Commendation Medal (ARCOM), 93, 222, 229-30, 247
Army Community Services (ACS), 124
Army Continuing Education System (ACES), 53, 55
Army Emergency Relief (AER), 124-25, 261, 307
Army Employment Network (AEN), 305
Army Family Action Plan (AFAP), 125-26
Army of Occupation Medal, 233, 234, 239, 247
Army Reserve Components Achievement Medal, 232, 233
Army Reserve Components Overseas Training Ribbon, 234, 239, 247
Army Service Ribbon, 233, 234, 238-39
Army Superior Unit Award, 232, 233
Army Training and Evaluation Program (ARTEP), 7, 47
Arrest in quarters, 150
Arrowhead, 248
Article 15, UCMJ, 145-48, 150-55
Assignment(s)
  career development programs, 283-87
  Drill Sergeant program, 285-86
  enlisted personnel assignment system, 278-79, 281-83
  exchange, 283
  of first sergeants, 286-87
  general policies/procedures, 277-78

319

Homebase and Advance Assignment
    Program, 282
  of married couples, 282–83
  overseas service, 287–88, 290–93
  Personnel Action Request, 278
  promotion, effect on, 101–2
  requests for PCS or deletion, 282–83
  staff, 23–26
Association of the U.S. Army (AUSA),
    63–64, 117
Awards and decorations. *See also*
    individual awards
  appurtenances, 245, 247–48
  badges and tabs, 240–45
  certificates and letters, 248–49
  criteria for, 219–20
  foreign individual, 248
  non-U.S. service, 239–40
  precedence of, 220–21
  service medals and ribbons, 233–39,
    245–46
  time limitation for, 220
  unauthorized wearing of, 223–24
  unit, 232–33
  wearing of medals and ribbons,
    221–32, 313

Bad conduct discharge, 301, 314
Badges, 213
  identification, 244–45
  security, 207
  types of, 240–44
Bank accounts, 116
Basic Allowance for Quarters
    (BAQ), 255
Basic Allowance for Subsistence
    (BAS), 254–55
Basic NCO Course (BNCOC), 49
Basic pay, 254
Basic Skills Education Program
    (BSEP), 55–56
Basic Technical Course (BTC), 51
Benefits
  burial, 314
  death, 314, 317
  disability, 312–13, 317, 318
  education, 58, 61, 263, 307, 316–17
  health care, 117, 143, 264–65,
    268–69
  veterans, 58, 61, 117, 143, 265, 268,
    307, 312–14, 316–18
Body escort detail, 29–32
Bonus
  enlistment, 260
  selective reenlistment, 260–61

Borrowing, 118, 120
Bronze Star Medal (BSM), 227–29, 247
Bugle calls, 179–81
Burial, 31, 314

Calling cards, 177
Cannon salutes, 168
Cards
  calling, 177
  identity, 272–73, 317
Career development programs, 283–87
Casualty notification, 26–28
Certificate of Achievement, 249
Chain of command, NCO and, 15–17
CHAMPUS (Civilian Health and
    Medical Program of the Uniformed
    Services), 117, 143, 308
  details of, 264–65, 268
Child care, 126
Civilian clothing
  allowance for, 259
  wearing of, 207
Clasps, 247
Classified information, 37–38
Clothing maintenance allowance, 258
Cohesion, Operational Readiness, and
    Training System (COHORT), 22
Collar brass insignia, 214, 216
College Level Examination Program
    (CLEP), 61
College programs and locations, 58–59
Combat leader's identification, 212
Commanders, responsibilities of, 79
Command Sergeant Major (CMS), 16
  retention program, 84
Commissary, 270–73, 308, 317
Commissary cards, 272–73, 317
Commission, applying for, 64–67
Community Counseling Center (CCC),
    138, 141
Conduct, personal, 118, 120–22
Confidential information, 37
Confinement, 150
Convenience of the government,
    discharge at the, 300–301
Correspondence courses, 9, 51–52, 62
Counseling
  description of, 128
  interview, conducting, 130–31
  interview, preparing for, 130
  performance, 69
  preseparation, 303
  recognizing problems, 129–30
  substance abuse and, 138, 141
  types of, 128–29

Index

Courtesy, 162–66, 168–70. *See also* Customs; Etiquette
Court of Military Appeals, 158–59
Court of military review, 158
Courts-martial
  appeals, 158–59
  challenges to, 158
  charges, who may prefer, 159–60
  charge sheets, preparation of, 160–61
  commander, action by immediate, 160
  composition of, 155–56
  convening authorities, 156
  general, 155–58, 160–61
  jurisdiction and punishments, 156–57
  NCO responsibilities, 161
  officers of the court, 157–58
  right to demand, 152–53
  sentences, effective date of, 159
  sentences, remission and suspension of, 159
  special, 155–58, 160–61
  summary, 155–57, 160–61
Custody, correctional, 150
Customs, 178–81. *See also* Courtesy; Etiquette

Date of rank, 96
Death benefit, 314, 317
Defense Activity for Nontraditional Education Support (DANTES), 60, 61
Defense Distinguished Service Medal (DDSM), 225
Defense Equal Opportunity Management Institute, 63, 135
Defense Meritorious Service Medal (DMSM), 228
Defense Superior Service Medal (DSSM), 226
Delta Dental Plan (DDP), 264, 268–69
Demolition pay, 259
Dental care, 264, 268–69, 317
Dependency discharge, 301
Dependent identification cards, 273
Dining-In, formal, 176–77
Dinner party, formal, 175–76
Disability benefits, 312–13, 317, 318
Discharge(s)
  bad conduct, 301, 314
  certificate of, 308, 314
  convenience of the government, at the, 300–301
  dependency, 301
  dishonorable, 301, 314
  general, 300, 313
  good of the service, for the, 301
  hardship, 301
  homosexuality, separation for, 302
  honorable, 300, 313
  misconduct, 302
  other than honorable, 300
  returning to Army after, 305–6
  uncharacterized separations, 301
Discipline of personnel, 3–4. *See also* Punishment
Discipline of supply, 43
Discrimination
  racial, 127, 135–37
  sexual, 127, 131–35
Dishonorable discharge, 301, 314
Distinguished Flying Cross (DFC), 227
Distinguished Service Cross (DSC), 225, 232
Distinguished Service Medal (DSM), 225–26, 247
Diving pay, 259
Dog tags, 207
Drawdown, the
  background of, 296–97
  tougher new standards, 297–99
  transition entitlements, 299–300
Drill Sergeant Program, 285–86
Drug abuse, 137–38
  effects of, 142
  testing for, 141
  tougher new standards, 298
Duty(ies). *See also* Assignment(s); Pay
  extra, 150
  NCO, 7–9, 11–12
  rosters for, 34, 36–37
  temporary, 101–2, 283

Education. *See also* Training
  Advanced NCO Courses, 49–50
  Advanced Skills Education Program, 55–56
  Army Continuing Education System, 53, 55
  Basic NCO Course, 49
  Basic Skills Education Program, 55–56
  benefits, 58, 61, 263, 307, 316–17
  college programs and locations, 58–59
  correspondence courses, 9, 51–52, 62
  degree programs, 56, 58
  dismissal from courses, 52–53
  Enlisted Personnel Management System, 45, 47, 49

Index

functional courses, 51-53
High School Completion Program, 56
Noncommissioned Officer
  Academies, 9, 49, 52-53
Noncommissioned Officer
  Development Program, 45-46
Noncommissioned Officer Education
  System, 9, 45, 47, 49-51
Officer Candidate School, 65
overseas, 58-59
Primary Leadership Development
  Course, 49, 298
Reserve Officer Training Corps,
  66-67
Service Members Opportunity
  Colleges Associate Degree
  Program, 56
services support, 61-62
Skill Recognition Programs, 59-60
U.S. Army Sergeants Major
  Academy, 47, 50-51
U.S. Military Academy, 65-66
Veterans Educational Assistance
  Program, 58, 61, 263
Employment assistance, veterans, 316
Enlisted Personnel Management
  System (EPMS), 45, 47, 49
Enlisted Standby Advisory Board
  (STAB), 107
Enlistment bonus, 260
Equal opportunity training, 63, 135
Etiquette, 170-71, 174-78. *See also*
  Courtesy; Customs
Evaluation reporting system, 68-69, 74,
  77-80
Experimental stress duty pay, 260

Family Separation Allowance
  (FSA), 258
First call, 179
First sergeant(s), 16-17
  course for, 51
  frocking of, 108
  promotion to, 103, 105
  selection and assignment of, 286-87
Flag courtesies, 166, 168-70
Flight pay, 259
Foreign duty pay, 259
Foreign individual awards, 248
Forfeiture of pay, 150-51
Formal Dining-In, 176-77
Formal dinner party, 175-76
Fraternization, 133-34
Frocking, 108
Funeral, 31

Gambling, 120
General discharge, 300, 313
GI Bills, 58, 61
GI loans, 316-17
Good Conduct Medal (GCM), 222,
  230-31, 247
Good of the service, discharge for, 301
Government life insurance, 263
Grade
  reductions in, 109-12, 150
  restoration to former, 111
Guest, house, 175

Hair styles, 200, 206
Harassment, sexual, 134-35
Hardship discharge, 301
Headgear
  authorized, 208-9
  wearing of, 184
  women and, 184, 208-9
Health care
  CHAMPUS, 117, 143, 264-65,
    268, 308
  dental, 264, 268-69, 317
  medical exam at separation, 302-3
  Uniformed Services Health Benefits
    Program, 311
  veterans, 143, 265, 268, 308,
    317, 318
High School Completion Program
  (HSCP), 56
Holidays, 276
Homebase and Advance Assignment
  Program (HAAP), 282
Homosexuality, separation for, 302
Honorable discharge, 300, 313
Hostile fire pay (HFP), 259
House guest, 175
Household goods, transportation
  of, 295
Housing, 122-24, 269-70
  allowances for, 255
Humanitarian Service Medal, 233, 234,
  237-38, 247

Identification
  badges, 244-45
  cards, 272-73, 317
  combat leader's, 212
  tags, 207
Income taxes, 118
Indebtedness, 109, 121-22
Individual Training and Evaluation
  Program (ITEP), 46-47
Inefficiency, 109-10
Infantry insignia, 213

Index

Information
  classified, 37-38
  sources of, 33-34
Initial Entry Training (IET), 22
Insignia
  airborne, 213-14
  collar brass, 214, 216
  infantry, 213
  of rank, 216, 218
  shoulder sleeve, 210-11
  unit, 212-14, 216
Insurance, 116-17, 263, 307, 314

Japan/Okinawa, educational opportunities in, 59
Jewelry, civilian, 206-7
Joint Service Achievement Medal (JSAM), 230
Joint Service Commendation Medal (JSCM), 229, 247

Kuwait Liberation Medal, 240

Language training, 63
Lapel buttons, 248
Leadership, NCO, 1-2
  competencies of, 2-3
Leave, 273-75
Leave and Earnings Statement (LES), 252
Legal assistance, 114
Legion of Merit (LM), 222, 226-28, 233, 245, 247
Lending, 118, 120
Letters of Commendation and Appreciation, 249
Lump-sum pay, 254
Lying, 121

Married couples, assignment of, 282-83
Master sergeant
  frocking of, 108
  promotion to, 103, 105
Medal of Honor (MOH), 221-22, 224-25, 245
Medals. *See also names of individual medals*
  miniature, 245-46
  non-U.S. service, 239-40
  service, 233-40, 245-46
  wearing of, 221-32, 313
Meritorious Service Medal (MSM), 228, 229
Meritorious Unit Commendation, 232, 233

Mess call, 179-80
Military identification cards, 272
Military Personnel Office (MILPO), 79
Military records, 102, 116, 154-55
Misconduct discharge, 302
Multinational Force and Observers Medal, 239, 247

Nameplates, 207-8
National Anthem, 166, 169
National Defense Service Medal, 222, 233, 234
NCO Professional Development Ribbon, 233, 234, 238, 247
Net Pay Advice (NPA), 252
New Army College Fund, 58, 61
New GI Bill, 58, 61
New GI Bill for Vietnam-era Soldiers, 58, 61
New Manning System (NMS), 22
Next of kin, notification of, 26-28
Noncommissioned Officer Academies (NCOAs), 9, 49, 52-53
Noncommissioned Officer Development Program (NCODP), 45-46
Noncommissioned Officer Education System (NCOES), 9, 45, 47, 49-51
Noncommissioned Officer Logistics Program (NCOLP), 63
Noncommissioned Officers Association (NCOA), 64, 117
Numerals, wearing of, 247

Oak-leaf cluster, 247
Officer Candidate School (OCS), 65
Officer-NCO relationship, 17-19
Official Military Personnel File (OMPF), 102, 154
Operations and Intelligence Course, 51
Orientation program, 294-95
Overseas education, 58-59
Overseas service
  approaches to, 287-88
  curtailment of tours, 292
  deferments, 290-91
  deletions, 291
  eligibility for, 291-92
  extension of tours, 292-93
  kinds of tours, 293
  policies, 288
  temporary deferments, 290
  volunteering for, 290
Overseas service bars, 209-10
Overseas Service Ribbon, 234, 239, 247

Parachute pay, 259-60
Passes, 275-76
Pay, 250. *See also* Allowances
   advance, 253-54
   allotments, 261, 263-64, 307-8
   basic, 254
   demolition, 259
   diving, 259
   enlistment bonus, 260
   errors in, 252-53
   experimental stress duty, 260
   flight, 259
   foreign duty, 259
   forfeiture of, 150-51
   hostile fire, 259
   Leave and Earnings Statement, 252
   lump-sum, 254
   Net Pay Advice, 252
   parachute, 259-60
   reporting for, 165
   reserve drill, 254
   retired, 309
   selective reenlistment bonus, 260-61
   separation, 299
   special duty assignment, 260
Performance counseling/checklist, 69
Personal affairs record, 115-16
Personal appearance, 200, 206-8
Personal conduct, 118, 120-22
Personal property, 117-18
Personnel Action Request, 278
Physical fitness, 298
   conditioning, 84, 86
   over age 40, 88-89
   weight control, 86, 88, 297
Platoon sergeant, 17
Pledge of Allegiance, 168
Post exchange, 270-72, 308, 317
Power of attorney, 114-15
Precedence and relative rank, 19, 22
Presidential Unit Citation, 232-33
Primary Leadership Development Course (PLDC), 49, 95, 298
Primary Technical Course (PTC), 51
Prisoner of War Medal (POWM), 230, 231
Professional development, 44-45.
   See also Education; Training
   applying for a commission or warrant, 64-67
   membership in professional organizations, 63-64
Promotion, 90-91
   acceptance of, 105, 107
   assignments and effect on, 101-2
   authority to promote, 91
   boards, 8-9, 11, 96, 99-103
   cutoff scores, 94
   date of rank, 96
   paper work needed for, 96, 99-101
   to private E-2 and private first class, 91-92
   recommended list, 96, 99
   recomputation of promotion points, 101
   reductions in grade, 109-12, 150
   reevaluation, 99
   removals from list, 100, 107-8
   school requirements, 95
   to senior NCO ranks, 102-3, 105, 107-8
   to sergeant and staff sergeant, 93-96
   service remaining obligations, 95-96
   to specialist or corporal, 92-93
   time in service and grade requirements, 94-95
   tougher new standards, 298
Property
   government (supply), 38-39, 41-43
   personal, 117-18
Punishment
   announcement of, 153-54
   appeals of, 153
   courts-martial, 152-53, 155-61
   nonjudicial, 145-48, 150-55
   records of, 146, 148, 154-55
   reductions in grade, 109-12, 150
   UCMJ, 145-48, 150-61, 301-2
Purple Heart (PH), 220, 226-28

Qualitative Management Program (QMP), 80-82, 84, 298
Qualitative retention subprogram, 81
Qualitative screening subprogram, 81-82, 84

Racial discrimination, 127, 135-37
Ranger training, 62
Rank
   comparable, among services, 19
   date of, 96
   insignia of, 216, 218
   precedence and relative, 19, 22
Rater qualifications/responsibilities, 77-78
Receptions, 174-75
Records
   discharge certificate, 308, 314
   emergency data, 116
   military, 102, 116, 154-55
   personal affairs, 113-16

Index

punishment, 146, 148, 154–55
  veterans, 317–18
Reduction boards, 110–11
Reductions in grade, 109–12, 150
Reenlistment
  bonus for, 260–61
  postdischarge, 305–6
  tougher new standards for, 298
Regimental System, 22
Relocation assistance, 293–95
Reporting for pay, 165
Reports
  annual, 69
  change-of-rater, 69
  commander intervention in, 77
  complete-the-record, 69, 74
  initial, 69
  relief-for-cause, 74
  restrictions in, 74
  special, 74
  of Survey, 42–43
Reserve drill pay, 254
Reserve Officer Training Corps (ROTC), 66–67
Responsibilities, NCO, 8, 13–15, 161
Retired Serviceman's Family Protection Plan (RSFPP), 263
Retirement, 306–13. *See also* Veterans benefits
Retreat, 168–70
Reveille, 168–69, 180
Reviewer qualifications/responsibilities, 78
Ribbons. *See also names of individual ribbons*
  service, 233–39, 245
  wearing of, 221–32, 313

Saluting, 162–64
Scarves, 211–12
Secret information, 37
Section leaders, 17
Security badges, 207
Security clearance, 105
Selection boards, 105
Selective Early Release Board (SERB), 299
Selective reenlistment bonus (SRB), 260–61
Self-perception, 122
Separation pay, 299
Sergeant Major of the Army (SMA), 16
Service bars, overseas, 209–10
Service medals, 233–39, 245–46
  non–U.S., 239–40

Service Members Opportunity Colleges Associate Degree Program (SOCAD), 56
Servicemen's Group Life Insurance (SGLI), 117, 263, 314
Servicemen's Opportunity Colleges Program, 61
Service ribbons, 233–39, 245
Service stars, 247
Service stripes, 209
Sexual discrimination, 127, 131–35
Sexual harassment, 134–35
Shoulder sleeve insignia, 210–11
Silver Star (SS), 226, 233
Skill Recognition Programs, 59–60
Smoking, 174
Soldier boards, 11–12
Soldiers' and Sailors' Civil Relief Act, 118
Soldier's Medal (SM), 227, 229
Southwest Asia Service Medal (SWASM), 237
Special duty assignment pay, 260
Special Separation Benefit (SSB), 299–300
Speech, proper, 170
Sponsorship program, 293–94
Squad leaders, 17
Staff assignments, 23–26
Stars, service, 247
Statements of Charges, 42
Station allowances, 258
Stripes, service, 209
Substance abuse
  ADAPCP and, 137–41, 298
  alcohol, 137–41, 298
  drugs, 137–38, 298
  tougher new standards, 298
Supply, 38–39, 41–43
Support channel, NCO, 16
Survivor Assistance Officer (SAO), 28–29
Survivor Benefit Program (SBP), 310

Tabs, 242–44
Tags, identification, 207
Taps, 180
Tattoo, 180–81
Team leaders, 17
Telephone etiquette, 171, 174
Temporary duty, 101–2, 283
Tobacco use, 174
Top secret information, 37
"To the Color," 166, 169, 170, 181
Training, 9. *See also* Education
  airborne, 62–63

Army Training and Evaluation
Program, 7, 47
conventional, 5
equal opportunity, 63, 135
Extension Course, 52
Individual Training and Evaluation
Program, 46–47
Initial Entry, 22
language, 63
New Manning System, 22
NCO trainer, 4–5, 12
Noncommissioned Officer Logistics
Program, 63
performance-oriented, 5–7
ranger, 62
Transfer points and facilities, 302–6
Transitions. *See also* Veterans benefits
discharges, 300–302, 308
drawdown, the, 296–300
retirement, 306–13
transfer points and facilities, 302–6
Travel and transportation allowances,
310–11

Uncovering, 165
Unemployment compensation,
veterans, 317
Uniform(s)
appearance of, 184–85
Army blue (female), 200
Army blue (male), 200
Army green classic service, 192
Army green service, 192
care and maintenance of, 185–87
changes to, 182
classification of, 183–84
clothing allowance system, 187–88
cold weather, 188, 192
combat vehicle crewman, 192
desert battle dress, 188
distinctive items, 208–12
fitting of, 187
flight, 192
green maternity service, 192
hospital duty (male), 192
hospital duty and maternity, 192
maternity work, 188
other authorized, 200
temperate and hot weather battle
dress, 188
types of, 188, 192, 200
wearing, 182–88, 313
when it is not to be worn, 184
when it is required, 184

Uniform Code of Military Justice
(UCMJ), 301–2
Article 15 (nonjudicial punishment),
145–48, 150–55
authority of NCOs under, 4, 146–47
courts-martial, 152–53, 155–61
Uniformed Services Health Benefits
Program, 311
Unit awards, 232–33
Unit insignia, 212–14, 216
United Nations Medal, 234, 239
U.S. Army Sergeants Major Academy
(USASMA), 47, 50–51
U.S. Military Academy (USMA), 65–66
U.S. Soldiers' and Airmen's Home
(USSAH), 311–12
Unit fund councils, 12

Valorous Unit Award, 232, 233
Variable Housing Allowance (VHA), 255
V Device, 247
VEAP-era Army College Fund, 61
Veterans benefits
correspondence/records and, 317–18
disability compensation, 312–13, 317
education, 58, 61, 263, 307
eligibility for, 313–14
employment assistance, 316
GI loans, 316–17
health care, 143, 265, 268, 308,
317, 318
insurance, 117, 314
Veterans Educational Assistance
Program (VEAP), 58, 61, 263
Veterans Group Life Insurance (VGLI),
117, 314
Vietnam Campaign Medal, Republic of,
234, 240
Vietnam Service Medal, 234, 236–37,
239, 240, 247, 248
Vocational rehabilitation, 318
Voluntary Separation Incentive (VSI),
299–300

Warrant, applying for, 64–67
Weight control, 86, 88, 297
Wills, 114
Women
courtesies to, 170–71
headgear and, 184
insignia and, 212, 214
personal appearance, 206
sexual discrimination, 127, 131–35
sexual harassment, 134–35